Sex Offender Treatment

A Case Study Approach to Issues and Interventions

Edited by Daniel T. Wilcox, Tanya Garrett, and
Leigh Harkins

D1807832

WILEY Blackwell

This edition first published 2015
© 2015 John Wiley & Sons, Ltd.

Registered Office
John Wiley & Sons Ltd, The Atrium, Southern Gate, Chichester, West Sussex, PO19 8SQ, UK

Editorial Offices
350 Main Street, Malden, MA 02148-5020, USA
9600 Garsington Road, Oxford, OX4 2DQ, UK
The Atrium, Southern Gate, Chichester, West Sussex, PO19 8SQ, UK

For details of our global editorial offices, for customer services, and for information about how to apply for permission to reuse the copyright material in this book please see our website at www.wiley.com/wiley-blackwell.

The right of Daniel T. Wilcox, Tanya Garrett and Leigh Harkins to be identified as the authors of the editorial material in this work has been asserted in accordance with the UK Copyright, Designs and Patents Act 1988.

Wiley also publishes its books in a variety of electronic formats. Some content that appears in print may not be available in electronic books.

Designations used by companies to distinguish their products are often claimed as trademarks. All brand names and product names used in this book are trade names, service marks, trademarks or registered trademarks of their respective owners. The publisher is not associated with any product or vendor mentioned in this book.

Limit of Liability/Disclaimer of Warranty: While the publisher and authors have used their best efforts in preparing this book, they make no representations or warranties with respect to the accuracy or completeness of the contents of this book and specifically disclaim any implied warranties of merchantability or fitness for a particular purpose. It is sold on the understanding that the publisher is not engaged in rendering professional services and neither the publisher nor the author shall be liable for damages arising herefrom. If professional advice or other expert assistance is required, the services of a competent professional should be sought.

Library of Congress Cataloging-in-Publication Data

Sex offender treatment : a case study approach to issues and interventions / edited by Daniel T. Wilcox, Tanya Garrett and Leigh Harkins.
     pages cm
   Includes bibliographical references and index.
   ISBN 978-1-118-67441-3 (cloth) – ISBN 978-1-118-67440-6 (pbk.)   1. Sex offenders–Psychology.   2. Psychosexual disorders–Treatment.   I. Wilcox, D. T. (Daniel T.) editor of compilation.   II. Garrett, Tanya, editor of compilation.   III. Harkins, Leigh, editor of compilation.
   HV6556.S425 2014
   616.85'83–dc23
                                        2014016399

A catalogue record for this book is available from the British Library.

Cover image: Sunset Watercolor. © mcswin /iStockphoto

Set in 11/13.5 pt SabonLTStd by Toppan Best-set Premedia Limited
Printed and bound in Malaysia by Vivar Printing Sdn Bhd

1   2015

Sex Offender Treatment

Contents

About the Editors

Daniel T. Wilcox is Managing Director of Wilcox Psychological Associates, a private clinical and forensic psychology practice. He is a registered clinical and forensic psychologist, an honorary associate professor at the University of Nottingham, School of Medicine (Division of Psychiatry), and an honorary research fellow at the University of Birmingham, Centre for Forensic and Criminological Psychology. He is widely published, on the editorial boards of several journals in the field, and Editor of *The Use of the Polygraph in Assessing, Treating and Supervising Sexual Offenders* (Wiley, 2009).

Tanya Garrett is a registered clinical and forensic psychologist in private practice and an honorary senior lecturer at the University of Birmingham Centre for Forensic and Criminological Psychology. Tanya's published research relates to sexual violations in therapy and clinical psychology training, ethical issues in therapy, and sexual offender treatment and evaluation.

Leigh Harkins is an assistant professor in the Faculty of Social Science and Humanities, University of Ontario Institute of Technology, Canada. She has experience working in treatment groups for sexual offenders, completing psychological assessments in prisons and community criminal justice settings in Canada and the UK. Leigh's published research focuses on sexual aggression, offender rehabilitation, and multiple-perpetrator offending.

About the Contributors

Gene Abel is a board-certified psychiatrist and the inventor of Abel Assessment for Sexual Interest™. Dr. Abel has directed six National Institute of Mental Health research projects on the evaluation of sexual problems and has published over 130 scientific articles. Currently, he is the medical director of Behavioral Medicine Institute of Atlanta and is a clinical professor of psychiatry at Morehouse School of Medicine and Emory University School of Medicine.

Geraldine Akerman is a therapy manager at HMP Grendon, and C. Psychol, C.Sci, AFBPsS, and PhD candidate at the University of Birmingham. She has publications in the areas of sexual offending, developing empathy with service-users with learning difficulties, therapeutic communities, and offence paralleling behavior. Her PhD thesis involves the development and validation of a psychometric measure of current sexual interest.

Anthony R. Beech, D.Phil, C.Sci, FBPsS, C.Psychol, has authored over 160 articles, 42 book chapters, and six books in the area of forensic science. Professor Beech was the 2009 recipient of the Senior Award from the Division of Forensic Psychology, British Psychological Society for a significant lifetime contribution to Forensic Psychology.

Adam Carter is a chartered and registered forensic psychologist with over 20 years experience working in National Offender Management Services (NOMS) and Her Majesty's Prison Service, predominantly in the assessment and treatment of sexual offenders. He received his PhD from Leicester University in 2009 and is currently Head of Offence Specialism for Sexual Offending Treatment Programmes in Interventions Services, NOMS.

Franca Cortoni received her PhD in clinical and forensic psychology from Queen's University at Kingston, Ontario. Since 1989, she has worked with and conducted research on male and female sexual offenders. Dr. Cortoni is Associate Professor at the School of Criminology of the Université de Montréal and Research Fellow at the International Centre of Comparative Criminology. Dr. Cortoni has edited a book on female sexual offenders and a book on criminal violence (in French), and has published extensively and made numerous presentations at national and international conferences on sexual offender issues. She is a member of the Editorial Board of *Sexual Abuse: A Journal of Research and Treatment* and of the International Advisory Board of the *Journal of Sexual Aggression*.

Leam A. Craig, BA (Hons), MSc, PhD, MAE, CSci, CPsychol, FBPsS, and EuroPsy, is a consultant forensic clinical psychologist and partner at FPP Ltd. He is Professor (Hon) of Forensic Psychology, University of Birmingham. He is a fellow of the British Psychological Society, a chartered scientist, holds the European Certificate in Psychology, and has dual registrations in forensic and clinical psychology. He was awarded the 2013 Senior Academic Award by the Division of Forensic Psychology. He has over 70 publications including six books.

Marguerite L. Donathy has a Certificate of Higher Education in Psychological Studies from the University of Birmingham, a BSc (Hons) in Psychology from the Open University and an MSc in Criminological Psychology from the University of Birmingham. She currently works in private practice as a trainee forensic psychologist and is completing a doctorate in Forensic Psychology Practice with the University of Birmingham. Ms. Donathy is Branch Secretary and Treasurer for the Midlands branch of the National Organisation for the Treatment of Abusers (NOTA).

Helen Jane Elliott is a research assistant working for SOCAMRU, having completed her MSc in forensic psychology in 2012, Ms. Elliott now works for Nottingham Trent University and a large part of her research focuses on understanding sexual offending through research at HMP Whatton. Ms. Elliott is also involved in research with offenders who have mental-health difficulties and prison-based Circles of Support and Accountability (CoSA).

Caroline M. Foss has an MSc in Forensic Psychology from the University of Birmingham, England, and MA in Professional Counseling from Lindenwood University, Missouri, USA. She currently works in private practice as a licensed professional counselor. Ms. Foss is a board member of the Missouri Association of Treatment for Sexual Abusers and a member of the Association for the Treatment of Sexual Abusers (ATSA).

Theresa A. Gannon is a professor of forensic psychology in the School of Psychology at the University of Kent. She obtained a First Class Honours Degree in Psychology from the University of Birmingham in 1998, a doctorate in psychology from the University of Sussex in 2003, and forensic psychologist practitioner status in 2007. Dr. Gannon has written over 100 peer reviewed journal articles and book chapters in the areas of sexual, violent offending, and firesetting. She has also edited numerous books in forensic psychology and assesses and treats offenders who have sexually offended or set fires on a weekly basis. Dr. Gannon is Editor of the Journal *Psychology Crime and Law*, and Associate Editor of the *Journal of Sexual Aggression*. She now leads the University of Kent's Centre of Research and Education in Forensic Psychology (CORE-FP) in the School of Psychology.

Rosie Gray, Registered Forensic Psychologist, works at Wilcox Psychological Associates Limited, where she undertakes risk assessments, offense-focused treatment, and safeguarding sessions. Dr. Gray is also a qualified probation officer and has worked with individuals who have committed offences in a range of settings, including the National Health Service and HM Prison Service. Her doctoral thesis explored diversity in sexual offender assessment and treatment and she is on the executive committee for the Midlands branch of the National Organisation for the Treatment of Abusers (NOTA).

Elizabeth Hayes is an expert advisor in criminal justice corrections, in the UK and internationally, with a particular emphasis on the assessment, treatment, and management of sexual offenders. She has a professional background in probation and criminal justice social work with established clinical experience followed by regarded expertise in practice, policy, and strategy development. Most recently Ms. Hayes was national Head of Probation Sex Offender Treatment in the Ministry of Justice for England and Wales; her advancements of practice whilst in post included the design and national implementation of the I-SOTP; an accredited treatment program exclusively for online sexual offenders. Ms. Hayes is now CEO of an NGO she has established, providing criminal justice services in the UK and abroad. In Europe, she is currently employed on a number of European Union-led projects, directed at advancing provisions for the effective management of sexual offenders across multiple jurisdictions. In the UK, Ms. Hayes is currently expert advisor to the Scottish Government Justice Department, where she has completed the design of a new national sex offender treatment program, providing for an integrated approach to the treatment of online sexual offenders and a unified provision for delivery across prisons and community correctional settings. Ms. Hayes is on international forums and registers of experts, present at professional conferences and symposia in the UK and abroad, and is published in her field.

Julie Hird is a consultant clinical psychologist in Greater Manchester Mental Health Trust and has worked in forensic NHS settings for 24 years. She has a special interest in sex offending and co-ordinates the Sex Offender Treatment Programme at the Edenfield Centre in Manchester.

Clive Hollin is Professor of Criminological Psychology in the School of Psychology at The University of Leicester, UK. He wrote the best-selling textbook *Psychology and Crime: An Introduction to Criminological Psychology* (2nd ed., 2013, Routledge). In all, he has published 22 books alongside over 300 other academic publications. As well as his various university appointments, he has worked as a psychologist in prisons, the Youth Treatment Service, special hospitals, and regional secure units.

Adarsh Kaul worked as a consultant forensic psychiatrist from 1994 onwards at secure psychiatric hospitals and in community forensic service managing medium and high risk mentally disordered offenders in the community. Having worked in prisons since 1988, Dr. Kaul moved fully into prison psychiatry with the formation of the Offender Health Directorate in Nottinghamshire Healthcare NHS Trust. He is Clinical Director of Offender Health, which provides healthcare to 11 prisons in the South Yorkshire and East Midlands regions of UK. He is a Fellow of the Royal College of Psychiatrists and has an MA in criminology. He was one of the founder members of Leicestershire Multiagency Public Protection Arrangements and worked for 7 years for the National Parole Board in England and Wales. He is currently a medical member of the Her Majesty's Courts & Tribunals Service and is also a member of the National Health and Justice Clinical Reference Group. Since 2010 he has worked at HMP Whatton, a prison exclusively for sex offenders in Nottinghamshire, where he has also started a prison based program of treatment with anti-libidinal drugs for high and very high risk sex offenders who have not adequately responded to psychological treatments.

Rebecca Lievesley is a research fellow for the Sexual Offences, Crime and Misconduct Research Unit (SOCAMRU) at Nottingham Trent University and a forensic psychologist in training. All of her research is focused on offenders, particularly sexual offenders, across a number of prison and forensic establishments and organizations. Ms. Lievesley is also undertaking a PhD on desistance and re-offending in short sentenced offenders.

William R. Lindsay, PhD, FBPS, FIASSID, AcSS, is a consultant clinical and forensic psychologist and Clinical Director in Scotland for Danshell Healthcare. He is Professor of Learning Disabilities at the University of

Abertay, Dundee and Honorary Professor at Deakin University, Melbourne. He has published over 300 research articles and book chapters, published five books, held around £2 million in research grants and given many presentations and workshops on cognitive therapy and the assessment and treatment of offenders with intellectual disability. His current research and clinical interests are in dynamic risk assessment, sex offenders, personality disorder, alcohol related violence, and CBT, all in relation to intellectual disability.

Caroline Logan is Lead Consultant Forensic Clinical Psychologist in Greater Manchester West Mental Health NHS Foundation Trust as well as an honorary research fellow in the Institute of Brain Behaviour and Mental Health at the University of Manchester. She has worked in forensic settings for almost 20 years, working directly with clients who are at risk to themselves and others and, in a consultancy role, with the multidisciplinary teams and local and national organizations that look after and manage them. She is a former Board Member of the Scottish Risk Management Authority, the DSPD Programme Expert Advisory Group, and the Project Board of Resettle, the Merseyside clinical risk and case management service for high-risk offenders. She is currently a member of the Advisory Panel for the Close Supervision Centres and Managing Challenging Behaviour Strategy in the HMPS Directorate of High Security. She is a coauthor of the *Risk for Sexual Violence Protocol*, a structured professional judgment approach to sexual violence risk assessment and management, and a coauthor of the 2007/9 Department of Health guidelines *Best Practice in Managing Risk in Mental Health Services*. Dr. Logan has research interests in the areas of personality disorder, psychopathy, and risk, and a special interest in gender issues in offending, on which she has published two books and many articles.

William L. Marshall is Director of Rockwood Psychological Services, a service that provides treatment for sexual offenders. He has over 400 publications including 20 books and has served on the editorial boards of 17 international journals. He is a fellow of the Royal Society of Canada and in 2006 he was appointed an Officer of the Order of Canada.

Amanda Michie, MA, PhD, CPsychol, AFBPsS, is a consultant clinical psychologist and lead psychologist for learning disability services in Edinburgh City and West Lothian. She has specialist expertise in the field of forensic ID and provides a clinical service to community and IP forensic settings across Lothian. She works closely with criminal justice staff; providing training, consultancy, and clinical input. She is also an established researcher, publishing regularly, particularly in the area of assessment and treatment of offenders with ID.

Christine Norman is a senior lecturer in psychology at Nottingham Trent University and a member of the Sexual Offences, Crime and Misconduct Research Unit (SOCAMRU). Dr. Norman's research and teaching interests are in the area of biological and cognitive psychology with application to psychiatric disorders, forensic psychology, and behavioral addictions. Her particular research interests are in the role of associative learning and reward sensitivity theory in obesity and eating disorders; the origins and development of sexual deviance and sexual preoccupation; the use of anti-libidinal medication in sexually preoccupied sex offenders; the role of traumatic brain injury in offending behavior; and associative learning in gambling behaviors.

Dawn Pflugradt received her doctoral degree in clinical psychology from the Wisconsin Professional School of Psychology. She is a licensed psychologist and works for the Wisconsin Department of Corrections – Division of Community Corrections as a chief psychologist/sex offender risk assessment specialist. Dr. Pflugradt is primarily a clinician providing assessment and treatment services directly to offenders. In addition to her clinical duties, Dr. Pflugradt conducts research on female sexual offenders and issues related to female offenders in general. She has coauthored multiple peer-reviewed articles and has provided workshops on female sexual offenders at national and international conferences.

David S. Prescott is Director of Professional Development and Quality Improvement for the Becket Family of Services in Northern New England. He has published 13 books and numerous articles and chapters on topics related to sexual violence and trauma. Mr. Prescott is on the International Advisory Board for the *Journal of Sexual Aggression* and a Section Editor for the formative journal *Motivational Interviewing: Training, Research, Implementation, Practice*. He currently writes articles for the NEARI Press Newsletter, which has a monthly circulation of over 4,000. He is a past president of the Association for the Treatment of Sexual Abusers (ATSA) and edited that organization's newsletter, *The Forum*, from 2002 to 2007. He is currently *The Forum*'s Review Editor. Mr. Prescott is also a member of the Motivational Interviewing Network of Trainers (MINT), an international organization devoted to a client-centered, directive method for enhancing intrinsic motivation to change by exploring and resolving ambivalence. Most recently, he has become a certified trainer with the International Center for Clinical Excellence, a worldwide community of practitioners, healthcare managers, educators, and researchers dedicated to promoting excellence in behavioral healthcare services.

Ethel Quayle is a senior lecturer in clinical psychology in the School of Health in Social Science at the University of Edinburgh and Director of COPINE research, which until September 2008 was based at University College Cork, Ireland. She is a clinical psychologist and as a practitioner worked with both sex offenders and their victims. For the last 14 years she has been conducting research in the area of technology-mediated crimes, collaborating internationally with government and nongovernment agencies in the context of research, policy, and practice. Her most recent book, with Kurt Ribsl from the University of North Carolina, was published in 2012 and is called *Internet Child Pornography: Understanding and Preventing On-line Child Abuse* and is published by Routledge Taylor-Francis. In addition to academic research activities she plays an active role in a number of government and nongovernment organizations.

Funmilayo Rachal is a forensic psychiatrist who currently works at the Behavioral Medicine Institute of Atlanta and is an adjunct assistant professor of psychiatry at Emory University School of Medicine. Dr. Rachal is a coauthor of the book *Professionalism in Psychiatry* and also coteaches the PBI Professional Boundary courses in Atlanta.

Phil Rich is a consultant and trainer specializing in work with sexually abusive youth. He holds a doctorate in applied behavioral and organizational studies and a master's degree in social work. He was the clinical director of a large treatment program for sexually abusive and sexually troubled children, adolescents, and young adults, and is the author of several books, as well as chapters and articles, which address work with sexually abusive youth.

Karen Thorne is a chartered and registered forensic psychologist. She specializes in the assessment and treatment of violent and sexual offender, with a special interest in noncontact sexual offenders. She has worked for HM Prison Service since 1995 and is currently a psychology service manager for East Midlands Forensic Psychology Service, Public Sector Prisons.

Tony Ward, PhD DipClinPsyc, is a professor of clinical psychology at Victoria University of Wellington, New Zealand. Professor Ward is the creator of the good lives model and has published a number of books, book chapters, and journal articles on this approach. His research interests include offender rehabilitation, forensic and correctional ethics, theoretical psychopathology, and cognition in offenders.

Jayson Ware is the Executive Director of Offender Services and Programs, Corrective Services New South Wales, Australia. He has worked with sexual offenders for the past 15 years and has authored over 20 journal articles or book chapters relating to the treatment of sexual offenders. He has a particular research interest in sex offender denial and is currently completing a PhD examining the effectiveness of treatment for sexual offenders who categorically deny committing a sexual offence.

Belinda Winder (PhD, Reader in Forensic Psychology, Nottingham Trent University) is Head of the Sexual Offences Crime and Misconduct unit (SOCAMRU). Dr. Winder works closely with HMP Whatton to facilitate an applied mixed-method program of research that makes a significant and practical contribution to our understanding of sexual offenders and sexual crime. Dr. Winder is leading the research team evaluating the use of anti-libidinal medication with sexually preoccupied sex offenders – work that has been ongoing since 2011. Dr. Winder is also involved with a number of other research studies, including denial, understandings of risk in Internet sex offenders, prison-based circles of support and accountability (CoSA), and religiosity in sex offenders. She is a trustee of the Safer Living Foundation – a charity set up in collaboration with HMP Whatton, Nottingham Police, and Probation Trust to offer prison-based CoSA for elderly and intellectually disabled high-risk sex offenders.

Foreword

The treatment of sexual offenders continues to be an important and challenging topic, particularly since the actual effectiveness of treatment continues to be debated in published works by "academic experts" more often than being improved upon by actual practitioners (some of whom may also be academics). This book is more about the latter than the former, and may result in practice improvements that may in turn improve outcomes in sexual offender treatment.

A perusal of the chapter titles from this book will impress upon its readers that the treatment of sexual offenders is very complex and that treatment approaches are as varied as the types of sexual offenders themselves. While many books have been written about the treatment of sexual offenders from an academic stance, this book is perhaps more "therapist-friendly" than most due to the use of the central organizing principle of case studies in all of the treatment chapters.

The book is very well laid-out with a convincing rationale for the utility of interventions designed for delivery at the individual client level rather than the usual group level intervention. This is a very useful and unusual approach, but much needed optic for addressing the needs of challenging clients. There are very few chapters that are not about treatment per se (e.g., the "Context Issues" section), but the majority of these also have provided case studies for examples. This approach will facilitate learning by practitioners and easy application for practice and supervision. I also can see that this book would be of great benefit to students who are interested in learning about sex offender treatment, as well for supervisory discussion, seminar material, and forensic coursework application.

For me as a practitioner, the "Offender Issues" and "Specialized Intervention" sections are of absolutely stellar value. Written by expert practitioners in their respective fields, these sections provide insights into how each of these authors thinks through and plans their intervention strategies. For all practitioners who wonder how to approach a difficult case, this approach is of incredible value as it will save time and energy for both the offender and therapist. I note that another Wiley book, written by William R. Lindsay, "The Treatment of Sex Offenders with Developmental Disabilities", was explicitly "A Practice Workbook", whereas the present book is perhaps more implicitly a compilation of best practice by client type. While the breadth of the scope of the book, in terms of types of offenders ("Offender Issues"; 12 chapters) and "Specialized Interventions" (3 chapters), could not allow comprehensive elucidation of all components of treatment, each of these intervention chapters in general provided a background rationale regarding the client type or intervention type, assessment issues, case description, case conceptualization, treatment plan, assessment of progress in treatment, and discussion of the treatment effectiveness plus recommendations regarding best practice.

The final chapter reiterates the rationale for the book's case study approach. In my opinion, the outstanding preceding 19 chapters should make most of this chapter, theoretically at least, redundant. There should be no doubt in any reader's mind that the case study approach used in the book is both useful and valuable by the time they read the last chapter! That said, I also have no doubt that the academics who are not clinicians, and who doubt the utility of sexual offender treatment, will see this book as a "How To" book in an area that is of speculative utility. However, this book is not about assessing effectiveness or utility, but about promoting and enhancing best practice with an incredible range of different types of sexual offenders utilizing case studies. The authors say it best: "although case studies cannot provide conclusive evidence for the overall effectiveness of a treatment approach, they can tell us what did or did not work when these approaches were implemented in real life practice with individuals who have multiple needs and this information can be used as a guide to inform future individualized work" (page 373).

In closing, I would like to congratulate the authors for putting a new twist on the important topic of sexual offender treatment and doing it so well. I also want to enthusiastically recommend this book to practitioners working with sexual offenders, whether on a group or individual basis. The book is a summary of current thinking about a wide range of subtypes of sexual offenders, best practice with such offenders, and a novel use of the case study approach that will allow practitioners to develop expertise with individual clients with complex needs. In my opinion, any practitioner in the field of sexual offender treatment would be very much remiss if this book was not on their real or virtual bookshelf.

Douglas P. Boer, PhD
Professor of Clinical Psychology
Centre for Applied Psychology
Faculty of Health, University of Canberra, Australia
President, International Association for the Treatment of Sexual
Offenders

Preface

A great many books have been written about sexual offenders. We hope that this book will not be viewed as just another run-of-the-mill volume to add to the list, to be purchased, put on the shelf, and forgotten. What we have tried to achieve here is something quite different. By bringing together top-notch international experts in the field, we hope to showcase the current state of play in sex offender treatment worldwide, with a focus on individual approaches. The treatment of sexual offenders is so often formulaic; yet, this client group is diverse and has varied needs. This is perhaps quite difficult to appreciate when so much of what is written is to do with risk assessment and group-based treatment. In this volume, we have sought to illustrate sexual offenders' diverse issues and treatment needs by emphasizing the need for individual formulation. We hope that this approach really brings alive this fascinating area of work.

We have been privileged to work with some inspiring clinicians and researchers in this field, whose influence and support we would like to acknowledge. These include Brian Thomas-Peter, David Middleton, Clark Baim, and many others who have been supportive, close, local colleagues. Birmingham, England, and the surrounding Midlands area has definitely had a history of punching above its weight, with the West Midlands Probation Service Sex Offender Unit developing the first Home Office-accredited group sex offender treatment program in the UK, and conducting the first polygraph trials with sex offenders that ultimately led to acceptance of the polygraph for use in the assessment and treatment of convicted sex offenders in the UK. The University of Birmingham, School of Forensic and Criminological Psychology was instrumental in the development of dynamic risk-assessment tools in Britain, and took the lead nationally in terms of both shaping and evaluating sex offender treatment programs in the UK. Many of the chapter authors emanate from this area and have authored or contributed to an extensive and impressive range of books on sex offender assessment, treatment, and community management. Working with our university, prison service, local authority, probation, and mental health services colleagues has always been a pleasure. Long may it continue.

This preface would not be complete without mention of the clients with sexual offending histories and those who have been sexually abused, with whom we have worked over the years. These clients, whether coming to us for assessment, treatment, or research purposes, have helped us to develop our understanding of this field in a way that we could not have done through academic pursuits alone. Often, they have shared their experiences bravely and openly. They have co-operated with us and have given us feedback about our work, and we have learned a great deal from them. We hope that, for our part, we have been able to be of some help to them.

This book has been a long time in the making. It was conceived of several years ago at the suggestion of Dan Wilcox, the first editor. He and I grappled with the idea on our own, but it never progressed to implementation stage because we always had other important "fish to fry." It was Dan's genius idea that brought our colleague Leigh Harkins on board as third editor, and Leigh has been a real catalyst in making the book happen, even though she has moved from the UK to Canada during the process, taking on various new responsibilities along the way. We seem to have become a great team and we miss her presence up the road from us at the University of Birmingham. However, Skype has proven to be a real boon, and we have met regularly in this way since Leigh's departure from the UK, to get the book finished. It has been a pleasure and a privilege for me to work with Dan and Leigh on this book. I shall miss our collaboration and meetings.

We have needed to be hard taskmasters with our contributors at times (ourselves as well), but we are grateful to all of the book authors who have stepped up to the mark, and do not seem to have minded the (sometimes quite considerable) demands we have placed on them. In fact, the chapter authors have exceeded all our expectations, and have gone above and beyond the call of duty to produce chapters which really do reflect the "state of the art" of sex offender treatment. We are grateful to them for the vast knowledge they have brought to this book, as well as their willingness, hard work, and co-operation.

A great many people contributed to the completion of this book; in particular, we would wish to express our thanks to Roz Wilcox, for her typing, amending, and editing assistance throughout. Thanks also to other WPA Ltd. staff who have all played some role in the completion of this book. The encouragement of Darren Read, early on, and Karen Shield, along with her assistant editor, Olivia Wells, at Wiley-Blackwell kept us on track and supported us throughout. Many thanks also go to Aileen Castell, Hairiani Rashid and Alec McAulay for their assistance in the final stages of completing this book. We are most grateful for their direction and guidance. Almost inevitably, there will be some errors and inaccuracies in a book of this length and we, the editors, take full responsibility for any such unfortunate occurrences. Lastly, we extend unreserved thanks and appreciation to our families and those closest to us who have borne the burden of our periodic preoccupation or unavailability over the last 2 years, and still managed to be both supportive and encouraging.

I'm sure I speak for the editors and all of the contributors when I say that we felt a great sense of achievement in taking this work through to completion. Lastly, in consideration of the vast experience of the chapter authors, it is our sincere hope that our readers will value this book as much as we enjoyed bringing it together.

Tanya Garrett
D. T. Wilcox
L. Harkins

Part I

Overview

1

The Continuing Need for Individualized Interventions with Sex Offenders

Daniel T. Wilcox, Tanya Garrett, and Leigh Harkins

Introduction

Among sex offenders, some do not deal well with the group process, while others can be disruptive in these settings. Still other offenders have complex treatment needs that cannot be fully met within a group treatment program. For this reason, although the authors are altogether supportive of group-based sex offender treatment programs (SOTPs), we consider that there are circumstances where either individualized interventions are required or a combination of group and one-to-one work is needed. For example, individuals with extremely high levels of assessed deviance or risk can, at times, have a marked adverse impact on standard SOTP groups.

Notably, individuals with significant psychopathic, paranoid or border-line personality features can also struggle in group treatment, demonstrating particular difficulties with group engagement concerning offense-related issues. They may also introduce an unhelpful dynamic in terms of inhibiting or otherwise interfering with the participation of other group members. Such offenders may, in the experience of the authors, benefit more from one-to-one sessions to explore their sexual interests and the pro-offending cognitive distortions that supported their offending behavior, or indeed as adjunctive treatment for any identified mental health related issues. However, the same individuals may progress better in a group setting in respect of developing better socio-affective skills and making necessary

Sex Offender Treatment: A Case Study Approach to Issues and Interventions, First Edition. Edited by Daniel T. Wilcox, Tanya Garrett, and Leigh Harkins. © 2015 John Wiley & Sons, Ltd. Published 2015 by John Wiley & Sons, Ltd.

self-management gains. In our experience, some offenders are also referred for individualized work because they lack the necessary coping abilities to contend with an SOTP. They may require individual clinical interventions to address inadequate emotional resilience and stress management abilities to be able to engage in an SOTP.

Perhaps unsurprisingly, in view of the unusual referral pathway that such individuals travel along, they almost invariably present as offenders with more complex needs than those taken through standard SOTP groups. In our experience, offenders referred for individualized treatment have more unusual and potentially challenging clinical or forensic histories and personality profiles. As such, even seasoned practitioners may at times be confronted with cases so unique that they would value the knowledge and experience of other professionals who have passed down similar roads before them.

Group Treatment

As a frame of reference, in Part II, Gray and Wilcox provide a summary of the assessment, treatment, and monitoring processes that are typically employed within accredited cognitive-behavioral-therapy-based SOTPs in North America, Europe, Australia/New Zealand and other parts of the world that are influenced by the Association for the Treatment of Abusers (ATSA), the National Organisation for the Treatment of Abusers (NOTA), the Australia and New Zealand Association for the Treatment of Sexual Abuse (ANZATSA), and the International Association for the Treatment of Sexual Offenders (IATSO). Research on treatment outcomes for these group-based SOTPs has consistently shown a significant positive effect, though in general not of a magnitude that would cause most professionals in this field to choose to rest on their laurels yet (Hanson, Bourgon, Helmus, & Hodgson, 2009; Hanson, et al., 2002; Hanson & Morton-Bourgon, 2005).

Over the last quarter of a century, assessment and treatment developments have been introduced and evaluated, giving much-needed structure to our work in this field (Beech, Craig, & Browne, 2009; Hanson & Bussière, 1998; Hanson & Morton-Bourgon, 2004; Hanson & Thornton, 2000; Laws, Hudson, & Ward, 2000; Maletzky, 1991; Marshall, Anderson, & Fernandez, 1999; Marshall, Laws, & Barbaree, 1990). However, professionals working with sex offenders in the past have seemingly been as vulnerable to manipulation and grooming as anyone else. Salter (1988, 2004) has tracked and chronicled this phenomenon, noting that even qualified professionals in the field have, at times, characterized sexual offenders as "harmless, unfairly judged or misguided" while directing a substantial weight of responsibility onto victims, impugning their characters, actions, and reputations. Further, Wilcox (2013) has noted that, even today, some professionals in practice continue to provide such explanations for the behaviors of abusers and victims. Nevertheless, while practitioners working with sex offenders on an individual case basis may be viewed as more vulnerable to manipulation and grooming than within the context of the structured group process (Wilcox, 2013), inevitably, this approach will be necessary in some circumstances to address identified needs and to reduce future risk of offending.

Fortunately, professionals in practice today have more tools available to assist them in maintaining an objective and informed perspective when applying structured professional judgment (Hart, 2013; Hart & Logan, 2011; Wilcox, 2013). From this starting point, sex offender workers may feel more equipped to develop treatment plans for offenders who do not fit into standard group-based intervention programs.

Case Formulation

The following chapters in this book describe the individualized interventions and the case formulations of acknowledged experts within which their assessment processes, intervention, and supervision plans are developed in relation to specific treatment issues or offender types. The book's central focus on case studies and case formulation draws from a rich theoretical and clinical/forensic-practice base, identifying the continuing need for individually-tailored interventions and recognizing the interrelationship between case conceptualization, applied behavioral analysis, and risk assessment. This is a rapidly developing field, with important contributions from, for example, Sturmey and McMurran (2011); Butler (1998); Eells (2007); Nezu, Nezu, Friedman, and Haynes (1997); and Tarrier (2005), which offer practitioners valuable guidance about case formulation in forensic settings.

We believe that case formulation is an essential tool in understanding offenders' behavior, the underpinning thoughts and feelings that influenced their actions, and those factors which have contributed to their risk of reoffending. This approach provides a structure for organizing and integrating information gained about the individual and about their presenting difficulties, such that causes and precipitating factors may be given full consideration along with the person-specific features that serve to maintain any propensity for offending. Comprehensive case formulation will also reveal protective features, as well as the various resilience potentials identified in the offender. These factors can be taken into account to provide the most robust assessment of risk possible, as well as an evaluation of desistance capacity (Harrison, 2010). Such a thorough review enables the treatment worker to develop a more comprehensive intervention and monitoring plan based on hypotheses drawn and tested from the case formulation. Eells (2007) has noted that effective case formulation does not concentrate on simply describing the offending behavior, but takes a further step to explain how the offending activity developed and progressed. Furthermore, Rich (2013) asserted that case formulation not only explains what happened, but more importantly offers a theory as to why the individual engaged in the sexually abusive behavior. Rich emphasized that a formulation-based approach to treatment cannot rely on a strict, inflexible, and predetermined strategy for intervention, or a manualized style of working. In a similar vein, Drake and Ward (2003) conclude that effective formulation is idiosyncratic and requires a comprehensive understanding of the underlying psychological characteristics of each individual being treated.

The Structure of This Book

Following this overview chapter, Part II describes the context within which sex offender work is undertaken. Prescott considers what impact working with sexual offenders has on professionals in the field, and focuses on therapist self-care. Ward explores the ethical framework for working with sex offenders, describing tensions between human rights and criminal justice perspectives with regard to treatment provision, and offers suggestions as to how they may be reconciled by professionals. Gray and Wilcox describe the typical journey of a convicted sexual offender by detailing accepted approaches to supervision, assessment, and treatment.

Part III focuses on offender issues, exploring treatment approaches applied with 12 different types of sexual offenders. These chapters variously take account of offender gender, age, deviant sexual preferences, mental state, and cognitive ability. It is hoped that the specificity of these offender-related chapters will assist workers in formulating their treatment approach with new and challenging cases. These chapters direct attention to treating those who sexually abuse children, men who sexually abuse adults, sexually abusive adolescents, intellectually disabled offenders, non-contact sexual offenders, and Internet offenders. A case study of a female sex offender is included, as well as a study of a sex offender with bipolar disorder. Professional sexual misconduct is addressed, as well as interventions with psychopathic sexual offenders, high deviance (zoophilic) offenders, and sexual killers.

Part IV describes specialist interventions employed with sexual offenders, with Ware and Harkins addressing denial issues and Marshall detailing techniques for changing deviant sexual interests. The final chapter in this part, by Winder and colleagues, explores the assistive role of anti-libidinal medication.

Part V of this book addresses future practice from the perspectives of the editors. It considers the training needs of practitioners and the skill base they require, as well as established and emerging assessment and treatment strategies that they may choose to employ. The authors are committed to the continuing development of responsive and focal treatment for sexual offenders and hope that the following chapters will offer novices and seasoned practitioners alike, helpful and relevant guidance tools that they can apply in their work with sexual offenders.

The continuing need for skilled individualized interventions is the central theme of this book and, relatedly, we recall the thoughts of Professor Simon Hackett when addressing the NOTA Annual General Meeting at the Edinburgh Conference in 2007. As the then outgoing editor of the Journal of Sexual Aggression, Simon advised, "The case study approach offers professionals in this field unique opportunities to link theory, research and practice". In support of this guidance it has been our intention, through producing this book, to play a part in forging these links.

References

Beech, A. R., Craig, L. A., & Browne, K. D. (2009). *Assessment and treatment of sex offenders: A handbook*. Chichester, UK: John Wiley & Sons.

Butler, G. (1998). Clinical formulation. In A. S. Bellack & M. Hersen (Eds.), *Comprehensive clinical psychology* (Vol. 6, pp. 1–24). Oxford, UK: Pergamon.

Drake, C. R., & Ward, T. (2003). Practical and theoretical roles for the formulation based treatment of sexual offenders. *International Journal of Forensic Psychology, 1*, 71–84.

Eells, T. D. (2007). *Handbook of psychotherapy case formulation*. New York: Guilford Press.

Hanson, R. K., Bourgon, G., Helmus, L., & Hodgson, S. (2009). The principles of effective correctional treatment also apply to sexual offenders: A meta-analysis. *Criminal Justice and Behavior, 36*, 865–891.

Hanson, R. K., & Bussière, M. T. (1998). Predicting relapse: A meta-analysis of sexual offender recidivism studies. *Journal of Consulting and Clinical Psychology, 66*(2), 348–362.

Hanson, R. K., Gordon, A., Harris, A. J. R., Marques, J. K., Murphy, W., Quinsey, V. L., et al. (2002). First report of the collaborative data outcomes project on the effectiveness of psychological treatment of sex offenders. *Sexual Abuse: A Journal of Research and Treatment, 14*, 169–194.

Hanson, R. K., & Morton-Bourgon, K. E. (2004). *Predictors of sexual recidivism: An updated meta-analysis.* Retrieved March 26, 2014, from http://www.static99.org/pdfdocs/hansonandmortonbourgon2004.pdf

Hanson, R. K., & Morton-Bourgon, K. E. (2005). The characteristics of persistent sexual offenders: A meta-analysis of recidivism studies. *Journal of Consulting and Clinical Psychology, 73*(6), 1154–1163.

Hanson, R. K., & Thornton, D. (2000). Improving risk assessments for sex offenders: A comparison of three actuarial scales. *Law and Human Behavior, 24,* 119–136.

Harrison, K. (2010). *Managing high-risk sex offenders in the community: Risk management, treatment and social responsibility.* Cullompton, UK: Willan.

Hart, S. D. (2013, September) Understanding, assessing and managing violence risk: The movement from formula to formulation. Keynote presentation at the European Association of Psychology and Law (EAPL) Conference. Coventry, UK: Coventry University.

Hart, S. D., & Logan, C. (2011). Formulation of violence risk using evidence-based assessments: The structured professional judgement approach. In P. Sturmey & M. McMurran (Eds.), *Forensic case formulation.* Chichester, UK: John Wiley & Sons.

Laws, D. R., Hudson, S. M., & Ward, T. (2000). *Remaking relapse prevention with sex offenders: A sourcebook.* Thousand Oaks, CA: Sage.

Maletzky, B. M. (1991). *Treating the sexual offender.* Newbury Park, CA: Sage.

Marshall, W. L., Anderson, D., & Fernandez, Y. (1999). *Cognitive behavioral treatment of sexual offenders.* New York: John Wiley & Sons.

Marshall, W. L., Laws, D. R., & Barbaree, H. E. (1990). *Handbook of sexual assault: Issues, theories and treatment of the offender.* New York: Plenum Press.

Nezu, A. M., Nezu, C. M., Friedman, S. H., & Haynes, S. N. (1997). Case formulation in behavior therapy: Problem-solving and functional analytic strategies. In T. D. Eells (Ed.), *Handbook of psychotherapy case formulation* (pp. 368–401). New York: Guilford Press.

Rich, P. (2013, September). The role of case study in work with sexually abusive adolescents. In "What we can learn from case studies in sex offender treatment?", Symposium for the National Organisation for the Treatment of Abusers (NOTA) National Conference. Cardiff City Hall, Cardiff, UK.

Salter, A. C. (1988). *Treating child sex offenders and victims: A practical guide.* Newbury Park, CA: Sage.

Salter, A. C. (2004). *Predators: Pedophiles, rapists and other sex offenders: Who they are, how they operate and how we can protect ourselves and our children.* New York: Basic Books.

Sturmey, P., & McMurran, M. (2011). *Forensic case formulation.* Chichester, UK: John Wiley & Sons.

Tarrier, N. (2005). *Case formulation in cognitive behaviour therapy: The treatment of challenging and complex cases.* Hove, UK: Bruner Routledge.

Wilcox, D. T. (2013). A forensic psychologist's involvement in working with sex offenders. In K. Harrison and B. Rainey (Eds.), *Legal and ethical aspects of sex offender treatment and management.* Chichester, UK: Wiley & Sons.

Part II

Context Issues

Part II

Context Issues

2

Motivation, Compassion, and Self-care in the Treatment of Sexual Offenders

David S. Prescott

Introduction

Professionals working with people who have sexually abused face challenges that are uncommon in other treatment settings. Many enter the field to help build safer communities and healthier lives, only to discover aspects of human experience well beyond anything they learned in their formal education. Some professionals find the experience deeply disturbing, and they begin questioning human nature and sexuality. Others find the work meaningful and rewarding despite the necessity of working with a population that is often unhappy about having to be in treatment. Some professionals begin to question elements of their own sexuality while others experience sexualized countertransference. Amid challenging perspectives on sexuality, they are often confronted with shifting expectations in their work, as well. For example, many professionals have found that the confrontational approaches advocated in the past (e.g., Salter, 1988) are less conducive to job satisfaction than other, more positive approaches (Harkins, Flak, Beech, & Woodhams, 2012).

This chapter explores compassionate, motivational treatment and the importance for professionals working with sexual offenders of taking excellent care of his or her self, physically and psychologically. It describes a therapist, Julie Hart, and a client, Marcus Paul. These characters are fabrications based on many people the author has encountered in nearly

Sex Offender Treatment: A Case Study Approach to Issues and Interventions, First Edition. Edited by Daniel T. Wilcox, Tanya Garrett, and Leigh Harkins. © 2015 John Wiley & Sons, Ltd. Published 2015 by John Wiley & Sons, Ltd.

30 years of practice. The institution in which this case study is based is also fictitious, but is representative of the strengths and challenges of numerous facilities like it.

Background Information: Theoretical and Research Basis

Julie had earned the appropriate credentials to accept a therapist position at the Calisota Civil Commitment Center (CCCC) only a few years before her arrival. The CCCC treats sexual offenders deemed by courts to be at high risk to reoffend after the expiration of their prison sentences and is one of approximately 20 such programs in the USA. The civil commitment of sexual offenders can be highly controversial (e.g., Schlank, 2005). Even the word "civil" can be ironic, given the highly adversarial processes involved. For example, legal defense professionals in these cases very frequently – and understandably – seek to minimize the harm done by their clients ("what we really have in these cases, your honor, is a case of some very intoxicated people"). It is even more common for legal defense professionals to seek to discredit both the assessment processes preceding treatment and the treatment program itself. Even setting aside the fact that civil commitment involves indefinite detention from which an individual might never be discharged, it is no surprise that many people enter these programs bitter, resentful, and in despair.

The interview process left Julie with a clear impression that the organizational structure of prisons and sexual offender civil commitment programs can appear paramilitary in comparison to traditional mental health treatment programs. Vernon Quinsey and his colleagues once quipped that, "The universe is homogeneous with respect to forensic institutions" (Quinsey, Harris, Rice, & Cormier, 2006, p. 12). The staffing numbers would bear much of this out; there were many more security staff than therapists, a fact that contributed strongly to the culture of the center. Typically there is intense financial pressure to have new staff members work directly with clients after the bare minimum amount of training considered necessary to ensure their safety. The bulk of introductory training for staff in civil commitment programs focuses on quelling disturbances, handling evidence, maintaining routines, and the like. Although they typically receive training in communication skills, conflict resolution, and what happens within sexual offender treatment, there are good reasons for the emphasis on safety and security. Prisons and civil commitment centers can be toxic environments at many levels. Even in programs where violence is rare, its potential is understood and felt at all times.

What receives far less attention in prisons and civil commitment programs is the importance of each staff member taking excellent care of him- or herself. There can be many reasons for this. Tight budgets and scant resources often make it necessary to teach only the basics of safety, supervision, and rehabilitation. Even the United States military has only recently developed positive psychology-based methods in the hope of reducing posttraumatic stress disorder (PTSD; Seligman, 2009). Prior to this, much of the military's efforts were about raising awareness that PTSD exists. The infrequency of organized attention to professional self-care can stem from many causes, but in the end there is one simple fact: long-term professional survival can depend on focusing efforts on managing short-term daily pressures.

When Julie reported for work on her first day, she filled out all of the usual paperwork and presented all the requisite documentation. A security captain gave her an identification badge containing a magnetic strip that would open locked doors in assigned areas to which she had access. Her badge would be stored in a locked cabinet requiring that she punch in a code. When she appeared slightly confused the security captain assured her that within two weeks, all of these procedures would fade into the background of her daily experience. She would come to realize that this was not only accurate, but a matter of some concern. Although not the subject of extensive research, it is nonetheless a common experience for staff not to notice how different the environment of a high-security setting is from the rest of the world. Likewise, when each workday flows smoothly into the next, it can be easy to minimize the level of depression and anxiety that many – perhaps most – clients experience. Likewise, it can be easy to underestimate the immense power that each staff member has in the life of the client.

This last point is worth a closer look. Authors on psychotherapy such as Michael Yapko (2005) have long noted a very simple element of human existence: whatever we focus on we amplify in our minds. In the mind of a professional working with sexual offenders, fulfilling documentation requirements can take center stage throughout much of a week. For Julie, this meant having case notes written in a timely fashion and focusing her efforts in a direction that would prevent upper management displeasure. To accomplish this, she might write more or less on a given day. She might select certain words for their expediency and in a way that would foster easy communication between clinicians in her immediate purview. Her clients, however, were clear in their own minds that Julie's observations could easily fall into the hands of a prosecutor who might use them to bring new charges. In Julie's mind, case notes became another obligation, while the clients viewed them as potential barriers to their freedom. Under these circumstances, Julie quickly became puzzled by the reluctance of those on her caseload to speak openly with her, just as the clients were quick to perceive her as not understanding or respecting their concerns.

Similar problems would emerge when Julie was assessing treatment progress. In her view, she might try to provide feedback about what work the client had yet to accomplish. Her clients came to view feedback as a litany of problems and unfulfilled tasks rather than processes to experience. Under these circumstances it was no wonder that when Julie walked into a treatment group without adequate rest or with something on her mind, her clients would recognize it immediately.

Case Introduction and History

Marcus was 42 years old when he arrived at the CCCC. The security staff inventoried his belongings and confiscated a number of items, including newspaper clippings about his crimes and legal documents related to his convictions. The assistant attorney general had personally contacted the program expressing concern that although Marcus was entitled by the laws of his state to have these documents while in prison, they were likely a source of pornographic fantasy to Marcus. In fact, they contained victim-impact statements; the assistant attorney general was concerned that Marcus would use these descriptions to invoke a euphoric recall of his past conquests.

Marcus had reached the end of his prison sentence and was aware that in accordance with the laws of 20 states and the federal government of the United States, there was a very good chance he would enter a facility where he would be detained indefinitely or until he could demonstrate that he had sufficiently reduced his risk by completing a treatment program. Marcus' age placed him at the exact median for residents in this kind of program; a few years older than the average in many prison populations (e.g., Wilson, Looman, Abracen, & Pake, 2012), this may have reflected the severity of his earlier prison sentence.

Marcus' most recent crime had involved kidnapping a woman, whom he had never met, in a parking lot and forcing her to drive to an area adjacent to a cemetery, where he sexually assaulted her. A factor that had made this crime particularly frightening was that Marcus wore a black hood and clothes typical of a member of an outlaw motorcycle gang (e.g., boots and a leather jacket with a club emblem sewn on the back). Following his arrest, police found handwritten narratives and maps describing his plan for this assault.

Following his admission, the staff escorted Marcus to a unit designated for those who had not yet consented to treatment. Upon finding out that he would share a room with another person, Marcus loudly threatened to assault the unit director, whereupon the security staff placed him immediately in a separation unit, reserved for those who posed an imminent risk to themselves and others. He would remain there for many months.

First Encounter: Presenting Complaints

As a therapist who was new to the institution and still inexperienced, Julie was assigned to the portion of the program that treats "conventional" clients, those with IQs in the average to above-average range, and who did not have high levels of psychopathic traits. Her work would involve the very first stages of treatment, which would seek to build amenability to treatment, improve decision making, provide education around thought patterns related to illegal behavior (called "thinking errors"), and help clients develop improved self-regulation. More than half of the clients in this treatment track had received diagnoses of Antisocial Personality Disorder and/or Pedophilia. Many carried more ambiguous diagnoses, such as Paraphilia, Not Otherwise Specified. In reviewing the diagnoses, Julie was fascinated by how few clients had received diagnoses in areas other than those related to sexual abuse. Her clients routinely expressed and displayed symptoms of anxiety, depression, Posttraumatic Stress Disorder, and Attention Deficit Hyperactivity Disorder that was either previously undiagnosed or untreated.

Part of Julie's responsibilities included making periodic attempts to engage the clients who refused treatment and those on the separation unit (SU). She was already aware of Marcus' presence, as his arrival had generated much discussion amongst the staff. Per institution policy, the treatment team held a meeting to review Marcus' placement 72 hours after his placement. These meetings often put therapists into a difficult role. By design, there were more security (a psychiatric security worker and a unit manager) than clinical staff (Julie) present. Although the rules for decision-making in SU placement matters were clear and explicit, a number of challenges still entered the background of the discussion. Some members of the security team, despite their training, were skeptical of their clientele's capacity to change and would prefer to err on the side of safety. Julie's supervisor had been clear with her that extended stays in the SU could quickly become the source of legal action, and urged Julie to do what she could to secure Marcus' commitment to treatment and placement on a unit for treatment participants. This put Julie into a bind; she could advocate for Marcus and risk creating an undesirable reputation with the security staff, or she could acquiesce to their wishes, creating doubts in her supervisor's mind. Although she told herself she would advocate according to her own assessment of the facts and Marcus' needs and rights, she was aware that she was also in a political bind and would likely be most successful in any situation where – as a local saying would explain – she could "go along to get along" with others. In this political calculus, Marcus' best interests could easily take second place to the institution's.

Fortunately, Marcus' situation was straightforward. His behavior had been stable for the full 72 hours, meaning that there was no reason to keep him on the SU. Julie then went to meet with Marcus. Her task was to explore Marcus' willingness to participate in treatment. The outcome of this discussion would determine whether he would move to a living unit for treatment participants or another unit for "refusers."

JULIE:	Good morning, Mr. Paul. My name is Julie Hart. I'm a social worker and therapist here at the CCCC. I wonder if we could speak for a few moments?
MARCUS (making direct, expressionless eye contact, dispassionately assessing her):	A few moments. I'm here for the rest of my life, and you want a few moments of it.
JULIE (aware of sensations in her abdomen and forehead, and unaware that her posture had begun to orient slightly back toward the door to the unit):	Yes, I was hoping to talk with you about the treatment program. I'll understand if it seems hopeless or if it's not the right time.
MARCUS:	I'm not interested.
JULIE (slight slouch, but prepared for this response):	Okay, thank you. I'll be on my way then, and hope to check up on you in the next week to see if you've had any additional thoughts. In the meantime, the staff can help you contact me if you like (gets up to leave and starts to walk away).

Assessment

In this instance, Julia had been prepared for a client's request not to meet. There is a central axiom in motivational interviewing (MI) that MI is something done for and with a client, not to and on them (Miller & Rollnick, 2013, p. 24). Under these conditions, the only acceptable answer to a client who does not want to talk is to thank them and leave; offering to be available to the client if they change their mind is also acceptable. Having this response at the ready is not only respectful toward the client, it is a building block of professional self-care. Professionals who attempt to force their interventions on unwilling clients are prone to greater levels of subjective distress and are less effective (Parhar, Wormith, Derkzen, & Beauregard, 2008). A helpful approach to any form of intervention in criminal justice is to remind one's self that the client's decisions, for better or worse, are between them and their future. Even as every professional wants the best outcomes for their clients and the community, an emotional investment in the outcome, which can easily become expressed in attempts to persuade or cajole, will bring disappointment and risk for burnout.

Another advantage to honoring the client's decision not to speak is that it is respectful of his or her autonomy. Within Julie's first hours at the CCCC, it became very clear that her clients had very few opportunities to make any decisions for themselves, much less function as autonomous beings. Julie made an explicit decision that she would work differently from how many people seemed to behave. Whereas prison and civil commitment environments can seem to encourage staff members tacitly to serve as reminders of their clients' restricted liberties, Julie was determined to be a person who found ways to offer appropriate choices when virtually all other choices had been taken away. For example, where other therapists might say, "Today we are going to review your treatment plan," she could say "What part of your treatment plan would you be willing to talk with me about today?" To this end, Julie was determined to approach interactions like the famous dancer Ginger Rogers. Rather than going to each interaction prepared to issue directions and provide feedback, Julie determined to engage in a kind of choreography with each client in much the way that Rogers did with her partner, Fred Astaire: by dancing backward and in heels. In real life, Ginger Rogers brought out the best in Fred Astaire. So it can be that in adopting a "choreography" mindset the professional can seek out evidence of strengths, autonomy, and positive attributes in each client and openly demonstrate understanding and respect for him or her.

A final advantage of Julie's prepared approach was that she did not have to engage in spontaneous guesswork. By relying on studied approaches such as MI or nonviolent communication, Julie could rely on a structure rather than her own wits. This left a great deal of energy and other psychological resources available to her and her clients.

First encounter continued: case conceptualization

As Julie got up to leave, Marcus demonstrated a change of heart that is familiar to those practicing MI under these circumstances. By respecting his autonomy she actually increased the likelihood that he would speak with her.

MARCUS:	Oh what the heck. I'll talk to you. Have a seat.
JULIE:	Okay, thank you, Mr. Paul.
MARCUS:	What do you want to talk about, anyway?
JULIE:	You've been in institutions a long time. I'm interested in whether there are any options you'd like to explore for getting off of this one? (Open-ended question)
MARCUS:	You're not the first person who's wanted me to get onto a regular unit. You know that, right?
JULIE:	I thought there might have been others.
MARCUS (smiling):	Yeah. I told them all to go to hell.

With this comment, Julie was now at a decision point. Marcus' comment appeared deliberately provocative, and could reflect many possible motivations. He might be assessing how far he could push her, and he could also simply be speaking his truth in his own language. Julie made a mental note that she may need to curtail the discussion at some point if Marcus were to escalate into abusive language. A dilemma in working in a larger institutional treatment program can be that there are standards for communication that are based on the culture of the institution; what might be acceptable to one person under specific circumstances can be different from what is acceptable to a large group of professionals in a specific program culture. As just one example, Julie had learned this quickly when she first started at the CCCC and received an informal tutorial on what was and was not considered acceptable professional dress and appearance. The relevance of these cultural considerations in the immediate discussion was that Julie was now making small decisions in the moment based upon myriad factors and not simply what was helpful to advancing her dialog with Marcus. For his part, Marcus had already been able to ascertain that

Julie was not listening fully and completely. Indeed, as the conversation continued she appeared to him as though she were mentally rehearsing her response before he had finished what he wanted to say. For her part, Julie deliberately continued the conversation knowing that she could always change course later if it proceeded into unhelpful directions.

> JULIE: So there's been all these staff trying to get you back onto a unit, and you don't want to. Tell me more about that.
>
> MARCUS: They want me to live in a room with a roommate. Look, I'm not a young man anymore. I don't want a roommate. I know there's no real choice, and I know overcrowding is a problem, but there's a point at which I have to take a stand.
>
> JULIE: This is about your autonomy, about standing up for what you believe in.

In this sentence, Julie wanted to understand Marcus' perspective at a deeper level. Instead of saying "tell me more," she tested her hypothesis by extending Marcus' "take a stand" into "standing up for what you believe in." If she was right, Marcus would agree; if not, he would tell her. This kind of reflective statement is virtually risk-free in high-stakes conversations such as this. A small but significant part of therapist self-care is to simply reflect back the client's statements (and their meaning) and seek to join up with them rather than correct, cajole, or work to persuade them. Julie's unspoken self-statement was that she would simply try to understand Marcus.

> MARCUS: Yes, that's right. What often gets forgotten in these places is that we are men. Not numbers, not just sex offenders, and definitely not cattle, or firewood to be stacked in some far-off corner.
>
> JULIE: So it seems to you that people aren't looking at you as a person.
>
> MARCUS (pursing lips): That's part of it, but – and please excuse me for saying this – you said person, I said man. If people looked at me as a man and not just a person (voice trails off). Look, what I'm trying to do is stand up for my rights and the rights of the other men here. It's pretty much all I have left. If you know anything about me, you know that no judge is ever going to let me out of here.
>
> JULIE: Even if you never get out of here, you want to hold on to your rights.

MARCUS:	Yes, that's very good, but I need to correct you on one small thing. I don't mean to be disrespectful. I appreciate your hopeful spirit that I might actually get out of here, but we both know that I will watch you retire from this place. This is my home (pointing to the unit) and this is my house (pointing to his cell, which in the CCCC was referred to as his "room").
JULIE:	So wherever you are in this institution, you'll be advocating for your rights and those of others.
MARCUS:	Yes.

Julie pondered this for a few moments. From one perspective, Marcus' indomitable attitude was a triumph of the human spirit. From another, he seemed hopeless about his chances for release. She found herself wondering if the emphasis he placed on manhood had not also factored in the sadistic nature of his sex crimes. A problem in working with sexual and violent offenders for therapists of both genders is that their behavior can often be so extreme that it is easy to forget that it is natural and healthy for men to consider their own masculinity. Teasing out the abuse-related attitudes and beliefs from those related to one's identity can be highly challenging to novices, and many men can become vulnerable to gender self-doubt (Bailey, Buchbinder, & Eisikovits, 2011). Perhaps most fascinating to Julie, however, was what seemed to be a continuum in Marcus' function, with his confident self-assertion on one end and his sadistic behavior on the other. She wondered what this said about men – and for that matter, women – in general.

JULIE (summarizing):	Let me make sure I understand. Your placement here in the separation unit is something of a protest about having to share a room with someone else, and you've seen no other way to make your concerns known or stand up for yourself.
MARCUS:	Yeah. I just want to be able to pass gas at 3 in the morning without being embarrassed.
JULIE:	I guess I'd never thought of it that way.
MARCUS (admiring her response):	I have to admit they're really not all that bad out there. You know, I heard they tried to fix me up with a bass player. I play guitar. I have to give them some credit. Maybe if there was some way to guarantee I could get out of my cell – have something to do – it might not be so bad.

JULIE:	You're thinking that if you are going to be here long enough to see me retire that there might be a way to make some things work.
MARCUS:	I don't know. I'd have to see what's possible.
JULIE (seeing the opportunity to offer a choice):	I would be happy to get you some information, or you can request it directly. It's up to you.
MARCUS:	Okay, I'll take you up on it. No promises. You know where to find me.
JULIE:	Thanks for that. I will be back with information tomorrow.

In many more traditional settings, a professional meeting with Marcus might have begun the encounter prepared to set the agenda and tell him what to do. For many newcomers to the field of sexual offender treatment, it can be difficult to set aside one's sense of morals, values, and abhorrence of sexual abuse and listen compassionately to a person who has caused the kind of harm that Marcus has. What is often called *compartmentalization* and defined as a defense mechanism elsewhere in the world can quickly become a job skill in the treatment of sexual offenders. In this instance, Julie found herself aware that many components of a person's drive for autonomy and independence can also contribute to a sexual offense process (Yates, Prescott, & Ward, 2010; Yates & Prescott, 2011). The end result can prompt a professional to examine their values, beliefs, gender, sexuality, and species in ways they never imagined they would. Some therapists have described their work, particularly when using motivational interviewing, as a process of observing themselves as well as their clients. The challenge for each practitioner becomes how comfortable they are examining their lives and those of others.

Course of Treatment: Deepening Engagement

Julie awoke a half hour early out of a horrible dream. The details were vague, but involved standing by a river as people who had been sexually victimized – all ages and genders – floated past silently. She realized she had to get upstream to the source to stop the abuse, but was unsure of what or where the source actually was. She walked along the side of the river until she saw a man with a hood. Making perfect sense in the twisted logic of dreams, he demanded to examine her "raw data."

Normally, Julie's automatic thought on awakening would be to remind herself that it was just a dream and that she was okay and had no reason to be anxious. Even before she was fully awake, however, she inventoried her memory to remember which assessments were coming due at work; she worried that she would face the wrath of her supervisor if she was late on any of them. In her calculations, she already brought enough eccentricities to her work without being late on deadlines. Julie drank some coffee and did a half-hour of yoga in front of an instructional DVD, practiced 20 minutes of meditation, and prepared to leave for work early.

Julie had settled on yoga and meditation as a morning routine while attending university. At that time of her life she was deep into her studies and at the same she was wrestling with the pros and cons of a difficult relationship that she would eventually leave. These activities compounded to produce anxiety on a daily basis. Yoga and meditation provided her with an opportunity to start each day observing her body and herself. While the physical exercise was excellent self-care in itself, Julie appreciated the opportunity to take time to simply notice what occurred in her body and thoughts as she practiced. For example, on this morning, she told herself that it was worth the time to practice yoga and meditation, because after taking good care of herself she would be better positioned to help others: "Let me take care of myself first, and then the whole world can have me for the rest of the day; by nightfall I will have been of service to myself and others." Even at university, she had noticed that many of her colleagues were so focused on pursuing goals that they spent almost no time on themselves. She noticed that the strain often showed on their faces. At her current job, she found that maintaining these practices allowed her to be present in all situations, and that she was able to remain grounded in the institution culture that demanded she "go along to get along."

Julie had become involved in yoga for purely physical reasons. As she came to the unfortunate end of a committed relationship, yoga provided constant reminders that her body was hers alone and no one else's. Further, it was unique to her, and different from others' bodies. During the course of even a half hour of practice, she noticed how much her body could transform itself – a living reminder that all situations, good and bad, ultimately change. Now that she had practiced for a few years, she was aware that yoga (a word cognate with "yoke," which means the joining of breath and body) takes many forms, only a few of which have anything to do with outsiders' preconceptions (e.g., dangerous contortions performed in a hot room to the sound of temple bells). Julie regarded yoga as a kind of single-study scientific exercise in which she examined herself in the moment. She could think about the rest of her life any time.

This focus on noticing physical transformation made Julie feel whole. In a parallel to providing treatment, she could be in a dialog with her body rather than telling it what to do or pushing its limits, as many more competitive people seemed to do. Julie quickly found that she could observe strengths and motivations in her body and mind that she had not known were there. This had a dramatic effect on how she worked with clients. Rather than try to impose motivation or push them into one direction or another in treatment, she worked simply to notice and observe their motivations and feed them back, one motivation and one client at a time.

On this morning, the benefits of yoga had nothing to do with Julie's physical movements. Having awoken out of a frightening dream, she was grateful for the opportunity to simply observe her anxiety and concerns and allow them to pass without judgment. Years earlier, she might have tried to ignore these thoughts and emotions, or talk herself out of them. She may have labeled her thoughts as "distorted cognitions" and analyzed the cognitive schemas on which they were based. While there is nothing inherently wrong in making judgments about one's thoughts and actions and making changes accordingly, the act of observing them nonjudgmentally prior to taking action provided Julie with a deeper sense of understanding, confidence, and wellbeing.

This nonjudgmental observation was particularly important to Julie at a time when she was troubled about the way forward with Marcus. Like many other clients at the CCCC, Marcus appeared to represent many extremes of human experience, including in the domains of sexuality, antisociality, and overall worldview. Taking a few moments to observe her responses to Marcus provided Julie with a renewed sense of her identity and purpose in taking on this work. "I am not the same as my work," she said to herself as she drove to work, "and my experience of humanity is not the same as my clients'."

After clearing security, Julie attended to the normal morning routines, compiled the information she had collected the day before, and headed for the separation unit to meet with Marcus. It was during the walk to the unit that Julie performed tasks that would contribute to self-care and effective professional practice. She deliberately slowed and lengthened each breath, ideally making each exhale twice as long as each inhale. By walking onto the unit in a calmed state, there was less likelihood that Marcus – irritable and impulsive on a good day – would become agitated. She would also be better poised both to respond helpfully and to understand his internal world and the motivations within it. This calming exercise seemed to work. Marcus emerged from his room looking as though he was prepared to make provocative statements and toy with

Julie in general. She took a few extra seconds before speaking and noticed Marcus take a deep breath and long exhale.

Julie explained the options she had gathered – recreational therapy schedules and other activities that would provide Marcus meaningful things to do outside of his room and the unit dayroom. Rather than provide assurances, Julie reflected back Marcus' concerns and made clear that only he could make his own decisions. Given that the entire institution was trying to persuade him to move to a regular unit peacefully, it made more sense to Julie to emphasize his autonomous decision-making. Marcus agreed that he would be willing to meet with the unit directors to discuss his move.

Because this had been far easier than she ever expected, Julie asked whether she could ask some questions for her own benefit. Marcus agreed.

JULIE: You and I are basically from different worlds. Of all the things you could have done to stand up for yourself, what made you threaten to assault a unit director?

MARCUS: You got me. I know better, and yet I do worse. Back in my cell I've got certificates of completion from all sorts of treatment modules: problem-solving, decision-making, anger management, thinking errors . . . I'm probably the most cognitively restructured guy you'll ever know. None of that treatment worked. I can teach those classes better than any social worker, and they still don't work for me. When I get near any power player, I go berserk. I don't think. Look, I've heard it all, about how I do think I just don't know it, and it's not true. I go straight to assault. What nobody gets is that violence isn't a problem for me, it's the solution. My body takes over. By the time I'm thinking it's too late. That's why I'm going to be here for the rest of my life. This (looking around) is my retirement community.

JULIE: It's like your brain is just wired differently.

MARCUS: Look I know I sound like I'm making excuses. I'm not.

JULIE: When the security staff people are walking towards you, you're so focused on the threat they might pose that you're not focused on yourself.

MARCUS: Well, I am after a while, it's only then that I can use all those fancy coping skills. I don't see these things coming, but I sure make them happen.

Assessment of progress and barriers to care

Marcus was a classic case of a mismatch between prior service delivery and the individual characteristics of the client. Referred to as the *respon-*

sivity principle in criminological studies (Andrews & Bonta, 2010), Marcus was typical of many clients in civil commitment programs. The CCCC appropriately matched itself to his level of risk (i.e. the *risk principle*) and like Marcus' prior treatment situations, provided programming that directly targets criminogenic needs (the *need principle*). The problem, it turned out, was that Marcus' life experiences had left him with implicit theories about the world being a dangerous and out-of-control place where might makes right and one has to fight to get even. A brain mapping of Marcus would likely have found deficits in the prefrontal cortex region, where much of the brain's capacity for self-observation and empathic response are located. Like Julie, Marcus would benefit from treatment exercises aimed directly at the very same kind of self-observation that Julie experienced in yoga and meditation.

Follow-up

Over time, Marcus became involved in recreational therapy that focused on observing one's body in space (proprioception) and self-observation (interoception). This eventually led to a dedicated meditation practice. By observing his thoughts, actions, body, and breath, he was better able to anticipate, notice, and allow situations to happen to which he previously would have responded violently. It was only then that the cognitive skills he had learned years earlier made sense at a far deeper level.

Implications and Recommendations to Clinicians and Students

Newcomers to the field of sexual offender treatment quickly find themselves examining their lives in response to the life histories and offense descriptions that they hear. Depending on one's setting, institutional pressure and intimidation by uninvested clients can become significant stressors. In a field where research emphasizes the importance of cognitive-behavioral therapy, it can be easy for programs to emphasize the cognitive aspects to the detriment of behavioral elements. All too frequently forgotten in the rush to complete treatment expediently is each client's capacity to observe themselves and explore their own personal and heartfelt reasons to live life differently.

The field of treating sexual aggression has made remarkable gains in matching the risk and need principles during the past 20 years. The stories of Julie and Marcus highlight the importance of self-care as a means to personal and professional longevity, and for building the inherent responsivity in every client.

References

Andrews, D. A., & Bonta, J. (2010). *The psychology of criminal conduct* (5th ed.). Cincinnati, OH: Anderson.

Bailey, B., Buchbinder, E., & Eisikovits, Z. (2011). Male social workers working with men who batter: Dilemmas in gender identity. *Journal of Interpersonal Violence, 26*, 1741–1762.

Harkins, L., Flak, V. E., Beech, A. R., & Woodhams, J. (2012). Evaluation of a community-based sex offender treatment program using a good lives model approach. *Sexual Abuse: A Journal of Research and Treatment, 24*, 519–543.

Miller, W. R., & Rollnick, S. (2013). *Motivational interviewing: Helping people change* (3rd ed.). New York: Guilford Press.

Parhar, K. K., Wormith, J. S., Derkzen, D. M., & Beauregard, A. M. (2008). Offender coercion in treatment: A meta-analysis of effectiveness. *Criminal Justice and Behavior, 35*, 1109–1135.

Quinsey, V. L., Harris, G. T., Rice, M. E., & Cormier, C. A. (2006). *Violent offenders: Appraising and managing risk* (2nd ed.). Washington, DC: American Psychological Association.

Salter, A. (1988). *Treating child sex offenders and victims*. Thousand Oaks, CA: Sage.

Schlank, A. (2005). The civil commitment of sexual offenders: Lessons learned. In W. L. Marshall, Y. Fernandez, L. E. Marshall, & G. Serran (Eds.), *Sexual offender treatment: Controversial issues*. New York: Wiley.

Seligman, M. (2009, December). *Positive psychology*. Invited address at the Evolution of Psychotherapy Conference, Anaheim, CA.

Wilson, R. J., Looman, J., Abracen, J., & Pake, D. R. (2012). Comparing sexual offenders at the Regional Treatment Centre (Ontario) and the Florida Civil Commitment Center. *International Journal of Offender Therapy and Comparative Criminology, 57*, 377–395.

Yapko, M. (2005). *Trancework*. New York: Routledge.

Yates, P. M., & Prescott, D. S. (2011). *Building a better life: A good lives and self-regulation workbook*. Brandon, VT: Safer Society Press.

Yates, P. M., Prescott, D. S., & Ward, T. (2010). *Applying the good lives and self regulation models to sex offender treatment: A practical guide for clinicians*. Brandon, VT: Safer Society Press.

3

Ethical Issues in the Treatment of Sex Offenders: Addressing the Dual Relationship Problem

Tony Ward

Introduction

The assessment and treatment of sex offenders relies on both scientific knowledge and ethical understanding. However, a variety of normative pressures involving value-laden questions and issues inevitably confront practitioners undertaking this type of work. These ethical flashpoints are typically associated with norms (i.e., rules or principles) that specify how clinicians should act and be accountable to one another. There are different types of norms, but the most relevant for sex offender clinicians are social and moral, or ethical norms. Social norms express professional duties and standards while ethical norms are broader in scope and obligate practitioners to act in ways that take the core interests and moral status of persons into account. Social norms stipulating what constitutes competent professional practice underpin all assessment and treatment tasks and provide standards that practitioners are expected to meet. In this case the relevant value dimension concerns how well a person does his or her job and, as such, whether the individuals who are treated benefit from such efforts or are harmed in some way. This first set of ethical or normative issues revolves around an individual's professional identity and sense of integrity, and the norms in question are essentially social norms that specify accountability conditions for a group of professionals (Brennan, Eriksson, Goodin, & Southwood, 2013). They are not ethical

Sex Offender Treatment: A Case Study Approach to Issues and Interventions, First Edition. Edited by Daniel T. Wilcox, Tanya Garrett, and Leigh Harkins.
© 2015 John Wiley & Sons, Ltd. Published 2015 by John Wiley & Sons, Ltd.

norms in the usual sense of that term. Thus, there is a conceptual relationship between competence standards, such as what is considered effective practice, and the obligations of being a sex offender therapist. Normative problems that emerge within professional practice are internal to that role and typically involve questions about professional competency in relation to issues such as gaining informed consent (which is defined with respect to specific roles and their requirements), conducting an accurate and relevant risk assessment, dealing with conflict between professional tasks (e.g., duty to warn versus maintaining client confidentiality as in the case of being an expert witness at a parole hearing when also serving as the offender's therapist), conducting a risk assessment, and so on.

Concerning ethical norms, within sex offender practice a number of significant ethical issues often emerge. Ethical problems typically revolve around concerns with how to treat *persons* as distinguished from *clients or patients*, and are associated with the use of terms such as *right, wrong, good, bad*, and so on. The kinds of ethical problems that confront practitioners include those created by civil detention assessments, deciding on the degree to which offenders' preferences and goals are factored into treatment plans, the components included in treatment and post-release plans, and opting for mandatory versus voluntary treatment. In the author's view, the key dilemma underpinning these ethical issues is how best to balance the welfare and freedom interests of offenders with the concern for safety of members of the community. In this case the ethical dimension centers on tension between public safety and protection and offender wellbeing (Birgden & Cucolo, 2011; Ward, 2013; Ward & Birgden, 2007; Ward & Salmon, 2011). The scope of the norms in question is much wider and goes beyond professional norms, the regulation of clinicians' actions, and the quality of their work. In essence, this wider set of norms is moral or ethical in nature and intended to apply to all members of the moral community no matter what group they belong to. They are universal in scope, impartial in application, and can be usefully described as "clusters of essentially practice-independent normative judgments" (Brennan et al., 2013, p. 72) that are intended to regulate the conduct and protect the key interests of *all individuals*, not simply members of specific groups such as psychologists, social workers, or psychiatrists.

There are formal social norms that cite practice standards for specific professional groups, working in particular settings, and overarching, superordinate personal ethical norms that function as standards against which to evaluate our actions towards each other in every day life. Practitioners are subject to both sets of norms in their working and day-to-day activities within and across the multiple domains of their lives. Of course, these two sets of norms do sometimes interact in work settings. For example, when a person acts unkindly towards another staff member, or fails to assist clients when they are suffering harm, ethical norms are relevant and questions of right and wrong, good and bad, legitimately emerge. However, for our purposes it is possible to distinguish between them and point to their different roles and challenges.

So far so good – where is the ethical problem? The problem as seen by the author is as follows: sex offender therapists have their professional roots in caring or helping professions and are subject to the social norms of these groups. However, they also work in correctional or forensic mental health settings and as such are subject to the social norms in these settings. These norms take the form of professional codes of practice of one kind or another. When both are applicable to a therapist there is a potential conflict of cultures, and this threatens to paralyze professional actions or even worse, result in loss of integrity and identity. Simply appealing to the respective sets of professional or social norms (i.e., those that guide the conduct of criminal justice and mental health practices) will not help much as they are at the same normative level. One set of norms (or professional code) determines the kinds of actions and practices that are acceptable for clinicians working with *offenders* while the other spells out what constitutes competent professional practice with *mental health* or therapy clients. It seems that the only solution is to go deeper, to moral norms that underpin both criminal justice and mental health cultures and their associated roles and practices. The above conflict of roles is known as the dual relationship problem and generates many of the significant ethical problems evident in sex offending practice. This chapter describes the dual relationship problem in more detail and then briefly outlines contemporary approaches to resolving it. The author then presents his own solution to the problem, based on human rights theory and relationship ethical theory, and a procedural model adapted from the bioethics literature. In my opinion, this framework can help sex offender therapists to identify ethical issues and to address them in an ethically nuanced and fruitful manner.

The Dual Relationship Problem in Sex Offender Treatment

The dual role or dual relationship ethical problem emerges in psychiatric and psychological practice in a number of ways depending on the specific nature of the task conflict in question. Often, it is used to refer to internal professional role or task conflicts rather than the kind of clash between practice cultures mentioned earlier. In a clash of cultures, which is an ethical as well as a professional practice clash, there is conflict between the distinct practices and norms associated with each role and their over-arching ethical and professional principles. In this type of conflict it becomes increasingly unclear as to whether an individual is a healer or a risk evaluator; it is not obvious how he or she can be both when working with the same client or patient. Thus, the most serious type of dual rela-tionship problem emerges when there is conflict between two relatively coherent sets of values, professional obligations, and practices (i.e., the specific professional activities engaged in, such as assessment, treating intimacy deficits, etc.).

Robertson and Walter (2008) usefully define the dual relationship problem as it occurs within a specific role (they label it the *dual role* problem) in the following way:

> The problem of the dual role, variably termed "dual agency", "overlapping roles", and "double agency", is a particular quandary in psychiatry. In this paper we refer to the "dual role" and define it as a quandary in which a psychiatrist faces the dilemma of conflicting expectations or responsibilities, between the therapeutic relationship on the one hand and the interests of third parties on the other. (p. 228–229)

As stated above, the broad, dual relationship problem in forensic and correctional practice emerges from conflict between two comparatively encapsulated sets of ethical norms: those associated with community protection and justice versus norms related to offender/defendant wellbe-ing and autonomy. These sets of norms are relatively coherent and guide the practice of those engaging in welfare-oriented practice and those working within a criminal justice context. When confronted with ethically problematic situations, clinicians refer to their respective sets of profes-sional principles and norms in order to formulate an ethically justified response. The problem for forensic and correctional clinicians is that because the two sets of values are embedded in distinct normative systems, reflection on them and the relevant case facts is likely to lead to different actions. When treating sex offenders should the focus be on their aims and aspirations or primarily on dynamic risk factors? Can it be on both? If so, should one set be prioritized over the other? How should or can the different values constituting the welfare/wellbeing and risk management perspectives be effectively integrated in a treatment program for sex offenders? Is this even possible?

What are the conceptual roots of the dual relationship problem in forensic and correctional practice? As mentioned earlier, the problem occurs because practitioners typically have their professional training in mental health or allied disciplines (such as psychiatry, clinical psychology, social work, etc.) and as such, often struggle to ethically justify aspects of forensic and/or correctional work. They are mental health professionals *and* criminal justice employees (whether as consultants or salaried workers), and therefore subject to (at least) two sets of norms and any associated professional ethical codes. While ethical codes and professional standards especially created for correctional forensic context describe or label the problem, arguably they do not provide ways of navigating past the obstacles (see the American Academy of Psychiatry and Law, 2005; International Association for Correctional and Forensic Psychology, 2010). Practitioners are advised to proceed with caution to avoid dual relationships, and if in them, seek advice. While the paper by Sawyer and Prescott (2011), in the recent special issue of *Sexual Abuse: A Journal of Research and Treatment*, does a good job of highlighting boundary issues associated with dual relationships, it does not really get to the conceptual heart of the problem. What is missing in papers on the topic and existing criminal justice or forensic codes is an analysis of the nature of the problem and, following on from this, some concrete suggestions for addressing it from an ethical standpoint. The pressing ethical issue for practitioners is that it is not possible to sidestep or avoid the dual relationship problem. It is ubiquitous.

This chapter does not afford sufficient space to present a comprehensive investigation of the dual relationship problem in both its narrow (within one rehabilitation culture) and broader (i.e., between cultures) senses, but a few comments will be made (see Ward, 2013). The author proposes that the problem of dual relationships is a manifestation of the wider underlying ethical issue of *value pluralism*. Value pluralism occurs when a number of distinct ethical codes (or if you prefer, sets of norms) exist within a society or community, none of which can be established as ethically superior by a rational, impartial observer (Engelhardt, 1986). The clash between the various ethical codes may be horizontal, between codes at the same level of abstraction (e.g., a professional ethical code versus a criminal justice employee code), or vertical, where professional norms conflict with more abstract principles (e.g., human rights norms might clash with those regulating staff conduct at a high-security prison). Thus, what is apparent at an abstract level in multicultural, complex societies also occurs at the level of professional practice and, more specifically, potentially within a single clinician. From this viewpoint, the conflict between risk management or safety values and their related practice issues and offender wellbeing concerns is a good example of a fundamental value conflict. The conceptual problem is that it is not possible to appeal to a third set of values or a master principle to resolve the value conflicts, because they are also values. The problem then becomes one of justifying why an appeal to such a master principle or value should trump the others. To cut a long story short, following Engelhardt (1986), it does not seem possible to resolve this problem rationally. There are multiple values associated with sex offender practice and ethical concerns that cannot be arranged hierarchically into less and more important ones. We simply have to find a way to deal with the dual relationship problem that accepts the existence of value pluralism. Both safety/community protection *and* offender welfare concerns are ethically legitimate practice concerns. Unfortunately, contemporary attempts to resolve the dual relationship problem have not managed to do so successfully, though they are briefly discussed below.

Contemporary Reponses to the Problem of Dual Relationships

An analysis of the forensic and correctional practice and ethical literature reveals three possible ways to resolve the dual relationship problem: (1) emphasizing either the mental health (wellbeing) or the criminal justice sets of values at the expense of the others, (2) developing hybrid models that seek to integrate the two sets of values, and (3) formulating procedural models that focus on process rather than arguing the case for the supremacy of specific practice-related values.

Single code primacy: mental health

The default position concerning the dual relationship problem is that traditional professional codes of practitioners (whether psychiatrists, psychologists, social workers, etc.) can satisfactorily resolve any ethical conflicts encountered when working in forensic or correctional contexts. It is assumed that ethical principles contained in ethical codes, or those specifically developed in bioethics, can be interpreted to provide guidance to practitioners in all assessment and treatment arenas (Weinstock, 2001). Thus, the traditional principles of beneficence, nonmaleficence, autonomy, and justice, if moderated by considerations of balance and the process of specification (i.e., translating principles into more concrete norms), can help practitioners to undertake risk assessments or offender treatment in ways that are ethically justified. The aim is to translate or tailor abstract ethical principles into specific action-guiding norms without losing their original meaning. Thus, the principle of autonomy might be specified in a risk assessment case in the following manner: the problem is to decide how much weight to give to a sex offender's self reports concerning his level of deviant sexual desires compared to his score on a measure of deviant sexual preferences and interests (Craig, Browne, & Beech, 2008). All of the major forensic professional codes contain a number of foundational ethical principles from which specific standards of practice are (loosely) derived. The principles function as a theoretical resource that are applied to cases arising in clinical work and can be used singly or in combination, depending on the nature of the case in question.

The trouble with this approach is that the issues of risk reduction and protection of the community only function as constraints on practice and do not centrally guide assessment and treatment. This is a problem because current sex offender practice squarely addresses dynamic risk factors in order to reduce reoffending. Furthermore, this focus is viewed as essential and is a core requirement of competent and ethical sex offender treatment. Mental health oriented treatment struggles to accommodate this focus. Thus, it appears that traditional mental health professional codes, and related principles, do not possess sufficient theoretical resources to satisfactorily resolve the dual relationship issue in forensic and correctional practice.

Single code primacy: criminal justice

In his landmark 1997 paper on forensic ethics, Paul Appelbaum formulated two forensic ethical principles for forensic practice truth-telling and respect for the person (he is referring to expert witness testimony but the present author's view is that his argument extends to treatment as well). The *principle of truth-telling* stipulates that the forensic psychiatrist ought to strive for objectivity and present the court with an accurate assessment of the defendant based on reliable and valid methods and theories. There should be honesty concerning the strengths and limitations of any methods of information gathering and its impact on the subsequent psychiatric report and testimony. The *principle of respect for persons* stipulates that in a forensic evaluation context the psychiatrist should be transparent, with the defendant conceding the fact that his or her client is the court rather than the defendant, and he or she will not function within the role of healer, therapist, or medical doctor. Appelbaum maintains that forensic ethical norms cannot be derived from medical professional heath norms because the values associated with each realm are distinct, and incommensurate with respect to the roles in question.

A weakness of Appelbaum's theory with respect to its solution of the dual relationship problem is that he has essentially *redefined* the practice of forensic psychiatry (and arguably correctional treatment) to include only assessment undertaken to help the court address legal questions. Nonlegal aspects of psychiatric work and those relevant to wellbeing are excluded from this sphere of practice by definition. The scope of forensic psychiatry (and by extension, all correctional assessment and treatment) has been shrunk to incorporate only those aspects that concern themselves directly with justice issues, and all other aspects of practice have been positioned on the nonforensic side of the professional role boundary. Thus, there is no dual relationship problem because, by definition, forensic psychiatry does not include traditional medical tasks, and their associated values of beneficence, nonmaleficence, autonomy, or even justice do not apply in this sphere of work. Once this line of thinking is extended to sex offender treatment it becomes the view that the community is the real client and the primary focus of intervention is to reduce risk of reoffending. Offenders' needs and entitlements are viewed as important but are always secondary to the goal of community protection. It seems to this author that the error is to overlook the crucial role that the professional training of sex offender therapists has in obtaining information and in communicating to offenders the message that they are there to help them. In such circumstances, there is a possible ethical issue of deception. However, fundamentally, the argument that the criminal justice cluster of values should dominate, with its primary aim of community protection, simply ignores the problem. The integrity and professional identities of sex offender therapists arguably partially reside in their capacity to assist offenders to live better lives alongside making the community safer.

Hybrid codes

The essential dilemma confronting forensic and correctional practitioners is that there are ethical tensions between their respective professional codes or systems (i.e., health related and criminal justice) and the ethical demands of working within the criminal justice system. One solution is to embrace the inherent complexity of the forensic role while still appreciating the added value conveyed by a mental health background. Theorists, such as Ward (2010), have suggested that more than one ethical theory will be required to justify and guide sex offender treatment. From this perspective, it is anticipated that there could be overlapping, although distinct, normative theories that deal with the risk management and the wellbeing-enhancing aspects of intervention, respectively. In this possible scenario, the nature of the practice tasks will dictate what ethical resources are drawn from at any point in time. The reality may well be that because of the complex combination of morality and treatment-related values apparent in the criminal justice domain it is not sensible, or even possible, to rely only upon one type of ethical framework (Ward & Salmon, 2009). However, unfortunately, aside from these comments, Ward (2010) has not outlined concrete steps for constructing such a hybrid ethical code.

Philip Candilis (2009) has developed a hybrid ethical code for forensic psychiatric practice based on the construct of robust professionalism, and narrative theory. According to Candilis, professional relationships between the forensic psychiatrist and offender or defendant, and other persons associated with the case, should be viewed as moral relationships. The forensic practitioner has an obligation to understand the story or narrative of the offender and other relevant individuals, and to accept that in forensic contexts there are multiple perspectives in play. In addition, there is an ethical responsibility to display integrity in his or her professional actions and to ensure that there is consistency between the way forensic tasks are undertaken and personal and broader ethical values. Candilis (2008, p. 433) states that practitioners ought to exhibit (1) sensitivity to vulnerable evaluees, (2) sensitivity to role problems, (3) awareness of personal biases and internal states, (4) honesty with respect to the facts of the case and in one's dealings with evaluees, and (5) ethical professionalism by ensuring one is kept up to date with the appropriate scientific and clinical facts and has a good grasp of ethical theories and perspectives.

The focus on the relationship with the offender is a strength of this approach; however, the failure to outline *a procedure* for implementing the model in practice situations is problematic. While the concept of robust professionalism, with its call to integrity and attention to personal narratives, is a necessary element of ethical assessment and treatment, it does not seem sufficient.

A Framework for Addressing Dual Relationship Problems

The moral acquaintance model is an ethical approach that is relational in orientation and respectful of the intrinsic value of other people. It claims that in a complex moral world with diverse ethical codes, systems, and cultural perspectives it is important to attend carefully to our concrete relationships (i.e., utilize a relational ethical perspective) with other people and to *engage* in dialogues that are open and intent on incorporating varying viewpoints (Bergum & Dossetor, 2005; Hanson, 2009; Ward, 2013). This is especially the case in forensic and correctional contexts where individuals' freedom and wellbeing is directly at stake. Furthermore, it is important to acknowledge the *dignity* of others, and not to act in ways that are *disrespectful* and that denigrate individuals' status as fellow human beings. Finally, according to the moral acquaintance perspective, the details or stories of individuals' lives ought to be the focus of moral decisions rather than simply abstract principles or norms. We need to construct personal narratives (an *embodiment* of their situation in a story) of each person involved in an ethically problematic situation and depict the relevant details, such as, what is at stake for them in an encounter.

In Hanson's (2009) formulation of the moral acquaintance model in bioethics, Engelhardt's distinction between moral friends, moral strangers, and moral acquaintances provides a helpful way of dealing with the issue of value pluralism (Engelhardt, 1986). The moral acquaintance framework agrees that in a pluralistic society there are a number of equally legitimate, competing, or alternative moral belief systems. The application of these different moral codes to concrete situations often results in varying responses to ethical problems. A moral acquaintance framework accepts that individuals with distinct moral codes may judge moral situations differently, and, in turn, justify their actions by appealing to competing sets of principles and theories, for example, religious beliefs, political theories, or codes of ethics. In effect, such individuals are *moral strangers* to each other as they have little in common with respect to their core moral beliefs and their underlying principles. They frame problems differently and as a result may arrive at diverse judgments concerning the right course of action to take. *Moral friends*, however, share the same ethical codes and are able to solve problems by carefully attending to the relevant facts, identifying the basic ethical principles, taking care to draw valid conclusions, and then acting in ways that reflect these conclusions. Disagreements amongst moral friends are most likely due to careless reasoning, mistaken factual beliefs, or inattention to problem definition.

It seems obvious that the dual-relationship problem in forensic and correctional practice contexts typically occurs between moral strangers rather than moral friends. That is, there is disagreement concerning what norms are foundational and therefore about how best to act professionally. The most problematic dual relationship scenario occurs *within a single* forensic or correctional practitioner, who struggles to align two distinct sets of ethical norms when engaging in practice. The practitioner has an obligation to accept the priorities of the criminal justice system when working in correctional or forensic contexts, but for the sake of his or her professional integrity is also obligated to act in accordance with his or her profession's code of ethics. The tension created by this clash of norms underpins the dual relationship ethical problem.

By contrast, *moral acquaintances* have some overlapping moral beliefs relating to the problem in question; they are not total strangers and can arrive at common decisions about how best to act (for a comprehensive discussion of the concept of moral acquaintances in bioethics, see Hanson, 2009). These overlapping beliefs may be based on a shared understanding of human nature and conditions (e.g., needs for warmth, food, water, relatedness, autonomy, safety, etc.) or be oriented around a specific issue, for example, the need to protect the community from harm, or the rights of offenders to receive educational vocational training and medical care. Moral acquaintances look for common, or overlapping, moral beliefs relating to a particular issue and view any actions proceeding from these common beliefs as justified if they are embedded within a coherent moral system, and if individuals with different sets of moral beliefs agree that their moral system is coherent. They may agree on what to do but have different reasons for doing so. The only requirement is that the reasons presented should be rationally derived from a coherent (i.e., noncontradictory and mutually supportive) set of moral norms. For example, one forensic practitioner might justify the implementation of treatment programs with sex offenders because of their lowering of recidivism rates. The underlying principle appealed to concerns an obligation to protect the community from the harmful actions of offenders. However, another forensic practitioner might argue that sex offenders ought to receive treatment because they have pressing psychological needs. This justification could have its grounding in human rights principles rather than community protection concerns. Yet, despite working from distinct – and equally coherent – ethical systems the two forensic practitioners might share a common moral belief that if a certain course of action can reduce human suffering without resulting in unjustified pain to others it ought to be undertaken. In the example being discussed here, a treatment approach that sets out to assist sex offenders improve their quality of life, by equipping them with the skills to manage their moods effectively, could also reduce their risk of offending. The two forensic practitioners are moral acquaintances – rather than strangers – by virtue of the fact that they share some moral beliefs that are directly linked to the issue in question: whether or not to fund programs for offenders. They justify the decision to fund such programs by recourse to different moral principles and theories. They are acquaintances not strangers on this issue, but they are not moral friends either as they do not share the same set of moral beliefs concerning the role of programs in the criminal justice system or, more broadly, the status of offenders and their entitlements. They accept that each other's decision to fund programs is based on good reasons, within a coherent moral system, although they do not subscribe to each other's particular moral system.

Moral Acquaintances and the Dual Relationship Problem: A Procedural Approach

From a moral acquaintance perspective, there are six steps to follow when addressing the dual relationship problem in the sex offender treatment domain (adapted from Hanson, 2009). Note that the author is focusing on the broader ethical issue of a "culture" clash between the risk management and offender wellbeing/welfare frameworks within sex offender treatment, and not on concrete ethical issues such as confidentiality or informed consent. However, one of the virtues of the procedural model being applied in this section is that it can help to deal with these professional practice issues as well.

In this example, a practitioner is asked to provide a report for the parole board on a sex offender's progress, which could affect his conditions of parole or determine whether or not parole is granted. The conflict occurs between considering what is truly in the offender's best interests versus what is in the community's best interests (i.e., a concern for community safety). The dual relationship problem in this situation has its origins in the fact that there are two ways of ethically framing the situation, each anchored in different sets of values and their respective practice norms. As stated above, there is no easy way of resolving the dilemma rationally because each ethical perspective (justice/community protection versus offender wellbeing) is internally consistent and based on sound foundational principles.

Discussion will focus on the six steps comprising the moral acquaintance model as they apply to the fictional case example of Hamish, who has applied for parole. The sex offender practitioner's job is to oversee the evaluation process and if possible to arrive at a plan for action that is ethically acceptable to all the participants. It is taken for granted that all of the key stakeholders accept that the offender has the same moral worth (status) as everyone else and that his core interests (e.g., work, relationships, freedom, autonomy, health, religions, freedom of speech, freedom from pain, leisure, etc.) and entitlements should be taken into account in any subsequent planning. The aim is to engage in an open and respectful dialogue that will incorporate all viewpoints and concerns. It is hoped that a plan will be formulated that will promote the goals of all the people who have a legitimate stake in the matter at hand.

The steps are as follows.

1. Define the practice task clearly and identify any ethical issues or problems. Note any factual errors and correct them. In any clinical situation there are significant matters of fact to note and also the use of specialist techniques and methods to gather clinically relevant information. It is important that these are competently administered and the information accurately recorded. This will include such information as risk level, the detection of specific dynamic risk factors, such as deviant sexual preferences, and pertinent environmental facts, such as the availability of local social and psychological resources (e.g., employment, training, support groups, family). In this case, the fact that the practitioner was Hamish's therapist is not a significant problem because his ethical decision-making will be conducted within the two ethical frameworks of a mental health professional *and* criminal justice employee/consultant. The task is to ensure that any plan can be ethically justified within both ethical frameworks, not just one. This, of course, is exactly the dilemma that constitutes the dual relationship problem.

2. Identify the relevant group of individuals who should be participants in the discussion. This is a crucial step as the moral acquaintance method depends on locating individuals and organizations that have a *legitimate stake* in the issue at hand. The issue in this case is the content of the practitioner's report and the degree to which any recommendations and subsequent arrangements are ethically justified from the viewpoints of *both* the forensic/criminal justice (community safety) and Hamish's wellbeing ethical frameworks. The acquaintance group includes Hamish, the therapist or evaluator, probation staff, prison authorities, Hamish's family, members of the parole board, and a community support group.

3. Construct a concise narrative of all involved individuals' unique situations, perspectives, and contributions to the task at hand. Try to identify the set of norms they are conceptualizing the case within. What is at stake and what are their stories? Hamish has a plan that involves learning to be a mechanic (a long-term hobby and interest)

and also wants to be able to spend time with his family (the relevant norms are all related to his personal happiness and desire to stay out of trouble). His family members are supportive of his goals but have some concerns about his alcohol use and anger problem and would like these to be addressed in a release plan (mixture of safety concerns and interests in their own and the offender's wellbeing). The community support group is a Christian organization that believes strongly in the possibility of redemption and giving people second chances. In contrast, the probation staff, parole board, and prison staff are primarily concerned with the offender's potential for reoffending and will be looking to construct a parole plan that contains robust monitoring procedures and evidence-based interventions that focus on his anger and alcohol problems (their values at play here are primarily those concerned with community safety and security). The degree to which Hamish's goals are explicitly considered is of secondary importance and is not a major concern.

4. In this phase it is suggested that a search for shared ethical norms across the participants is undertaken. If the conflict occurs within a single practitioner, it is recommended that he or she look for any common elements between the different sets of norms held. This step is crucial. In this particular case the practitioner undertaking the assessment has ethical obligations derived from two distinct roles, that of therapist and those of the legal and criminal justice system. Aligned with the latter are also responsibilities to his or her fellow citizens and their right to live in a safe environment. The practitioner carefully scrutinizes the ethical and professional viewpoints of all members of the acquaintance group and looks for common norms or beliefs. In this case it is noted that all members of the group share a commitment to human rights and the entitlement of all individuals to have access to a set of core health, freedom, educational, and social goods. They also share the belief that once people have been punished they should be allowed to resume their lives in the community, providing any risk to the community is taken into account in a subsequent release plan. The primary values held by prison, probation, and criminal justice staff are those pertaining to community safety, and consideration of Hamish's wellbeing as a lesser, although still significant, priority. Hamish's family, support group, and Hamish, weigh the relevant values in the reverse order, but still view protection and safety as essential elements of any parole plan. However, they are looking for a solution to the problem of competing interests that will promote Hamish's goals (and meet his core needs) alongside reducing his risk of further offending.

5. Once any shared or common norms have been detected it is important to tailor them to the case at hand, using techniques such as specification (i.e., translating abstract ethical principles into more concrete norms) and balancing, and arriving at an agreed plan of action. It is crucial to ensure that each participant can justify the plan arrived at within their own ethical code or set of norms. In the report, the practitioner notes that while Hamish's risk level is moderate to high he has made good progress in reducing his drinking and aggressive behavior. He recommends that Hamish be provided with the opportunity to attend a community course to learn basic car mechanics. In addition, Hamish will be asked to participate in anger management and substance abuse maintenance programs to ensure that the progress he has made in these areas is maintained. The Christian support group has agreed to provide social support and to recruit a small number of volunteers to assist Hamish in a socialization program. In effect, this involves accompanying him to sports events and church activities. From Hamish's viewpoint this is a plan that incorporates important personal goals. He is willing to accept the conditions specifying further therapeutic interventions and monitoring because he understands that (a) it will assist him to stay out of prison, and (b) importantly, control of his drinking and anger means that he will be allowed greater access to woodworking tools and thus be able to acquire skills that he highly values. It is likely that criminal justice staff will be satisfied with the plan because they will see that the offender's high-risk characteristics will continue to be a focus of clinical attention and he will be monitored on an ongoing basis both by the church group (whom he is aligned to) and probation staff. Hamish's family is happy with the plan as well. Thus, the plan has the merits of being justified within both criminal justice (community protection/risk management) and offender wellbeing frameworks. Criminal justice personnel are happy because there is sufficient attention focused on risk management and monitoring, while the family, offender, and support groups appreciate that Hamish will have a chance to start a more productive and personally meaningful life. On this occasion, looking for common norms and beliefs has enabled the practitioner to arrive at a plan that has dual ethical justification and, therefore, avoids the implications of the dual relationship. As an aside, one of the virtues of strength-based intervention treatment framework is that it is able to accommodate risk management and offender wellbeing enhancing elements relatively well. Some of the gains acquired while learning the skills for occupations, such as car mechanics, will directly reduce offenders'

criminogenic needs (e.g., they are skills that are likely to strengthen emotional and behavioral regulation). Further, the fact that an offender is pursing goals that are personally meaningful to him may well increase his motivation to work harder on risk-reducing programs.

6. If satisfied that the proposed plan can be justified within the different ethical codes and sets of norms, the next step is to implement it and evaluate its subsequent effectiveness from both ethical and prudential viewpoints (i.e., benefits both the offender and meets Hamish's ethical obligations to the community and other key stakeholders). In the case under discussion, it would be important to have meetings of the relevant acquaintance groups on a regular basis and to compare notes in terms of how well the plan is being implemented. If there are problems, then a solution should be sought using the above procedure. Because the dual relationship problem is inescapable for forensic and correctional practitioners, it is incumbent for them to act in ways that can be justified by both ethical systems.

In the above example, the initial conflict between the two rehabilitation cultures of risk management/community safety and offender wellbeing (agency, autonomy, etc.) threatened to force practitioners to adopt either one or the other framework or fall back on a hybrid model where the two sets of norms coexist rather uneasily. The danger was that well-meaning sex offender therapists would either seek to help Hamish attain his personal goals and improve his level of wellbeing or else relegate what mattered to him to the background and instead concentrate on reducing his array of dynamic risk factors. The moral acquaintance model outlined above provides one way of formulating a treatment plan that can be ethically justified within both frameworks. Often, common ground is discovered where the stakeholders accept that a particular course of action will further their own, and each other's goals. This is an ethical matter as well as a practical one. The right course of action is one that takes into account Hamish's entitlements and wishes, and balances them against the right of the community not to be exposed to an unjustified risk of further offending.

Conclusions

It is suggested in this chapter that an ethical decision-making procedure based on relational ethics and the concept of moral acquaintance has greater utility than traditional approaches in addressing the dual relationship problem in forensic and correctional domains. An advantage of this model is that it is inclusive, and encourages practitioners to search for areas of agreement, or moral kinship with others, rather than become preoccupied with differences. The fact that human beings have a common set of needs and are equally vulnerable to social and physical deprivations means there will be a good chance of arriving at some common ground. Even when consensus is not possible and a practitioner – or groups of practitioners – cannot agree on what constitutes an ethically acceptable course of action, a procedural model ought to diminish dogmatism and promote more openness to alternative viewpoints. Forensic and correctional sex offender practice is professionally demanding because of its straddling of both health and criminal justice jurisdictions. In view of its level of complexity it makes sense to adopt ethical models that reflect the multilayered nature of such work and promote an open and respectful ethical dialogue.

Acknowledgement

I would like to thank Elsevier Science for giving permission to use part of the following paper in this chapter: Ward, T. (2013). Addressing the dual relationship problem in forensic and correctional practice. *Aggression and Violent Behavior, 18*, 92–100.

References

American Academy of Psychiatry and Law (2005). Ethical guidelines for the practice of forensic psychiatry. Retrieved March 29, 2014, from http://www.aapl.org/pdf/ethicsgdlns.pdf

Appelbaum, P. S. (1997). A theory of ethics for forensic psychiatry. *Journal of the American Academy of Psychiatry and Law, 25*, 233–247.

Bergum, V., & Dossetor, J. (2005). *Relational ethics: The full meaning of respect.* Hagerstown, MD: University Publishing Group.

Birgden, A., & Cucolo, H. (2011). The treatment of sex offenders: Evidence, ethics, and human rights. *Sexual Abuse: A Journal of Research & Treatment, 23*, 295–313.

Brennan, G., Eriksson, L., Goodin, R. E., & Southwood, N. (2013). *Explaining norms.* New York: Oxford University Press.

Candilis, P. (2008). The MacArthur Competence Assessment Tool for Treatment (MacCAT-T). In B. Cutler (Ed.), *Encyclopedia of Psychology and Law* (p. 433). Thousand Oaks, CA: Sage Publishing.

Candilis, P. J. (2009). The revolution in forensic ethics: Narrative, compassion, and a robust professionalism. *Psychiatric Clinics of North America, 32,* 423–435.

Craig, L. A., Browne, K. D., & Beech, A. R. (2008). *Assessing risk in sex offenders: A practitioner's guide.* Chichester, UK: John Wiley & Sons.

Engelhardt, H. T. (1986). *The foundations of bioethics.* New York: Oxford University Press.

Hanson, S. S. (2009). *Moral acquaintances and moral decisions: resolving conflicts in medical ethics.* New York: Springer.

International Association for Correctional and Forensic Psychology (2010). Standards for psychology services in jails, prisons, correctional facilities, and agencies (3rd ed.). *Criminal Justice and Behavior, 37,* 449–808.

Robertson, M. D., & Walter, G. (2008). Many faces of the dual-role dilemma in psychiatric ethics. *Australian and New Zealand Journal of Psychiatry, 42,* 228–235.

Sawyer, S., & Prescott, D. (2011) Boundaries and dual relationships. *Sexual Abuse: A Journal of Research and Treatment, 23*(3), 365–380.

Ward, T. (2010). Punishment or therapy?: The ethics of sexual offending treatment. *Journal of Sexual Aggression, 16,* 286–295.

Ward, T. (2013). Addressing the dual relationship problem in forensic and correctional practice. *Aggression and Violent Behavior, 18,* 92–100.

Ward, T., & Birgden, A. (2007). Human rights and clinical correctional practice. *Aggression and Violent Behavior, 12,* 628–643.

Ward, T., & Salmon, K. (2009). The ethics of punishment: Correctional practice implications. *Aggression and Violent Behavior, 13,* 239–247.

Ward, T., & Salmon, K. (2011). The ethics of care and treatment of sex offenders. *Sexual Abuse: A Journal of Research and Treatment, 23,* 397–413.

Weinstock, R. (2001). Commentary: A broadened conception of forensic psychiatric ethics. *Journal of the American Academy of Psychiatry and Law, 29,* 180–185.

4

Standard Sex Offender Assessment, Supervision, and Group Treatment

Rosie Gray and Daniel T. Wilcox

Introduction

Sexual offending is an international problem that has significant social and psychological effects (Kendall-Tackett, Williams, & Finkelhor, 1993; Pereda, Guilera, Forns, & Gómez-Benito, 2009). Therefore, reliable methods for assessing risk of sexual harm, and effective treatment programs, are of paramount importance. Over recent years, the research base has increased exponentially and this, in turn, has facilitated significant advances in risk assessment techniques, as well as the development of psychological interventions that have been associated with reductions in sexual recidivism (Hall, 1995; Hanson, Bourgon, Helmus, & Hodgson, 2009; Lösel & Schmucker, 2005). This chapter seeks to provide an overview of the "standard" approach to sex offender assessment and treatment, by considering the case example of Mr. N, who was supervised by the National Probation Service (NPS) for England and Wales. The broad approach adopted by the NPS towards assessing, managing, and reducing risk of sexual harm is reflective of most forensic organizations, including custodial and inpatient settings, and services within other jurisdictions (see Brown, 2011).

Sex Offender Treatment: A Case Study Approach to Issues and Interventions,
First Edition. Edited by Daniel T. Wilcox, Tanya Garrett, and Leigh Harkins.
© 2015 John Wiley & Sons, Ltd. Published 2015 by John Wiley & Sons, Ltd.

Theoretical and Research Developments

Assessment

In order to develop a treatment plan and reduce the risk presented by a sexual offender, it is firstly necessary to assess the likelihood of, and factors associated with, their recidivism (Craig & Beech, 2010). Until the 1970s and 1980s, due to the paucity of research evidence, forensic risk assessments were largely completed using *unstructured clinical judgment* (Bonta & Andrews, 2007; Wilcox, 2013a). This approach involved gathering information about the case and, from these data, drawing conclusions "without any significant *a priori* list or theory to prioritise the relative importance of the data obtained" (Craig, Beech, & Harkins, 2009, p. 55). Using this method, sexual offenders were generally considered to pose a high risk of reoffending purely on the basis of the nature of their crimes (Mann & Marshall, 2009). However, as the evidence base developed, it became apparent that there was significant variability in sexual offending recidivism data and that more reliable assessment methods were required. Indeed, unstructured clinical judgment, often referred to as "first generation risk assessment," has consistently demonstrated low predictive validity (Hanson & Morton-Bourgon, 2007). As well as public protection implications, this raises an important ethical issue as, for example, risk assessments are often used to inform decisions relating to sentencing and other restrictions on liberty. Therefore, "optimal precision" is required in order to balance offender rights against public safety concerns (Bengtson & Längström, 2007, p. 136; Vess, 2011; Wilcox, 2013b).

The advent of *actuarial* risk tools represented the "second generation" of forensic risk assessment. Developed using statistical techniques, actuarial scales comprise scorable items that have been empirically associated with recidivism and which are static and/or largely unchangeable through treatment, such as prior sexual offenses, victim gender, and the offender's current age. An offender's overall score on an actuarial assessment tool is translated into a risk band: low, medium, or high (Craig et al., 2009). This yields a probabilistic estimate of recidivism over a specified time period, based on the number of reoffenses amongst those falling in the same risk category within the standardization sample (Tully, Chou, & Browne, 2013).

As well as being relatively straightforward to score and interpret, actuarial tools have generally demonstrated strong predictive validity (Hanson & Morton-Bourgon, 2009). However, by their nature, they have inherent limitations which must be considered during the assessment and case formulation process. Firstly, they reflect a nomothetic approach to risk assessment, as they only include factors that have been derived from data concerning large forensic samples. Therefore, features that are unique to the individual being assessed may be missed (Craig & Beech, 2010). Secondly, actuarial tools cannot be used to indicate the likely nature, severity, or imminence of a reoffense: factors that are of paramount importance when considering public protection issues. In addition, they do not assist in identifying targets for change, nor can they be used to reassess risk level following treatment (Hanson, 1998).

In relation to this issue, "third generation" sexual offending risk assessment tools include dynamic risk factors: characteristics that have been empirically associated with sexual recidivism and are amenable to change, such as offense-supportive attitudes, sexual preoccupation, and poor self-regulation (Hanson & Morton-Bourgon, 2005, 2009; Mann, Hanson, & Thornton, 2010). Third generation tools overcome some of the limitations of actuarial methods, for example, they reflect an idiographic approach to risk assessment, giving consideration to person-specific risk factors (Tully et al., 2013). They can also be used to inform treatment planning and to reassess risk following program completion or other changes in circumstance. Third generation tools tend to rely on the clinical judgment of the assessor to determine overall risk level and, unlike actuarial tools, they have no recidivism data relating to each risk category. However, their format is structured (this method of assessment is often referred to as *structured professional judgment*) and they have garnered promising empirical support (Tully et al., 2013). In practice, it is common for clinicians to use a third generation tool in addition to an actuarial instrument when completing a risk assessment, as this combination of methods indicates both treatment need and likelihood of recidivism, and increases the reliability of overall judgment (Wilcox, 2013b).

Treatment

Alongside developments in assessment technique, there have also been significant changes in treatment approaches for sexual offenders. Behavioral methods (e.g., aversion therapy) were popular during the 1970s, as it was considered that sexual offending resulted from deviant sexual interests that had been learnt and reinforced through "accidental experiences with sexually deviant behavior" and repeated masturbation to fantasies of this nature (Brown, 2011; Laws & Marshall, 2003, p. 77). Over time, however, it became increasingly apparent that while deviant sexual interests and arousal were important contributory factors, sexual offending was in fact more complex than had previously been believed.

Therefore, still drawing on behavioral principles, treatment providers sought to enhance appropriate sexual interests and encounters via methods such as masturbatory reconditioning and social skills practice (Brown, 2011). During the 1980s, cognitive psychology became increasingly popular, and elements of this approach were soon incorporated into sex offender treatment (Marshall & Laws, 2003). For example, cognitive restructuring techniques were used to develop perspective-taking skills and enhance victim empathy. This integration of cognitive principles and behavioral methods was to become known as the "cognitive-behavioral" approach (Brown, 2011).

The aforementioned programs tended to be based on theoretical assumptions rather than empirical research findings. However, over time, the developing research base and increasingly sophisticated data analysis techniques allowed for more comprehensive evaluations of offender treatment. Indeed, the majority of current sex offender treatment programs (SOTPs) are based on the risk–need–responsivity (RNR) model, which was derived from meta-analytic reviews that were undertaken during the 1980s and 1990s (see Bonta & Andrews, 2007). These meta-analyses involved the integration of results from a number of independent research studies and revealed three key findings, often referred to as the "what works" principles. In brief, the what works principles suggest that in order to effectively reduce recidivism, the intensity or "dosage" of treatment should be proportionate to the offender's level of risk ("risk principle"); the material should target the factors associated with their offending behavior ("need principle"); and program methods or delivery style should reflect their learning style and abilities ("responsivity principle"). While these findings were originally drawn from samples of general offenders, they appear to also hold true for those who have committed sexual offenses (Hanson et al., 2009).

During the 1990s, the what works principles had a significant influence on international forensic practice (Brown, 2011). An evidence-based practice agenda was established and correctional treatment programs were required to meet certain standards, for example, they had to have a clear model of change; be supported by research; target dynamic risk factors; and utilize methods that had proven effective. In order to ensure that such programs were delivered as intended ("treatment integrity"), they were manualized and carefully monitored. While this has given rise to criticisms in terms of restricting new knowledge and innovation (Marshall, 2009), others have argued that it helps to prevent "treatment drift" and, in line with the need principle, to maintain focus on empirically identified dynamic risk factors (Mann, 2009).

Cognitive-behavioral programs, which adopted a participatory delivery style, were generally considered to be the most effective form of treatment. They continue to be delivered across the US, Canada, Australia, New Zealand, Ireland, and the UK, in both secure and community settings (see Brown, 2011, for a fuller description of these programs). Broadly speaking, cognitive-behavioral SOTPs aim to change the internal processes (thinking patterns, feelings, and physiological arousal) that are associated with sexual offending, and also to replace maladaptive learned behaviors with those that are expected to reduce the likelihood of recidivism (Dennis et al., 2012). Treatment goals tend to include: raising the offender's awareness of the link between thoughts, feelings, and behavior; reducing offense-supportive attitudes and reasoning biases; increasing self-monitoring abilities; identifying future risk scenarios; and developing alternative, adaptive coping (relapse prevention) strategies in order to reduce the likelihood of recidivism (Dennis et al., 2012; Laws, Hudson, & Ward, 2000).

Over time, the focus of cognitive-behavioral SOTPs has changed slightly. Indeed, for a period the value placed upon cognitive factors in sex offender treatment expanded such that behavioral elements (deviant sexual interests and social skills training) were often overshadowed (Brown, 2011; Mann & Marshall, 2009). However, more recently there has been a greater emphasis on problem-solving skills, emotional regulation abilities, and general interpersonal effectiveness and, in this respect, observers have commented that sex offender treatment "traversed something of a circle" (Mann & Marshall, 2009, p. 341). Even more recently, treatment providers have started to place greater emphasis on protective factors, future goals, and personal potential in order to promote desistance from offending (see Good Lives Model: e.g., Ward, Collie, & Bourke, 2009). However, the underlying cognitive-behavioral approach to sex offender treatment is retained in the majority of current SOTPs.

There appear to be more similarities than differences in the various SOTPs that exist across settings and jurisdictions. For example, they tend to be delivered in a group format (generally up to ten members), with sessions being run on at least a weekly basis (Brown, 2011). This group modality appears to hold a number of potential benefits, for example, it offers peer support or challenge, provides vicarious learning opportunities, and can assist in overcoming treatment-related difficulties such as denial (Ware, Mann, & Wakeling, 2009; Wilcox, 2013a). It is also generally recognized that process variables such as group cohesion and therapist style can influence treatment outcomes, and staff are highly trained to demonstrate empathy, use open questions, and adopt a motivational style (e.g., Beech & Fordham, 1997; Garrett, Oliver, Wilcox, & Middleton, 2003; Marshall, 2005).

While treatment aims to target dynamic risk factors, the monitoring and management of acute risk is also important in maximizing public protection. Acute risk factors are those that are readily subject to change, including response to supervision, access to victims, and other relevant changes in life circumstances, such as a relationship breakdown or increase in substance use (Hanson & Harris, 2000). In the NPS, supervision of acute risk is typically the purview of the individual's probation officer, and they work closely with treatment staff, police, and others in undertaking this role. In some instances where individuals are judged to be particularly high-risk, more intensive measures can be employed, including electronic monitoring ("tagging"), periodic polygraph examinations, and regular interagency reviews (Kemshall, 2008; Wilcox, 2009; Wilcox & Gray, 2012).

Case Introduction

Mr. N was a Caucasian 26-year-old male who received a 3-year Community Order with a requirement to complete a sexual offending treatment program after being convicted for indecently assaulting a 14-year-old girl. Mr. N's parents and the victim's parents had been friends for several years and the offense took place when Mr. N was babysitting for the victim and her younger brother while the two sets of parents went out together. On the evening concerned, after the brother had gone to bed, Mr. N initiated a discussion with the victim about relationships, including, for example, asking questions about her sexual experiences. He began to stroke her leg and, when she did not physically resist, touched her breasts. At this point, the victim moved away and Mr. N stopped. Her parents arrived home shortly thereafter and she disclosed the offense to them after Mr. N had left. Mr. N was convicted for one count of indecent assault, though the case documentation suggested that Mr. N had initiated inappropriate discussions and contact with the victim on other occasions prior to the offense, including allegedly showing her an adult pornography website "as a joke" and "hugging" or "stroking" her whilst they had watched television. These behaviors leading up to Mr. N's offense occurred over a 3-month period.

History

Mr. N described a fairly unremarkable childhood, except to note that he had few friends and experienced some bullying at school. He left aged 16 with "average" grades and had worked in a mail-sorting office since that time. Although he enjoyed his job, he said that when asked to undertake additional duties by managers or colleagues, he had difficulty in saying no and this resulted in him often staying late, as well as feeling annoyed when his helpfulness was neither acknowledged nor reciprocated.

Mr. N described a limited support network. He occasionally socialized with colleagues after work, though these relationships appeared somewhat superficial. Indeed, even when out with others, he described that he often felt lonely and left out. Mr. N reported a heterosexual orientation and stated that he had his first sexual experience while on holiday at the age of fourteen, with a girl who was two years older. He recalled some mixed feelings about this encounter, noting that the girl had commented on his relative sexual immaturity, which had contributed to concerns about inadequacy. He had never had a long-term intimate relationship and reported a strong desire for a partner. Relatedly, Mr. N stated that approximately 6 months prior to his offense he had made advances towards an adult female whom he met through a colleague and had liked for some time, though she had turned him down. He reported that he had always felt under-confident around adult females and that he had taken this rejection badly.

Mr. N had no history of involvement with mental health services and there were no indications of substance misuse. He had no prior convictions and there had been no other allegations of sexual offenses made against him in the past.

Assessment

In terms of static risk level, Mr. N was assessed using the Risk Matrix 2000 (RM2000; Thornton, 2007; Thornton et al., 2003). The RM2000 is used widely in UK forensic services to indicate the likelihood of sexual reconviction (Grubin, 2011; Khiroya, Weaver, & Maden, 2009). Another similar actuarial tool, the Static-99 (Hanson & Thornton, 2000), is more commonly applied in the US and Canada, though the RM2000 perhaps better reflects police and court recording processes within the UK (Thornton, 2007). The RM2000 comprises seven scorable items, each of which has been empirically associated with increased risk of recidivism. They include the number of previous sexual offenses, the offender being single (i.e. having had no history of a marital-type relationship), and offense-specific factors, such as the victim being male, a stranger, or subject to a noncontact offense.

Table 4.1   Content of the Structured Assessment of Risk and Need

Risk domain	Risk factor items
Sexual interests	Sexual preoccupation
	Sexual preference for children
	Sexualized violence
	Other offense-related sexual interest (e.g., paraphilias)
Distorted attitudes	Adversarial sexual attitudes
	Sexual entitlement beliefs
	Child-abuse supportive beliefs
	Rape supportive beliefs
	Beliefs that women are deceitful
Socio-affective functioning	Feelings of inadequacy
	Distorted intimacy balance (emotional congruence with children)
	Grievance thinking style
	Lack of emotional intimacy with adults
Self-management	Lifestyle impulsiveness
	Poor problem-solving
	Poor emotional control

Note. Adapted from Mann et al. (2004), *Structured Assessment of Risk and Need (Sexual Offenders): Manual v.2*, and Webster et al. (2006) Inter-rater reliability of dynamic risk assessment with sexual offenders, *Psychology, Crime and Law, 12,* 439–452.

The Structured Assessment of Risk and Need (SARN; Mann et al., 2004; Thornton, 2002; Webster et al., 2006) was used to assess Mr. N's level of dynamic risk and treatment need. As detailed in Table 4.1, the SARN includes 16 empirically-supported dynamic risk factors which are clustered into four domains: sexual interests; distorted attitudes; socioaffective functioning; and self-management. Assessors are required to assess the presence and weighting of each item using evidence gathered via clinical interview, psychometric testing, and case documentation (e.g., Police National Computer Report and Crown Prosecution Service evidence). It is widely acknowledged that this tripartite approach is likely to reduce bias and contribute to a more comprehensive and reliable assessment (Wilcox, 2000).

In line with the responsivity principle, Mr. N's cognitive and literacy abilities were also assessed. He was administered the Shipley Institute of

Living Scale (Zachary, 1991), which is an intellectual functioning screening measure that estimates an individual's level of verbal comprehension and abstract reasoning ability. Adapted treatment programs, in which concepts are simplified and material is more accessible, tend to be considered for those achieving an IQ score below 80 (Brown, 2011).

Case conceptualization

The information gained from Mr. N's assessment was organized and synthesized in a manner that clearly indicated the contributory factors to his offense; protective factors that could be developed and/or consolidated; and potential future high-risk scenarios. Effective treatment methods and potential barriers to progress were also considered. This process of case formulation provides a working hypothesis of offending behavior, from which treatment and supervision plans can be drawn. It also offers a gauge for measuring change (Eells & Lombart, 2011).

Mr. N's overall score on the RM2000 placed him within the medium risk band. Amongst those producing similar scores (i.e. sharing similar characteristics) in the validation sample, 13% were reconvicted for a sexual offense over a 5-year period, and 19% were reconvicted for a sexual offense over 15 years. In terms of dynamic risk, Mr. N's greatest difficulties related to the socioaffective functioning domain. His psychometric test results, which indicated low self-esteem, externalized locus of control, feelings of emotional loneliness, and assertiveness deficits, were consistent with his clinical presentation (see Beech, Fisher, & Beckett, 1998). Mr. N's offending behavior was considered to reflect the *intimacy deficits* pathway; it had occurred during a period of prolonged loneliness, within the context of a relatively recent rejection, and appeared to be an attempt to compensate for a lack of intimacy (Ward & Siegert, 2002). While his offense was committed against a child, there was no other evidence to suggest deviant sexual interests. Rather, he described feeling as though, at that time, his relative seniority and greater life experiences would have been attractive to the victim and, in turn, this had contributed to positive affect. Nonetheless, his behavior suggested a capacity for arousal to children under certain circumstances and, therefore, this, too, was identified as an area for exploration during treatment. In terms of protective factors, Mr. N evidenced a relatively stable lifestyle, with supportive familial relationships and employment that he reported enjoying.

Mr. N achieved an IQ estimate of 85, which fell within the low average intellectual functioning range. He demonstrated no significant difficulties in relation to reading, writing, and general communication, although in comparison to his peers, his skills in these areas were somewhat under-developed. Therefore, while it was considered that an adapted SOTP was not required, it was agreed that Mr. N would be offered support by his Probation Officer to complete homework exercises between sessions of the mainstream program. It is also important to note that although it was known that Mr. N had shown his victim internet (adult) pornography, he was not allocated to the internet offense-focused SOTP, as this was developed for men convicted of downloading indecent images of children. Another responsivity factor that was taken into account was Mr. N's working hours. Since his employment was considered to reflect a protective feature, efforts were made to offer an evening treatment program in order that this was not interrupted.

Treatment

Early exercises aimed to enhance group members' motivation to change by, for example, exploring their values and the benefits of self-development. They were also encouraged to develop their own "group rules" in order to promote group cohesion and a greater sense of safety in sharing personal information with one another.

Following on from this, Mr. N completed an "offense account" exercise, which he presented to the group. The aim was to promote greater insight into the thoughts, feelings, and behaviors that preceded his offending in order that he could start to self-identify the changes he needed to make in order to reduce the likelihood of reoffending. Another benefit of this type of exercise is that it can yield further information for the individual's risk assessment, as well as enable treatment facilitators to tailor future program exercises so that they are relevant and responsive. Initially, Mr. N tended to suggest that his offense was impulsive, unplanned, and that his actions were the result of a "miscommunication" between himself and the victim about her feelings towards him. He also said that he would not reoffend as he had "learned the hard way" and he would not make any sexual advances towards anyone in the future unless he was "sure" that these were wanted. However, with some exploratory questions posed by both facilitators and other group members, Mr. N acknowledged that the victim had in fact been a child and also that the offense for which he was convicted reflected a culmination of grooming behaviors that he had engaged in over several months beforehand. In addition, Mr. N self-identified that he would benefit from developing his intimacy and problem-solving skills so that, in the future, he would be better equipped to develop appropriate adult relationships and to manage difficult feelings or situations in more adaptive ways (which, in turn, would reduce the likelihood of a further offense). Mr. N was offered positive reinforcement for increased levels of responsibility taking over the course of this exercise, as well as his contributions to other group members' offense accounts, in order to start the process of improving his self-esteem and developing a sense of self-efficacy.

As the program progressed, Mr. N was further encouraged to consider how he might improve his cognitive and problem-solving style. For example, during a session that focused on self-esteem and the role of self-beliefs upon behavior, Mr. N identified a number of unhelpful thoughts that he had had, not only in the lead up to his offense, but in his life more generally and which had hindered his goal of developing successful interpersonal relationships: for example, "I'm not as successful, good-looking or funny as other people … no-one would want to spend time with someone like me, so there's no point trying to make friends or find a girlfriend." He then identified a number of "replacement thoughts" which could support and reinforce positive change: for example, "I have a lot of good qualities … Nobody is good at everything – even though I get nervous when I speak to new people, if I keep going out of my way to avoid doing this, then I'll never get better at it … Nothing bad will happen if I get something wrong – practice makes perfect."

Following on from this, Mr. N participated in a skills practice, wherein he rehearsed how he might start or contribute to a conversation, with the aim of improving his confidence and abilities in this area. In preparation, Mr. N broke down this skill into smaller steps, for example, giving forethought as to what he might want to say, identifying helpful self-talk techniques, and thinking about appropriate verbal and nonverbal behaviors. A more confident group member was asked to model the skill before Mr. N took part in a role-play. Mr. N practiced on several occasions and, after each practice, he was encouraged to identify what he had done well and to give himself praise, as well as to consider how he might further improve his performance. Using similar principles, Mr. N was also encouraged to increase his assertion skills. During this particular session, Mr. N said that he planned to practice these the next time that he felt he was unfairly asked to undertake additional duties at work. This situation arose several days later and Mr. N reflected on how he had managed this at the next session. He received positive feedback from other group members, which appeared to increase his confidence in this area.

During the program, Mr. N was also asked to consider how he might better deal with rejection in the future, as this had happened shortly before his offense. Again, he was able to identify a number of unhelpful thinking patterns and behaviors that he had engaged in at that time, such as "I'm not good enough for her ... people are probably laughing at me, it's so embarrassing" and isolating himself for several days afterwards. He then considered more adaptive coping mechanisms, including telling himself "everybody gets rejected at some point in their lives, it's not the end of the world and it doesn't mean that it's something about me." He also recognized that, in such circumstances, it would be helpful to speak to someone about his feelings; engage in positive, enjoyable activities in order to relieve negative affect; and to reward himself for having done something that he finds challenging.

While Mr. N denied that deviant sexual interests preceded his offense, he acknowledged that he had engaged in inappropriate fantasies about having sexual intercourse with his 14-year-old victim. As such, he self-identified that he would benefit from monitoring the content of his sexual thinking in the future, particularly if he was struggling to manage feelings of loneliness or rejection. Mr. N considered a number of strategies that he could use to curb inappropriate sexual fantasy in the future, including "fantasy blockers" (e.g., recalling the details of his arrest and the memory of his mother's face when the police told her about his offense) and keeping "positive reminder cards" in close proximity (e.g., pictures of his family, who had been supportive through the treatment process). Mr. N also undertook a number of victim awareness exercises, wherein he considered the potential short- and long-term effects of sexual abuse in order to build an empathic response that would help to support the management of deviant sexual arousal.

Towards the end of treatment, Mr. N was encouraged to reflect on personal "warning signs" of increased risk and how he could apply newly developed coping strategies for managing high-risk thoughts, feelings, behaviors, and situations. The final sessions also emphasized approach-goal setting: looking at what group members could achieve rather than solely what they should avoid. For example, Mr. N discussed steps that he might take towards developing an increased social support network and greater independence in his life, such as joining a local adult badminton club and, in the future, moving out of the family home.

Supervision

Alongside treatment, Mr. N attended regular appointments with his probation officer, wherein session material was reviewed and reinforced. In addition, information was routinely shared between Mr. N's probation officer and treatment staff in order to effectively monitor for and manage any changes in acute risk level. This close liaison proved useful when, during the group, Mr. N reported that a cousin had found out about his offense and effectively "rejected" him. His supervision appointments with his probation officer allowed more time to discuss and consider how he could manage this issue, as well as greater opportunity to monitor its effect upon his risk level. Mr. N's probation officer also visited the family home and met with Mr. N's parents, in order to assess and reduce the likelihood of contact between Mr. N and his victim (as their parents were friends). This collaborative approach resulted in a much more comprehensive risk management plan than the treatment program would have allowed for alone.

Assessing treatment change

The process of groupwork appeared to increase Mr. N's social confidence and he engaged well with the program material. Over the course of treatment, he developed good working relationships with staff. However, it is important to note that rapport and other positive interpersonal features can influence clinician's judgments concerning risk and treatment progress (Moore, 1996). Therefore, in assessing change, several other types of outcome data were considered, including: examples of applied learning; psychometric reassessment; feedback from and reflection discussion with Mr. N; and evidence of further offending or offense-type behaviors. This information was then used to review Mr. N's dynamic risk assessment and case formulation.

As indicated above, Mr. N provided examples of applied learning during treatment. For example, he described how he had managed difficult thoughts and feelings following an argument with a family member. He also reported effectively using the skill of assertion in the workplace. Towards the end of the program, Mr. N started to give greater consideration to ways he might further increase his social support network, and this was identified as an area of posttreatment work during his ongoing supervision appointments.

Mr. N was readministered psychometric tests following his completion of treatment, and his scores were examined for clinically significant change – that is, whether they were indistinguishable from the nonoffender sample, *and* whether that change was statistically reliable (see Beech et al., 1998; Beech, Fisher, & Beckett, 2005; Fisher, Beech, & Browne, 1999). As referenced previously, Mr. N's pretreatment scores had indicated that his greatest difficulties related to the socioaffective functioning domain. His posttreatment scores on measures of assertiveness, self-esteem, emotional loneliness, and locus of control "moved" in the desired directions and passed the "cut-off" distinguishing between dysfunctional and functional responding (though this change was not statistically reliable in the case of emotional loneliness). Research suggests that positive change on measures relating to the socioaffective functioning risk domain is associated with reduced recidivism (Barnett, Wakeling, Mandeville-Norden, & Rakestrow, 2013).

There was no evidence to suggest that Mr. N had reoffended during the course of treatment, either from self-report or official sources. In addition, a review of his SARN assessment suggested that his level of dynamic risk had reduced. There was no evidence to suggest that any previously unidentified dynamic risk factors were now present (e.g., child abuse supportive beliefs). Further, as described above, there was evidence of positive change in features associated with the socioaffective functioning domain.

Although Mr. N had made a number of internal and interpersonal changes, he agreed that he would benefit from support in further developing his level of social activity. He also identified that "booster" exercises concerning monitoring and challenging negative self-talk would be helpful in maintaining treatment gains. Therefore, this information was shared with Mr. N's probation officer, who agreed to continue this work during individual posttreatment sessions.

Conclusion

Through the use of a case example, this chapter has described the current *standard* approaches to sex offender assessment, treatment, and supervision. A developing evidence base concerning effective practice has informed these. Nonetheless, it is widely acknowledged that the heterogeneity of the sexual offender population warrants further research efforts. Indeed, there are a substantial number of individuals for whom such standard approaches appear less effective. Due to factors such as high deviance, unique criminogenic needs, or certain personality features, these individuals may require tailored or one-to-one interventions, alongside or separate to a mainstream treatment program. Single case study evaluations which explore individualized interventions, such as those described in the following chapters, can, therefore, provide clinicians with a rich source of information to draw upon when assessments and formulation indicate specialist treatment needs.

References

Barnett, G. D., Wakeling, H. C., Mandeville-Norden, R., & Rakestrow, J. (2013). Does change in psychometric test scores tell us anything about risk of reconviction in sexual offenders? *Psychology, Crime and Law, 19*(1), 85–110.

Beech, A. R., Fisher, D., & Beckett, R. C. (1998). *STEP 3: An evaluation of the prison sex offender treatment programme.* London: Home Office.

Beech, A. R., Fisher, D., & Beckett, R. C. (2005, November). *Background to calculation of treatment change.* Paper presented at National Probation Service "STEP" Training Event, Birmingham, UK.

Beech, A. R., & Fordham, A. S. (1997). Therapeutic climate of sex offender treatment programs. *Sexual Abuse: A Journal of Research and Treatment, 9,* 219–237.

Bengtson, S., & Längström, N. (2007). Unguided clinical and actuarial assessment of reoffending risk: A direct comparison with sex offenders in Denmark. *Sexual Abuse: A Journal of Research and Treatment, 19,* 135–153.

Bonta, J., & Andrews, D. A. (2007). *Risk–need–responsivity model for offender assessment and rehabilitation* (User Report No. 2007-06). Ottawa, Canada: Public Safety and Emergency Preparedness Canada.

Brown, S. (2011). *Treating sex offenders: An introduction to sex offender treatment programmes.* Oxford, UK: Routledge.

Craig, L. A., & Beech, A. R. (2010). Towards a guide to best practice in conducting actuarial risk assessments with sex offenders. *Aggression and Violent Behavior, 15,* 278–293.

Craig, L. A., Beech, A. R., & Harkins, L. (2009). The predictive accuracy of risk factors and frameworks. In A. R. Beech, L. Craig, & K. D. Browne (Eds.), *Assessment and treatment of sex offenders: A handbook* (pp. 53–74). Chichester, UK: John Wiley & Sons.

Dennis, J. A., Khan, O., Ferriter, M., Huband, N., Powney, M. J., & Duggan, C. (2012). Psychological interventions for adults who have sexually offended or are at risk of reoffending. *Cochrane Database of Systematic Reviews 2012/12.*

Eells, T. D., & Lombart, K. G. (2011). Theoretical and evidence-based approaches to case formulation. In P. Sturmey & M. McMurran (Eds.), *Forensic case formulation* (pp. 3–32). Chichester, UK: John Wiley & Sons.

Fisher, D., Beech, A. R., & Browne, K. D. (1999). Comparison of sex offenders to non-sex offenders on selected psychological measures. *International Journal of Offender Therapy and Comparative Criminology, 43,* 473–491.

Garrett, T., Oliver, C., Wilcox, D. T., & Middleton, D. (2003). Who cares? The views of sexual offenders about the group treatment they receive. *Sexual Abuse: A Journal of Research and Treatment, 15*(4), 323–338.

Grubin, D. (2011). A large-scale evaluation of Risk Matrix 2000 in Scotland. *Sexual Abuse: A Journal of Research and Treatment, 23*(4), 419–433.

Hall, G. C. N. (1995). Sexual offender treatment recidivism revisited: A meta-analysis of recent treatment studies. *Journal of Consulting and Clinical Psychology, 63*, 802–809.

Hanson, R. K. (1998). What do we know about sex offender risk assessment? *Psychology, Public Policy and Law, 4*, 50–72.

Hanson, R. K., Bourgon, G., Helmus, L., & Hodgson, S. (2009). The principles of effective correctional treatment also apply to sexual offenders: A meta-analysis. *Criminal Justice and Behavior, 36*, 865–891.

Hanson, R. K., & Harris, A. J. R. (2000). *The Sex Offender Need Assessment Rating (SONAR): A method for measuring change in risk levels* (User Report No. 2000-01). Ottawa, Canada: Public Safety and Emergency Preparedness Canada.

Hanson, R. K., & Morton-Bourgon, K. E. (2005). The characteristics of persistent sexual offenders: A meta-analysis of sexual offender recidivism studies. *Journal of Consulting and Clinical Psychology, 73*(6), 1154–1163.

Hanson, R. K., & Morton-Bourgon, K. E. (2007). *The accuracy of recidivism risk assessments for sexual offenders: A meta-analysis* (User Report No. 2007-01). Ottawa, Canada: Public Safety and Emergency Preparedness Canada.

Hanson, R. K., & Morton-Bourgon, K. E. (2009). The accuracy of recidivism risk assessments for sexual offenders: A meta-analysis of 118 prediction studies. *Psychological Assessment, 21*(1), 1–21.

Hanson, R. K., & Thornton, D. (2000). Improving risk assessments for sex offenders: A comparison of three actuarial scales. *Law and Human Behavior, 24*, 119–136.

Kemshall, H. (2008). *Understanding the community management of high risk offenders*. Maidenhead, UK: Open University Press.

Kendall-Tackett, K. A., Williams, L. M., & Finkelhor, D. (1993). Impact of sexual abuse on children: A review and synthesis of recent empirical studies. *Psychological Bulletin, 113*(1), 164–180.

Khiroya, R., Weaver, T., & Maden, T. (2009). Use and perceived utility of structured violence risk assessments in English medium secure forensic units. *The Psychiatrist, 33*, 129–132.

Laws, D. R., Hudson, S. M., & Ward, T. (2000). *Remaking relapse prevention with sex offenders: A sourcebook*. Thousand Oaks, CA: Sage.

Laws, D. R., & Marshall, W. L. (2003). A brief history of behavioral and cognitive behavioral approaches to sexual offenders: Part 1: Early developments. *Sexual Abuse: A Journal of Research and Treatment, 15*(2), 75–92.

Lösel, F., & Schmucker, M. (2005). The effectiveness of treatment for sexual offenders: A comprehensive meta-analysis. *Journal of Experimental Criminology, 47*, 653–663.

Mann, R. E. (2009). Sexual offender treatment: The case for manualization. *Journal of Sexual Aggression, 15*(2), 121–132.

Mann, R. E., Hanson, R. K., & Thornton, D. (2010). Assessing risk for sexual recidivism: Some proposals on the nature of psychologically meaningful risk factors. *Sexual Abuse: A Journal of Research and Treatment*, 22(2), 191–217.

Mann, R. E., & Marshall, W. L. (2009). Advances in the treatment of adult incarcerated sex offenders. In A. R. Beech, L. Craig, & K. Browne (Eds.), *Assessment of treatment of sex offenders: A handbook* (pp. 329–347). Chichester, UK: John Wiley & Sons.

Mann, R. E., Milner, R., O'Brien, M., Rallings, M., Ray, N., Thornton, D., et al. (2004). *Structured Assessment of Risk and Need (Sexual Offenders): Manual v.2*. London: HM Prison Service.

Marshall, W. L. (2005). Therapist style in sex offender treatment: Influence on indices of change. *Sexual Abuse: A Journal of Research and Treatment*, 17(1), 109–116.

Marshall, W. L. (2009). Manualization: A blessing or a curse? *Journal of Sexual Aggression*, 15(2), 109–120.

Marshall, W. L., & Laws, D. R. (2003). A brief history of behavioral and cognitive behavioral approaches to sexual offender treatment: Part 2. The modern era. *Sexual Abuse: A Journal of Research and Treatment*, 15(2), 93–120.

Moore, B. (1996). *Risk assessment: A practitioner's guide to predicting harmful behaviour*. London: Whiting & Birch.

Pereda, N., Guilera, G., Forns, M., & Gómez-Benito, J. (2009). The international epidemiology of child sexual abuse: A continuation of Finkelhor (1994). *Child Abuse and Neglect*, 33(6), 331–342.

Thornton, D. (2002). Constructing and testing a framework for dynamic risk assessment. *Sexual Abuse: A Journal of Research and Treatment*, 14(2), 139–153.

Thornton, D. (2007). *Scoring Guide for Risk Matrix 2000.9/SVC*. Retrieved March 31, 2014, from http://www.birmingham.ac.uk/Documents/college-les/psych/RM2000scoringinstructions.pdf

Thornton, D., Mann, R. E., Webster, S. D., Blud, L., Travers, R., Friendship, C., et al. (2003). Distinguishing and combining risks for sexual and violent recidivism. *Annals of New York Academy of Science*, 989, 225–235.

Tully, R. J., Chou, S., & Browne, K. D. (2013). A systematic review on the effectiveness of sex offender risk assessment tools in predicting sexual recidivism of adult male sex offenders. *Clinical Psychology Review*, 33, 287–316.

Vess, J. (2011). Ethical practice in sex offender assessment: Consideration of actuarial and polygraph methods. *Sexual Abuse: A Journal of Research and Treatment*, 23(3), 381–396.

Ward, T., Collie, R. M., & Bourke, P. (2009). Model of offender rehabilitation: The good lives model and the risk–need–responsivity model. In A. R. Beech, L. Craig, & K. Browne (Eds.), *Assessment of treatment of sex offenders: A handbook* (pp. 293–310). Chichester, UK: John Wiley & Sons.

Ward, T., & Siegert, R. J. (2002). Towards a comprehensive theory of child sexual abuse: A theory knitting perspective. *Psychology, Crime and Law*, 8, 319–351.

Ware, J., Mann, R. E., & Wakeling, H. C. (2009). Group versus individual treatment: What is the best modality for treating sexual offenders? *Sexual Abuse in Australia and New Zealand*, 2(1), 2–13.

Webster, S. D., Mann, R. E., Carter, A. J., Long, J., Milner, R. J., O'Brien, M. D., et al. (2006). Inter-rater reliability of dynamic risk assessment with sexual offenders. *Psychology, Crime and Law*, 12, 439–452.

Wilcox, D. T. (2000). Psychometric testing in care and family proceedings. *Family Law*, 30, 268–271.

Wilcox, D. T. (Ed.). (2009). *The use of the polygraph in assessing, treating and supervising sex offenders*. Chichester, UK: John Wiley & Sons.

Wilcox, D. T. (2013a). Ethical practice and the use of the polygraph in working with sex offenders. In K. Harrison & B. Rainey (Eds.), *Legal and ethical aspects of sex offender treatment and management* (pp. 388–405). Chichester, UK: John Wiley & Sons.

Wilcox, D. T. (2013b). A forensic psychologist's involvement in working with sex offenders. In K. Harrison & B. Rainey (Eds.), *Legal and ethical aspects of sex offender treatment and management* (pp. 251–270). Chichester, UK: John Wiley & Sons.

Wilcox, D. T., & Gray, R. (2012). The use of the polygraph with sex offenders in the UK. *European Polygraph*, 6(19), 55–68.

Zachary, R. A. (1991). *Shipley Institute of Living Scale (SILS): Revised manual*. Los Angeles: Western Psychological Services.

Part III

Offender Issues

5

Treating Child Sex Abusers: A Person-Centered Approach

Geraldine Akerman, Leam A. Craig,
and Anthony R. Beech

Introduction

The aim of this chapter is to examine the role of sexual fantasy in offending through the presentation of a case study. The authors have drawn on the rich fantasy life of Mr. P and the current literature on case study as a method, alongside assessment and treatment of sexual interest to measure risk and manage current sexual interest. Adult sexual offender assessment is often used to inform estimations of risk potential as well as treatment need and risk management options for those offenders in the community. While these are, of course, paramount, such assessment information can be of limited value unless it is drawn into a detailed understanding as to the function of the offending for that individual. The use of actuarial risk assessment scales (ARAS) can potentially inform on levels of reoffending, and act as proxies to psychological vulnerabilities (Beech & Ward, 2004), but do not inform a greater understanding as to what leads an individual to commit offenses, such as their motivations and the reinforcing elements of their offending. Hence, ARAS are based on historical information that cannot be changed. Dynamic risk assessment attempts a more holistic understanding as to the factors which are important to an individual's risk of reoffending, and which are seen as more amenable to change. The recent direction in sex offender assessment is towards combining actuarial, dynamic, and detailed formulation together as a manner of clearly

Sex Offender Treatment: A Case Study Approach to Issues and Interventions,
First Edition. Edited by Daniel T. Wilcox, Tanya Garrett, and Leigh Harkins.
© 2015 John Wiley & Sons, Ltd. Published 2015 by John Wiley & Sons, Ltd.

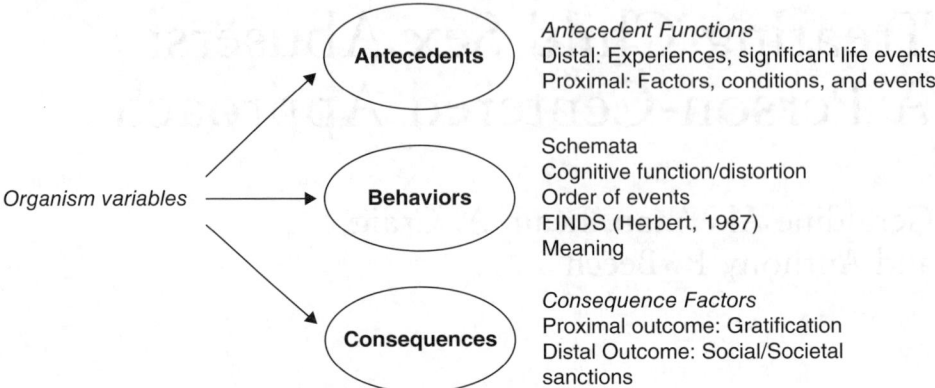

Figure 5.1   Antecedents, Behaviour, and Consequences Model. (Adapted from Craig, Browne & Beech, 2008).

understanding risk and what may be unique to each offender (see Ireland & Craig, 2011). Such an approach to assessment aims to draw together a detailed understanding as to what led the individual to commit the offense/s, the identifying of potential future triggers and destabilizers, the factors that may be maintaining such unhelpful behaviors, as well as an understanding of potential protective factors for the individual (see figure 5.1).

In many ways it attempts to tell the offender's story, from developmental influences to clinical presentation, in order to identify clear areas for treatment and to support the individual in managing their risk and to enhance their potential for a life that is offense free. It is important to stress that "case formulation" and "functional assessment" are often used interchangeably in the literature, and refer to the same principle. Henceforth, formulation will be used in this chapter.

Butler (1998) suggested that formulation should be used to test hypotheses and relate theory to practice. Eells (1997) further defines case formulation as a way of developing understanding of how the problems (psychological, interpersonal, and behavioral) began, developed, and were maintained. Therefore, the key aspects of formulation are hypotheses as to a person's difficulty, in this case sex offending, while referring to relevant theoretical models. The most important factor is to arrive at this formulation collaboratively, in a way that is understood by the client. Such a formulation is then used to inform treatment by identifying key areas of change for the individual (Tarrier & Calam, 2002). Figure 5.2 illus-

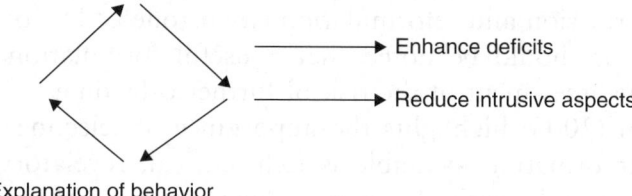

Integration of formulation on:

- Formative experiences

- Innate capacities/abilities

- Situational events

- Behavioral sequences

→ Enhance deficits

→ Reduce intrusive aspects

Explanation of behavior

- Areas of intervention

- Risk of repeating behavior

Figure 5.2 Psychological Assessment Model. (Craig & Stringer, 1999 and Ireland & Craig, 2011: Adapted from Lee-Evans, 1994 and Herbert, 1981.)

trates the importance of examining all aspects of functioning in order to develop a robust case formulation.

Butler (1998) offers a detailed description as to the purpose of formulation. This includes the need to clarify the hypotheses with the client through careful questioning by the professional. The hypotheses should be developed early on in the assessment to facilitate a greater level of understanding as to the client's problems, both in the client and the professional, and to identify the key factors in the individual's problematic behaviors. Butler argues that formulation can assist in determining the most crucial factors, as opposed to what may initially be felt to be of importance. Formulation can also help to consider the possible barriers and challenges to an individual when engaging in later therapies. For example, if triggers for an individual's offending are more likely during periods of inadequacy, then a later intervention would need to consider any possible areas which may trigger such feelings of inadequacy during the therapy, and to put supportive mechanisms in place should this occur. In doing so, this reduces the risk of inadequacy affecting the ability to successfully engage and make progress during the intervention work. As such, a detailed formulation can contribute towards assessing the best potential methods and interactions, which may increase the prospect of a more successful outcome.

Individual formulations often take the form of case studies and synthesize the core problems of the client, such as their sexual offending. They aim to show how the client's difficulties relate to one another through drawing on appropriate theories and scientific ideas. Additionally, they attempt to explain how an individual has developed such difficulties, which can assist with intervention planning. Importantly, all formulations are open to revision and reformulation (Johnstone & Dallos, 2006). Following this, it should be noted that a useful formulation should link theory to the assessment of the risk of further offending.

Johansson (2003) highlights the importance of selecting a case study where the information available is rich, critical, revelatory, unique, or extreme. Case study methodologies encourage the use of triangulation of data in order to improve the credibility of a qualitative study (Frechtling & Sharp, 1997; Patton, 1987). This technique of data analysis allows for the comparison of various types and sources of data gained throughout the study in order to achieve consistency of results. Frechtling and Sharp (1997) defined triangulation as the attempt to get "a fix" on a phenomenon by approaching it via several independent routes. Patton (1987) described triangulation as comparing observational data with interview data; thus comparing what people say in public with what they say in private. Patton highlighted the need to assess the consistency of what people say over time and compare the perspectives of people who may have different points of view. Furthermore, information should be validated through interviews, checking program documents, and other written evidence that can corroborate what interview respondents report.

Case Introduction

In this chapter, we offer a case formulation of Mr. P using triangulation of data as described above and through linking his case information to the literature. Mr. P was arrested and convicted of possessing indecent images of children and incitement to commit a sexual offense (inciting others to kidnap). He had discussed his fantasies of sexually abusing a child with other men via the Internet and had gone as far as trying to buy chloroform. He was sentenced to an Indeterminate Sentence for Public Protection.[1] Mr. P's accounts of past and present behavior were examined and analyzed by comparing the records available from the court, his work on the Core Sex Offender Treatment Programme[2] (CSOTP) and postprogram information, his psychometric information from CSOTP and induction for his current intervention and recent treatment information, and interview. In addition, his self-reported current sexual interests and observations made by staff where Mr. P is located are reported.

Personal history

Mr. P described being an only child brought up by both parents until his father died suddenly of a heart attack when Mr. P was 15 years old. Mr. P discovered his father's body and was deeply traumatized by the loss, having tried unsuccessfully to resuscitate him. Mr. P recalls being very close to his father: "Dad was my idol; we did everything together. I didn't know how to react. I was hurt, upset." He placed this in the context of the deaths of several close family members (grandparents), and his father's death was followed 2 weeks later by the death of his father's brother and a few years later by the death of Mr. P's school friend. Despite these bereavements he described having had a happy childhood, with the exception of experiencing a good deal of bullying at school, "I was weak, not out-going." He recalled that his parents were warm and kind and encouraged him to express his emotions readily, supporting him through the difficulties at school. He speaks of his school days as industrious and unaffected by the bullies. He had always planned to join the armed forces, like his father and grandfather before him. Initially he enlisted with the Royal Navy but was asked to leave after 6 weeks, having failed physical tests. He then joined the Army, where he was employed until his arrest, seeing active service in Northern Ireland, Cyprus, Iraq, and Afghanistan.

Psychosexual development

Mr. P reported that his first experience of sexual intercourse was at 21 years of age with a woman whom he had a relationship with for two years. He later met and married his wife and denied ever having been unfaithful to her. He described them as having what he saw as a "normal" sex life, including them role-playing (uniforms, Mr. And Mrs. Claus, schoolgirl, nurse, his forces outfit, French maid, air hostess), bondage, use of pornography, discussions of threesomes, and sex in the car in the countryside. He explained, "We were at it like rabbits." He recalled they maintained their sex lives while he was stationed away through "dirty letters, pictures and phone calls." As Mr. P worried that his wife would be lonely when he was deployed abroad she lived with his mother, and Mr. P visited at weekends. He had been having financial difficulties having taken out a

£5,000 loan to "spoil my wife" and being overdrawn at the bank by £1,600. He reported no problems with drug or alcohol misuse, depression, mental illness or mental effects following exposure to trauma, or personality disorder.

Mr. P reported that while he was stationed in Iraq he began to have daydreams relating to the wish to be more involved on the frontline and fantasies about kidnapping, tying up, and using chloroform to sedate a victim for sexual pleasure.

The role of sexual fantasies will now be discussed further.

The role of sexual fantasy

Leitenberg and Henning (1995) defined a sexual fantasy as any imagery that is sexually arousing or erotic to the individual and is deemed more elaborate than a fleeting thought. Kahr (2007) added that the fantasy would produce pleasurable mental and/or physical sensations. Through his work in psychotherapy and undertaking the British Sexual Fantasy Research Project with 19,000 respondents, Kahr (2007, p. 11) described how sexual fantasies can both provide immense pleasure and feelings of shame, anxiety, guilt, and confusion, and should they be used for masturbation and result in orgasm, they can be seen as "masturbatory paradox." He suggested that sexual fantasies could serve a number of purposes, including wish-fulfillment, trial action (experiencing a new thought or action), self-comfort and medication, discharge of aggression, mastery of trauma, defense against intimacy, and defense against negative mood states. Bartels and Gannon (2011) discuss the role of sexual fantasy in offending, highlighting the links between sexual fantasy, managing mood, and risk. Quayle, Vaughan, and Taylor (2006) suggest that sexual deviation can be a form of self-medication used to avoid anxiety, loneliness, or depression, thus reducing stress. As such, Mr. P being placed in a warzone may have triggered the use of sexual fantasy to manage anxiety, fear, and boredom.

Kahr (2007) also described fantasy as a means of managing aggression, discussing the Abu Ghraib Syndrome, alluding to the way in which American soldiers humiliated a group of Iraqi prisoners, including stripping them naked, posing them in humiliating sexual positions, and forcing them to eat food not permitted in the Muslim diet. Kahr draws on psychotherapeutic theories to understand and explain such behavior, suggesting that the soldiers are overcoming their own trauma in the situation by inflicting their feelings onto their captives. However, although Mr. P was familiar with this story he reported no conscious awareness of such trauma, stating that his time in Iraq was rather mundane and that he yearned to be on the frontline with those "kicking the doors in." Interestingly, although he painted a picture of monotony, carrying out routine tasks behind a safe perimeter fence, he also recalled being "scared stiff." As such, it does not appear to be in his conscious awareness that he is using fantasy to escape fear, but this term is informative.

Offending history

Mr. P had no criminal convictions prior to his arrest. His high level of risk-taking is indicated by his use of a public computer to engage in conversations about, and ultimately trying to purchase, chloroform. His conversations with other web users related to drugging and kidnapping girls aged 7 or 8 years old, having sex with teenage girls, and encouraging others to do the same. The owner of the Internet café reported the activity to the police. Following his arrest, Mr. P was found in possession of 30 indecent images on his laptop. Twenty-three of the images were at Level 1 on the Sentencing Advisory Panel scale (SAP; Sentencing Guidelines Council, 2007),[3] one at Level 3, five at Level 4, and one at Level 5. Beech, Elliott, Birgden, & Findlater (2008) highlight that there is little research into the relationship between categorization of indecent images of children and the offender's risk of reoffending.

Mr. P had visited a chat room called "teen girls for older men." He acknowledged that he did chat to 16- or 17-year-olds, "but just chit chat." He told a psychiatrist at the time of his trial that he had five or six orgasms per day, indicating a high level of sexual preoccupation. Mr. P stated he had no intention of carrying out his plans but was interested in how far his Internet contact fantasies would go, and he was "fuelling" his fantasies. Long, Alison, and McManus (2013, p. 388) surmise that if an offender is looking for images in particular age-ranges this would indicate preference in that area, referring to an "anchor point" representing the prominent interest of the offender.

During chats online, Mr. P stated "I offer a kidnap service" and that he wanted to drug and kidnap a 7–8-year-old child. In a discussion with another man (Mr. Q) in the chat room they spoke of two young girls who lived next door to Mr. Q and how they might drug them for the purpose of sexual assault. Mr. P suggested that Mr. Q should "grab them as they walk home." In conversation with another man (Mr. R), he asked if Mr. R would pick a girl up so they could "both do her," stating he could get to Mr. R's home in two and a half hours. Mr. P refers to the use of chloroform, "just grab and chloro her and do what we want with her." Mr. P's images are described as featuring naked and semi-naked girls aged between 6 and 15 years; one girl aged between 10 and 12 was being digitally penetrated while bound and blindfolded. The file names clearly indicated content, for example, "Anita 7 yr gives her uncle a nice blowjob." Therefore, it would be difficult to claim that the content is a surprise. He had used search terms "chloroform" and "chloroformed girls."

Risk assessment

Mr. P's risk potential and treatment needs were assessed using the Structured Assessment of Risk and Need (SARN; Thornton et al., 2003). The SARN is a research-guided multi-step framework for assessing the risk presented by a sex offender and provides a systematic way of going beyond static risk classification. Deviance is defined in terms of the extent to which the offender's functioning is dominated by the psychological factors that contribute to his offending – high deviancy means that the dynamic risk factors underlying offending are relatively intense and pervasive (Thornton, 2002). These are based on potentially changeable, but relatively stable psychological factors, organized into four domains: sexual interests, offense supportive attitudes, relationships (socio-affective functioning), and self-management.

Mr. P was assessed as low risk on the RM2000/S using the Risk Matrix 2000[4] (Thornton et al., 2003), a measure of static risk. His dynamic risk factors were identified from the treatment files and interviews as follows.

Sexual interests domain
1. Obsession with sex: Mr. P role-played with his wife, including her dressing as a nurse, air hostess, etc. He also suggested a threesome to her, which he stated she had agreed to, but they had not done. Mr. P stated that he used chat rooms while on operational tours, but these discussions have not been accessed. He was spending increasing time on the computer and risk-taking by using a public computer.
2. Sexual preference for children: Mr. P took little responsibility for possession of the images blaming a virus for them being on his laptop, even though he had used terms such as "child porn fetish" in search engines. One discussion he had with Mr. S involved Mr. S asking, "how low age would you go to fuck," to which Mr. P replied "eight up." In discussion about sex with young girls, Mr. P stated the youngest girl he had had sex with was "fifteen, but want younger." In discussion about a 7-year-old girl, Mr. P suggested "hold back and follow if she goes down an alley alone and then grab and kidnap and have fun." Mr. P acknowledged that he had used the search terms "teen

pics" and was interested in girls in uniform. Mr. P denies ongoing fantasy in this area, but as described previously it is difficult for an offender to acknowledge such a fantasy to him- or herself, let alone to a treatment provider (Akerman 2010, 2011, 2012; Akerman & Beech, 2013; Dowdswell, Akerman, & "Lawrence", 2010). Further, Mr. P's incarcerated circumstances can also affect the nature and content of his fantasies. Mann, Thornton, Wakama, Dyson, and Atkinson (2010, p. 124) noted that, "a prison, a confined environment where no children are present produces few triggers for this propensity, and manifestations consequently are less likely, or may be weaker."

3. Preferring sex that includes violence and humiliation: This item was indicated by Mr. P being aroused by images of abduction and coercion, and discussing this with others. He acknowledged feeling excited by fantasies of violence for many years, including scenes of kidnap, abduction, and torture, and having begun research as to how to carry these plans out. He acknowledged that these plans would have probably led to rape had he not been caught, and that he had used these fantasies to distract himself from negative aspects of his life. He had role-played a sexual attack on his wife (he states this was with her consent) indicating an escalation from fantasy to reality. He also stated he and his wife engaged in spanking, raising the dilemma of respondents gaining sexual pleasure through hurting others. While in custody, Mr. P had tried to order films containing scenes of torture and kidnap, namely Saw III, Hostel, Kiss the Girls, The New York Ripper, and The Cell 2, which depicts a serial killer kidnapping and torturing victims until they beg to die, indicating ongoing interest. He demonstrated a lack of insight into this link with his offending in thinking he could watch horror films and censor them himself.

4. Other offense-related interests: This item includes both the interest in kidnap and in teenage girls, which Mr. P has not discussed in-depth to date.

Relationships domain

1. Feeling inadequate: The inadequacy cluster includes low self-esteem, feeling lonely, and believing others have control over what happens to you. Mr. P has stated that he feels different from others around him. Although he thought that the army would provide him with a sense of belonging, instead he experienced difficult emotions linked to his position and level of acceptance. He described himself as "just a subordinate" and felt helpless to change his circumstances and "outcast" and "isolated" in the army.

Self-management domain

1.   Impulsive unstable lifestyle: Mr. P was deemed to have had an unstable lifestyle, even though he had a secure job and relationship, because he had moved frequently in his job, was in debt, and made impulsive decisions.
2.   Poor problem solving: Mr. P responds emotionally and feels overwhelmed by emotions, particularly negative ones, using fantasy to escape.
3.   Out-of-control emotions and urges: Mr. P referred to feeling "like the Incredible Hulk" at times and described the anger building in him as like a "monster" and a "beast," released only by "going into a war zone where you can release all your anger through your gun." In CSOTP he felt distracted by this anger, which made it more difficult to make full use of the program. It would be useful to ascertain what evoked this anger.

Following treatment in the CSOTP, Mr. P's treatment needs still included his sexual interests, emotional management, and relationship skills. In terms of risk reduction, recent research (Wakeling, Beech, & Freemantle, 2013) reported that those who showed clinically significant change in the four domains of the SARN, so that their scores were in the "normal range" in psychometric tests after treatment, were reconvicted at a significantly lower rate than those whose scores were not. Further, those who were deemed "changed" overall on three of the four risk domains were reconvicted at a lower rate than those who were deemed not to have changed on these domains.

Case conceptualization

At present, Mr. P is undertaking treatment at HMP Grendon, a prison-based therapeutic community (TC), which houses Category B (medium secure) and Category C (lower security) offenders who have volunteered for treatment. The prison is comprised of six democratic therapeutic communities (including the assessment unit) housing up to 235 adult men who are typically more damaged, disturbed, and dangerous than the average inmate (Shine & Newton, 2000). The facility is accredited by the Correctional Services Advice and Accreditation Panel[5] of the UK, which is designed to address holistic change with a focus on risk, and by the Community of Therapeutic Communities, which is part of the Royal College of Psychiatrists' Centre for Quality Improvement.[6]

During the course of treatment it will be important for Mr. P to be able to discuss the content of his sexual fantasies. Wood (2013) stated that the escalation of sexual fantasy is evident in those using the Internet to access images, as external censorship is removed, leaving the user in a more infantile state. Wood explains that the Internet can expose more primitive, previously unconscious fantasies, more raw, infantile and taboo (id-driven). Sexual interests become normalized, as the user will always find someone else with similar interests, thus, without needing to leave their home or risk exposing their interest publicly, they are invited (by drop-down menus) to sample limitless images. As there is no censorship (or super-ego) to say no, the options are boundless.

Wood (2013) notes that perversions (in psychodynamic terms) are defined on the basis of the behavior, rather than the behavior itself, asking what purpose it serves. Psychodynamic theory suggests that behavior defends the user against anxiety and depression. Wood highlights that escalation is almost always towards younger adults or children, and becomes more violent as habituation takes hold, rather than the other trajectory. In Mr. P's case it will be important to understand when his feelings of anger started and if the increase in sexual preoccupation served to defend him from these feelings. In discussion with Mr. P he was unsure as to the basis of these fantasies. He recalled struggling to get a girlfriend when he was at school and girls laughing at him when they heard he "fancied" them. It is interesting that Mr. P's fantasy of being more power-ful and dominant developed at a time when he felt "scared stiff"; his psyche may have returned to other times when he felt powerless, such as the loss of his father, being bullied, and not being successful with girls, all of which happened when he was a teenager. The fantasies that Mr. P described contained components to overcome powerlessness, such as being dominant. It could be hypothesized that by tying someone up, he could prevent them leaving, thus overcoming the loss of his father. Kahr (2007) described several case studies in which the basis of sexual fantasies could be traced back to incidents of trauma in the person's history. It could also be hypothesized that the death of his father and Mr. P's inability to resuscitate him could be re-enacted in a scenario where he sedates another but is able to rouse them. Therefore, it may be useful for him to express his underlying emotions relating to this event and assess his sexual fantasies once he has done this.

As he has not acknowledged adverse feelings about the bullying, rejec-tion by girls, loss of his father, or his state of fear in war zones, it may be that his fantasies become a defense at such times, a means of alleviat-ing his negative mood states. He stated that his wife was aware of the discussions he was having on the Internet and she was not willing to role-play the kidnap fantasy. He had promised her he would not carry out the things he had talked about in chat room discussions, but said "I may have been going to break that promise."

Barriers to treatment and how to overcome them

One barrier to treatment could be Mr. P's lack of understanding of his offending. It is known that those who offend via the Internet may distance themselves from the impact of offending by their view of their own behavior (Henry, Mandeville-Norden, Hayes, & Egan, 2010). The use of cognitive distortions, such as "I did not see them as a person" and "I did not see the abuse," distances the image-viewer from contact offending (Akerman, 2003; DeLong, Durkin, & Hundersmarck, 2010). Mr. P has yet to acknowledge the impact of his inciting others to abuse children in order to produce images. Mr. P described discussions in the chat rooms: "I didn't care," "I didn't think I was harming anyone," "It [the Internet] was better, easier, more exciting, allowed me to talk to others so I didn't think I was doing anything wrong … Now I do. It didn't dawn on me I was talking about children. I might have been fuelling someone else's fantasies and they might have done it," "I created victims in the images, and telling men to kidnap the girls," "I don't know how it changed; I didn't change it on purpose. My wife was very young looking, she was old enough, legal but it made me go for it. I didn't have an attraction to children at the time. In the conversation it changed, I had never discussed kidnapping children before yet I offered to go and help. I don't know if I would have – I'm glad I was arrested. I know I was ordering chloroform, there was a possibility I would have gone and helped those people." He stated he was not preoccupied with thoughts of the Internet when he was away from it, but acknowledged his preference was for girls aged 13 to 18 in school uniform. Although he has not acknowledged this, the decision for his wife to live with his mother may have been to allow him free time to pursue his sexual interests on the Internet. It may also have related to his motives of his wife being "very young looking but … old enough." Akerman (2003) encourages the use of role play to place the perpetrator in the role of the victim at different stages of their life, for instance, when informed by the police that their images are on the Internet and cannot be removed, when they travel abroad, aware that people throughout the world could have viewed the images, and when they have their own children. Quayle et al. (2006) suggest the use of mindfulness techniques to make associations between viewed images and contact offending clearer.

Treatment implications for Mr. P

In order to assess current risk, Mr. P's offense paralleling behavior (OPB) is examined and discussed as a means of assessing change and thus reducing risk. Several authors give definitions of OPB, for example, Akerman (2011, 2012), Akerman and Beech (2013), Genders and Player (1995), Jones (1997, 2004, 2010, 2011), and Shine and Morris (2000). Jones (2004, p. 38) described it as "any form of offense-related behavior (or fantasized behavior) pattern that emerges at any point before during or after an offense. It does not have to result in an offense; it simply needs to resemble, in some significant respect, the sequence of behaviors leading up to the offense." Emphasis is placed on the *sequence* of behaviors rather than on individual behavior, such as acting in an aggressive manner. However, it is also noted that in addition to individual or internal traits in the sequence of behaviors precipitating an offense, the environment has a role to play when considering OPB and access to the sequence of factors that precipitated an offense. Therefore, behavior within the confines of prison may well be less obvious than that in the community. It will be important to find out what precipitated Mr. P's increased sexual preoccupation and how it may be manifested in a different environment.

Davies, Jones, and Howells (2010) suggest assessing what change has occurred and been maintained on an individual basis. However, they caution that clinicians working in treatment with the service-user may give a biased response, as they will have an interest in change having occurred. They highlight the need for independent assessment; to this end, a checklist, the Sexual Offence Paralleling Behaviour Checklist (SOPBC) was developed by Akerman and Beech (2013) in order to provide an alternative to self-reporting. The measure is based on a range of risk factors identified as based on sexual interests (Mann, Hanson, & Thornton, 2010; Marshall, 1993; Ó Ciardha, 2011; Ward, Hudson, & McCormack, 1997), holding offense-supportive cognitions (Gannon, Keown, & Polaschek, 2007; Mann & Beech, 2003; Mann & Hollin, 2010; Maruna & Mann, 2006; Ó Ciardha, 2011; Ó Ciardha & Gannon, 2011), and self-regulation problems (Ireland & Craig, 2011; Ward, Hudson, & Keenan, 1998).

In order to formulate Mr. P's ongoing risk, his current OPB is organized into the relevant domains as identified on SOPBC by staff working with him in treatment:

- Sexual interests domain: using sexual banter, sexualizing non-sexual situations, using pornography excessively, writing to a number of women in a sexual manner, and alluding to offense accounts.

- Displaying offense-supportive attitudes: minimizing his offending.
- Having negative associates.
- Self-regulation problems: missing groups, impulsivity, failing to make plans for the future, and poor emotional control.
- Poor relationship skills.

There was no evidence that he showed poor coping techniques in terms of use of medication, self-harm, or excessive use of the gym, paralleling his time prior to offending. Therefore, as described above, Mr. P continued to demonstrate behavior linked to ongoing risk, albeit less obvious, within the confines of prison.

Course of treatment and assessment of progress

Mr. P participated in ongoing research using the newly developed Current Sexual Interest Measure (CSIM; Akerman, Bishopp, & Beech, 2014). The CSIM is a psychometric measure developed through gathering a wide range of views of those with a knowledge of sexual offending, including perspectives of offenders, researchers, and academics working in the field in the UK, US, and Canada. The measure contains items relating to a wide range of sexual interests. Preliminary findings indicate a structure of four factors: sexual interest in children, hurting others, sexual preoccupation, and, in one case, lack of interest in hurting others. The measure asks for the relevance of each item for the participant in the past 6 months. Mr. P's profile indicated ongoing sexual preoccupation and sexual interest in hurting others; these would form the focus of treatment. His poor problem solving and emotional control, lack of self-agency, and interpersonal skills can be addressed within the TC, as these are core skills developed in a TC program. In order to manage his sexual interests he could be assessed for the Fantasy Modification Programme (FMP; Akerman, 2008), or when he transfers to another establishment for the Healthy Sexual Functioning Programme (HSFP; Operational Services and Interventions Groups, 2012). Like the TC model, both programs aim to help participants identify strengths in line with the Good Lives Model (Ward & Gannon, 2006) and set goals to develop weaker areas. The FMP and HSFP help participants develop their understanding of the role of fantasy in their life and develop the skills, knowledge, and competency to gain their primary goals in an acceptable manner in prison and on release. Each program also develops intimacy skills and teaches behavioral modification techniques in order to reduce offense-related arousal.

Problems encountered

The main barrier to care has been the extent to which Mr. P denies aspects of his sexual arousal. For instance, he finds it difficult to acknowledge a sexual interest in children and yet admits that he has spent time fantasizing about and discussing abducting and sexually abusing a child. At interview, he stated "I didn't have an attraction to children at the time, but I had images. One image of a girl tied to a chair was arousing. I didn't want to be attracted to children. I wish I could cut it out. In the conversation [on the Internet] I didn't care, I moved to children. I never discussed kidnapping children before. I offered to go and help – I don't know if I would have. I'm glad I got arrested." He also possessed and traded images of children being abused, some at the highest level of seriousness. He admits that he still has offense-related fantasies and so, by instructing him on behavioral methods of managing deviant sexual arousal, he could apply these skills to the fantasies of children. However, this would rely on his being willing to give these fantasies up, requiring him to develop alternate methods of managing emotions. Given society's view of those who offend sexually against children it would follow that those who have sexual fantasies about doing so would need to use cognitive distortions such as "I am not doing them any harm," or deny having such fantasies to reduce the dissonance. They would need a supportive and encouraging environment in which to discuss current sexual interest.

Follow-up

Having completed treatment, Mr. P's ongoing risk can be assessed through his responses on the CSIM, the views of staff on SOPBC, and through interview. As he develops more trust in those supporting him in treatment and personally (for instance, having frank discussions as to his risk with his partner), robust relationship and intimacy skills can be followed up throughout the remainder of his sentence and on release.

Conclusion

This chapter discussed the incarceration of an individual based on their discussion of fantasy rather than actions. Further, it addressed the difficulties implicit in requesting an individual to identify and divulge these most intimate sexual fantasies in a prison setting, knowing that society (and they themselves) find these sexual fantasies abhorrent. Various methods of assessment have been considered and the importance of collaboration with the client in order to develop an accurate case formulation is emphasized. Clinicians are encouraged to consider how difficult it would be to disclose such information to others, thus developing empathy for the client in order to help achieve the goal of helping the client to manage their risk. This chapter emphasizes that in order to assess current sexual interest, data needs to be gathered from a range of sources in addition to self-reporting through triangulation in order to assess ongoing risk.

Acknowledgement

Sincerest thanks to Mr. P for being so willing to discuss something he finds so shameful and abhorrent, in the hope that it would, as he put it, "help someone else."

Endnotes

1   An Indeterminate Sentence for Public Protection is a prison sentence whereby the court sets the minimum term of imprisonment an offender must serve before becoming eligible to be considered for release by the Parole Board.
2   CSOTP helps offenders develop understanding of how and why they have committed sexual offenses. The program also increases awareness of victim harm. The main focus is to help the offender develop meaningful life goals and practice new thinking and behavioral skills that will lead them away from offending.
3   SAP rating systems were created in Ireland and used in the United Kingdom to categorize the severity of images of child sex abuse, and thus used in the sentencing of offenders in a UK court of law. The Sentencing Advisory Panel (SAP) scale is defined thus: 1. Nudity or erotic posing with no sexual activity; 2. Sexual activity between children or solo masturbation by a child; 3. Non-penetrative sexual activity between adult(s) and child(ren); 4. Penetrative sexual activity between child(ren) and adult(s); 5. Sadism or bestiality.
4   The Risk Matrix 2000 is a static risk assessment tool designed to predict sexual and nonsexual violent reconviction among men (aged at least 18) who have been convicted of a sexual offense. It classifies an offender into one of four groups based on some simple facts about his criminal and personal history. RM2000 consists of three scales: risk of sexual offending, risk of violent offending, and a combined scale, which predicts sexual or other violence.
5   The Correctional Services Advice and Accreditation Panel is a nonstatutory body that helps the Ministry of Justice to develop and implement high quality offender programs. Its main work is to accredit programs for offenders.

6   The Community of Therapeutic Communities is a standards-based quality improvement network for national and international therapeutic communities.

References

Akerman, G. (2003). Developing ways to enhance victim empathy with men who have committed offences via the Internet. *Nota News, 45*, 23–24.

Akerman, G. (2008). The development of a fantasy modification programme for a prison-based therapeutic community. *International Journal of Therapeutic Communities, 29*, 180–188.

Akerman, G. (2010). Undertaking therapy at HMP Grendon with men who have committed sexual offences. In E. Sullivan & R. Shuker (Eds.), *Grendon and the emergence of forensic therapeutic communities: Developments in research and practice* (pp. 171–182). Chichester, UK: John Wiley & Sons.

Akerman, G. (2011). Offence paralleling behaviour and the custodial good life at HMP Grendon. *Forensic Update, 104*, 20–25.

Akerman, G. (2012). Sexual offenders, offence paralleling behaviour and how it relates to risk. *Forensic Update, 105*, 17–24.

Akerman, G., & Beech, A. R. (2013). Exploring offence paralleling behaviours in incarcerated offenders. In J. Fuhrmann & S. Baier (Eds.), *Prisons and prison systems: Practices, types and challenges* (pp. 1–24). Hauppauge, NY: Nova.

Akerman, G., Bishopp, D., & Beech, A. R. (2014). *The development of a psychometric measure of current sexual interest*. Manuscript submitted for publication.

Bartels, R. M., & Gannon, T. A. (2011). Understanding the sexual fantasies of sex offenders and their correlates. *Aggression and Violent Behavior, 16*, 551–561.

Beech, A. R., Elliott, I. A., Birgden, A., & Findlater, D. (2008). The Internet and child sexual offending: A criminological review. *Aggression and Violent Behavior, 13*, 216–228.

Beech, A. R., & Ward, T. (2004). The integration of etiology and risk in sex offenders: A theoretical model. *Aggression and Violent Behavior, 10*, 31–63.

Butler, G. (1998). Clinical formulation. In A. Belack & M. Hersen (Eds.), *Comprehensive clinical psychology* (pp. 1–24). Oxford, UK: Pergamon.

Craig, L. A., & Stringer, I. (1999). Psychological assessment model. Unpublished manuscript. Available from the authors at: Forensic Psychology Practice Ltd, The Willows Clinic, 98 Sheffield Road, Boldmere, Sutton Coldfied, UK.

Craig, L. A., Browne, K. D., & Beech, A. R. (2008). *Assessing risk in sex offenders: A practitioner's guide*. Chichester, UK: John Wiley & Sons.

Davies, J., Jones, L., & Howells, K. (2010). Offence paralleling behaviour: Evaluating individual change. In M. Daffern, L. Jones, & J. Shine (Eds.), *A case formulation approach to offender assessment and intervention* (pp. 287–302). Chichester, UK: John Wiley & Sons.

DeLong, R., Durkin, K., & Hundersmarck, S. (2010). An exploratory analysis of the cognitive distortions of a sample of men arrested in Internet stings. *Journal of Sexual Aggression, 16,* 59–71.

Dowdswell, H., Akerman, G., & "Lawrence." (2010). Unlocking offence paralleling behaviour in a custodial setting – A personal perspective from members of staff and a resident in a forensic therapeutic community. In M. Daffern, L. Jones, & J. Shine (Eds.), *A case formulation approach to offender assessment and intervention* (pp. 231–243). Chichester, UK: John Wiley & Sons.

Eells, T. D. (1997). Psychotherapy case formulation: History and current status. In T. D. Eells (Ed.), *Handbook of psychotherapy case formulation* (pp. 3–32). New York: Guilford Press.

Frechtling, J. A., & Sharp, L. M. (Eds.). (1997). *User-friendly handbook for mixed method evaluations.* Arlington, VA: NSF, Directorate for Education and Human Resources, Division of Research, Evaluation, and Communication.

Gannon, T. A., Keown, K., & Polaschek, D. L. L. (2007). Increasing honest responding on cognitive distortions in child molesters: The bogus pipeline revisited. *Sexual Abuse: A Journal of Research and Treatment, 19,* 5–22.

Genders, F., & Player, E. (1995). *Grendon: A study of a therapeutic prison.* Oxford, UK: Oxford University Press.

Henry, O., Mandeville-Norden, R., Hayes, E., & Egan, V. (2010). Do internet-based sexual offenders reduce to normal, inadequate and deviant groups? *Journal of Sexual Aggression, 16,* 33–46.

Ireland, C. A., & Craig, L. A. (2011). Adult sexual offender assessment. In D. P. Boer, R. Eher, L. A. Craig, M. H. Miner, & F. Pfäfflin (Eds.), *International perspectives on the assessment and treatment of sexual offenders: Theory, practice and research* (pp. 13–34). Chichester, UK: John Wiley & Sons.

Johansson, R. (2003, September). *Case study methodology.* A keynote speech at the International Conference "Methodologies in Housing Research," organized by the Royal Institute of Technology in co-operation with the International Association of People–Environment Studies, Stockholm. Retrieved from http://www.infra.kth.se/BBA/IAPS%20PDF/paper%20Rolf%20Johansson%20ver%202.pdf

Johnstone, L., & Dallos, R. (2006). Introduction to formulation. In L. Johnstone & R. Dallos (Eds.), *Formulation in psychology and psychotherapy: Making sense of people's problems* (pp. 1–16). London: Routledge.

Jones, L. F. (1997). Developing models of managing treatment integrity and efficacy in a prison-based TC: The Max Glatt Centre. In E. Cullen, L. Jones, & R. Woodward (Eds.), *Therapeutic communities for offenders* (pp. 121–157). Chichester, UK: John Wiley & Sons.

Jones, L. F. (2004). Offence paralleling behaviour (OPB) as a framework for assessment and interventions with offenders. In A. Needs & G. Towl (Eds.),

Applying psychology to forensic practice (pp. 34–63). Oxford, UK: Blackwell.

Jones, L. F. (2010). History of the OPB construct and related concepts. In M. Daffern, L. Jones, & J. Shine (Eds.), *Case formulation approach to offender assessment and intervention* (pp. 3–23). Chichester, UK: John Wiley & Sons.

Jones, L. F. (2011, February). History and practice issues for working with OPB. Paper presented at Offence Paralleling Behaviour: A case formulation approach to offender assessment and intervention Conference. Rampton Hospital, Nottingham, UK.

Kahr, B. (2007). *Sex and the psyche: The truth about our most secret fantasies.* London: Penguin.

Leitenberg, H., & Henning, K. (1995). Sexual fantasy. *Psychological Bulletin, 3,* 469–496.

Long, M. L., Alison, L. A., & McManus, M. A. (2013). Child pornography and likelihood of contact abuse: A comparison between contact child sexual offenders and noncontact offenders. *Sexual Abuse: A Journal of Research and Treatment, 25,* 370–395.

Mann, R. E., & Beech, A. R. (2003). Cognitive distortion, schemas and implicit theories. In T. Ward & S. M. Hudson (Eds.), *Sexual Deviance: Issues and Controversies* (pp. 135–153). Thousand Oaks, CA: Sage.

Mann, R., & Hollin, C. (2010) Self-reported schemas in sexual offenders. *Journal of Forensic Psychiatry & Psychology, 6,* 834–851.

Mann, R. E., Hanson, R. K., & Thornton, D. (2010). Assessing risk for sexual recidivism: Some proposals on the nature of psychologically meaningful risk factors. *Sexual Abuse: A Journal of Research and Treatment, 22,* 191–217.

Mann, R. E., Thornton, D., Wakama, S., Dyson, M., & Atkinson, D. (2010). Applying the concept of offence paralleling behaviour to sex offender assessment in secure settings. In M. Daffern, L. Jones, & J. Shine (Eds.), *Case formulation approach to offender assessment and intervention* (pp. 121–136). Chichester, UK: John Wiley & Sons.

Marshall, W. L. (1993). The role of attachment, intimacy and loneliness in the etiology and maintenance of sexual offending. *Sexual and Marital Therapy, 8,* 109–121.

Maruna, S., & Mann, R. E. (2006). Fundamental attribution error? Rethinking cognitive distortions. *Legal and Criminological Psychology, 11,* 155–177.

Ó Ciardha, C. (2011). A theoretical framework for understanding deviant sexual interest and cognitive distortions as overlapping constructs contributing to sexual offending against children. *Aggression and Violent Behavior, 16,* 493–502.

Ó Ciardha, C., & Gannon, T. A. (2011). The cognitive distortions of child molesters are in need of treatment. *Journal of Sexual Aggression: An International, Interdisciplinary Forum for Research, Theory and Practice, 17,* 130–142.

Operational Services and Interventions Group (2012). *The healthy sexual functioning programme: Guidance for staff carrying out assessments for suitability*. Retrieved March 31, 2014, from http://www.justice.gov.uk/downloads/offenders/probation-instructions/pi-01-2012-psi-07-2012-accredited-programmmes.doc

Patton, P. (1987). *How to use qualitative methods in evaluation* (5th ed.). Thousand Oaks, CA: Sage.

Quayle, E., Vaughan, M., & Taylor, M. (2006). Sex offenders, Internet child abuse images and emotional avoidance. The importance of values. *Aggression and Violent Behavior*, *11*, 1–11.

Sentencing Guidelines Council. (2007). *Sexual Offences Act 2003: Definitive guidelines*. London: Sentencing Guidelines Council.

Shine, J., & Morris, M. (2000). Addressing criminogenic needs in a prison therapeutic community. *Therapeutic Communities*, *21*, 197–218.

Shine, J., & Newton, M. (2000). Damaged, disturbed and dangerous: A profile of receptions to Grendon therapeutic prison 1995–2000. In J. Shine (Ed.), *A compilation of Grendon research* (pp. 151–172). Available from HM Prison Grendon, Grendon Underwood, Aylesbury, Buckinghamshire, UK.

Tarrier, N., & Calam, R. (2002). New developments in cognitive behavioral case formulation. *Behavioural and Cognitive Psychotherapy*, *30*, 311–328.

Thornton, D. (2002). Constructing and testing a framework for dynamic risk assessment. *Sexual Abuse: A Journal of Research and Treatment*, *14*, 139–152.

Thornton, D., Mann, R., Webster, S., Blud, L., Travers, R., Friendship, C., et al. (2003). Distinguishing and combining risks for sexual and violent recidivism. In R. Prentky, E. Janus, & M. Seto (Eds.), *Annals of the New York Academy of Sciences, Sexually Coercive Behavior: Understanding and Management*, *989* (pp. 225–235).

Wakeling, H., Beech, A. R., & Freemantle, N. (2013). Investigating treatment change and its relationship to recidivism in a sample of 3773 sex offenders in the UK. *Psychology, Crime and Law*, *19*, 233–252.

Ward, T., & Gannon, T. (2006). Rehabilitation, etiology, and self-regulation. The good lives model of rehabilitation for sexual offenders. *Aggression and Violent Behavior*, *11*, 77–94.

Ward, T., Hudson, S. M., & Keenan, T. (1998). A self-regulation model of the sexual offence process. *Sexual Abuse: A Journal of Research and Treatment*, *10*, 141–157.

Ward, T., Hudson, S. M., and McCormack, J. (1997). Attachment style, intimacy deficits, and sexual offending. In B. K. Schwartz and H. R. Cellini (Eds.), *The sex offenders: New insights, treatment innovations and legal developments* (vol. 2, pp. 1–2: 14). Kingston, NJ: Civic Research Institute.

Wood, H. (2013). The nature of the addiction in "sex addiction" and paraphilias. In M. Bower, R. Hale, & H. Wood (Eds.), *Addictive states of mind* (pp. 151–174). London: Karnac.

6

Treatment of Men Who Have Sexually Abused Adults

Theresa A. Gannon

Introduction

The assessment and treatment of men who sexually abuse adults is a challenging and complex task. The sexually inappropriate behaviors associated with these men are wide ranging and may include exhibitionism, inappropriate sexual touching, voyeurism, sexual sadism, and rape. Furthermore, a good proportion of men who sexually abuse adults also abuse children. No single text, however detailed, will be able to provide the clinician with specific guidance on how to provide effective intervention for each unique case that they will encounter over the period of their practice. When tasked with the responsibility of treating a particularly complex case involving myriad offense behaviors, the author would recommend consulting Laws and O'Donohue (2008), Marshall, Marshall, Serran, and O'Brien (2011), and Schwartz (2012) in addition to the case study materials presented in this book.

Within this chapter, in order to provide focus, the author will examine clients who rape or attempt to rape adult women. Rape is typically a legal term and, although its exact definition varies across jurisdictions, it is generally used to refer to vaginal or anal penetration without legitimate consent. The author will begin by describing the characteristics, psychopathologies, and treatment needs that the research literature suggests are particularly pertinent to this client group. The author will then examine

Sex Offender Treatment: A Case Study Approach to Issues and Interventions, First Edition. Edited by Daniel T. Wilcox, Tanya Garrett, and Leigh Harkins. © 2015 John Wiley & Sons, Ltd. Published 2015 by John Wiley & Sons, Ltd.

contemporary knowledge regarding the treatment of rapists before describing rehabilitative models and techniques which the author uses in her treatment approaches. Finally, the author will introduce and discuss a case study description before drawing key conclusions.

Key Features of Men Who Rape

Thorough knowledge of the evidence base describing the features of men who rape is essential for developing a clear understanding of pertinent assessment and treatment issues. While there is some good evidence to draw upon (see Gannon, Collie, Ward, & Thakker, 2008 or Thakker, Collie, Gannon, & Ward, 2008), the evidence base associated with men who rape adults is limited relative to research examining men who sexually abuse children.

Characteristics and interpersonal features

Men who rape appear broadly similar to the general prison population on factors relating to socioeconomic status. For example, men who rape appear to be characterized by low socioeconomic status, poor education, and employment in unskilled professions (Bard et al., 1987; Crowell & Burgess, 1996). In terms of developmental experiences, men who rape – similarly to the general prison population – tend to report poor childhood attachment experiences characterized by sexual and physical abuse (Dhawan & Marshall, 1996; Haapasalo & Kankkonen, 1997; Smallbone & Dadds, 1998; Ward, Hudson, & Marshall, 1996). When compared with men who sexually abuse children, men who rape adults appear to be younger (Dickey, Nussbaum, Chevolleau, & Davidson, 2002), less passive in their social interactions (Christie, Marshall, & Lanthier, 1979), more socially competent (Dreznick, 2003; Segal & Marshall, 1985), less anxious (Chantry & Craig, 1994), and more likely to have experienced an intimate relationship (Christie et al., 1979). Yet, despite their apparent competence and ability to form intimate relationships, rapists are also noted as holding hostile and combative sexual beliefs about women (Malamuth, 1986; Polaschek & Gannon, 2004).

Associated psychopathologies

It is not uncommon for professionals to highlight psychopathologies among men who rape that fit contemporary diagnostic criteria (Hillbrand,

Foster, & Hirt, 1990; Långström, Sjöstedt, & Grann, 2004). For example, Långström et al. (2004) inspected retrospective inpatient ICD psychiatric diagnoses for men who had raped adults ($n = 535$) or sexually abused children ($n = 522$) and who had been discharged from Swedish prisons between 1993 and 1997. In short, the most prevalent diagnoses for men who had raped were – in order of prevalence – alcohol abuse or dependence (9.3%), drug abuse (3.9%), personality disorder (2.6%), and psychosis (1.7%). Notably, although these prevalence rates appear low, they were significantly higher than those noted for men who had sexually abused children. In terms of specific personality disorders, relative to men who sexually abuse children, men who rape appear more likely to be diagnosed as being psychopathic or holding psychopathic traits (Abracen, Looman, Di Fazio, Kelly, & Stirpe, 2006; Firestone, Bradford, Greenberg, & Serran, 2000; Vess, Murphy, & Arkowitz, 2004).

Treating Men Who Rape

Within group treatment programs worldwide, men who rape are typically treated alongside men who sexually abuse children. In fact, some professionals have estimated that – at least in the UK Prison Service – only 15% of group sexual offender clients are rapists (Beech, Oliver, Fisher, & Beckett, 2005). The problem with this state of affairs is that the majority of treatment modules and theories of sexual offending, although broadly applicable to men who rape, may be translated in a way that is likely to be more meaningful to men who sexually abuse children. The majority of group treatment program evaluations have tended to focus on treatment effectiveness more generally, rather than focusing more specifically on effectiveness in relation to men who rape (e.g., Hall, 1995; Lösel & Schmucker, 2005). Consequently, our knowledge of "what works" for men who rape lags behind that available for men who sexually abuse children, although, in general terms, key treatment targets typically addressed in work with men who sexually abuse adults are: inappropriate sexual interest, emotional regulation, offense supportive attitudes and beliefs, and intimacy and relationships (see Thakker et al., 2008). A number of professionals have proposed that men who rape should be treated separately from men who sexually abuse children (Eccleston & Owen, 2007; Polaschek & King, 2002). This is because, as noted earlier, men who rape are likely to be more antisocial and hostile relative to men who sexually abuse children, and are also likely to hold more notably hostile beliefs in relation to women. However, no research appears to have focused on the treatment effects of partitioning men who rape from other sexual offenders.

Theoretical Frameworks Underpinning Treatment

Specific sexual offender models

For the practitioner seeking an overarching model of sexual offending that focuses specifically on men who rape, there is some choice (see Hall & Hirschman, 1991; Malamuth, 1986, 1996). Each of these rape-specific theories, among other factors, emphasizes the role of inappropriate sexual arousal (e.g., sexual arousal to aggressive or violent sex), offense-supportive thinking (e.g., acceptance of rape myths and associated hostility towards women), personality issues (e.g., antisocial characteristics), and anger or affective dyscontrol in the commission of rape. These models are useful for highlighting the types of factors that should be investigated within the assessment and treatment process. However, when examined carefully, each of these theories lacks the explanatory depth required to fully explain why rape occurs (Ward, Polaschek, & Beech, 2005).

General rehabilitation approaches

When providing treatment for sexual offenders (i.e., generally cognitive behavioral therapy oriented), the author typically draws upon a wide range of guiding theoretical frameworks in order to ensure that the treatment is strength-based, collaborative, and grounded within contemporary empirical evidence. The overarching rehabilitation theory underpinning the author's work is the good lives model (Ward, 2002; Ward & Gannon, 2006; Ward & Marshall, 2004). The good lives model approaches the task of offender rehabilitation in a strength-based, positive way. Essentially, the key question posed by this approach is "how can we enable the client to lead a fulfilling and prosocial good life?" In other words, the focus of the model rests upon how to establish skills, contexts, attitudes, and behaviors that automatically reduce the problems or criminogenic needs associated with sexual offending. To illustrate, a client who has raped may come to treatment with a series of offense-supportive attitudes that espouse hostility towards women and a lack of social skills (i.e., the criminogenic needs). These aspects may severely block the client's ability to lead a prosocial "good" life since they are unable to achieve prosocial experiences with women in both intimate and nonintimate contexts (i.e., work). Thus, by working collaboratively with this client to identify the key mechanisms underlying this blockage and providing them with the key skills required to socialize more effectively with women (e.g., social skills, attitudes, self-esteem), they will become more able to communicate and maintain relationships with females, automatically reducing problems experienced in the area of intimacy and relationships. In other words, problems are addressed by instilling strengths and capabilities within the client.

A common misconception made by professionals is that adopting treatment using a good lives approach – particularly within individual treatment – results in treatment that is at odds with the risk–need–responsivity model of offender rehabilitation (RNR; Andrews & Bonta, 2010). However, Ward and his colleagues propose that the good lives model can be integrated with, and enhance, traditional RNR approaches (Ward & Gannon, 2006; Ward, Yates, & Willis, 2012; Willis, Yates, Gannon, & Ward, 2013). Three main principles are particularly pertinent within the RNR approach: risk (i.e., offenders deemed to be of higher risk require more intensive treatment), need (i.e., treatment should focus on factors that have been empirically associated with reductions in recidivism), and responsivity (i.e., treatments should be molded to ensure good fit with the characteristics and learning abilities of the client). In short, the good lives model is able to encapsulate these important evidence-based principles within a strength-based format. Therefore, what differs about these rehabilitation models is their overarching conceptualization of risk and of how best to promote change. The RNR approach views the primary purpose of intervention as being the reduction or eradication of criminogenic risk factors. The good lives model, on the other hand, tackles the problem of risk or criminogenic need by looking first at the client and how their life may be improved through paying particular attention to the personal identity and values of the client (i.e., responsivity in its deepest sense). For the high-risk client, instilling the skills and attitudes to live a good life is likely to take a lengthy period of time. Clearly then, key RNR principles may be naturally embedded within an overarching good lives framework.

There are numerous treatment approaches and methods of communication that fit very well within the good lives model of rehabilitation, and the author tends to draw on these variously and flexibly throughout the treatment process. In particular, in engaging collaboratively and respectfully with men who have raped – especially in the face of resistance – the author has found motivational interviewing (Miller & Rollnick, 2012) an invaluable framework, in addition to Knowles and Linn's (2004) "Alpha and Omega" strategies, adapted for use with sexual offenders by Flinton and Scholz (2006), and Wachtel's (2011) guidance on effective therapeutic communication. In combining these powerful approaches, an emphasis is placed upon empathic, genuine, and nonconfrontational interactions and communication, which support the client to make important discoveries about their behavior while respecting their autonomy and capacity to change. These frameworks are critical for establishing the genuine therapeutic alliance that is deemed to be critical for promoting behavior change in men who have sexually offended (Marshall & Burton, 2010; Marshall et al., 2011).

Case Study Description

In this section, a case study of individualized treatment with a client who has raped will be presented. Individual treatment is sometimes necessitated due to client or contextual circumstances. For example, a client may require specialist, individually tailored treatment due to substantial mental health problems (see Chapter 12). The case study client described here was initially referred for a group sex offender treatment program (SOTP) by his clinical team. However, individualized treatment was necessitated by the fact that there were not enough patients at the hospital who required sexual offense work to form a group. The described case study is intended to provide guidance on the issues – and benefits – of individualized assessment and intervention, as well as unanticipated challenges that permeate practice in this area. In order to provide the most comprehensive case with associated "how to" advice, as well as for the sake of brevity, I have amalgamated details from two similar cases.

Background case presentation

Guy was a 61-year-old white male of average intelligence. He held a longstanding schizoaffective disorder diagnosis and was detained in a medium secure forensic hospital under Section 37/41 of the Mental Health Act (1983). Guy's index offenses involved two counts of sexual assault. In the first, Guy entered a female acquaintance's home while only partially clothed and informed the victim that he "had" to rape her. Guy grabbed the victim and touched her inappropriately until she was eventually able to break free and call neighbors for help. In the second count of sexual assault, while residing in hospital for the first sexual assault, he sexually assaulted a female staff member in a manner almost identical to the first sexual assault. Guy had a long history of previous sexual offenses spanning almost 30 years, which included rape, frotterism, and inappropriate sexual touching. His victims were all adult women and his offending appeared to occur almost exclusively in the context of mental health deterioration. Guy's mental health would typically deteriorate after he ceased taking medication due to the various unpleasant side effects that he experienced. As a result, he had spent varying periods of time in both hospital and prison during his adult life. Guy did not have any nonsexual offenses on his offense record and there were no reports of generally antisocial behavior, personality disorder, psychopathy, or alcohol or drug abuse or dependence. He was deemed to be of moderate risk of sexually reoffending.

Previous sexual offense work

Despite his significant history of sexual offending and detention in secure establishments across a 30 year time period, Guy had engaged with very little psychological work. In part, this appeared to be due to the fact that he had generally not been detained long enough to engage in any substantial piece of work. In addition, Guy did not appear motivated to receive treatment, stating that his sexual offenses were "in the past," and that they would not occur again as he was now mentally stable. He also stated that he was unable to recall his offenses in any meaningful detail.

Assessment

Guy's assessment consisted of a basic clinical interview which took place over two sessions. This interview was used to develop a basic formulation of sexual offending that could be updated throughout treatment. As part of this interview, Guy was asked a series of questions about his personal life goals and values (i.e., the key experiences described in the good lives model) and how these may have related to his sexual offending behavior (see Yates, Kingston, & Ward's [2009] Good Lives Checklist for Guidance). Questionnaire assessments were then used preintervention to provide additional information regarding treatment need, and also postintervention to gain information on treatment gain. There is a range of assessments available that may be used to aid the clinician in determining relevant treatment needs for men who have raped. For this particular client, the following assessments were used: the RAPE Scale (Bumby, 1996), the Sex Fantasy Questionnaire (Wilson, 1978), the Victim Empathy Scale (Beckett & Fisher, 1994), the Emotional Loneliness Scale (Russell,

Peplau, & Cutrona, 1980), the Self Esteem Questionnaire (Thornton, 1989), the Relapse Prevention Questionnaire (Beckett, Fisher, Mann, & Thornton, 1998), and the Paulhus Deception Scale (Paulhus, 1999).

During assessment, Guy appeared to be shameful about his offending and stated that he was unable to recall his offending in any meaningful detail. At this stage, Guy was reassured that his lack of memory in relation to his offense would not interfere with his treatment plan and that he may, in time, come to recall aspects of his offense that would allow us to work with plausible "hypotheses" concerning his offense behavior. He appeared surprised at this feedback, stating that he felt that he was "not treatable" given his lack of memory for his offense. It was unclear whether Guy's lack of memory reflected dissimulation associated with shame or genuine compromised memory function associated with schizoaffective disorder (Beatty, Jocic, Monson, & Staton, 1993).

With guidance, Guy was able to provide a sketchy and operational account of his childhood and basic adolescent and adult functioning. However, Guy maintained that he could not recall anything of the events immediately surrounding any of his sexual offenses. Guy appeared more comfortable engaging fully with questions concerning personal life goals and values. Guy was able to identify that the most important goal to him was to achieve more creativity in his life (i.e., through art and poetry), which would impact on his sense of mastery as well as his self-direction. Guy also acknowledged with some regret that although his family relationships were important to him, he no longer had any contact with his sister or brother as he had lost touch with them approximately 5 years ago as a result of his hospitalizations. Guy scored relatively low on impression management and declined to complete the victim empathy scale, stating that it was impossible for him to know how his victim might feel as a result of his sexual offending. On all other scales, his scores appeared largely unremarkable, although he scored particularly low in the area of self-esteem. Furthermore, Guy's scores on the relapse prevention questionnaire (4/18 for awareness and 2/18 for strategy) indicated that he had relatively poor understanding of the factors associated with his sexual offending or of the strategies that he could use in order to minimize future risk of sexual offending.

In the absence of any self-reported information in relation to Guy's offending, file records were consulted; they indicated that Guy's offending appeared to be linked with approach goals associated with auditory hallucinations ("I have to rape women"). Guy was asked if he would be willing to partake in an extended collaborative assessment in which we would examine his file records and witness statements concerning his offense so that we could work together on a series of hypotheses concerning his offense behavior. Guy agreed to this but stated that he felt he would need to take the process slowly as it would be "difficult." Guy was assessed for any possible symptoms of posttraumatic stress disorder prior to this work in order to ensure that he would not experience any significantly distressing symptomology as a result of explorations in relation to his offending (see Clark et al., in press). This assessment did not highlight any concern and enabled us to continue with an extended period of assessment over five sessions.

Extended collaborative assessment

During the extended period of assessment, a number of witness statements were identified as being appropriate to share with Guy. He was informed that he was in control of the sessions and could choose how much or how little of the witness statements we worked through at one time. He was informed that due to the nature of human memory and associated eyewitness testimony it was unlikely that the witness statements would provide a flawless account of his offending behavior. However, Guy was informed that the witness statements were likely to provide an important platform from which to understand his behavior and the possible factors underlying it. Although he appeared understandably apprehensive at the task he was about to undertake, he stated that he felt "in control" of the pace of the sessions and was ready to "take the plunge." During the first session, Guy stated that he had actively avoided hearing any information about his offense, as he did not want to know what type of person he became when he was mentally unwell. He was reassured that he held positive attributes that were not all offense-related, that he was in control of the sessions, and that although the process would be difficult, it would provide him with important information that would enable him to desist from offending in the future. Some preparatory shame-related work was also undertaken with him.

Guy asked that the witness statements be read aloud to him. At times, he covered parts of his face in apparent shock and disgust. However, at the end of the witness statements (there were five in total, including two victim accounts), Guy stated that he was learning "an important lesson" about what he was like when he was unwell. Guy appeared to feel particularly uncomfortable when he heard accounts stating that he was shouting "I want to rape women, they have to be raped" prior to his offenses.

When Guy was asked to reflect upon the reports regarding his behavior and was introduced to the range of key treatment needs typically addressed in work with men who rape adults (i.e., inappropriate sexual interest, emotional regulation, offense supportive attitudes and beliefs, intimacy and relationships, and mental health), Guy focused predominately on his mental health. However, explorations of Guy's life around the time of his offending highlighted that he had not experienced an intimate relationship for over two decades. Nevertheless, following exploration, Guy stated that he held positive views of women and respected them a great deal. Guy appeared to find it extremely challenging to consider how his sexual arousal and beliefs may have played a role in his offending behavior and declined to explore this issue on a number of occasions.

Formulation

Individual case formulation represents the continuing procedure of testing clinical hypotheses so that an overall "best fit" picture of the factors resulting in the client's inappropriate sexual behavior – as well as their strengths – may be developed in a collaborative manner (see Marshall et al., 2011). In Guy's case, because he stated that he was unable to recall aspects of his offense, and because he found it challenging to consider exploring his sexual interests and beliefs, the development of a preliminary formulation was difficult. However, from file information and Guy's presentation, a number of key aspects were informative in guiding the treatment that followed. Most notable, perhaps, was the fact that Guy appeared to experience significant shame – and low self-esteem – in relation to his offending, which would require work to ensure that it did not impede Guy's ability to make important treatment changes. Other key aspects, which appeared important possible vulnerabilities related to Guy's offending behavior, were intimacy and relationships (i.e., absence of intimate relationships over the decades). These appeared to be associated with significant mistrust and possible hostility or anger towards women (i.e., negative affect). These appeared to present most seriously when Guy was mentally unwell. It was unclear how or whether sexually inappropriate interests were related to Guy's offending, although it appeared that these aspects were likely to warrant some exploration. Finally, Guy's strengths were highlighted as being his creativity and his motivation to explore his offending behavior. However, it was clear that Guy had – for many years – dealt with his overwhelming shame by accounting for all of his offense behaviors as being the product of poor mental health, which had enabled him to avoid exploring other underlying issues.

Treatment

Guy's individual treatment took place over a period of 8 months. Within this time, his overall treatment plan and associated formulation was updated collaboratively at regular intervals. Guy attended all of the scheduled sessions.

When faced with an array of factors that require exploration and possible treatment it can be difficult to ascertain what to focus on first. In this case, however, the author felt that Guy's shame was likely to provide a significant blockage to therapy if this was not tackled early on. Given Guy's presentation in this respect, as well as the possibility that he had problems trusting women, it was also of paramount importance to establish, as best as possible, a secure therapeutic relationship and a positive and "safe" experience with the author, as a female therapist. Thus, treatment began – and continued – to focus on enhancing Guy's self-esteem, reducing his experiences of shame, and working with him in a manner that was thoroughly co-operative and transparent. For example, in order to enhance self-esteem and reduce experiences of shame, Guy was asked, with support from myself and the therapeutic team, to develop a series of positive statements about himself and his key qualities that reflected who he was as a person (see also Marshall, Marshall, Serran, & Fernandez, 2006; Marshall et al., 2011). He was asked to recount these qualities regularly outside of the sessions, and the therapeutic team was asked to reinforce these qualities on a regular basis. The purpose behind this assessment was to establish a positive self-concept over the course of treatment and to instill in Guy a sense of hope that he would be able to take control of his offending behavior. He was also encouraged to think of himself as comprising a whole of many "parts" and to view his offending behavior as only one particular "part" that was within his power to change (see Marshall et al., 2011). One particularly problematic session involved Guy struggling to see that he had any positive "parts" and stating that there was "no point" in continuing, as he could not be treated. However, after Guy was provided with significant reassurance and care was taken to consistently address the normality of such feelings given Guy's circumstances, Guy began to exhibit a more positive perception of himself and his ability to change his offending behavior. As part of the collaborative process, the author made a strong effort to be fully transparent with Guy. For example, at the beginning of each session, the author would bring along the notes that had been made from the previous session (including those which were disseminated to his clinical team) and encouraged him to examine and reflect upon them in full. This appeared to aid in the development of a trusting relationship, which enabled Guy to talk more openly about his "hypotheses" in relation to his offending behavior.

Over a series of sessions, using a Good Lives focus, Guy was, for the first time, able to provide a short autobiographical account of his life, both developmentally and in the lead up to each of his key offenses. There were times when he appeared to be lost for words and so, drawing on his creativity, Guy was encouraged to draw or write poetry in an attempt to describe his key thoughts, feelings, and circumstances. A notable feature of Guy's descriptions about his early life was the fact that his mother worked excessively during his childhood and so he had been left in the family home for long periods of time with a female nanny who abused him from the age of 6 to 9 years, which affected his ability to trust others (i.e., relationships). During Guy's description of his life around the time of his key offenses, he appeared to overemphasize mental health deterioration to the exclusion of other factors. Early on in treatment, the author worked with Guy and his multidisciplinary team to examine his medication and see if any changes could be made to ensure that side effects were minimized. Guy appeared to be happy with a key change in medication and stated that the side effects were minimal in comparison to his previous medication. This aspect was key since Guy had previously stopped his medication in the community for this reason. During collaborative discussions with Guy, he was reassured that while mental health deterioration was most certainly a factor associated with his offending, there were likely to be some other issues associated with his offending that could be explored together and which may, in part, be reflected by some of his symptoms when unwell. Guy appeared to find it extremely challenging to perceive himself as holding any treatment needs other than those associated with his mental health, and so efforts were concentrated on further enhancing his self-concept. He was also provided with some key resources concerning the association of mental illness with offending (adapted from Sahota & Chesterman, 1998), outlining that, in many cases, even severe command hallucinations are unlikely to be the direct cause of sexual offending behavior.

This appeared to represent a significant breakthrough in the work undertaken with Guy. After considering the resources, he came to his session stating that he was "ready" to explore his behavior and functioning further. We began by looking at some of his command hallucinations in more detail (e.g., "I have to rape women") and he was asked to consider how these hallucinations might reflect his wider experiences and attitudes towards women. At this stage, Guy tearily disclosed that, although he tried hard to respect women, he found it difficult to relate to them or trust them as a result of his childhood experiences. Guy also disclosed having experienced one significant 6 year intimate relationship beginning when he was 22 years old. Guy stated that this woman walked out on him to be with another man very suddenly, leaving him to deal with the shared home and all of its expenses. Further explorations revealed that he appeared to hold a schema or implicit theory of "women as dangerous" (see Polaschek & Gannon, 2004).

This opened up a whole new branch of discussion with Guy and enabled the sessions to focus on exploring his childhood abuse, his attitudes and feelings towards women, and his intimacy and communication skills. A good deal of this work focused on supporting him in establishing connections between these concepts and also to validate the feelings that he experiences as a result of his previous encounters with women. Throughout our collaborative work together, the author endeavored to ensure that Guy's experience with me as a female was boundaried yet positive, through remaining highly transparent, honest, and warm. For example, the author was unable to get to one of the sessions because of snow. Although nursing staff stated that they would pass the message on it was ensured that the author spoke with Guy on the phone about the session change personally. Of particular importance was that this relationship should be one that Guy perceived as being safe and secure; in order to provide him with a somewhat different experience of women. The work was directed towards developing strategies for dealing more effectively with his attitudes, affect, and automatic thoughts about women through cognitive restructuring which continued throughout the work undertaken. A particularly useful aspect of this work was asking Guy to write an assignment in which he supported his view of women as dangerous and then another one challenging these views. This provided an important springboard for developing some positive challenges to his negative beliefs about women. However, although Guy appeared to engage well with cognitive restructuring and reported practicing these skills regularly in the ward environment, he still found it difficult to think of himself ever possibly engaging in another intimate partnership, stating that even if he could begin to trust, he could not see how he could enter any relationship meaningfully given his offense history. At this stage, work was conducted to prepare Guy for disclosing his offense history to any potential partner. Issues such as choosing the right *time* and *place* to disclose, allowing the person *space* to reflect on the disclosure, and *coping with negative responses* or possible rejection as a result of a disclosure were all covered. Guy reported finding this work "informative." He was encouraged to practice his social skills with females – which were reasonable – on his day leave experiences from the unit.

Throughout each of our sessions, Guy would report back on his experiences (including any problems with negative automatic thoughts about women) and reflect on them in treatment to strengthen his skills and improve his confidence. Both Guy himself and ward staff reported some improvements in his ability to interact with females socially in a positive manner. Alongside this work, he was also supported to reconnect his relationship with his family through writing a letter to them about how he felt about losing contact with them. This reconnection turned out to be vital both for Guy's self-esteem (i.e., "I'm not so bad, my family want to see me again") and for his Good Lives management plan (i.e., a key part of his plan was to build and further develop his familial relationships).

Although Guy engaged well in the treatment, and his engagement was pointing towards the discovery of important treatment needs that we were able to work on, he appeared unwilling or unable to explore his sexual interests. On numerous occasions, Guy stated that he did not want to discuss this area, despite reassurance that he could control the amount of information he disclosed. Nursing reports did not appear to highlight Guy as engaging in any notable sexual activity, and none of his previous reports from when he was younger suggested any general preoccupation or unusual levels of masturbation during periods of significant stress (i.e., sexual coping). However, Guy's reluctance to explore these issues or even provide any detail about the appropriateness of his sexual interests suggested that Guy might hold some inappropriate interests and/or conservative attitudes surrounding sex and sexuality that were functioning to trigger his experiences of shame. Given that inappropriate sexual interests have been highlighted as being a key predictor of sexual reoffending (Hanson & Morton-Bourgon, 2005), this is a factor that cannot be set aside; even if a client is reluctant or unable to fully detail the nature of their sexual interests and associated attitudes. Phallometry is not used within our practice, and is not used widely in the UK. Thus, in the absence of any specific information about Guy's sexual interests, he was invited to talk about sexual concepts in the third person (i.e., commenting on a series of hypothetical cases that the author had constructed). This enabled me to present him with key educational materials associated with healthy sexual expression adapted from a variety of resources (e.g., Litvinoff, 2001; Stoppard, 2003) in a manner that was clearly more comfortable for him to process. In particular, using third person hypothetical cases, Guy was able to ask questions and discuss the concept of appropriate versus inappropriate sexual interests and fantasy without specifically referring to himself. Most important, perhaps, was the fact that within this context, the author was able to present Guy with key masturbatory reconditioning exercises and appropriate information regarding how to choose appropriate sexual images for use in this procedure (see Marshall et al., 2011). Guy was clearly very interested in this technique, and asked a series of meaningful questions about it. He was also reassured that many individuals masturbate to images and fantasies that they would like to alter or switch (e.g., married individuals who think about a past partner; individuals who think about rough sex). It was at this point that Guy appeared to allow himself to speak more personally about masturbatory reconditioning. While Guy was never able to fully disclose the nature of his sexual interests, he stated that there were elements of his fantasy life that he would like to adapt using the masturbatory reconditioning principles that we had talked about. This enabled Guy to "check in" with the author at regular intervals about how he was finding the exercises and what was "working" without having to fully disclose the nature of his images or interests. Towards the end of the author's work with Guy, he was able to inform me that his sexual interests had been "less than ideal" previously, but that he felt more able to control them if he "put the work into it." Guy also noted that, when well, he could just about handle his problems in this area but when unwell he found it to be totally impossible. He was encouraged to continually practice his masturbatory reconditioning exercises in preparation for the inevitable challenges that he was likely to face when discharged from the hospital setting.

During the latter parts of the treatment, Guy began to show a good awareness of his own personal vulnerabilities associated with sexual offending. In particular, he was able to consider the possible links between his command hallucinations and other pre-existing factors (e.g., hostility towards women). Guy developed a plan for his *good life* that appeared realistic and thoughtful. In the posttreatment assessments, Guy again did not appear to score high on impression management. He declined to complete the victim empathy and Wilson sex fantasy scales. Among many seemingly unchanged scores, Guy's score on self-esteem had increased dramatically. Guy's scores on the relapse prevention questionnaire had also increased to 12/18 for awareness and 10/18 for strategy. A key lesson learnt from these pre- and posttest assessment results perhaps, is that they should be viewed as supplementary. Clients often refuse to complete them, evidence difficulties connecting with and understanding them, or may show complex socially desirable responses. As a result, it is important that the clinician looks past any concrete conclusions drawn solely on the basis of psychometric tests. Guy made numerous gains that were seemingly not captured by the tests used and perhaps arguably never could be. Guy was discharged soon after treatment completion and has been living in the community offense-free for some years.

Conclusion

In this chapter, the author has described individualized treatment for a client who has raped adults. There are many reasons why individual treatment may be required for clients like Guy in clinical settings (see Chapter 1). For example, group treatment may not be an option because there are not enough clients to make up a group, or alternatively a client may require specialist, individually tailored treatment due to substantial mental health problems. One common anxiety voiced by clinicians faced with the task of providing individualized treatment is that individualized treatment may be less "powerful" than group treatment due to the absence of peer feedback. It is perhaps worth noting, however, that Serran, Marshall, Marshall, and O'Brien (2013) have recently reviewed the literature available within this area and concluded that individual and group treatments are likely to be equally effective with sexually abusive clients. There is much more evidence to gather in this particular area before definitive conclusions can be drawn. However, in the author's personal view, clinicians tasked with treating men who rape adults individually rather than in a group should view themselves as being in a rather unique and privileged position. Individual treatment enables the clinician to become fully flexible to the needs of the client and develop a trusting therapeutic alliance (Flinton & Scholz, 2006). Given the specific characteristics of men who abuse adults, which may not receive specialist attention within generic sexual offender treatment programs, individualized treatment provides a highly flexible platform to attend to these needs in a manner that is fully in tune with best practice forensic psychological principles.

References

Abracen, J., Looman, J., Di Fazio, R., Kelly, T., & Stirpe, T. (2006). Patterns of attachment and alcohol abuse in sexual and violent non-sexual offenders. *Journal of Sexual Aggression, 12*, 19–30. DOI: 10.1080/13552600600722963.

Andrews, D. A., & Bonta, J. (2010). *The psychology of criminal conduct* (5th ed.). Cincinnati, OH: Anderson.

Bard, L. A., Carter, D. L., Cerce, D. D., Knight, R. A., Rosenberg, R., & Schneider, B. (1987). A descriptive study of rapists and child molesters: Developmental clinical, and criminal characteristics. *Behavioral Sciences and the Law*, 5, 203–220. DOI: 10.1002/bsi.2370050211.

Beatty, W. W., Jocic, Z., Monson, N., & Staton, D. (1993). Memory and frontal lobe dysfunction in schizophrenia and schizoaffective disorder. *The Journal of Nervous and Mental Disease*, 181, 401–465. DOI: 10.1097/00005053 -199307000-00008.

Beckett, R. C., & Fisher, D. (1994, November). *Assessing victim empathy: A new measure*. Paper presented at the 13th Annual Conference of the Association for the Treatment of Sexual Abusers, San Francisco, CA.

Beckett, R. C., Fisher, D., Mann, R., & Thornton, D. (1998). The relapse prevention questionnaire and interview. In H. Eldridge (Ed.), *Therapist guide for maintaining change: Relapse prevention for adult male perpetrators of child sexual abuse*. London: Sage.

Beech, A. R., Oliver, C., Fisher, D., & Beckett, R. C. (2005). *Step 4: The sex offender treatment programme in prison: Addressing the offending behavior of rapists and sexual murderers*. Birmingham, UK: The Centre for Forensic and Family Psychology.

Bumby, K. (1996). Assessing the cognitive distortions of child molesters and rapists: Development and validation of the MOLEST and RAPE scales. *Sexual Abuse: A Journal of Research and Treatment*, 8, 37–54. DOI: 10.1177/107906329600800105.

Chantry, K., & Craig, R. J. (1994). Psychological screening of sexually violent offenders with the MCMI. *Journal of Clinical Psychology*, 50, 430–435. DOI: 10.1002/1097-4679(199405)50:3<430::AID-JCLP2270500314>3.0 .CO;2-W.

Christie, M. M., Marshall, W. L., & Lanthier, R. D. (1979). A descriptive study of incarcerated rapists and child molesters (a report to the Solicitor General of Canada). Ottawa, Canada: Office of the Solicitor General.

Clark, L., Tyler, N., Gannon, T. A., & Kingham, M. (in press). Eye movement desensitisation and reprocessing (EMDR) for offence related trauma in a mentally disordered sexual offender. *Journal of Sexual Aggression*. DOI :10.1080/13552600.2013.822937. Retrieved April 1, 2014, from http:// www.tandfonline.com/doi/abs/10.1080/13552600.2013.822937# .UzsZPqLGCPQ

Crowell, N. A., & Burgess, A. W. (1996). *Understanding violence against women*. Washington, DC: National Academy Press.

Dhawan, S., & Marshall, W. L. (1996). Sexual abuse histories of sexual offenders. *Sexual Abuse: A Journal of Research and Treatment*, 8, 7–15. DOI: 1079-0632/96/0100-0007509_50/0.

Dickey, R., Nussbaum, D., Chevolleau, K., & Davidson, H. (2002). Age as a differential characteristic of rapists, pedophiles, and sexual sadists. *Journal of Sex and Marital Therapy*, 28, 211–218. DOI: 10.1080/009262302760328253.

Dreznick, M. T. (2003). Heterosocial competence of rapists and child molesters: A meta-analysis. *Journal of Sex Research*, 40, 170–178. DOI: 10.1080/ 00224490309552178.

Eccleston, L., & Owen, K. (2007). Cognitive treatment "just for rapists": Recent developments. In T. A. Gannon, T. Ward, A. R. Beech, & D. Fisher (Eds.), *Aggressive offenders' cognition: Theory, research and practice* (pp. 135–153). Chichester, UK: Wiley-Blackwell.

Firestone, P., Bradford, J. M., Greenberg, D. M., & Serran, G. A. (2000). The relationship of deviant sexual arousal and psychopathy in incest offenders, extrafamilial child molesters, and rapists. *Journal of the American Academy of Psychiatry and Law, 28,* 303–308.

Flinton, C. A., & Scholz, R. (2006). *Engaging resistance: Creating partnerships for change in sexual offender treatment.* Bethany, OK: Wood "N" Barnes.

Gannon, T. A., Collie, R. M., Ward, T., & Thakker, J. (2008). Rape: Psychopathology, theory and treatment. *Clinical Psychology Review, 28,* 982–1008. DOI: 10.1016/j.cpr.2008.02.005.

Haapasalo, J., & Kankkonen, M. (1997). Self-reported childhood abuse among sex and violent offenders. *Archives of Sexual Behavior, 26,* 421–431. DOI: 10.1023/A:1024543402906.

Hall, G. C. N. (1995). Sexual offender recidivism revisited: A meta-analysis of recent treatment studies. *Journal of Consulting and Clinical Psychology, 63,* 802–809. DOI: 10.1037/0022-006X.63.5.802.

Hall, G. C. N., & Hirschman, R. (1991). Toward a theory of sexual aggression: A quadripartite model. *Journal of Consulting and Clinical Psychology, 59,* 662–669. DOI: 10.1037/0022-006X.59.5.662.

Hanson, R. K., & Morton-Bourgon, K. E. (2005). The characteristics of persistent sexual offenders: A meta-analysis of recidivism studies. *Journal of Consulting and Clinical Psychology, 73,* 1154–1163. DOI: 10.1037/0022-006X.73.6.1154.

Hillbrand, M., Foster, Jr., H., & Hirt, M. (1990). Rapists and child molesters: Psychometric comparisons. *Archives of Sexual Behavior, 19,* 65–71. DOI: 10.1007/BF01541826.

Knowles, E. S., & Linn, J. A. (2004). *Resistance and persuasion.* Mahwah, NJ: Lawrence Erlbaum.

Långström, N., Sjöstedt, G., & Grann, M. (2004). Psychiatric disorders and recidivism in sexual offenders. *Sexual Abuse: A Journal of Research and Treatment, 16,* 139–150. DOI: 10.1023/B:SEBU.0000023062.56389.ed.

Laws, D. R., & O'Donohue, W. T. (Eds.). (2008). *Sexual deviance: Theory, assessment, and treatment* (2nd ed.). London: Guilford Press.

Litvinoff, S. (2001). *Relate sex in loving relationships.* London: Vermilion.

Lösel, F., & Schmucker, M. (2005). The effectiveness of treatment for sexual offenders: A comprehensive meta-analysis. *Journal of Experimental Criminology, 1,* 117–146. DOI: 10.1007/s11292-004-6466-7.

Malamuth, N. M. (1986). Predictors of naturalistic sexual aggression. *Journal of Personality and Social Psychology, 50,* 953–962. DOI: 10.1037/0022-3514.50.5.953.

Malamuth, N. M. (1996). The confluence model of sexual aggression: Feminist and evolutionary perspectives. In D. B. Buss & N. M. Malamuth (Eds.), *Sex, power, conflict: Evolutionary and feminist perspectives* (pp. 269–295). New York: Oxford University Press.

Marshall, W. L., & Burton, D. L. (2010). The importance of therapeutic processes in sexual offender treatment. *Aggression and Violence Behavior: A Review Journal, 15*, 141–149. DOI: 10.1016/j.avb.2009.08.008.

Marshall, W. L., Marshall, L. E., Serran, G. A., & Fernandez, Y. M. (2006). *Treating sexual offenders: An integrated approach.* New York: Routledge.

Marshall, W. L., Marshall, L. E., Serran, G. A., & O'Brien, M. D. (2011). *Rehabilitating sexual offenders: A strength-based approach.* Washington, DC: American Psychological Association.

Miller, W. R., & Rollnick, S. (2012). *Motivational interviewing: Preparing people for change* (3rd ed.). London: Guilford Press.

Paulhus, D. L. (1999). *Paulhus deception scales.* Toronto, Canada: Multi-Health Systems.

Polaschek, D. L. L., & Gannon, T. A. (2004). The implicit theories of rapists: What our questionaires tell us. *Sexual Abuse: A Journal of Research and Treatment, 16*, 299–315. DOI: 10.1023/B:SEBU.0000043325.94302.40.

Polaschek, D. L. L., & King, L. (2002). Rehabilitating rapists: Reconsidering the issues. *Australian Psychologist, 37*, 215–221. DOI: 10.1080/0005006021000 1706896.

Russell, D., Peplau, L. A., & Cutrona, C. E. (1980). The revised UCLA loneliness scale: Concurrent and discriminant validity evidence. *Journal of Personality and Social Psychology, 39*, 472–480. DOI: 10.1037/0022-3514.39.3.472.

Sahota, K., & Chesterman, P. (1998). Sexual offending in the context of mental illness. *Journal of Forensic Psychiatry, 9*, 67–80. DOI: 10.1080/ 09585189808402196.

Schwartz, B. K. (Ed.). (2012). *The sex offender: Current trends in policy and treatment practice.* Kingston, NJ: Civic Research Institute.

Segal, Z. V., & Marshall, W. L. (1985). Heterosexual social skills in a population of rapists and child molesters. *Journal of Consulting and Clinical Psychology, 53*, 55–63. DOI: 10.1037/0022-006X.53.1.55.

Serran, G. A., Marshall, W. L., Marshall, L. E., & O'Brien, M. D. (2013). Group or individual therapy in the treatment of sexual offenders. In L. A. Craig, L. Dixon, & T. A. Gannon (Eds.), *What works in offender rehabilitation: An evidence-based approach to assessment and treatment* (pp. 452–467). Chichester, UK: Wiley-Blackwell.

Smallbone, S. W., & Dadds, M. R. (1998). Childhood attachment and adult attachement in incarcerated adult male sex offenders. *Journal of Interpersonal Violence, 5*, 555–573. DOI: 10.1177/088626098013005001.

Stoppard, M. (2003). *Healthy sex* (Rev. ed.). London: Dorling Kindersley.

Thakker, J., Collie, R. M., Gannon, T. A., & Ward, T. (2008). Rape: Assessment and treatment. In D. R. Laws & W. T. O'Donohue (Eds.), *Sexual deviance: Theory, assessment, and treatment* (pp. 356–383). New York: Guilford Press.

Thornton, D. (1989). *Self esteem scale.* Unpublished Manuscript. Snad Ridge Secure Treatment Center, Mauston, WI.

Vess, J., Murphy, C., & Arkowitz, S. (2004). Clinical and demographic differences between sexually violent predators and other commitment types in a state forensic hospital. *Journal of Forensic Psychiatry and Psychology, 15*, 669–681. DOI: 10.1080/14789940410001731795.

Wachtel, P. (2011). *Therapeutic communication: Knowing what to say when* (2nd ed.). London: Guilford Press.

Ward, T. (2002). Good lives and the rehabilitation of offenders: Promises and problems. *Aggression and Violent Behavior: A Review Journal, 7*, 513–528. DOI: 10.1016/S1359-1789(01)00076-3.

Ward, T., & Gannon, T. A. (2006). Rehabilitation, etiology, and self-regulation: The comprehensive good lives model of treatment for sexual offenders. *Aggression and Violent Behavior: A Review Journal, 11*, 77–94. DOI: 10.1016/j.avb.2005.06.001.

Ward, T., Hudson, S. M., & Marshall, W. L. (1996). Attachment style in sex offenders: A preliminary study. *Journal of Sex Research, 33*, 17–26. DOI: 10.1080/00224499609551811.

Ward, T., & Marshall, W. L. (2004). Good lives, aetiology and the rehabilitation of sex offenders: A bridging theory. *Journal of Sexual Aggression, 10*, 153–169. DOI: 10.1080/13552600412331290102.

Ward, T., Polaschek, D. L. L., & Beech, A. R. (2005). *Theories of sexual offending*. Chichester, UK: Wiley-Blackwell.

Ward, T., Yates, P. M., and Willis, G. M. (2012). The good lives model and the risk–need–responsivity model: A critical response to Andrews, Bonta, and Wormith (2011). *Criminal Justice and Behavior, 39*, 94–110. DOI: 10.1177/0093854811426085.

Willis, G. M., Yates, P. M., Gannon, T. A., & Ward, T. (2013). How to integrate the good lives model into treatment programs for sexual offending: An introduction and overview. *Sexual Abuse: A Journal of Research and Treatment, 23*, 123–142. DOI: 10.1177/1079063212452618.

Wilson, G. D. (1978). *The secrets of sexual fantasy*. London: J. M. Dent & Sons.

Yates, P. M., Kingston, D. A., & Ward, T. (2009). *The self regulation model of the offense and relapse process (Vol. 3)*. Pacific Psychological Assessment Corporation.

7

The Role of Case Studies in Work with Sexually Abusive Adolescents

Phil Rich

Introduction

It is not possible to describe the development of sexually troubled behavior in children and adolescents as though there is a single developmental pathway or characterological profile that defines or describes all sexually abusive youth, or suggests that they are all alike. They are not. To be sure, there are clear and definite features and attributes frequently found in the lives of sexually abusive youth that contribute to and shape the development of sexually abusive behavior. However, it is equally true that there is no clearly defined or single set of risk factors or markers, and no definite developmental history that sets into motion a pathway leading to juvenile sexually abusive behavior. In fact, we may well argue that a statement about differences is more accurate than a statement about similarities; that is, despite commonalities, the forces that shape and drive sexually abusive behavior are different in the case of each youth. This is a diverse population of individuals, among whom heterogeneity is described by Caldwell as "one of the most resilient findings in the research on juvenile sexual offenders" (2002, p. 296). Indeed, paraphrasing Kluckhohn and Murray (1953), we can say that every sexually abusive youth is, in some respects, like all other sexually abusive youth, in some respects like some other sexually abusive youth, and in some respects like no other sexually abusive youth.[1]

Sex Offender Treatment: A Case Study Approach to Issues and Interventions,
First Edition. Edited by Daniel T. Wilcox, Tanya Garrett, and Leigh Harkins.
© 2015 John Wiley & Sons, Ltd. Published 2015 by John Wiley & Sons, Ltd.

If we fail to recognize and acknowledge these differences we not only overlook and ignore heterogeneity and individuality, but also risk building a "one-size-fits-all" mentality in which we approach assessment and treatment in the same manner in every case, and thus fail to understand each client with whom we work as an individual. Put another way, the root of sexually troubled behavior in juveniles is multi-determined, involving individual, family, peer, school, and community variables (Letourneau, Schoenwald, & Sheidow, 2004), as well as biology (O'Connor & Rutter, 1996), temperament (Kagan & Snidman, 2004), and socioeconomics (Lipsey & Derzon, 1998). Thus, despite the many developmental commonalities and shared features in the lives of sexually troubled youth, the development of sexually troubled behavior is a complex phenomenon that develops under conditions and through circumstances that are different for each person. Hence, even though the pathway for many sexually abusive youth often starts at a common point, we cannot predict the eventual outcome of the pathway because the pathway is influenced by various subtle factors, many of which we are unaware, or do not recognize at the time.

In their case study of a sexually abusive youth, Latham and Kinscherff (2013) ask whether the details of each case, including the youth's age, diagnosis, intellectual capacity, personal history, history of behavioral problems, or relationship with others, matters in work intended to prevent further sexually abusive behavior. They answer Yes, details and differences do matter, and in so doing make clear the importance of understanding the circumstances specific to each case as we think about and plan treatment. Put another way, it is not simply the behavior alone upon which our aim is set, without regard for the individual engaging in that behavior and the circumstances of his or her life. It is the individual engaging in the behavior we are treating, and not simply the behavior, and it is therefore the individual in whom we are most interested.

Not only does individuality matter in terms of our capacity to understand the individual we intend to assess and treat, in terms of his or her developmental history and the circumstances of the problematic behavior, but individuality *also* matters with respect to how we approach the case and engage in treatment interventions. Just as there is no one-size-fits-all method for understanding juvenile sexually abusive behavior, there is also no universal or single best model for treating every sexually abusive youth, no single approach and set of interventions to be used in the treatment of every case. In the well-developed case study, we do not merely describe the details and facts of the case, but formulate the case in a manner that provides understanding and adds context and depth, and, therefore, a foundation upon which treatment may be built. Thus, case studies can be used to bring ideas about heterogeneity to life, bringing these ideas into the real world of assessment and treatment, not merely summarizing each case but also, and more importantly, bringing understanding to each case and its individual characteristics.

The Case Study Approach: Differences and Similarities

Although we may generalize to the larger population, case studies illuminate the case of just one client. Accordingly, there is simply no way to meaningfully understand sexually abusive behavior in all juveniles through a single case study. However, even though the case study focuses upon only one case, and despite significant differences among cases, the case study approach also allows us to think about cases in terms of shaping influences that affect the behaviors and relationships of *all* sexually abusive youth, although the details will vary widely in each case. Despite heterogeneity, we see common elements in each case that can, in turn, help us to draw reasonable conclusions about the nature, dynamics, and development of sexually abusive behavior in juveniles, and in turn help us to understand the population as a whole. Sexually troubled youth do, in fact, engage in similar behaviors and we are bound to see similarities, not just in their behaviors and in their prior and current developmental experiences, but also in their approach to life, in their relationships, in their psychological mindedness, and in their cognitive schema.

Two Case Studies

A single case study can tell us a lot about the individual client, but not a great deal about *all* sexually abusive youth. Two cases can do little more. However, two studies can begin to show, not only differences in developmental pathways to improve problem sexual behavior, but also similarities across cases, both evident in the two case studies presented in this chapter. Perhaps most of all, they can help us recognize the complexity of each case, at the same time presenting a process that we can apply to each of the complex cases with which we work.

Case one introduction: Juan

Juan is a 13-year-old adolescent of Hispanic descent, and appears smaller and younger than his stated age. He has a Full Scale IQ of 123, although his actual IQ may be several points higher based on prior testing.

Presenting complaint   At age 12, while on an out-of-state visit to his extended adoptive family, Juan sexually abused his 4-year-old male cousin while they were playing together unsupervised in his cousin's home, including oral sex and attempted penile-anal penetration. The behavior was the first report of sexually troubled or sexually abusive behavior, and occurred just 9 days after Juan's completion of treatment and discharge from a residential program where he had done relatively well and was deemed appropriate for return home.

History   Juan has an extensive and complex history of multiple and persistent out-of-home placements dating back to age 4, when he was removed from the care of his biological parents due to significant domestic violence and a history of severe neglect and physical abuse. By age 4, Juan was displaying increasingly defiant behavior, as well as behavior danger-ous to himself, including attempting to "fly" out of a fifth floor window in the family apartment. By age 7, he had experienced multiple foster care and residential placements, as well as three psychiatric hospitalizations. At age 7, he was transitioned into the care of foster parents who later adopted him. Juan's biological mother lives in the same state as him, but has had limited contact since he was age 10, and he has not seen his mother or had any contact for the past 18 months. Of his six biological siblings, ranging from age 3 to 18, four have been adopted and the young-est two live with Juan's mother. His father was deported when Juan was age 9 due to criminality, but Juan had little contact with him from age 4 on. Juan's adoptive parents are two married gay women, both of whom hold professional positions, with no other children.

Even after his adoption, Juan continued to require ongoing and persist-ent treatment, including several psychiatric hospitalizations, intensive day treatment, and several short- and long-term residential treatment pro-grams. His earliest placements were due to increasing aggression and severe noncompliance, including theft in school and in his adoptive home, and significant aggression toward his adoptive parents.

Juan's most recent residential placements were due to his sexual abuse of a significantly younger cousin.

Upon discovery, the behavior resulted in immediate admission to short-term residential care, eventually leading to a longer and more specialized residential placement. Although he responded well to the longer treatment program, engaging appropriately in treatment and demonstrating rela-tively few behavioral problems, Juan's parents did not feel comfortable having him return to their home before engaging in treatment specifically designed to address sexually abusive behavior in young adolescents. Juan was admitted to a specialized residential treatment program where he remained for an additional 5 months before being discharged to his adoptive parents' home.

Course of treatment and assessment of progress   Juan was easily able to manage his behaviors during the time that he was in the program, although he demonstrated difficulty remaining focused and could be rude and oppositional with both adults and peers. He engaged in such behaviors when frustrated or anxious, but in general demonstrated good behavioral self-regulation and usually responded well to staff redirection, as well as the ability to regulate and manage his moods and emotions. This represented a significant shift in Juan's behavior compared to earlier treatment placements in which his behavior could easily spiral out of control, resulting in significant problems for Juan and others. A bright child, with an above-average IQ, Juan sometimes attempted to manipulate staff in order to get his needs met, although this behavior diminished significantly throughout his placement.

Typical of the higher and often more intensive level of treatment provided in residential care, Juan received individual, group, and family treatment. In group therapy, Juan showed leadership skills, and consistently helped his peers talk about their issues and behaviors, providing them with advice and suggestions for the future. However, in terms of his own work in group, Juan minimally shared his issues with others and engaged only reluctantly in discussions regarding his sexually troubled behavior, stating that he did not like or know his peers well enough. Overall, Juan did not form any significant relationships with staff or peers, and although he did demonstrate awareness of others and their needs, he showed little depth in his concern for others, and, even after taking into account his age, he did not appear to experience any significant level of empathy for others.

Juan did not engage in individual therapy in any depth. He spent time processing events and his experiences in the residential treatment unit, as well as time discussing his experiences during family and weekend home visits, which began several weeks after his admission. However, despite cognitive strengths, Juan remained superficial in his individual treatment and showed little insight into his own behaviors, or interest in exploring them. His focus in treatment seemed to be aimed more at self-regulation than self-discovery, at staying out of trouble. He was minimally involved and not really motivated to engage in treatment, focusing more on "getting by." Much of Juan's treatment centered on learning essential cognitive behavioral concepts and tools regarding safe behavior. However, even in this area Juan showed little real interest and, despite his IQ, poor retention and application of ideas. He showed a minimal understanding of the motivators that drove his sexually abusive behavior, and little interest in discovery. This, in large part, seemed an outgrowth of his lack of any real engagement or motivation, as well as the fact that, again bearing in mind his age (13) and despite his IQ, Juan was neither psychologically minded nor especially insightful and, of importance, was not motivated to think deeply. In fact, even in the completion of required treatment tasks, such as the development of a safe behavior plan, Juan frequently did not complete the assignment, waited until the last minute, minimally engaged in the task, misplaced the completed work, and/or more simply reported that he had forgotten that he had a treatment "homework" assignment.

Juan made the most progress in family therapy, although his parents' involvement and the high bar they set for his involvement in sessions drove this. A primary focus included educating Juan on behavioral choices he could make and identifying how his choices affect family members. Juan and both of his parents were receptive to trying new strategies to help anticipate and mitigate potential conflicts. However, Juan rarely took the lead, and followed the path set by his parents in treatment. As sessions progressed, both parents increased their understanding of Juan's continued need for treatment and had a more thorough sense of his avoidance in engaging in treatment and completing treatment tasks. Once family home visits began, family therapy discussed both the dynamics of the visits and treatment tasks to be worked on during visits. Both parents were effectively engaged in family sessions and able to identify their concerns as they arose. One notable dynamic in the family was the anxiety that both parents and Juan experienced, which became recognizable as a family pattern, as well as an individual characteristic in each family member. This pattern was not merely a reactive anticipation of possible problems, given Juan's history of multiple treatment placements, but also actively contributed to and created family problems, as well as creating difficulties in the engagement of family members with one another, and "family anxiety" became a major focus in family therapy.

Assessment With regard to work that specifically addressed his sexually abusive behavior, although Juan began to discuss his sexual behavior with his clinician within weeks of admission, he tended to avoid any detailed discussion in individual, group, or family therapy. As was the case in general, Juan showed limited insight or concern, and seemed only superficially concerned about any harm he may have caused his young cousin. He did, however, recognize that his behaviors had caused great damage in his extended family and family relationships, and this did seem to concern him, though perhaps more in terms of the effect that his behavior had on his own life rather than the lives of others. In discussing his sexually abusive behavior, he refrained from providing details, and it was easier for him to discuss the precipitating events rather than the actual behaviors. In general, even by the time of discharge, Juan had not completed a well-considered safe behavior plan, and although he had a basic understanding of the tools and concepts of treatment, he lacked the ability to apply those concepts to his sexual and nonsexual behaviors.

Follow-up postdischarge Juan was discharged to his adoptive parents' home, and continued in outpatient individual, group, and family therapy with a focus on continuing his work on material specific to his sexually abusive behavior.

Upon discharge, Juan was assessed to have a moderate level of risk for reengaging in sexually troubled behavior, in part driven by "static," or historical, features of his prior antisocial behaviors. These included the sexually abusive behavior itself, Juan's history of adverse childhood experiences, his extensive history of nonsexual behavioral problems, a significant treatment history followed by continued problems, and the fact that Juan engaged in sexually abusive behavior quite literally within days of discharge from prior treatment. "Dynamic" risk factors, or those associated with current behaviors, thoughts, and relationships, included Juan's limited sense of personal responsibility, weak relationships, and lack of any significant engagement or interest in treatment for sexually abusive behavior. On the other hand, a number of protective factors were evident, including Juan's increased capacity for self-regulation, his cognitive (rather than emotional) recognition that sexually abusive behavior is harmful to others, and a family environment that was stable and supportive, with generally positive family relationships.

Case conceptualization Given his early and significant history, Juan can best be described as an emotionally reactive child entering adolescence, with a significant history of severe emotional and behavioral dysregulation in the face of distress or frustration and a tendency to escalate quickly and with little provocation, often in the service of avoiding or controlling distressing situations and/or getting his immediate needs met without regard for others or his own long-term benefit. Over time in treatment, Juan showed a strong increase in self-regulation and understanding of behavioral expectations, despite minimal involvement in more intensive aspects of his treatment. However, the fact that Juan has lived in a highly structured treatment environment while engaging in frequent contact and engagement with his parents may also have served as an important emotional and behavioral anchor and control mechanism.

In terms of his only known incident of sexually abusive behavior, Juan appears to have acted out his sexual interests and curiosity by intentionally and knowingly using his 4-year-old cousin in an opportunistic manner. In addition, that behavior seems to highlight his disconnection from how his behavior may affect himself or others. At that time, lacking strong self-regulation, secure and reciprocal connections to others, perhaps having a distorted view of the future, and a lack of insight into or concern for the needs and experiences of others, when presented with an opportunity to develop sexual experience Juan seized the moment, also believing that his status as the elder, and, therefore, in-control cousin would allow him to take advantage of the situation without discovery.

With literally a lifetime of physical disruptions in his living and emotional environment, and an early history of severe adversity and complete disconnection from his biological family, we might reasonably argue that Juan has been and continues to be in survival mode, taking care of his own experienced needs, acting out his stress under times of emotional volatility, and concerned more about getting caught than the consequences of his behavior to himself or others. As he entered puberty and at the time of his sexually abusive behavior, after years of treatment, Juan began to demonstrate greater self-regulation, but at the same time continued to engage in behavior, now of a sexual nature, that met his needs. Juan's adopted parents are a great source of support for him, and although engaged with them and valuing their love, he also values what they can offer him on a practical level (not so unusual for any child). Indeed, it is family treatment and the constant support of his parents that has perhaps most helped Juan over the years, as well as his developing social skills, including an increased self-regulation along with the greater development of his executive functioning skills as he enters puberty. Nevertheless, Juan remains somewhat distant in his relationship to both parents, and we may say that he has an attachment style that is detached and disconnected at times, and at other times enmeshed and anxious. To this degree, in addition to arrested or limited moral development, we can understand Juan's capacity to engage in antisocial behaviors, including sexually troubled behavior, fueled by a weakened sense of social connection and attachment in which, despite improvement, Juan does not show great concern or empathy for others, including his parents.

Treatment implications: generalizing from this case   When it comes to empathy, Whittaker, Brown, Beckett, and Gerhold (2006) found that juveniles who sexually abuse children showed less sexual knowledge and a weak sense of empathy when compared to nonoffending adolescents, concluding that this combination may be critical in understanding the development of sexually abusive behavior towards children in juveniles. However, it is important to note that Whittaker et al. are describing a combination of at least two factors, as it is not likely that a lack of empathy is in itself sufficient to explain the capacity to engage in sexually abusive behavior. Nevertheless, it is probably a mistake not to consider empathy a significant factor. Adding to this conceptualization, Keenan and Ward (2000) suggest that problems with victim empathy may be the result of a lack of mentalization (or the ability to reflect upon and imagine one's own mental experiences and the experiences of others, also known as metacognition), rather than a lack of empathy per se.

Despite this, if we think of and judge adolescent empathy in adult terms, we risk seeing a lack of empathy in adolescents as pathological, rather than an unfolding developmental process. Here, it is important to remind ourselves that empathy in adolescents is not as well developed or clear as empathy in adults (D'Orazio, 2002). Adolescent empathy is thus best understood in the context of cognitive and emotional development, partly driven or impeded by either social connection or social disconnection. In fact, it may be more relevant for us to consider empathy in juvenile sexual offenders as not simply the capacity to recognize and care about emotion in others, which may be limited in many adolescents, but also to feel connected to others. Here, we might consider the development of empathy in adolescents as, not simply a feature of cognitive and emotional development, but also a feature and measure of social connection and belonging. When potentiated by and melded with other factors, limited empathy in adolescents may be reflected in a sense of disconnection and unrelatedness to others, and perhaps to social values as a whole.

Moving from the development of empathy to another critical component of social connection and social behavior, that of moral development, Ashkar and Kenny (2007) propose that sexually abusive youths have arrested moral development. However, they suggest that the level of moral reasoning is tied to the context in which decision making occurs, and although sexually troubled youths may be capable of a higher level of moral decision making, they are most likely to use less developed moral reasoning in situations in which their primary goal is to meet their own needs, including their engagement in sexually abusive behavior. Similar to ideas about the capacity for empathy and the experience of empathic distress (i.e., feeling sorry for others), this suggests that sexually abusive juveniles either have not developed or are able to switch off a higher level of moral reasoning, allowing them the ability to be sexually abusive without the feelings of guilt associated with such behavior.

Ideas about empathy and morality are inevitably connected, because the two constructs are developmentally and cognitively linked, with morality serving as the attitudinal and behavioral equivalent of empathy (Rich, 2006, 2011). To this end, empathic concern for others translates into and becomes congruent with moral reasoning and behavior. In this regard, empathy is a precondition for moral decision making, in which moral development is contingent upon the development and experience of empathy (Hoffman, 2000; Kagan, 1984; Vetlesen, 1994).

Case two introduction: Martin

Martin is a 14-year-old adolescent, described by his clinician as "sad, guarded, anxious, and controlling," with a low average IQ of 87, a few points above borderline intellectual functioning. Martin's parents divorced when he was 5, and his father moved to Ohio, remarried, and had infrequent contact with him until he was admitted to residential care at age 13. His mother remarried, and Martin sexually abused the children from this second marriage (Martin's half-siblings). Martin was himself sexually abused by a male teenage babysitter between the ages of 4 and 9, including the use of pornography, oral sex, and anal penetration, and between ages 7 and 8 by a 20-year-old male cousin, involving reciprocal fondling and mutual fellatio. In both cases, Martin reported experiencing the relationships as special and nonabusive.

Presenting complaint   Between the ages of 9 and 13, Martin sexually abused his younger half-brother (aged 3 to 7) and half-sister (aged 1 to 5). His offenses included fondling and fellatio, including ejaculating into his brother's mouth, cunnilingus, and attempted vaginal penetration for which he was adjudicated as a juvenile sexual offender and placed on probation.

History   Martin was exhibiting conduct-disordered behavior by age 4, continuing throughout elementary and middle school. By the time of his half-brother's birth, Martin, age 6, was demonstrating severe oppositional behavior with his mother and stepfather. As he got older, he began bullying both younger siblings, which later included sexually abusing them. Martin describes sexual discussion among schoolmates, viewing of pornography, and television with overt sexual content as prompts to his sexually abusive behavior, as well as his own sexual victimization, which occurred until he was age 9. He also described missing the contact with his babysitter after his own victimization ended. Between ages 9 and 12, Martin lit at least nine minor fires and described being fascinated and relaxed by fire. Martin engaged in troubled behavior throughout elementary and middle school, and failed to form any friendships, often and most typically garnering attention through persistent acting out, and often lashing out verbally and physically at peers and adults in the school setting. Upon admission to residential care, he was described as oppositional, conduct disordered, anxious, and obsessive, as well as easily irritated, depressed, easily stressed, quickly overwhelmed, and having periodic sleeping difficulties. Diagnoses included conduct disorder, anxiety disorder, dysthymic disorder, pyromania, and sexual abuse of a child. Axis II diagnoses were deferred given his age, but included narcissistic and histrionic traits.

Course of treatment and assessment of progress   Martin demonstrated poor self-regulation, although he showed slow and incremental improvement over the course of 14 months in residential care. Nevertheless, he was easily overwhelmed by emotions, most of which involved uncertainty, self-doubt, and a sense of not being heard or valued by others, leading to a disintegration of behavioral control. Although this led to significant physical acting out, most of the time Martin's negative behaviors involved loud, sarcastic, critical, and demanding statements directed to peers and staff, intended to put others in their place and demonstrate a sense of self as superior and in control. During the first 10 months of Martin's treatment, he frequently demonstrated excessive reactions to stimuli, including prolonged and severely destructive behaviors designed to gain full staff attention and take control over situations. On two occasions, Martin tore up an entire carpet, piece by piece, in a time out room, and on another he gouged at a plasterboard wall until he had worked his way through it and began to tear at electrical and phone wires in an attempt to cause significant damage. Although these behaviors significantly diminished, Martin nevertheless remained labile, gravitating at times towards infantile, destructive, and excessive behaviors. These involved hurting and depriving others, taking control, and being unmistakably seen and recognized by others.

Martin was not able to form strong relationships with peers because of his frequently childish behavior, and at other times his demanding and rude interactions in which he showed little concern for the feelings or needs of peers. Martin wanted to be liked and often acted as "class clown" in therapeutic and work environments, hoping to align himself with peers, but instead appeared silly and unfocused. At other times, although attempting serious participation in groups, he came across as pseudo-mature and awkward, lecturing his peers and telling them what to do, and how to do it. As his therapist wrote, Martin's "mixture of anxiety, silliness, and oppositionality causes him huge difficulties, driving away and alienating the very people he wants to attract and from whom he seeks support and admiration." Martin struggled to be in tune with others but did, at times, offer support to peers. However, Martin experienced a limited ability to feel or maintain a feeling of empathy for anyone. In fact, Martin frequently failed to recognize any other point of view, particularly when upset, and instead intentionally lashed out at others with the intention of causing emotional harm.

In treatment at all levels, including individual, group, family, and in the residential milieu, Martin was often narcissistic, demanding, silly, and pseudo-mature, and at times resorted to transparent lies and deceit for no apparent reason. Although later providing multiple, and sometimes contradictory, reasons for being dishonest with others, including his parents during family sessions, his explanations were invented, lacking coherence and consistency.

Martin began family therapy with his mother and stepfather and with his father in separate family sessions as the divorced parents would not meet together. With his father, Martin began to express feelings of sadness and rejection due to his experience of abandonment by his father following the divorce at age 5. In sessions with mother and stepfather, Martin described his feelings of being emotionally abused and uncared for in their household, and stated his lack of trust in his mother. He also described feeling ready to begin the process of disclosing his sexually abusive behavior to them, as well as victim clarification (in which he would begin the process of meeting in face-to-face sessions with the siblings he had sexually victimized). However, Martin was impatient with his parents and therapist because they did not feel he was ready for victim clarification, and he became frustrated, angry, and impatient because his stepfather was not willing to hear details of Martin's sexually abusive behavior against his children. As on the residential unit, although doing some real work, Martin significantly acted out and was self-defeating in family sessions. On the whole, family therapy moved slowly, despite some significant gains over time. However, Martin's parents were never able to come together for blended family sessions, continuing to place their own needs and differences above the needs of Martin.

Assessment   Although Martin's behaviors, including his sexually abusive behavior, are more complex than simply attachment-driven, we may nevertheless take an attachment-informed approach as a foundation for understanding his case. From this perspective, Martin can be seen as insecurely attached,[2] in which he largely fits a model of anxious attachment, although at times also appears detached (an avoidant form of attachment), struggling with and distancing himself from the very people with whom he desires connection, including both family and peers. To this degree, attachment style can be seen as dimensional, rather than categorical; that is, attachment patterns and styles shift over time and under different circumstances, rather than being fixed and placed into one attachment category or another (Bartholomew & Horowitz, 1991; Brennan, Clark, & Shaver, 1998; Crittenden, 2000a; Fraley & Spieker, 2003; Fraley & Waller, 1998; Rich, 2006).

Martin is neither a coherent nor cohesive thinker, to the point where his behaviors and cognitions are often purely reactive, accomplishing no clear purpose other than lashing out at others, taking control through acting out, or impulsively meeting immediate emotional needs. To this degree, Martin can be considered not only insecure in and ambivalent about relationships, but also disorganized in his thinking and strategies for building and maintaining social relationships. At times, he shows significant, if not frank, disorganization (Hilburn-Cobb, 2004), acted out in extreme physical behaviors that have no clear purpose and represent a collapse of emotional and cognitive resources, and disconnected, seemingly purposeless, and poorly integrated behavioral interactions with others when under stress.

Follow-up postdischarge Martin showed improvements in all domains over time, but despite progress and growth continued to show great difficulty in his relationship and decision-making skills, affect regulation, and executive functioning. Rather than remaining in residential care and continuing to build upon his progress in a highly-contained, well controlled, and safe environment, Martin was instead discharged to the home of his maternal grandparents and enrolled in an intensive outpatient and wraparound program that provided services in the home and community. However, more emotional and behavioral containment was required, and his behaviors began to quickly deteriorate, returning to the same behavioral and relationship problems evident in his history prior to and during his first months in residential treatment, and even escalating. The capacity of Martin's grandparents to manage his behaviors quickly deteriorated, as did his relationship with them and other family members. Although Martin did not re-engage in known sexually abusive behavior, he ran away from home after several weeks, accompanied by an older man, and when found was placed into a state correctional facility for breaking the terms of his probation.

Case conceptualization   Despite a mix of attachment styles, for the most part Martin demonstrates an anxious ambivalent pattern of attachments and social connections. In addition, related to his early experiences and development of attachment to caregivers, Martin's capacity for reflection and self-awareness, and hence his ability to understand his own mental and emotional state and that of others, is impoverished, as is his sense of control and mastery. Limitations in his capacity for reflective awareness make it difficult for Martin to recognize or understand any perspective other than his own, highlighting not simply a level of narcissism but a more significant failure of both perspective taking and metacognition. Indeed, Martin feels, and likely believes, that others should want what *he* wants and recognize and adopt *his* point of view. Martin does not understand that others may not share his feelings and ideas, a basic realization that forms in most children at an early age as they develop metacognition.

Instead, Martin displays coercive behaviors, with great emphasis placed on emotional decision-making processes to interpret the world and act out attachment strategies. Indeed, as described, Martin is neither coherent nor cohesive in his thinking, especially when under stress or emotionally stimulated. By his frequent reactive behavior and acting out against others, Martin thus fails to build the relationships he seeks or accomplish goals he hopes to meet, with virtually no use of cognitive strategies for social engagement, relationship development, and goal accomplishment. Instead, Martin implicitly expects that people are unlikely to be naturally drawn to him or recognize or tend to his needs, and to this degree cannot be counted on. His coercive behaviors, coy at times and angry at others, and always emotionally driven, are designed to ensure active proximity to and the presence of others who *will* recognize his presence and respond to his needs, one way or another. Failing to develop an adequate capacity for metacognition creates major obstacles in Martin's ability to experience or maintain empathy for others, something clearly evident in his relationships and his view of others, including family members and peers. Indeed, the basis for both moral behavior and self-agency lies in the development of metacognition and perspective taking, in which a failure to develop metacognition contributes to the capacity of individuals to devalue and victimize others and construct a world of self-serving behaviors, in which they genuinely may fail to recognize their responsibility for their own behaviors (Fonagy, 2004; Fonagy et al., 1997a, 1997b). In Martin's case, this also allows for behaviors that create a sense of control and influence over others, however self-defeating, antisocial, and socially isolating in nature.

Martin's experience of being sexually victimized was positive, in which he reported feeling close to both perpetrators, and served as a surrogate relationship for otherwise lacking secure parental attachments. In addition to experiencing a sense of estrangement and lack of nurturance from his parents, Martin also resented the intrusion into his life by his younger siblings, who diverted even more of his parents' attention away from him. At the same time, he was increasingly unable to form meaningful or close relationships with peers outside of the family, a persistent pattern through-out his childhood and early adolescence. Instead, he seemed to find his greatest sense of himself in his control over others and a fascination with experiences in which he felt in control, such as fire play, conduct-disorder behaviors, deceit, coercion, and the bullying and sexual abuse of his younger siblings, serving as punishment as well as control. Although Martin's relationship with his younger siblings was absent of any form of supportive or caring behavior, his abuse of them perhaps also helped him to re-experience some of the pleasurable and positive feelings he experienced through his own sexual victimization.

Treatment implications: generalizing from this case   Although childhood sexual abuse is a risk factor in the lives of many sexually abusive youth, it is nonetheless incorrect to assume that most sexually abusive youth have themselves been sexually victimized. Instead, sexually abusive behavior is the product of a multitude and complex set of factors that come together to produce the behavior, including developmental history, personal psychology, and socioenvironmental forces. Consequently, it is naïve to believe that sexually abusive youth are merely playing out or reliving their own history of victimization, or somehow engaging in sexually abusive behavior to take control over prior distressing experiences, for instance. Indeed, the very experience of being sexually victimized is different for each victim, and most victims of childhood sexual abuse do not later perpetrate sexual abuse toward other children.

However, in Martin's case, it is likely that being sexually victimized *is* relevant to his sexually abusive behaviors, especially as he experienced his sexual abuse as positive and desirable. In fact, Martin's sexual abuse of his younger siblings began shortly after his own sexual victimization ended. Here, then, we can see a clear link between being victimized and later victimizing others, and thus the case study reflects circumstances where being a victim of sexual abuse may significantly contribute to later sexually abusive behavior. In general, in Martin's case, from which we can extrapolate to the larger population of sexually abusive youth, we see a set of early and persistent childhood experiences that reflect insecure attachment and weak emotional bonds with parents and other family members, which in turn contribute to delays in the development of metacognition and resulting limitations in the development of empathy, moral reasoning, and important social relationships. Of course, Martin's case is unique to Martin, and thus illustrates heterogeneity. At the same time, his case captures the power, importance, and relevance of early experience in shaping our sense of self and others, what we can expect from others and the world-at-large, and the development of cognitive schema that shape our relationships and behaviors, in some cases paving the way for antisocial behaviors when shaping circumstances come together.

We can also draw generalizations about the importance of connected peer relationships, or in Martin's case the absence of such relationships throughout his childhood. On this point, Miner and colleagues (2010) point to the importance of peer relationships in adolescent healthy and well-adjusted behavior, and the possibility that sexually abusive youth expect adult and peer rejection.

Recommendations to Clinicians

Bear in mind the diversity of each case and the goal of the case study in not only better understanding the case, but also recognizing the individuality of each client. As in the two cases presented above, it is important to understand *current* behaviors in both children and adolescents as partial outgrowths of developmental experiences, not only earlier in their lives but also in their recent and current lives. In both cases, understanding developmental and attachment experiences is key to making sense of the presenting problems, helping build treatment around treatment needs that are well-understood for each client. Also, of note is that time in treatment counts. Some sexually troubled youth require more treatment over a longer period of time, while others require far less treatment and treatment that is less intense.

Think, then, in developmental terms, about the behavior of youth in treatment and the rise of that behavior, and about social, emotional, and relational needs that will need to be addressed in treatment if we are to decrease risk and build strengths.

Conclusion: Case Studies as a Driving Force in Understanding Juvenile Sexually Abusive Behavior

At its strongest, the case study approach does not simply summarize cases. Instead, it adds insight, depth, and understanding. In so doing, it requires that clinicians understand the psychological problems and vulnerabilities for each client, rather than utilizing a cookbook approach to understanding behavior (Drake & Ward, 2003; Eells, 2007; Eells & Lombart, 2011). To this degree, the case study approach also addresses and meets the principles established by the risk–need–responsivity model (Andrews, Bonta, & Hoge, 1990; Wormith, Gendreau, & Bonta, 2012), in which case formulation provides a foundation for the type of treatment provided for each client, including intensity, duration, and the setting in which it occurs. For Juan and Martin, this involved residential care and included individual, group, and family therapy.

Although each of the two cases presented in this chapter reflects a different pathway to sexually abusive behavior, they also clearly reflect commonalities, one of which involves the role of early and ongoing caregiver relationships, highlighted by West, Rose, Spreng, Sheldon-Keller and Adam, who describe adverse family experiences as "a relentless threat" to the development of secure and confident attachments to others and sense of self (1998, p. 662).

Perhaps most of all, my goal has been to describe some of the features that some, and perhaps many, sexually abusive youths have in common, while at the same time demonstrating the perspective that no two youths are the same, that the pathways that lead to sexually abusive behavior are different in each case despite broad similarities, and that case study and case formulation provide a means for evaluating, understanding, and making sense of each individual case presented to us.

Endnotes

1 Every person is in some ways like all other people, in some ways like some other people, and in some ways like no other people (Kluckhohn and Murray, 1953).

2 Although there are a number of models that describe types, patterns, or styles of attachment, most consider attachment in terms of secure or optimal forms of attachment in contrast to insecure, or suboptimal, forms, in which there is a sense of uncertainty, ambivalence, or lack of security in self and/or others (for instance, Bartholomew & Horowitz, 1991; Crittenden, 2000b; Goldberg, 2000; Main & Solomon, 1986).

References

Andrews, D. A., Bonta, J., & Hoge, R. D. (1990). Classification for effective rehabilitation: Rediscovering psychology. *Criminal Justice and Behavior*, 17, 19–52. DOI: 10.1177/0093854890017001004.

Ashkar, P. J., & Kenny, D. T. (2007). Moral reasoning of adolescent male offenders: Comparison of sexual and nonsexual offenders. *Criminal Justice and Behavior*, 34, 108–118. DOI: 10.1177/0093854806288118.

Bartholomew, K., & Horowitz, L. M. (1991). Attachment styles among young adults: A test of a four-category model. *Journal of Personality and Social Psychology*, 61(2), 226–244. DOI: 10.1037/0022-3514.61.2.226.

Brennan, K. A., Clark, C. L., & Shaver, P. R. (1998). Self-report measurement of adult attachment: An integrative overview. In J. A. Simpson & W. S. Rholes (Eds.), *Attachment theory and close relationships* (pp. 46–76). New York: Guilford Press.

Caldwell, M. F. (2002). What we do not know about juvenile sexual reoffense risk. *Child Maltreatment*, 7, 291–302. DOI: 10.1177/107755902237260.

Crittenden, P. M. (2000a). A dynamic-maturational approach to continuity and change in pattern of attachment. In P. M. Crittenden & A. H. Claussen (Eds.), *The organization of attachment relationships: Maturation, culture, and context* (pp. 343–383). Cambridge, UK: Cambridge University Press.

Crittenden, P. M. (2000b). Introduction. In P. M. Crittenden & A. H. Claussen (Eds.), *The organization of attachment relationships: Maturation, culture, and context* (pp. 1–10). Cambridge, UK: Cambridge University Press.

D'Orazio, D. (2002). *A comparative analysis of empathy in sexually offending and non-offending juvenile and adult males*. Unpublished doctoral dissertation. California School of Professional Psychology at Alliant University, Fresno.

Drake, C. R., & Ward, T. (2003). Practical and theoretical roles for the formulation based treatment of sexual offenders. *International Journal of Forensic Psychology*, 1, 71–84.

Eells, T. D. (2007). Psychotherapy case formulation: History and current status. In T. D. Eells (Ed.), *Handbook of psychotherapy case formulation* (2nd ed., pp. 3–32). New York: Guilford Press.

Eells, T. D., & Lombart, K. G. (2011). Theoretical and evidence-based approaches to case formulation. In P. Sturmey & M. McMurray (Eds.), *Forensic case formulation* (pp. 3–32). Chichester, UK: John Wiley & Sons.

Fonagy, P. (2004). The developmental roots of violence in the failure of mentalization. In F. Pfafflin, & G. Adshead (Eds.), *A matter of security: The application of attachment theory to forensic psychiatry and psychotherapy* (pp. 13–56). London: Jessica Kingsley Publishers.

Fonagy, P., Target, M., Steele, M., Steele, H., Leigh, H., Levinson, A., et al. (1997a). Morality, disruptive behavior, borderline personality disorder, crime, and their relationships to security of attachment. In L. Atkinson & K. J.

Zucker (Eds.), *Attachment and psychopathology* (pp. 223–274). New York: Guilford Press.

Fonagy, P., Target, M., Steele, M., & Steele, H. (1997b). The development of violence and crime as it relates to security of attachment. In J. D. Osofsky (Ed.), *Children in a violent society* (pp. 150–177b). New York: Guilford Press.

Fraley, R. C., & Spieker, S. J. (2003). What are the differences between dimensional and categorical models of individual differences in attachment? Reply to Cassidy (2003), Cummings (2003), Sroufe, (2003), and Waters and Beauchaine (2003). *Developmental Psychology, 39*, 423–429. DOI: 10.1037/0012-1649.39.3.423.

Fraley, R. C., & Waller, N. G. (1998). Adult attachment patterns: A test of the typological model. In J. A. Simpson & W. S. Rholes (Eds.), *Attachment theory and close relationships* (pp. 77–114). New York: Guilford Press.

Goldberg, S. (2000). *Attachment and development.* London: Arnold.

Hilburn-Cobb, C. (2004). Adolescent psychopathology in terms of multiple behavioral systems: The role of attachment and controlling strategies and frankly disorganized behavior. In L. Atkinson & S. Goldberg (Eds.), *Attachment issues in psychopathology and intervention* (pp. 95–135). Mahwah, NJ: Lawrence Erlbaum.

Hoffman, M. L. (2000). *Empathy and moral development: Implications for caring and justice.* Cambridge, UK: Cambridge University Press.

Kagan, J. (1984). *The nature of the child.* New York: Basic Books.

Kagan, J., & Snidman, N. (2004). *The long shadow of temperament.* Cambridge, MA: Harvard University Press.

Keenan, T., & Ward, T. (2000). A theory of mind perspective on cognitive, affective, and intimacy deficits in child sexual offenders. *Sexual Abuse: A Journal of Research and Treatment, 12*, 49–60. DOI: 10.1177/107906320001200106.

Kluckhohn, C., & Murray, H. A. (1953). *Personality in nature, society, and culture* (2nd ed.). New York: Alfred Knopf.

Latham, C., and Kinscherff, R. (2013). *A developmental perspective on the meaning of problematic sexual behavior in children and adolescents.* Holyoke, MA: NEARI Press.

Letourneau, E. J., Schoenwald, S. K., & Sheidow, A. J. (2004). Children and adolescents with sexual behavior problems. *Child Maltreatment, 9*, 49–61. DOI: 10.1177/1077559503260308.

Lipsey, M. W., & Derzon, J. H. (1998). Predictors of violent and serious delinquency in adolescence and early adulthood: A synthesis of longitudinal research. In R. Loeber & D. P. Farrington (Eds.), *Serious and violent juvenile offenders: Risk factors and successful interventions* (pp. 86–105). Thousand Oaks, CA: Sage.

Main, M., & Solomon, J. (1986). Discovery of a new, insecure-disorganized/disoriented attachment pattern. In T. B. Brazelton & M. W. Yogman (Eds.), *Affective development in infancy* (pp. 95–124). Norwood, NJ: Ablex.

Miner, M. H., Robinson, B. E., Knight, R. A., Berg, D., Swinburne, R., & Netland, J. (2010). Understanding sexual perpetration against children: Effects of attachment style, interpersonal involvement, and hypersexuality. *Sexual Abuse: A Journal of Research and Treatment, 22,* 58–77. DOI: 10.1177/1079063209353183.

O'Connor, T. G., & Rutter, M. (1996). Risk mechanisms in development: Some conceptual and methodological considerations. *Developmental Psychology, 32,* 787–795. DOI: 10.1037/0012-1649.32.4.787.

Rich, P. (2006). *Attachment and sexual offending: Understanding and applying attachment theory to the treatment of juvenile sexual offenders.* Chichester, UK: John Wiley & Sons.

Rich, P. (2011). *Understanding juvenile sexual offenders: Assessment, treatment, and rehabilitation* (2nd ed.). Hoboken, NJ: John Wiley & Sons.

Vetlesen, A. J. (1994). *Perception, empathy, and judgment: An inquiry into the preconditions of moral performance.* University Park, PA: Pennsylvania University Press.

West, M., Rose, M. S., Spreng, S., Sheldon-Keller, A., & Adam, K. (1998). Adolescent attachment questionnaire: A brief assessment of attachment in adolescence. *Journal of Youth and Adolescence, 27,* 661–673. DOI: 10.1023/A:1022891225542.

Whittaker, M. K., Brown, J., Beckett, R., & Gerhold, C. (2006). Sexual knowledge and empathy: A comparison of adolescent child molesters and non-offending adolescents. *Journal of Sexual Aggression, 12,* 143–154. DOI: 10.1080/13552600600823621.

Wormith, J. S., Gendreau, P., & Bonta, J. (2012). Deferring to clarity, parsimony, and evidence in reply to Ward, Yates, and Willis. *Criminal Justice and Behavior, 39,* 111–120. DOI: 10.1177/0093854811426087.

8

Intervention Issues with a Sex Offender with Intellectual Disability

William R. Lindsay and Amanda M. Michie

Theoretical and Research Basis for Treatment

Several of the theoretical developments that underpin cases in other chapters of this book are relevant to sex offenders with intellectual disability. However, one theoretical framework has been developed specifically for this client group. Counterfeit deviance was first developed by Hingsburger, Griffiths, and Quinsey (1991) and has recently been updated by Griffiths, Hingsburger, Hoath, and Ioannou (2013). These authors noted that people with intellectual disability tend to live in relatively protected circumstances in which appropriate heterosexual relationships and sexual development may not be supported. They developed a counterfeit deviance hypothesis as a way of explaining some inappropriate sexual behavior that has its genesis in restricted sexual and social development rather than deviant sexuality. The authors emphasize that some inappropriate sexual behavior in men with intellectual disability is indeed brought about by sexual deviance and that, regardless of the cause of the behavior, the effect on victims is likely to be traumatic. But they also stress the importance of differentiating counterfeit and true deviance. In this way, some inappropriate sexual behavior can be explained by poor or faulty learning such as inadequate understanding of privacy, poor appreciation of the extent to which nakedness is an appropriate or underdeveloped sexual knowledge.

Sex Offender Treatment: A Case Study Approach to Issues and Interventions, First Edition. Edited by Daniel T. Wilcox, Tanya Garrett, and Leigh Harkins.
© 2015 John Wiley & Sons, Ltd. Published 2015 by John Wiley & Sons, Ltd.

Lindsay (2009, 2013) has reviewed recent research and evaluated the way in which it supports and adjusts the counterfeit deviance hypothesis. He noted a number of studies that have tested this hypothesis directly through the assessment of sexual knowledge in sex offenders with intellectual disability and control participants with intellectual disability. The counterfeit deviance hypothesis would suggest that the sex offenders would have poorer sexual knowledge and understanding of sexual relationships giving rise to inappropriate sexual behavior based on this misunderstanding. However, several studies have demonstrated that sex offenders with intellectual disability have better sexual knowledge than nonsexual offenders with intellectual disability (Lockhart, Guerin, Shanahan, & Coyle, 2010; Michie, Lindsay, Martin, & Grieve, 2006; Talbot & Langdon, 2006).

While this might suggest that the counterfeit deviance hypothesis is unlikely, Lindsay (2013) has interpreted these findings to suggest that while some men with intellectual disability understand that certain sexual behaviors are wrong, they may not understand the extent to which they are condemned by society. There is supporting evidence investigating the validity of the Ward and Hudson (2000) self-regulation pathways model of sexual offending for men with intellectual disability. In summary, the pathways have two distinct ways of establishing offense-related goals (approach or avoidance) and two strategies of self-regulation or means of achieving these goals (active or passive). Keeling and Rose (2005) suggested that sex offenders with intellectual disability would conform to more passive self-regulation styles because of the lack of cognitive capacity to actively plan offending. However, Langdon, Maxted, and Murphy (2007), Lindsay, Steptoe, and Beech (2008), and Ford, Rose, and Thrift (2009) found that the majority of sex offenders with intellectual disability in their studies were allocated to pathways with approach goals, with around half employing simple active strategies for offending. Lindsay (2013) suggested that men with intellectual disability might not have understood the extent to which inappropriate sexual behavior is against interpersonal conventions. He also suggested that a poor understanding of the threat posed by society towards the commission of inappropriate sexual behavior also contributed to men with intellectual disability behaving in this way. In doing this, he invoked the theoretical construct of the "threat threshold," in which Hall and Hirschman (1992) suggested that the threat threshold should be sufficiently high to counterbalance the motivation to commit the sexual offense. In this way, the counterfeit deviance hypothesis can be adapted to accommodate new research findings.

Research on sex offenders with intellectual disability has increased considerably over the last 15 to 20 years. In terms of support for theoretical positions, the main findings have been in the area of adversity in childhood. Several authors have shown that people with intellectual disability in general are considerably more at risk of experiencing adversity in childhood than people in the general population. Emerson and Halpin (2013) investigated this directly by looking at antisocial behavior. They conducted a secondary analysis of data from the Longitudinal Study of Young People in England, which included 15,772 young people, 532 of whom were identified as having mild intellectual disability. For the group as a whole, indicators of social, economic, and environmental adversity were significant risk factors for contact with the police and antisocial behavior. Teenagers with intellectual disability were significantly more likely than other teenagers to be exposed to all risk factors, including living with a single parent, living in an area of deprivation, living in rented accommodation, living in a workless household, and being eligible for free school meals. Although teenagers with mild intellectual disability were significantly more likely to have police contact and to report antisocial behavior, when these risk factors were controlled intellectual disability itself was significantly associated with lower rates of antisocial behavior. The study, on a very large data set, suggests that while intellectual disability on its own may not be a risk factor, it is associated with higher rates of childhood adversity.

Marshall and Barbaree (1990) developed an integrated theory in which they emphasized adolescence as a critical period in the development of personal understanding of aggressive and sexual impulses, the development of social and interpersonal skills, and the development of problem-solving and self-regulation skills for aggression and sexuality. They focused on developmental experiences and, in the light of research on developmental adversity and intellectual disability, this is important. Lindsay, Steptoe, and Haut (2012) compared the physical and sexual abuse histories of 156 sexual and 126 nonsexual offenders with intellectual disability. They found that 33% of the sexual offenders and 18% of the nonsexual offenders had experienced sexual abuse in childhood, while 16% of the sexual offenders and 33% of the nonsexual offenders reported physical abuse in childhood. These trends were significant, suggesting that sexual abuse was associated with sexual offending while physical abuse was associated with violent offending. However, it is important to note that around two-thirds of participants did not report childhood sexual and physical abuse and that a small percentage of violent offenders reported sexual abuse but did commit sexual offenses. Novaco and Taylor

(2008) also found that witnessing parental violence in childhood was significantly associated with anger and aggression in adulthood in men with intellectual disability. These studies support the importance of childhood adversity in the development of offending in adulthood.

Research on the efficacy of treatment

Early reports on the efficacy of treatment were generally very positive. Griffiths, Hingsburger, and Quinsey (1989) developed a comprehensive treatment service for sex offenders with intellectual disability and reported no reoffending after 4 years for 40 cases. However, this report suffered from one of the difficulties that have beset outcome studies for sex offenders with intellectual disability, in that all of the participants continued to be monitored with 24-hour supervision. This difficulty has made evaluation problematic, since, presumably, the men have had little opportunity to offend because of the supervision arrangements (e.g., Craig, Stringer, & Moss, 2006; McGrath, Livingston, & Falk, 2007). Lindsay and colleagues (1998a, b, c) reported case studies in the treatment of sex offenders with intellectual disability who had unescorted access to the community and were followed up for at least 4 years. They reported one case of reoffending among a total of 15 cases.

More recent studies have reported low reoffending rates in sex offenders who have received group treatment and have continued to have free access to the community. Rose, Rose, Hawkins, and Anderson (2012) conducted an evaluation of a program with 12 participants who were living in the community and attended over 40 weekly sessions. Participants were assessed before and after treatment using the Questionnaire on Attitudes Consistent with Sexual Offending (QACSO; Lindsay, Whitefield, & Carson 2007), which has become a widely used assessment to evaluate the effects of treatment in sex offenders with intellectual disability. The QACSO assesses attitudes that mitigate or justify sexual offenses in the areas of rape and attitudes to women, exhibitionism, voyeurism, stalking, dating abuse, offenses against men, and offenses against children. It also has a social desirability scale to assess the extent to which respondents answer in a socially conformist fashion. Because of literacy deficits in participants, each item is read to the individual who then responds by endorsing the item or disagreeing. The QACSO has good reliability, internal consistency, and discriminative validity (Lindsay et al., 2007), and will be used as an assessment for the current case study. Rose et al. (2012) also assessed locus of control and sexual knowledge. Following treatment there were highly significant improvements in sexual knowledge and attitudes relating to sexual offending. There were also shifts towards greater external locus of control, suggesting that offenders have a better appreciation of the influence of others in their behavior, including inappropriate sexual behavior. In this study, participants had free access to the community during the 18-month follow-up period and there was only one incident of reoffending.

Craig, Stringer, and Sanders (2012) evaluated a program for 14 sex offenders with intellectual disability living in the community. They completed assessments of sexual knowledge and empathy and used the QACSO. Sessions were conducted weekly for 14 months and they found significant improvements in attitudes (QACSO), victim empathy, and sexual knowledge. They followed up all participants for 6 months and six participants for 12 months. All had access to the community and so were able to commit further incidents. No further incidents of inappropriate sexual behavior were reported. Lindsay, Michie, Steptoe, Moore, and Haut (2011) conducted a treatment evaluation of 15 people who had offended against children and 15 who had offended against adults. All were living in community settings and all had unescorted access to the community throughout the study. The treatment program lasted 3 years and all participants were followed up for at least 3 years. Assessment using the QACSO demonstrated that both groups improved significantly as treatment progressed and at the 3 year follow up reoffending (official and unofficial reports) was between 20 and 25%. As the groups did not differ significantly from each other, it brings into focus the main drawback of all these evaluations. The field of sex offenders with intellectual disability is severely lacking in studies that employ an appropriate treatment control condition. Lindsay and Smith (1998) is the only meaningful comparison study, where they found that a group treated for 2 years improved significantly more than those treated for 1 year and that reoffending was significantly lower in the 2-year group. However, there were only seven participants in each group and the study was seriously underpowered.

Two final treatment studies with lengthy follow-up have been completed recently. Murphy et al. (2010) reported on 48 sex offenders with intellectual disability who had been treated for 1 year and assessed them on sexual knowledge, victim empathy, and the QACSO. They found significant improvements in sexual knowledge and attitudes consistent with sexual offending. In their follow up of 34 of these individuals for an average of 44 months, Heaton and Murphy (2013) reported continued improvements in sexual knowledge and attitudes consistent with sexual offending. In this study, 32% (11 participants) had committed another sexual incident, although only two appeared in court. Lindsay et al. (2012) reported on 156 sexual offenders with intellectual disability followed up for up to 20 years. They found that 16% of the men committed at least one further incident of inappropriate sexual behavior. They also calculated harm reduction of over 95% for the whole cohort, comparing the number of incidents 2 years prior to referral and up to 20 years after referral. In both studies, the drawback in reaching conclusions is lack of appropriate control conditions. In the Heaton and Murphy (2013) study there was no control or comparison. In the Lindsay et al. (2012) study, the comparisons were male nonsexual offenders and female offenders. Therefore, it is difficult to draw firm conclusions, but the weight of evidence would suggest that treatment for sex offenders with intellectual disability reduces offending over long follow-up periods (Lindsay & Michie, 2013).

Case Introduction

William is a 37-year-old man who was referred for treatment after conducting inappropriate sexual behavior with two females aged 17 and 23. The incidents happened over a period of 3 weeks and both occurred in the same area around the park close to where his father stayed. The first incident happened when he followed the 17-year-old female off the bus towards the local park. He had been travelling to his father's house and saw the female when on the bus. They happened to get off at the same stop and he assaulted her on the path from the road to the park. He stopped her, held her, and made an attempt to force his hand down her trousers but she shouted at him and he ran off. She did not report the incident to the police. The second incident happened 2 weeks later when he had left his father's house and saw the 23-year-old female walking across the park. He asked her if she wanted to kiss him and when she told him to go away, attempted to push her behind a large clump of bushes while trying to put his hand underneath her skirt. She pushed him off while shouting for help and, on this occasion, as he ran off he was stopped by others in the park. They called for the police who took him to the station and charged him. After some publicity for the incident, the previous victim came forward and he was charged with both offenses. William admitted to both charges and was sentenced to 3 years probation with court-ordered treatment.

History

William had one previous incident of inappropriate sexual behavior which had not been referred to the criminal justice system. Five years previously, when he was 31, he had tried to assault his then 25-year-old female cousin at a family gathering. They had both been consuming alcohol and had been sitting in the garden talking while other family members were in the house. The family members had heard her shout the words "pervert" and "stop that." When they went into the garden she said that he had tried to hold her, kissed her, and put his hand underneath her clothing and between her legs.

William had a history of mild learning disabilities. He was the youngest of three brothers and his two elder siblings did not have intellectual disability. His parents separated when he was 5 years old and while the other brothers remained with their mother, William was thought to be more difficult to manage and was fostered for some time before moving in with his grandparents. He had attended the local primary school but it was soon identified that he was falling behind in his schoolwork. He then went to the special needs school where he remained until he left. Periodically there had been behavioral problems at school, and he had been excluded on two occasions at ages 12 and 14 for fighting. On both of these occasions he had been arguing with boys of his own age and the suspensions were only for 1 day. There had also been complaints when he was around 15 years of age that he had pestered some girls in the cloakroom but there was no specific complaint of inappropriate sexual behavior. However, he had been told to refrain from spending time in the cloakroom.

On leaving school, he attended the special needs class in the local college. He then gained supported employment 2 days per week in the mail room with the local council. In his early 20s he began to consume alcohol and had his first episode of serious depression. During this time he was charged and convicted with stealing alcohol from a local shop and causing an affray when he was apprehended by the shopkeeper. William was given 6 months probation for the offense and referred to the local learning disability service. The depression was treated but he continued to consume alcohol at increasingly serious levels. During an interview in his early 20s he said that he was depressed about not being able to have a girlfriend and relationship. He again became depressed in his 30s immediately prior to the incident of inappropriate sexual behavior with his cousin. The family attributed the inappropriate sexual behavior to his low mood and he was treated in the local learning disability service.

Following his court appearance and disposal for the two sexual offenses in the local park, he was referred to the forensic learning disability service for treatment.

Assessment

Assessment was conducted by the consultant clinical psychologist and consultant psychiatrist on referral from court, prior to sentencing. The psychologist carried out a number of assessments including the WAIS 3, where William achieved an IQ of 64, in the middle of the range of mild intellectual disability. His verbal abilities were slightly stronger than his nonverbal abilities. On the Static 99 index, nonsexual violence, previous nonsexual violence, stranger victims, unrelated victims, and relationship status contributed to placing him in the range of medium to high risk for future sexual offenses. Assessment of his sexual knowledge revealed significant deficits in areas of relationships, although his knowledge of parts of the body, both male and female, was good. Assessment on the QACSO revealed that he endorsed attitudes consistent with offending in the sections on rape and attitudes to women, exhibitionism, voyeurism, dating abuse, and stalking at a rate consistent with or higher than the average for the standardization group of sex offenders with intellectual disability and well above the averages for nonsexual offenders.

During interview, William accepted that he had committed the offenses but was reluctant to acknowledge previous incidents that had been reported. For the first incident, walking from the bus to the park, he said that he did not know what had come over him. He had been coming home from work where others in the mail office had been teasing him. He said that the teasing was fairly usual and was normally about relationships and sexual behavior. It seems that he had taken this seriously because he was in a bad mood. For some days prior to the event he had been feeling very low again. However, he had not reported his low mood to anyone. In relation to the second incident, in the park, he had had an argument with his father and had been stressed and angry. He said that when he saw the woman he became sexually aroused and thought that she might be willing to have sex with him. It became clear after some further interviewing that he had been in the park for some time and it was likely that he was looking for an opportunity for social or sexual interaction.

Case conceptualization and formulation

Mild intellectual disability was identified in William from an early age. This undoubtedly compromised his ability to assimilate information throughout his life. He had some difficulties with his peers in childhood, to the extent that arguments and disputes have resulted in short periods of suspension from school. Perhaps the most important set of events contributing to the formulation are his parents' divorce and the subsequent breakup of the family. Crucially, his brothers stayed with his mother while he stayed with his grandparents. There are two possible consequences, the first of which is associated with the negative social comparison between William, who was fostered, and his normally able brothers, who stayed with his mother. The stigma associated with this may have had a lasting consequence on his self-concept and emotional regulation. The second consequence is the disruption of emotional relationships firstly with his mother and father, then with his foster parents, and then moving onto his grandparents. Disrupting, establishing, and re-establishing these emotional bonds may have been challenging developmental experiences that have contributed towards the development of William's emotional self-regulation.

In addition to the disruption and establishment of emotional relationships, it is likely that there was a breakdown of friendships with others at school. All of these difficulties are consistent with the theoretical position described earlier. William's intellectual limitations will have made it difficult for him to assimilate these experiences. Indeed, there may have been some attempt to protect him from knowledge about what was happening in the family by limiting his information, paradoxically resulting in even more confusion. These limitations and developmental experiences are precisely the difficulties referred to in the counterfeit deviance hypothesis and work by Marshall and Barbaree (1990). The adverse consequences for William appeared to have taken the form of inappropriate relationship skills and a corresponding use of alcohol in bolstering self-image and feelings of social self-competence.

In relation to the two sexual offending incidents leading to referral, both involved emotional dysregulation immediately prior to the event. For the first, he had been teased at work about lack of relationships and this had come on top of a period of days in which he had been feeling low and had increased his alcohol use. For the second incident, it became clear that he had been in the park for some time looking for an opportunity for social and sexual interaction. He was already emotionally aroused following the argument with his father and the emotional arousal affected his perception of the threat threshold presented by approaching an unknown woman with a view to sexual intercourse. William's intellectual limitations will also have reduced his ability to understand how inappropriate it is to approach strangers for sex.

Psychometric assessment revealed a level of sexual knowledge somewhat better than other men with intellectual disability, but a poor understanding of relationships. Assessment using the QACSO revealed a profile of cognitive distortions consistent with his inappropriate sexual behavior towards females. His attitudes were inappropriate in areas of sexual assault against women, exhibitionism, voyeurism, stalking, and dating abuse. His attitudes to inappropriate sexual behavior with both men and children were consistent with nonsexual offenders.

In terms of the Ward and Hudson (2000) self-regulation pathways, both the present and previous incidents conform to a man who has approach goals and a variety of self-regulation strategies. In the incident with his cousin and the incident between the bus and the park he did not seem to have actively planned the offense. With his cousin, they had both been drinking and William began to imagine that sexual interaction might be appropriate. In the bus incident he said that he had not been thinking about sexual contact but had been in low mood and upset about teasing from his workmates. The opportunity presented by the 17-year-old female walking in close proximity instigated thoughts and actions about sexual contact. The incident in the park seemed different since he was there for some time looking for an opportunity for social and sexual interaction. Therefore, in addition to having an approach goal, he had developed a simple strategy for sexual contact. Treatment should focus on emotional regulation, understanding and compensating for adverse developmental experiences, reviewing these behavioral cycles leading to offending, understanding the importance of inappropriate attitudes towards women and the extent to which they contribute to mitigation and justification of sexual offending, and some teaching on the way in which appropriate relationships are formed and maintained.

Course of treatment and assessment of progress

We conducted treatment following guidelines set out by Lindsay (2009). This framework is detailed but the author advises that the guidelines can be used flexibly, either in a closed or open treatment group for sex offenders with intellectual disability. The present authors have been running open groups for sex offenders with intellectual disability for many years, beginning in 1988 (see Lindsay et al. 2012). The format of treatment follows that outlined in several standard sex offender treatment programs and includes modules on offense disclosure, dealing with attitudes and cognitions that support inappropriate sexual behavior, problem-solving scenarios and exercises, issues related to personal physical and sexual abuse, reviewing the cycle of offending and self-regulation pathway, victim awareness and empathy, use of pornography and sexual fantasy, developing attachments and relationships, promoting lifestyle change, and preventing relapse (including issues of quality of life or the good lives model).

While those working in sex offender treatment easily recognize these modules, the important aspect of work in intellectual disability is the way in which the therapist needs to alter their approach and deliver treatment. The essential underlying principle is that treatment should be accessible, and if it is presented with complex language, cognitive concepts and procedures, it will simply not be accessible to men with intellectual disability. While this sounds a fairly straightforward process, i.e. simplifying one's approach, in our experience, observation, and practice, it is very difficult to do. We have known people who have worked for many years in the field of intellectual disability who find it difficult to ensure that clients understand the material being dealt with. Therefore, while the principles remain the same, the methods are adapted to suit the client group.

One of the most basic difficulties is that very few of the men, if any, have any motivation to attend. While motivation is not a specific treatment module, constant consideration should be given to promoting motivation to attend, change, and maintain prosocial behavior. Two broad tenets underpin treatment: firstly, dealing with personal psychological issues associated with the sex offense, such as cognitive distortions, cycle of offending, and victim awareness; and, secondly, promotion of engagement with society with subsequent exposure to prosocial influences, attachment to the conventions of society, and engagement with occupational and educational activity. The latter is crucially important and is related to the good lives model.

The good lives model (Ward & Gannon, 2006; Ward & Stewart, 2003) is a relatively recent recognition that sex offenders should be treated by introducing them to alternative sources of prosocial engagement and relationships (rather than sexual offending) as well as attending to risk. In the field of intellectual disability, quality of life has been a mainstay of services since the 1980s. Quality of life is automatically incorporated into any approach for people with intellectual disability in general, and sex offenders with intellectual disability in particular. Therefore, sessions and exercises on the development of relationships and appropriate engagement with the community have always been incorporated into treatment. In addition, a focus on quality of life is important for motivation. By developing a fulfilling life for the sex offender, the therapist has a focus for maintaining appropriate relationships and self-regulation. It is common for therapists to have sessions that emphasize how much a client has gained in treatment in terms of quality of life with discussion on how easy it is to lose these fulfilling activities through a single act of inappropriate sexual behavior. In this way, the good life model is not a recent addition to treatment for sex offenders with intellectual disability but a fundamental principle of treatment and services.

We also promote engagement with treatment through transferring to group members as much ownership of sessions as possible. One method is to allow group members themselves to develop their own group rules.

While this may feel an uncertain way to proceed, in practice group members make up sensible rules. As facilitators, the two essential rules are attendance and confidentiality. If group members do not mention these, we will add them. Exercises for promoting engagement and motivation include encouraging group members to record all of the information discussed, reviewing possible outcomes for reoffending, considering community reactions to offending, role-playing the consequences of reoffending situations, and reviewing these consequences in imagination.

Language needs to be simplified and uncluttered. As we have indicated, simplifying one's language is not a natural process and can be difficult for those unused to working with people with intellectual disability. Facilitators should use short sentences that contain a single concept and constantly monitor their own language for its linguistic and syntactical complexity. It is a good technique to ask clients to review and summarize previous sections of a session in order to assess their understanding and retention of information. It is better to avoid didactic explanations and employ inductive methods that support and encourage clients to develop information for themselves. This Socratic dialogue allows the therapist to develop a series of questions that will lead clients to the appropriate information. An important caution is that people with intellectual disability may expect to be told what to do see because they have had repeated experience of directed interactions. They may also be worrying about "giving the wrong answer" as a result of experience in repeated failure and negative social comparison. Therefore, facilitators should be aware of and try to avoid the temptation constantly to lead the session and provide answers and information. Allow clients to review their own evidence in the development of arguments. In this way they will gain an understanding through their own cognitive processes rather than attempting to grasp information presented by someone else. One significant drawback to this process is that it is much slower than providing the person with information, but facilitators can have greater confidence that clients have understood, promoting greater retention.

William responded to treatment in a way not unfamiliar to the authors. He was extremely reluctant to engage during the first weeks. He made a number of statements such as "I have learned my lesson ... the judge has told me not to do it and I won't ... I don't need your sessions because I know what to do ... I'm not doing that again and just staying in the house from now on." However, as sessions progressed he engaged with other group members who were supportive of his attendance and his difficulties. When he disclosed details of his offending he was extremely reluctant but was supported by other group members with statements such as "we found it difficult ... it's always hard when you're talking about what you did ... you may as well get it over with."

Other group members directly challenged his attitudes towards women, which were found to be extremely problematic during assessment. Open groups for sex offender treatment provide opportunities for more experienced group members on the one hand to support new members with difficulties they have during the initial weeks and months and on the other to challenge directly their attitudes and behavior towards victims and themselves. These sessions are conducted repeatedly through role-play, rehearsal in imagination, and problem-solving scenarios (Lindsay, 2009). Over the course of treatment we included modules of victim empathy, dealing with personal abuse and adversity in childhood, developing and maintaining appropriate relationships, and maintaining occupational placements.

Complicating factors (including medical management)

One difficult issue for William was the link between alcohol and mood. His understanding was that arguments, particularly those with his father, led to his depression, and his depression resulted in his drinking. Both we and the psychiatrist working with the service felt that his alcohol use and low mood were related, in that one would lead to the other and vice versa. These in turn lead to disruption of his relationships. This was difficult to deal with in detail during group sessions because other group members became disengaged with the entirely personal nature of these discussions. They were happy to discuss the importance of alcohol control in relation to sexual offending but less interested in the specifics of William's low mood. Therefore, facilitators conducted some individual sessions as preparatory work for dealing with these issues in a group. In this way William became clearer about the importance of avoiding excessive alcohol intake in order to control his mood and help with his relationships.

Review of progress

William was assessed on the QACSO on two occasions prior to beginning group sessions and regularly throughout the treatment, which lasted 3 years. He was also assessed on four occasions up to 3 years after treatment. Because there were a number of assessments throughout his contact with services, we have averaged the pretreatment scores, the scores on each year of treatment and the four follow-up results. The repeated measures can be seen in Table 8.1. As will be remembered, his attitudes towards offenses with children and offenses with men were consistent with those

Table 8.1   William's Responses on the QACSO during the Course of Treatment and Follow-up

QACSO section	Pretreat	Year 1	Year 2	Year 3	FU1	FU2	FU3	FU4
Rape	7.5	0.25	3	2	2	1	1	2
Exhibitionism	6	1	0.5	0.5	1	1	1	1
Voyeurism	6.5	2	0.5	0.5	2	1	2	1
Dating abuse	6	1	3	0.5	1	0	0	0
Stalking	7.5	0.25	0.5	1	1	1	1	0

of nonoffenders, they did not change throughout treatment and are therefore not reported in the table. Only those sections of the QACSO in which he demonstrated problematic attitudes are inserted.

The QACSO has standardization norms for sex offenders with intellectual disability in all sections. William's responses showed problematic attitudes in these sections. At the pretreatment stage, his average score was above the average for the standardization group of sexual offenders with intellectual disability. On all scales, the results were at least one standard deviation above the mean for nonsexual offenders with intellectual disability and on the rape, exhibitionism, dating abuse, and stalking scales he was two standard deviations above the mean for nonsexual offenders. Therefore, on these sections, his attitudes were assessed as being particularly problematic. On the social desirability scale he had a score of five, which is a maximum.

Over the course of treatment, his opinions became more socialized. This is true for all of the scales in which he had previously shown a high number of attitudes consistent with sexual offending. The items that were last to respond to treatment were in the stalking scale. Indeed, it became apparent during treatment that following women had been a more common cycle of behavior for him than had been previously indicated. Therefore, it seems that the sexual assault between the bus and the park may have been an extension of this behavioral script.

Follow-up

These improvements maintained throughout all the follow-up assessments. There were setbacks from time to time because of his alcohol use. In the second year of treatment, he went through a phase of abusing alcohol for a while and, while this did not result in any offending, he did become more oppositional and argumentative. This was reflected in one of the assessments where his attitudes became generally confrontational and as a result he endorsed a number of attitudes suggesting that he was becoming antagonistic towards women (a slight rise in average scores in Table 8.1 in Year 2).

Because learning disability services are relatively well coordinated in the UK, it is usually possible to follow up offenders with intellectual disability over lengthy periods of time. Many have a care coordinator and most will be reviewed at some point at least every 3 to 12 months by a clinical social work team. Therefore, facilitators will remain aware of the progress of most clients. William continued to live with his father and managed to control his drinking throughout the follow-up period. He did have sessions on two occasions with the forensic intellectual disability team aimed at reviewing and controlling his alcohol intake. Because of these various arrangements, we remained well aware of his progress and there was no reoffending or inappropriate sexual behavior throughout treatment or follow-up period.

There were two periods when those working with him noticed that his mood was deteriorating. On these occasions, the consultant psychiatrist reviewed and treated him. Following his appearance in court, he lost his supported employment in the council offices but during treatment he was accepted for a special-needs course in college and continued with the course for 3 years. After he finished college, he worked for a year in a horticultural placement and remained in the placement for 2 days a week thereafter. We continue to monitor him through attendance at clinics and invitations to alcohol awareness sessions.

Recommendations to Clinicians and Students

- Treatment for inappropriate sexual behavior in men with intellectual disability requires considerable adaptation so that it can be accessible and meaningful. Training is required to understand the way in which treatment should be adapted. There are a number of publications that can assist program developers to organize treatment relevant to people with intellectual disability (e.g., Lindsay, 2009).
- There are specific theoretical considerations that incorporate the alternative developmental experiences of people with intellectual disability. The principle theoretical position that has been developed for men with intellectual disability is the counterfeit deviance hypothesis (see Lindsay & Michie, in press).

- Quality of life and the good lives model have been germane to work with people with intellectual disability for decades, and this has extended to sex offenders with intellectual disability as a natural process.
- Important pretreatment considerations for facilitators include accessibility, use of language, ownership, and motivation. This is particularly relevant to the skills and considerations required for facilitators of treatment programs for this client group.
- There are specific assessments for sex offenders with intellectual disability, and these require alternative methods of administration. Some of these assessments have been illustrated in the current chapter and the primary consideration for the assessor is that few if any of the offenders will have well developed literacy skills.
- There are a number of studies showing treatment effectiveness but they lack appropriate experimental control.

References

Craig, L. A., Stringer, I., & Moss, T. (2006). Treating sexual offenders with learning disabilities in the community. *International Journal of Offender Therapy & Comparative Criminology, 50*, 111–122.

Craig, L. A., Stringer, I., & Sanders, C. E. (2012). Treating sex offenders with intellectual limitations in the community. *The British Journal of Forensic Practice, 14*, 5–20.

Emerson, E., & Halpin, S. (2013). Antisocial behaviour and police contact among 13–15 year English adolescents with and without mild/moderate intellectual disability. *Journal of Applied Research in Intellectual Disabilities, 26*, 362–369.

Ford, H., Rose, J., & Thrift, S. (2009). An evaluation of the applicability of the self-regulation model to sexual offenders with intellectual disabilities. *Journal of Forensic Psychiatry and Psychology, 20*, 440–457.

Griffiths, D., Hingsburger, D., Hoath, J., & Ioannou, S. (2013). Counterfeit deviance revisited. *Journal of Applied Research in Intellectual Disabilities, 26*, 471–480.

Griffiths, D., Hingsburger, D., & Quinsey, D. (1989). *Changing Inappropriate Sexual Behavior: A Community-Based Approach for Persons with Developmental Disabilities.* Baltimore: Paul H Brookes.

Hall, G. C. N., & Hirschman, R. (1992). Sexual aggression against children: A conceptual perspective of etiology. *Criminal Justice and Behaviour, 19*, 8–23.

Heaton, K., & Murphy, G. (2013). Men with intellectual disabilities who have attended sex offender treatment groups: A follow up. *Journal of Applied Research in Intellectual Disabilities, 26*, 489–500.

Hingsburger, D., Griffiths, D., & Quinsey, V. (1991). Detecting counterfeit deviance: Differentiating sexual deviance from sexual inappropriateness. *Habilitation Mental Health Care Newsletter, 10,* 51–54.

Keeling, J. A., & Rose, J. L. (2005). Relapse prevention with intellectually disabled sex offenders. *Sexual Abuse: A Journal of Research & Treatment, 17,* 407–423.

Langdon, P. E., Maxted, H., & Murphy, G. H. (2007). An exploratory evaluation of the Ward and Hudson offending pathways model with sex offenders who have intellectual disabilities. *Journal of Intellectual & Developmental Disabilities, 32,* 94–105.

Lindsay, W. R. (2009). *The treatment of sex offenders with developmental disabilities. A practice workbook.* Chichester. UK: Wiley-Blackwell.

Lindsay, W. R. (2013). Criminal behavior, offending and pathways into forensic intellectual disability services. In R. Hastings & J. Rojahn (Eds.) *Challenging behavior* (pp. 105–142). Amsterdam, Netherlands: Elsevier.

Lindsay, W. R., Marshall, I., Neilson, C. Q., Quinn, K., & Smith, A. H. W. (1998b). The treatment of men with a learning disability convicted of exhibitionism. *Research on Developmental Disabilities, 19,* 295–316.

Lindsay, W. R., & Michie, A. M. (2013) Individuals with developmental delay and problematic sexual behaviors. *Current Psychiatry Reports, 15,* 350–356.

Lindsay, W. R., & Michie, A. M. (in press) Theoretical approaches for sex offenders with intellectual and developmental disabilities. In A. Beech & T. Ward (Eds.), *Theoretical approaches for sex offenders.* Chichester, UK: Wiley-Blackwell.

Lindsay, W. R., Michie, A. M., Steptoe, L., Moore, F., & Haut, F. (2011). Comparing offenders against women and offenders against children on treatment outcome for offenders with intellectual disability. *Journal of Applied Research in Intellectual Disability, 24,* 361–369.

Lindsay, W. R., Neilson, C. Q., Morrison, F., & Smith, A. H. W. (1998a). The treatment of six men with a learning disability convicted of sex offences with children. *British Journal of Clinical Psychology, 37,* 83–98.

Lindsay, W. R., Olley, S., Jack, C., Morrison, F., & Smith, A. H. W. (1998c). The treatment of two stalkers with intellectual disabilities using a cognitive approach. *Journal of Applied Research in Intellectual Disabilities, 11,* 333–344.

Lindsay, W. R., & Smith, A. H. W. (1998). Responses to treatment for sex offenders with intellectual disability: A comparison of men with 1 and 2 year probation sentences. *Journal of Intellectual Disability Research, 42,* 346–353.

Lindsay, W. R., Steptoe, L., & Beech A. R. (2008). The Ward and Hudson pathways model of the sexual offence process applied to offenders with intellectual disability. *Sexual Abuse: A Journal of Research and Treatment, 20,* 379–392.

Lindsay, W. R., Steptoe, L., & Haut, F. (2012). The sexual and physical abuse histories of offenders with intellectual disability. *Journal of Intellectual Disability Research, 56,* 326–331.

Lindsay, W. R., Whitefield, E., & Carson, D. (2007). An assessment for attitudes consistent with sexual offending for use with offenders with intellectual disability. *Legal & Criminological Psychology, 12*, 55–68.

Lockhart, K., Guerin, S., Shanahan, S., & Coyle, K. (2010). Expanding the test of counterfeit deviance: Are sexual knowledge, experience, and needs a factor in the sexualised challenging behaviour of adults with intellectual disability? *Research in Developmental Disabilities, 31*(1), 117–130.

Marshall, W. L., & Barbaree, H. E. (1990). An integrated theory of sexual offending. In W. L. Marshall, D. R. Laws, & H. E. Barbaree (Eds.), *Handbook of sexual assault: Issues, theories and treatment of the offender* (pp. 257–275). New York: Plenum Press.

McGrath, R. J., Livingston, J. A., and Falk, G. (2007). Community management of sex offenders with intellectual disability: Characteristics, services and outcome of a Statewide program. *Intellectual and Developmental Disabilities, 45*, 391–398.

Michie, A. M., Lindsay, W. R., Martin, V., & Grieve, A. (2006). A test of counterfeit deviance: A comparison of sexual knowledge in groups of sex offenders with intellectual disability and controls. *Sexual Abuse: A Journal of Research & Treatment, 18*, 271–279.

Murphy, G. H., Sinclair, N., Hays, S. J., et al. (SOTSEC-ID) (2010) Effectiveness of group cognitive-behavioural treatment for men with intellectual disabilities at risk of sexual offending. *Journal of Applied Research in Intellectual Disabilities, 6*, 537–555.

Novaco, R. W., & Taylor, J. L. (2008). Anger and assaultiveness of male forensic patients with developmental disabilities: Links to volatile parents. *Aggressive Behaviour, 34*, 380–393.

Rose, J., Rose, D., Hawkins, C., & Anderson, C. (2012). Sex offender treatment group for men with intellectual disabilities in community settings. *Journal of Forensic Practice, 14*, 21–28.

Talbot, T. J., & Langdon, P. E. (2006). A revised sexual knowledge assessment tool for people with intellectual disabilities. *Journal of Intellectual Disability Research, 50*, 523–531.

Ward, T., & Gannon, T. A. (2006). Rehabilitation, etiology and self-regulation: The comprehensive good lives model of treatment for sexual offenders. *Aggression & Violent Behaviour, 11*, 214–223.

Ward, T., & Hudson, S. M. (2000). A self-regulation model of the relapse prevention process. In D. R. Laws, S. M. Hudson, & T. Ward (Eds.), *Remaking relapse prevention with sex offenders: A source book* (pp. 79–101). Thousand Oaks, CA: Sage.

Ward, T., & Stewart, C. A. (2003). The treatment of sex offenders: Risk management and good lives. *Professional Psychology, Research & Practice, 34*, 353–360.

9

Working with Non-Contact (Offline) Sexual Offenders

Karen Thorne

Theoretical and Research Basis for Treatment

This chapter explores the challenges of assessing and treating noncontact sexual offenders, using the case of Colin,[1] to highlight the issues faced with this complex group of offenders. It discusses treatment work undertaken over a 5-year period to address risk of sexual offending.

The three most common offline, noncontact sexual offenses are exhibitionism, voyeurism, and telephone scatologia. The assessment and treatment of noncontact sexual interests is a relatively unstudied area, and most of the existing research is over 20 years old. But noncontact sexual offenses, particularly exhibitionism, have some of the highest recidivism rates of all sexual offenses (Firestone, Kingston, Wexler, & Bradford, 2006), suggesting that they are more than just nuisance behaviors.

Within criminal justice (Abel, Becker, Cunningham-Rathner, Mittelman, & Rouleau, 1988), clinical (Bradford, Boulet, & Pawlak, 1992), and general population samples (Långström & Seto, 2006; Templeman & Stinnett, 1991) voyeuristic and exhibitionistic acts are among the most common sexual offenses observed. Further, research (Abel et al., 1988; Bradford et al., 1992; Fedora et al., 1992; Freund, Seto, & Kuban, 1997) has found considerable overlap of exhibitionism and voyeurism within criminal justice and clinical samples, a finding which also emerged in a national survey of the Swedish population (Långström & Seto, 2006).

Sex Offender Treatment: A Case Study Approach to Issues and Interventions,
First Edition. Edited by Daniel T. Wilcox, Tanya Garrett, and Leigh Harkins.
© 2015 John Wiley & Sons, Ltd. Published 2015 by John Wiley & Sons, Ltd.

This suggests the overlap between different types of noncontact interests is not simply explained by sampling bias. Research has also found that they can move from one pattern of offending to another, such as from noncontact to contact, or adult to child victims (Abel et al., 1988). Thus, there is a high degree of crossover among sex offenders with noncontact interests.

The *Diagnostic and Statistical Manual of Mental Disorders* (5th ed.; *DSM-5*; American Psychiatric Association, 2013) defines exhibitionism and voyeurism respectively as follows: "Over a period of at least 6 months, recurrent, intense sexually arousing fantasies and sexual urges or behaviors" involving "exposing one's genitals to an unsuspecting stranger" and "the act of observing an unsuspecting person who is naked, in the process of disrobing or engaging in sexual activity." Where individuals have acted on these sexual urges with nonconsenting persons, or the interest causes significant distress or impairment for the individual, a diagnosis of exhibitionistic or voyeuristic disorder is possible. These definitions identify a commonality of experience for the affected individuals, who report intense and recurrent fantasies and urges to engage in exhibitionism or voyeurism (Gebhard, Gagnon, Pomeroy, & Christianson, 1965; Grant, 2005; Langevin et al., 1979). But some authors (Mann, Ainsworth, Al-Attar, & Davies, 2008; Morin & Levenson, 2008) have suggested that criteria such as these do not adequately cover the range and types of behaviors observed in offending populations who would not necessarily meet the diagnostic criteria in *DSM-5*. For example, an interest in watching others toileting would not meet the criteria for voyeuristic disorder. Therefore, it is important not to rely entirely on a DSM diagnosis to provide information about a client's sexual interests.

Långström (2010) argues that it is likely that those whose paraphilic interests are acted out through offline noncontact sexual offenses will have additional risk factors for sexual offending, separate from the paraphilic interest itself. Research (Långström & Seto, 2006) has suggested that, within a representative national Swedish sample, exhibitionism and voyeurism are positively associated with being male, having more psychological problems, low satisfaction with life, alcohol and drug use, greater interest in actual sexual activity (including higher numbers of sexual partners), greater ability to be sexually aroused, higher frequency of masturbation and pornography use, and greater likelihood of a same-sex partner. These findings suggest that alongside the paraphilic interest, high levels of hypersexuality are observed in those with noncontact interests, indicating that treatment might usefully focus on addressing these factors in order to reduce risk of reoffending. Research also suggests (Kafka &

Hennen, 1999) that exhibitionists and voyeurs may be generally hypersexual in that they exhibit high sexual appetite, sexual preoccupation, and repeated engagement in sexual behaviors.

There are differing hypotheses about the drivers of noncontact sexual interests and a number of explanations have been proposed. Individuals with noncontact interests frequently describe urges to engage in sexual behaviors even though they know the behavior to be self-destructive and have negative consequences (Abouesh & Clayton, 1999; Adams & Robinson, 2001; Goodman, 1997, 2001). Indeed, many noncontact offenders report persistent thoughts of acting in a voyeuristic or exhibitionist way, and find those thoughts sexually exciting. So, the problem can be explained using a sexual addictions model (Grant, 2005; O'Keefe et al., 2009; Stroebel et al., 2010) or viewed as a manifestation of obsessive compulsive disorder (Abouesh & Clayton, 1999).

Others have proposed physiological explanations. Kafka (1997) proposes that noncontact interests may be explained by low levels of neurotransmitters, such as serotonin (5HT), which have been associated with sexual and violent offending (for a review see Raine, 1993). Kafka suggests this could possibly account for the difficulty in inhibiting sexual behavior of voyeurs and exhibitionists. This explanation is clinically useful because it suggests a clear treatment pathway. Hormonal treatment shows encouraging results (Lösel & Schmucker, 2005; Schmucker & Lösel, 2008) although research specifically investigating the impact of hormonal treatment with noncontact offenders is limited. The use of selective serotonin reuptake inhibitors (SSRIs) has proven effective in reducing deviant arousal and urges, and in mitigating sexual impulsivity in paraphilic populations (Abouesh & Clayton, 1999; Adi et al., 2002; Greenberg & Bradford, 1997). Kafka and Prentky (1992) found statistically significant results in hypersexual symptoms in men with paraphilias and paraphilic-related disorders, including noncontact interest when SSRIs were used to treat them. However, biological explanations do not account for all noncontact offending. Morin and Levenson point out that "sexual offending is not totally or even primarily physiologically driven for most men and that hormone treatment in the absence of cognitive behavioral treatment is likely to be ineffective" (2008, p. 97). In practice, biological treatments might, therefore, be considered alongside cognitive behavioral treatment when the primary driver for noncontact sexual offending is deviant sexual preference.

Drawing on social learning and conditioning theories, some authors (Laws & Marshall, 1990; McGuire, Carlisle, & Young, 1965; Swindell et al., 2011) argue that noncontact sexual interests are acquired through a conditioned learning process. Voyeurs and exhibitionists frequently report early experiences by which they are exposed to seeing someone undressed or naked. Laws and Marshall (1990) argued that, as with all sexual interests, noncontact interests are learnt through repeated associations between stimuli and reinforced through masturbation, leading to high sexual arousal to the stimulus. These explanations suggest that individuals will obtain paraphilic sexual arousal through undetected illegal behaviors if opportunities for normal sexual interests are disrupted. Maletzky (1997) provides a review of a range of behavioral techniques, such as ammonia aversion therapy, masturbatory reconditioning, and covert sensitization, that could be used to treat noncontact offenders.

Another explanation of noncontact sexual offending is courtship disorder theory (Freund 1990). Freund conceptualized noncontact sexual offenses as relating to problems in the courtship process. According to this theory, voyeurism is a distortion in the partner selection phase. Exhibitionism and telephone scatologia are distortions of the "interacting with partner" phase of courtship. The few empirical investigations of this model have mixed results (Freund & Seto, 1998; Lang, Langevin, Checkley, & Pugh, 1987).

Some explanations of noncontact interests highlight the fact that individuals may have problems in a number of areas of functioning that make it difficult for them to have conventional sexual relationships (McGuire et al., 1965; Ward & Siegert, 2002). Deviant interests may increase by weakening the belief that access to appropriate sexual outlets is possible. Thus, deviant sexual interests may not be the key driver in the noncontact offending, and treatment pathways should address the other areas of problematic functioning. The majority of sexual offender treatment programs adopt a cognitive behavioral treatment model (Marshall, Anderson, & Fernandez, 1999; McGrath, Cumming, Burchard, Zeoli, & Ellerby, 2010). Cognitive behavioral programs generally aim to address deficits in offender functioning, including: improving offense responsibility, improving understanding and control of deviant arousal, cognitive restructuring, relationship skills, social skills, victim impact/empathy, relapse prevention skills, and family support (McGrath, Cumming, & Burchard, 2003). Evidence suggests that deviant arousal can be modified without any specific cognitive behavioral treatment component aimed at modifying that deviant sexual interest (Marshall, 1997), but other treatment elements are required to address these other areas of problematic functioning.

Although there is limited research specifically addressing the treatment of noncontact sexual offenders (Mann et al., 2008; Morin & Levenson, 2008) treatment approaches can be informed by the wider literature on treatment effectiveness. Some researchers (e.g., Hanson, Broom, &

Stephenson, 2004) fail to note any differences in recidivism rates between treated and untreated offenders; others have found a difference in recidivism of up to 40% (Lösel & Schmucker, 2005). The most effective treatment interventions for sexual offenders generally are matched to the risk level of the offender (e.g., higher-intensity treatment to higher-risk offenders), target criminogenic needs (i.e., potentially changeable factors that have a relationship with reoffending), and are delivered in a way which is responsive to the individuals' needs – the risk–need–responsivity principles (Andrews & Bonta, 2003). Hanson, Bourgon, Helmus, and Hodgson (2009) suggest greater treatment effectiveness when the risk–need–responsivity principles are a key feature of the treatment design and implementation uses a cognitive behavioral approach. It is, therefore, reasonable to conclude that effective treatment for noncontact interests should also be based on these principles.

The literature shows that there are cognitive, behavioral, and physiological components to noncontact offending and that treatment intervention with paraphilias, including exhibitionism and voyeurism, should be incremental (Bradford, 2000; Krueger & Kaplan, 2002; Mann et al., 2008). Less restrictive interventions should be used first, with progression on to pharmacological type therapies if necessary.

Case Introduction

Colin is a 58-year-old Caucasian British male prisoner serving a life sentence for the murder of an adult male. Colin is of average intellectual ability.

Colin, and another man, committed the offense when he was 21 and serving in the army. He had no history of violence before the offense but did have an addiction to alcohol that contributed to problems functioning in many areas of life. He was released on life license on two occasions but was recalled to prison from both because of concerns about his conduct towards women. The first recall occurred 1 year after his release from prison as a result of his conviction for common assault on a 16-year-old girl. Colin only acknowledged his intention to rape the victim some time later. During this period Colin had been stealing women's underwear from washing lines and had vivid masturbatory fantasies about watching unsuspecting women voyeuristically. Three years later, Colin was again released from prison on life license. He was recalled again after 2 years because of concerns about his inappropriate sexual behavior towards a married woman with whom he had been having a sexual relationship.

When she tried to end the affair he coerced her into sexual activity by threatening to tell her husband of the affair unless she showed him her underwear. He then forced her to remove her underwear and touched her sexually. Over the 2 years he was in the community on license, Colin kept a diary with thousands of entries detailing sightings he had made of women, alongside descriptions of their underwear. It was during this period that he disclosed a longstanding interest in voyeurism.

Colin was referred for the Core Sex Offender Treatment Programme (CSOTP), a cognitive behavioral group work program offered by the National Offender Management Service (NOMS). The program's primary treatment objectives are to improve the offender's acceptance of responsibility for his offending behavior, improve victim empathy, assist in identifying risk areas, and teach him relapse prevention skills. Following CSOTP, Colin completed further cognitive behavioral treatment interventions, including the Extended Sex Offender Treatment Programme (ESOTP) to address his schemas, an accredited cognitive skills program, emotional management program, and substance misuse program. Colin also completed 18 months in a therapeutic community prison, but was removed from therapy because of difficulties in forming trusting relationships with other community members. He was transferred to a sex offender prison and, despite these difficulties with trusting relationships, he was assessed as having progressed well in addressing his sexual interests.

Presenting complaints

Colin was referred to the author by prison staff who had discovered pornographic magazines in his cell during a routine search. They also found a quantity of magazine and newspaper articles featuring paparazzi style shots of individuals who had been photographed in states of undress and photographs of women with underwear exposed. When interviewed by the author Colin presented with two specific problems: a general preoccupation with sex and a very active voyeuristic interest and inability to manage this using the strategies he had learned on CSOTP or ESOTP.

History

Colin was one of two children born to a middle-class family. His family moved frequently as a result of his father's work in military service, and he spent many of his childhood years living abroad. He describes a happy childhood and a good relationship with his parents. However, Colin was bullied at school and he spent his early years feeling socially isolated.

Colin described being curious about watching others, beginning at around the age of 10. He was clear about the onset of his paraphilic interest and provided vivid descriptions of his first memory of observing others. Having climbed a tree in his garden he observed a neighboring family using an open-air toilet and was fascinated by this. He went on to spend many hours sitting in the tree watching and waiting to see the family toileting. Colin identified several other experiences that reinforced his interest in voyeurism. At the age of 13, he observed his mother getting out of bed and caught a glimpse of her pubic region and was ashamed but curious about this. At the age of 14, he saw a friend's older sister ironing her clothes while dressed in her bra and pants. He observed her for some time and later masturbated to the image he had seen. He became obsessed with her and would pursue every opportunity to see her in a state of undress. This pattern of observing her, and others, became a pervasive feature of his life, and he became skilled at setting up opportunities to engage in voyeurism with girls and women.

A socially awkward boy, Colin found engaging with girls difficult. His interest in observing people, sexual curiosity, and difficulties in relating to girls led Colin to try to observe girls in a state of undress or see their knickers by lifting their skirt. His difficulties were compounded by several incidents when he was confronted by girls who had noted him watching them. They humiliated him and ridiculed him in front of others. Such experiences fueled a mistrust of girls, and, as time progressed, voyeurism became a way of having a relationship on his terms with limited threat of rejection or ridicule.

Colin became sophisticated in his techniques and methods for engaging in voyeurism, with all of them providing visual stimulus he could later fantasize about and masturbate to. Colin's confidence grew as he became more skilled at engaging in voyeurism without being caught and was able to meet his sexual needs this way. His high sex drive, growing sexual preoccupation, and personal confidence led to a wider pattern of sexually motivated manipulation of women. His view of women as sexual objects was reinforced by an army culture that saw men as superior and promoted an adversarial engagement with women. He would compete with other soldiers for impersonal sexual conquests. His lifestyle reinforced his difficulties in establishing reciprocally meaningful relationships with women. Colin did have a couple of short-lived relationships, although these were primarily motivated by sex. In the first relationship he was mostly interested in his partner's willingness to reveal her underwear to him. Colin reported little, if any, arousal to consenting adult intercourse and used voyeuristic or coercive fantasy during sex to maintain arousal.

Assessment

The assessment of noncontact sexual interests should capture the breadth, frequency, and severity of the interest in order to effectively target treatment (Doren, 2002; Marshall et al., 1999). Mann et al. (2008) highlight that there are no measures that have been specifically designed to assess the onset or maintenance of noncontact sexual interests. Therefore, assessment should include a clinical interview to ensure that these factors are captured. A clinical interview was undertaken with Colin and covered: breadth, frequency, and severity of the interest; hypersexuality; sexual and emotional intimacy (including attachment); the content of sexual fantasy; beliefs about the deviance; sexual self-esteem; impact on relations and social functioning; and lifestyle and environment.

In the general population, exhibitionism and voyeurism have a high rate of co-occurrence (Långström & Seto, 2006). Researchers (Abel & Rouleau, 1990; Gebhard et al., 1965; Price Kafka, Commons, Gutheil, & Simpson, 2002) agree that in clinical samples, noncontact offenses are seldom observed as solitary disorders. The Multiphasic Sex Inventory (Nichols & Molinder, 1984) was used to support the assessment of Colin's noncontact sexual interests and of specific concern was the presence of other paraphilic interests or hypersexuality. The Multiphasic Sex Inventory has favorable psychometric properties, and is considered comparable to, if not better than, phallometric assessment (Day, Miner, Sturgeon, & Murphy, 1989). Colin was generally open in acknowledging his paraphilic interests in voyeurism, but minimized the extent of the problem, and therefore the Multiphasic Sex Inventory was used to understand the extent and range of that interest. The results showed elevated scores in relation to rape fantasy, rape sexual assault, paraphilia fetish, and paraphilia voyeurism. The assessment confirmed the presence of multiple paraphilic interests but did not specifically support the presence of sexual obsession.

The Structured Assessment of Risk and Need (SARN; Webster et al., 2006) was used in Colin's case to analyze clinical data to identify psychological factors associated with future sexual offending. SARN assessment considers 15 dynamic risk factors in four domains: sexual interests, offense-supportive beliefs, socioaffective functioning, and self-management. The following were assessed as fully present: sexual preoccupation, other paraphilic interests, inadequacy, emotional loneliness, adversarial attitudes, and poor problem-solving. The presence of psychological risk markers in four domains resulted in Colin's treatment needs being assessed as high and this assisted in determining the amount of treatment required.

As part of the preintervention assessment process, Colin undertook a Penile Plethysmograph (PPG) assessment. The use of PPG assessments for exploration of noncontact sexual interests has received some support. Hanson and Harris (1997) said the PPG might have some applicability in assessing noncontact interests. Maletzky (1991) found modest arousal in a minority of exhibitionist offenders to the use of audio stimulus and argued that this may be more successful as it allows the individual's imagination to do its work. However, others have not supported this finding (Langevin et al., 1979). The PPG assessment used was NOMS[2] (National Offender Management Service, 2008) standardized assessment protocol that presented the Marshall auditory stimulus sets (Rockwood Psychological Services) – female adult and female child. These stimulus sets do not specifically contain material aimed at measuring noncontact interest in offenders. Colin's PPG profile indicated a clinically significant interest[3] in passive, coercive, and sexual violence against pubescent females and coercive sexual activity with adults. The assessment supported the presence of comorbid paraphilic interests but did not add anything further to our understanding of his voyeuristic interests. The PPG, as a biofeedback mechanism, did facilitate discussions with Colin about these interests and their relevance to his general offending and case formulation (Maletzky, 1997). Colin was surprised he had become aroused to the violent stimulus, as he did not feel he was mentally enjoying the material, although acknowledged he was physically aroused. His high levels of sexual preoccupation were considered to be a possible explanation for the levels of arousal seen.

Case conceptualization

The outcome of the assessment process was consistent with the evidence suggesting that noncontact sexual interests develop following early life interest in watching others or exposure to nudity (Laws & Marshall, 1990; Swindell et al., 2011). His account of the development of his interests reflects the conditioning model in action. Consistent with research (Abouesh & Clayton, 1999), Colin reported recurrent and persistent urges to engage in voyeuristic behavior, which he found sexually exciting and compulsive. Colin's core beliefs about women were a key factor in him avoiding engaging in healthy relationships with women and viewing his noncontact interests as safer and more rewarding.

All of the above factors indicated that a cognitive behavioral intervention with a behavior-modification module would be an effective treatment for Colin's voyeuristic interests and sexual preoccupation. The aim of the treatment was to reduce the frequency of the voyeurism and increase the frequency of appropriate sexual interests (Langevin, 1983). Specific treatment targets identified for Colin included: identify and manage triggers to offense related fantasy, increase arousal to healthy sexual fantasies, decrease arousal to unhealthy sexual fantasies, develop skills to help manage sexual preoccupation, and develop intimacy skills. The Healthy Sexual Functioning (HSF) program (National Offender Management Service, 2004) was recommended.

Course of treatment and assessment of progress

Treatment consisted of approximately twenty 1- to 1.5-hour sessions delivered on a weekly basis over five modules: assessment and introduction, developing a healthy sexuality, assessing and learning to manage patterns in sexual arousal, behavioral strategies for promoting healthy sexual interests, and relapse prevention. Treatment also requires offenders to complete work between sessions. Therapist discretion is exercised to determine which of the modular exercises to use with the client, depending on treatment needs and presenting issues. Therapists may also set non-manualized tasks which meet treatment goals, provided they are consistent with the aims and principles of the treatment program.

Colin agreed to attend the HSF program although ambivalence about change was noted during orientation sessions. Although Colin stated he was happy to attend any treatment that the Parole Board directed, he was angry that the Parole Board had revoked a prior decision to send him to an open prison to undertake the HSF program. As the treatment progressed Colin expressed greater understanding of the negative effects of his voyeuristic interest, more optimism about the benefits of the work, and indicated that he was motivated to achieve sustainable change. He was open about his concerns about working with a female therapist, recognizing that it was likely he would find the sessions arousing. This was discussed openly with his therapist and a process of feeding this back and taking action to manage the situation were agreed in the event that he did begin to feel aroused or if his therapist suspected this may be the case.

The first HSF module also explored the origins of Colin's voyeuristic interest. He recognized he had put a great deal of time and effort into his voyeuristic and deviant fantasies, and such thoughts were now automatic when he saw a woman. Colin said he often felt compelled to look at women voyeuristically, even when he tried not to, or wanted to stop. His difficulty in controlling this feeling of compulsion triggered an "I'm useless" schema.

Colin was initially reluctant to complete out-of-session work, and exploration with his therapist revealed a schema about needing to be perfect. If his work was not perfect, Colin experienced significant personal discomfort and would attempt to control the situation so that it would meet his high expectations or he would take action to avoid the discomfort (e.g., not complete between session work). However, as treatment progressed, Colin did complete self-monitoring sheets, schema diaries, and between-session work set by the therapist.

The second module of treatment, developing a healthy sexuality, provided factual information to help Colin reassess his beliefs about sex, which had been based on myth and wrong information. He completed exercises to identify his core beliefs and expectations of others and consider how these beliefs had affected his engagement with women. For Colin, this focused on his mistrust of women and patriarchal gender-role beliefs. Colin had a particularly strong belief that women should make noise during intercourse and if they did not then he believed he was not good at sex. This was a critical belief that promoted insecurity in his relationships with women. Colin undertook exercises to monitor and challenge his beliefs using self-talk. The work showed that Colin not only challenged his thinking about women by taking an opposing view to his beliefs but by adding real meaning to his "new thoughts" about women. Colin had a good understanding of healthy sexual thoughts although he was aware that his masturbating to nonhealthy thoughts reinforced these beliefs. By the end of the module, Colin expressed more confidence in choosing a partner and during role-plays practiced the skills he would need both to approach a woman and also deal with a rejection.

Module three helped Colin to understand the antecedents to his sexual arousal in preparation for module four, which focused on providing behavioral strategies to manage sexual arousal. Colin had good insight into triggers for his arousal but found it hard to control this arousal effectively. Treatment focused on providing two behavior-modification techniques to assist in managing his interest. Initially, Colin was taught directed masturbation techniques (Kremsdorf, Holmen, & Laws, 1980) to further develop his limited appropriate sexual interests. Colin initially reported high levels of intrusive offense related thoughts and thematic shift techniques were reinforced to help manage this. Colin still found it difficult to maintain arousal to ejaculation using healthy sexual thoughts but, equally, when experiencing intrusive offense-related thoughts did not masturbate to ejaculation. Colin's offense-related sexual interests were targeted through the use of ammonia aversion therapy (Earls & Castonguay, 1989) with the aim of reducing their positive reward. Colin preferred this technique and would use his ammonia salts regularly to stop his arousal to voyeuristic or offense related thoughts. Colin started to voice concerns about the gap that would be left in his life if he did not have voyeurism. His sense of self was constructed with voyeurism as part of his identity. Treatment therefore focused on considering the costs of continuing the interest, encouraging Colin to recognize the distinction between his sense of identity and his behavior, and to consider other prosocial ways in which he could achieve the rewards voyeurism had bought him. By the end of module five Colin no longer felt he needed to have voyeurism in his life.

Following the program, Colin made improvements in his understanding of his noncontact sexual interests, his triggers, and risky situations and how to control them. Colin reported a sense of excitement about his future and his ability to achieve change and gradually distance himself from his old identity as a voyeur. His ability to recognize warning signs and triggers to offense-related thinking was more developed than his range of coping strategies, but he was able to use these strategies to manage his risk. Colin reported lower frequency of sexual arousal and the conscious stopping of offense-related thoughts.

Although Colin found the directed masturbation technique hard to use he also reported ongoing use of the ammonia aversion technique. Colin maintained positive progress for some time but then stopped using the ammonia aversion technique and recognized he had become complacent about his need to continue with the technique because he felt his voyeuristic interests were under control. Treatment staff continued to encourage the use of the technique but there were no concerns about his conduct or the material he was accessing while not using the technique.

Complicating factors

Approximately 12 months after Colin completed the program, the treatment team were contacted by staff asking for clarification about voyeuristic sexual fantasy scripts found during another routine search of Colin's cell. Colin had described them as HSF homework to the wing staff, which they were not. In discussions with treatment staff about the scripts, Colin disclosed continuing sexual preoccupation of a voyeuristic nature. Colin also disclosed that he had had a number of intrusive urges to look down female staff's top during a group session. He had managed this risky situation by moving away from the member of staff, but acknowledged that he had struggled to manage the urges.

Bradford (2000) provides a treatment algorithm for use in pharmacological interventions. Where the paraphilia is a mild to moderate sexual deviation, such as noncontact interests, Bradford suggests treatment should commence with SSRIs. If there is insufficient benefit observed then treatment should move on to hormonal treatments, such as cyproterone acetate (CPA). Bradford suggests hormonal treatment is combined with SSRIs where the client reports both hypersexuality and sexual preoccupation. Selecting the correct treatment for those with paraphilic interests can be a matter of client choice (Mann et al., 2008) and, therefore, following discussion with Colin, he was referred for pharmacological treatment to assist in managing his hypersexuality and sexual preoccupation.

Following initial assessment by a consultant forensic psychiatrist, Colin was prescribed an SSRI to help manage his preoccupation. After initially noting some benefits from the SSRI Colin's progress leveled off and the dosage of SSRI was increased. He was later prescribed CPA.

Access and barriers to care

Although this was not an issue in the management of Colin's case, accessing services for prescribing psychopharmacological interventions to sexual offenders can be difficult for individuals requiring this specialist service. Service availability and prescribing protocols may vary between settings (e.g., custodial versus secure forensic mental health). Within the prison system, access to such a service is limited to a small national prescribing system and a regional clinic based in a prison in the East Midlands (refer to chapter 19).

Follow-up

Colin completed his HSF treatment 5 years ago but attended regular "check in" sessions with his therapist. Whilst he continued to report finding the behavior-modification techniques difficult to implement, he continued to use cognitive strategies to manage arousal. Colin has been on psychopharmacological treatments for 12 months and his compliance with them has been good. Baseline psychometric data were collected using the Sexual Compulsivity Scale (Kalichman & Rompa, 1995). Colin's scores on the Sexual Compulsivity Scale decreased progressively across the 12 month follow up period and have stabilized lower levels below baseline (see Table 9.1).

Table 9.1   Follow-up Scores on the Sexual Compulsivity Scale (up to 12 Months)

	Baseline	3-month follow-up	6-month follow-up	9-month follow-up	12-month follow-up
Sexual Compulsivity score	3.30	1.50	1.0	1.0	1.0

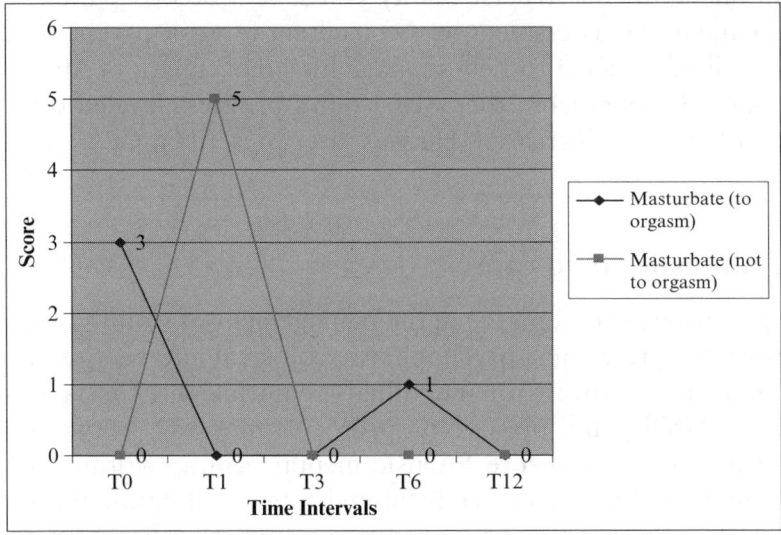

Figure 9.1   Follow-up: masturbatory practice over 12 months.

Colin also reported a reduction in the intensity and frequency of voyeuristic thoughts and improvements in impulse control in terms of his ability to discontinue masturbation to voyeuristic fantasies over a 12-month period (T0–T12, see Figure 9.1).

To date there have been no additional institutional issues with possession of voyeuristic material or with the sexualization of female staff. Colin reports that, whilst he is aware of the opportunities to look at female staff voyeuristically, he is no longer overcome by sexual urges and finds using his cognitive strategies easier to implement. Colin attends regular appointments with his offender supervisor and reports a significant reduction in the frequency of noncontact sexual thoughts. When sexual thoughts do occur, Colin uses cognitive techniques to challenge them.

Treatment implications

Colin presented with multiple paraphilic interests and limited nonoffense-related sexual arousal. The experience of working with Colin supports the view that treatment can be approached on an incremental basis with cognitive behavioral treatment interventions as the starting point for all noncontact offenders. Treatment should progress on to other interventions if sufficient benefit is not derived from cognitive behavioral treatment alone, or for offenders where paraphilic interests are a primary driver to offending. The case particularly lends weight to the effectiveness of pharmacological treatments for noncontact sexual offenders, and the combination of cognitive behavioral, behavioral, and physiological techniques to enable clients to maximize the effectiveness of each treatment approach.

Treatment also needs to recognize the role noncontact interests have in shaping an individual's identity, and reference to the literature on identity may be useful in this process. In this case, Colin's identity was constructed around his paraphilia. It is necessary to acknowledge the role this has had and to assist the offender to construct an identity that is not based on the paraphilla in order to promote change.

Colin also highlighted the importance of therapeutic relationships that encourage open discussions about treatment impact. He was embarrassed to report to staff that techniques he had learned were not working for him. When clinicians undertake treatment, it is essential to create opportunities for the client to say it is not working without feeling shame or embarrassment.

Significant shortfalls remain in our understanding of noncontact offenders, but, hopefully, Colin's case has contributed to our understanding of the effectiveness of treatment approaches for this population.

Author's Note

The content is the sole responsibility of Dr Kerensa Hocken and does not necessarily represent the views of the National Offender Management Service or Her Majesty's Prison Service.

Acknowledgements

I would like to thank Colin for allowing the use of his case details in this chapter. Thanks also go to Kerensa Hocken, Chartered and Registered

Forensic Psychologist, and Peter Wright, Prison Governor, for their helpful comments on earlier drafts of this chapter.

Endnotes

1   Colin (not his real name) provided fully informed consent for his case assessment and treatment to be used in this chapter. He has reviewed the chapter in draft form and provided useful comments, which were incorporated into the text prior to submission.
2   NOMS PPG assessment protocol is constructed in line with British Psychological Society and ATSA guidelines for the use of phallometric testing (ATSA Professional Issues Committee, 2002; The British Psychological Society, 2000).
3   A stimulus category was considered interpretable if the mean peak minus baseline response was greater than 3 mm of circumferential change. If this criterion was met, clinically significant sexual interests were identified if the client's arousal to sexual or violent assault was at or above 80% of his arousal to appropriate sexual stimuli (adult consenting) AND/OR the client's arousal to sexual or violent assault that was equivalent to 30% full erection (approximately 9mm circumferential change from baseline, NOMS PPG interpretation guidelines).

References

Abel, G. G., Becker, J. V., Cunningham-Rathner, J., Mittelman, M., & Rouleau, J.-L. (1988). Multiple paraphilic diagnoses among sex offenders. *Journal of the American Academy of Psychiatry and the Law*, 16, 153–168.

Abel, G. G., & Rouleau, J.-L. (1990). The nature and extent of sexual assault. In W. L. Marshall, D. R. Laws, & H. E. Barbaree (Eds.), *Handbook of sexual assault: Issues, theories and treatment of the offender* (pp. 9–21). New York: Plenum Press.

Abouesh, A., & Clayton, A. (1999). Compulsive voyeurism and exhibitionism: A clinical response to paroxetine. *Archives of Sexual Behaviour*, 28, 23–30.

Adams, K. M., & Robinson, D. W. (2001). Shame reduction, affect regulation, and sexual boundary development: Essential building blocks of sexual addiction treatment. *Sexual Addiction & Compulsivity*, 8, 23–44.

Adi, Y., Ashcroft, D., Browne, K., Beech, A., Fry-Smith, A., & Hyde, C. (2002). Clinical effectiveness and cost-consequences of selective serotonin reuptake inhibitors in the treatment of sex offenders. *Health Technology Assessment*, 6, 1–66.

American Psychiatric Association. (2013). *Diagnostic and statistical manual of mental disorders* (5th ed.). Washington, DC: American Psychiatric Association.

Andrews, D. A., & Bonta, J. (2003). *The psychology of criminal conduct* (3rd ed.). Cincinnati, OH: Anderson.

ATSA Professional Issues Committee. (2002, January). *Practice standards and guidelines for members of the association of for the treatment of sexual abusers.* Available from The Association for the Treatment of Sexual Abusers, 4900 S.W. Griffith Drive, Suite 274 Beaverton, Oregon 97005.

Bradford, J. M. W. (2000). The treatment of sexual deviation using a pharmacological approach. *Journal of Sex Research*, 37, 248–257.

Bradford, J. M., Boulet, J., & Pawlak, A. (1992). The paraphilias: A multiplicity of deviant behaviors. *The Canadian Journal of Psychiatry*, 37, 104–108.

Day, D. M., Miner, M. H., Sturgeon, V. H., & Murphy, J. (1989). Assessment of sexual arousal by means of physiological and self report measures. In D. R. Laws (Ed.), *Relapse prevention with sex offenders* (pp. 115–123). New York: Guilford Press.

Doren, D., (Ed.). (2002). *Evaluating sexual offenders: A manual for civil commitments and beyond.* Thousand Oaks, CA: Sage.

Earls, C. M., & Castonguay, L. G. (1989). The evaluation of olfactory aversion for a bisexual paedophile with a single case study multiple baseline design. *Behaviour Research and Therapy*, 20, 137–140.

Fedora, O., Reddon, J. R., Morrison, J. W., Fedora, S. K., Pascoe, M. D. H., & Yeudall, L. T. (1992). Sadism and other paraphilias in normal controls and aggressive and nonaggressive sex offenders. *Archives of Sexual Behaviour*, 21(1), 1–15.

Firestone, P., Kingston, D. A., Wexler, A., & Bradford, J. M. (2006). Long-term follow-up of exhibitionists: Psychological, phallometric, and offense characteristics. *Journal of the American Academy of Psychiatry and the Law*, 34(3), 349–359.

Freund, K. (1990). Courtship Disorder. In W. L. Marshall, D. R. Laws, & H. E. Barbaree (Eds.), *Handbook of sexual assault: Issues, theories and treatment of the offender* (pp. 195–206). New York: Plenum Press.

Freund, K., & Seto, M. C. (1998). Preferential rape in the theory of courtship disorder. *Archives of Sexual Behaviour*, 27(5), 433–443.

Freund, K., Seto, M. C., & Kuban, M. (1997). Frotteurism and the theory of courtship disorder. In D. R. Laws & W. T. O'Donohue (Eds.), *Sexual deviance: Theory, assessment, and treatment* (pp. 111–130). New York: Guilford Press.

Gebhard, P. H., Gagnon, J. H., Pomeroy, W. B., & Christianson, C. V. (1965). *Sex offenders: An analysis of types.* New York: Harper & Row.

Goodman, A. (1997). Sexual addiction: Diagnosis, etiology, and treatment. In J. H. Lowinson, R. B. Millman, P. Ruiz, & J. G. Langrod (Eds.), *Substance abuse: A comprehensive textbook* (3rd ed., pp. 340–354). Baltimore: Williams and Wilkins.

Goodman, A. (2001). What's in a name? Terminology for designating a syndrome of driven sexual behaviour. *Sexual Addiction & Compulsivity: The Journal of Treatment and Prevention*, 8, 191–213.

Grant, J. E. (2005). Clinical characteristics and psychiatric co-morbidity in males with exhibitionism. *Journal of Clinical Psychiatry*, 66(11), 1367–1371.

Greenberg, D. M., & Bradford, J. M. W. (1997). Treatment of paraphilic disorders: A review of the role of the selective serotonin reuptake inhibitors. *Sexual Abuse: A Journal of Research and Treatment*, 9(4), 349–360.

Hanson, R. K., Bourgon, G., Helmus, L., & Hodgson, S. (2009). The principles of effective correctional treatment also apply to sexual offenders a meta-analysis. *Criminal Justice and Behaviour*, 36(9), 865–891. DOI: 10.1177/0093854809338545.

Hanson, R. K., Broom, I., & Stephenson, M. (2004). Evaluating community sex offender treatment programs: A 12-Year follow-up of 724 offenders. *Canadian Journal of Behavioural Science*, 36(2), 85–94.

Hanson, R. K., & Harris, A. (1997). Voyeurism: Assessment and treatment. In D. R. Laws & W. O' Donohue (Eds.), *Sexual deviance: Theory, assessment and treatment* (pp. 311–331). New York: Guilford Press.

Kafka, M. P. (1997). A monoamine hypothesis for the pathophysiology of paraphilic disorders. *Archives of Sexual Behaviour*, 26, 343–358.

Kafka, M. P., & Hennen, J. (1999). The paraphilia-related disorders: An empirical investigation of non-paraphilic hypersexuality disorders in outpatient males. *Journal of Sex & Marital Therapy*, 25(4), 305–319.

Kafka, M. P., & Prentky, R. (1992). Fluoxetine treatment of non-paraphilic sexual addictions and paraphilias in men. *Journal of Clinical Psychiatry*, 53(10), 351–358.

Kalichman, S. C., & Rompa, D. (1995). Sexual sensation seeking and sexual compulsivity scales: Validity, and predicting HIV risk behaviour. *Journal of Personality Assessment*, 65(3), 586–601.

Kremsdorf, R. B., Holmen, M. L., & Laws, D. R. (1980). Orgasmic reconditioning without deviant imagery: A case report with a pedophile. *Behaviour Research and Therapy*, 18(3), 203–207.

Krueger, R. B., & Kaplan, M. S. (2002). Behavioural and psychopharmacological treatment of the paraphilic and hypersexual disorders. *Journal of Psychiatric Practice*, 8(1), 21–32.

Lang, R. A., Langevin, R., Checkley, K. L., & Pugh, G. (1987). Genital exhibitionism: Courtship disorder or narcissism? *Canadian Journal of Behavioural Science*, 19(2), 216.

Langevin, R. (1983). *Sexual strands: Understanding and treating sexual anomalies in men*. Hillsdale, NJ: Lawrence Erlbaum.

Langevin, R., Paitich, D., Ramsay, G., Anderson, C., Kamrad, J., Pope, S., et al. (1979). Experimental studies of the etiology of genital exhibitionism. *Archives of Sexual Behaviour*, 8, 307–331.

Långström, N. (2010). The DSM diagnostic criteria for exhibitionism, voyeurism, and frotteurism. *Archives of Sexual Behaviour*, 39(2), 317–324. DOI: 10.1007/10508009957774.

Långström, N., and Seto, M. C. (2006). Exhibitionistic and voyeuristic behaviour in a Swedish national population survey. *Archives of Sexual Behaviour*, 35(4), 427–435. DOI: 10.1007/s1050800690426.

Laws, D. R., & Marshall, W. L. (1990). A conditioning theory of the aetiology and maintenance of deviant sexual preferences and behaviour. In W. L. Marshall, D. R. Laws, & H. E. Barbaree (Eds.), *Handbook of sexual assault: Issues, theories and treatment of the offender* (pp. 209–227). New York: Plenum Press.

Lösel, F., & Schmucker, M. (2005). The effectiveness of treatment for sexual offenders: A comprehensive meta-analysis. *Journal of Experimental Criminology*, 1, 117–146.

Maletzky, B. M. (1991). *Treating the sexual offender*. Newbury Park, CA: Sage.

Maletzky, B. M. (1997). Exhibitionism: Assessment and treatment. In D. R. Laws & W. T. O'Donahue (Eds.), *Sexual deviance theory, assessment and treatment* (pp. 40–74). New York: Guilford Press.

Mann, R. E., Ainsworth, F., Al-Attar, Z., & Davies, M. (2008). Voyeurism: Assessment and treatment. In R. D. Laws & W. T. O'Donahue (Eds.), *Sexual deviance theory, assessment and treatment* (2nd ed., pp. 320–335). New York: Guilford Press.

Marshall, W. L. (1997). Paedophilia: Psychopathology and theory. In R. D. Laws & W. T. O'Donahue (Eds.), *Handbook of sexual deviance: Theory and application*. New York: Guilford Press.

Marshall, W. L., Anderson, D., & Fernandez, Y. (1999). *Cognitive-behavioural treatment of sexual offenders*. Chichester, UK: Wiley.

McGrath, R. J., Cumming, G. F., & Burchard, B. L. (2003). *Current practices and trends in sexual abuser management: The safer society 2002 nationwide survey*. Brandon, VT: Safer Society Foundation.

McGrath, R. J., Cumming, G. F., Burchard, B. L., Zeoli, S., & Ellerby, L. (2010). *Current practices and emerging trends in sexual abuse management: The Safer Society North American Survey*. Brandon, VT: Safer Society Press.

McGuire, R. L., Carlisle, J. M., and Young, B. J. (1965). Sexual deviations as conditioned behaviour: A hypothesis. *Behaviour Research and Therapy*, 2, 185–190.

Morin, J. W., & Levenson, J. S. (2008). Exhibitionism: Assessment and treatment. In R. D. Laws & W. T. O'Donahue (Eds.), *Sexual deviance theory, assessment and treatment* (2nd ed., 76–107). New York: Guilford Press.

National Offender Management Service. (2004). *Healthy sexual functioning programme manual*. London: Ministry of Justice.

National Offender Management Service. (2008). *PPG interpretation manual*. London: Ministry of Justice.

Nichols, H. R., & Molinder, I. (1984). *Multiphasic sex inventory manual*. Firecrest, WA: Nichols and Molinder Assessments.

O'Keefe, S. L., Beard, K. W., Stroebel, S. S., Berhie, G.,Bickham, P. J., & Robinett, S. R. (2009). Correlates of inserted object assisted sexual behaviours in women: A model for development of paraphilic and non-paraphilic urges. *Sexual Addiction & Compulsivity*, *16*, 101–130.

Price, M., Kafka, M., Commons, M. L., Gutheil, T., & Simpson, W. (2002). Telephone scatologia comorbidity with other paraphilias and paraphilia related disorders. *International Journal of Law and Psychiatry*, *25*, 37–49.

Raine, A. (1993). *The psychopathology of crime: Criminal behaviour as a clinical disorder*. San Diego, CA: Academic Press.

Schmucker, M., & Lösel, F. (2008). Does sexual offender treatment work? A systematic review of outcome evaluations. *Psicothema*, *20*, 10–19.

Stroebel, S. S., O'Keefe, S. L., Beard, K. W., Robinett, S., Kommor, M. J., & Swindell, S. (2010). Correlates of inserted object-assisted sexual behaviours in men: A model for development of paraphilic and non-paraphilic urges. *Sexual Addiction & Compulsivity*, *17*, 127–153.

Swindell, S., Stroebel, S., O'Keefe, S., Beard, K. W., Robinett, S., & Kommer, M. (2011). Correlates of exhibition like experiences in childhood and adolescence: A model for development of exhibitionism in heterosexual male. *Sexual Addiction & Compulsivity*, *18*, 135–156.

Templeman, T. L., & Stinnett, R. D. (1991). Patterns of sexual arousal and history in a "normal" sample of young men. *Archives of Sexual Behaviour*, *20*(2), 137–150.

The British Psychological Society. (2000). *Code of conduct, ethical principles and guidelines*. Available from The British Psychological Society, St Andrews House, 48 Princess Road East, Leicester LE1 7DR.

Ward, T., & Siegert, R. J. (2002). Towards a comprehensive theory of child abuse: A theory knitting perspective. *Psychology, Crime and Law*, *9*, 315–351.

Webster, S. D., Mann, R. E., Carter, A. J., Long, J., Milner, R. J., O'Brien, M., et al. (2006). Inter-rater reliability of dynamic risk assessment with sexual offenders. *Psychology, Crime & Law*, *12*, 439–452.

10

Interventions with an Internet Sexual Offender

Ethel Quayle and Elizabeth Hayes

Theoretical and Research Basis for Treatment

In 2001, Buttell and Carney published research examining treatment provider awareness of the possible impact of the Internet on the treatment of sex offenders in the United States. The majority of practitioners surveyed were unaware of any potentially negative impacts, had no policies restricting Internet use, and felt that probation and parole would be of little assistance in monitoring Internet use. While a decade on we are aware of the impact in terms of the availability of indecent images of children (IIOC), the ease of producing illegal content, and the role that the Internet might play in facilitating the sexual solicitation or grooming of children, we are still struggling to understand what the treatment needs may be and whether these offenders warrant a distinct treatment approach (de Almeida Neto et al., 2013a). Central to the debate about the assessment, treatment, and management of these "Internet offenders" is whether they belong to a separate group of sex offenders or to a group already known to us who commit contact sexual offenses against children and who are merely using a new technology to carry out their offending (Babchishin, Hanson, & Hermann, 2010).

Internet sex offenders clearly use the Internet, via a computer, mobile device, games console, smart TV, and so on, to commit a crime, and can be seen in this way as similar to other cybercrimes, such as identity theft

Sex Offender Treatment: A Case Study Approach to Issues and Interventions,
First Edition. Edited by Daniel T. Wilcox, Tanya Garrett, and Leigh Harkins.
© 2015 John Wiley & Sons, Ltd. Published 2015 by John Wiley & Sons, Ltd.

or phishing (Hunton, 2011). The term "Internet offenders" is often used to describe people whose index crime is possession of IIOC, but in fact the range of sexual crimes against children involving the Internet includes the production of images, their distribution, and online solicitation or grooming. All of these are relatively new crimes and in many jurisdictions what we have seen is a "proliferation of laws" (Adler, 2001) which, in the UK, now involves "prohibited images of children" (PIOC) which was created to tackle the demand for nonphotographic images of child sexual abuse. These were already illegal to publish or distribute (but not to possess) in the UK under the Obscene Publications Act 1959 (Antoniou, 2013). This law, therefore, refers to computer-generated child sexual abuse images, as well as manga images, private cartoons, and drawings depicting the sexual abuse of children. These categories of offending are clearly not discrete, and it is increasingly likely that all involve IIOC (including online solicitation and grooming, as seen in Briggs, Simon, and Simonsen's 2011 study).

The question of the similarity or difference of Internet offenders to existing offender groups is in debate, as it is apparent that some of those who commit Internet-related offenses will also have committed, or will go on to commit, non-Internet-related contact offenses against children. In research samples, these are often called mixed offenders (Elliott, Beech, & Mandeville-Norden, 2013; Neutze, Grundmann, Scherner, & Beier, 2012) or generalist sexual offenders (Wakeling, Howard, & Barnett, 2011). However, the distinction between these groups largely depends on a known conviction for an additional contact offense, or a known disclosure, with differences between the two. For example, Seto, Hanson, and Babchishin (2011), in a meta-analysis of studies examining histories of contact offending by online offenders, found that approximately one in eight had an officially known contact offense sexual history, but in the six studies that used self-report data one in two offenders admitted to a contact offense. For many practitioners, particularly when trying to establish the level of risk of future offending, this poses considerable challenges and has led to the suggestion that the use of polygraphs may have utility for Internet offenders and result in the disclosure of previously unknown contact offenses or risk factors for reoffending (Robilotta, Mercado, & De Gue, 2008). In studies that have used the polygraph (e.g., Bourke & Hernandez, 2009; Buschman, Wilcox, Krapohl, Oelrich, & Hackett, 2010) there were differences between the self-reported and polygraph-confirmed elicited disclosure concerning grooming behaviors and contact behaviors towards children in men whose index offense was possession of IIOC. In addition to possible underreporting, the Buschman et al.

(2010) study also indicated that these offenders overestimated the ages of the children in the images collected and underestimated the level of sexual victimization within the images.

To date, the majority of studies have used contact offenders (with no known history of offenses related to IIOC) or mixed offenders as comparison groups in relation to risk, recidivism, or across a number of largely self-reported variables. More recently, comparisons have been made between Internet offenders who have been convicted of the possession of IIOC and those convicted of online grooming or solicitation. One further challenge in relation to these groups is our lack of knowledge in many of these studies as to whether the mixed offender group committed crimes that related to the production of IIOC, which have been uploaded to the Internet or distributed through other means such as a mobile phone. Where this has happened it might be argued that these are also Internet offenses, as image production may have been in the service of the commission of further Internet crimes (Taylor & Quayle, 2003).

Differences between Internet and contact offenders have also been examined in relation to other characteristics. Elliott et al. (2013) examined the psychological profiles of Internet, contact, and mixed Internet/contact sex offenders using self-report measures, assessing: offense supportive beliefs; socio affective functioning; emotional management; and socially desirable responding. Their multivariate general linear model indicated a mixed offender profile that was more similar to the Internet offender group than the contact offender sample. The contact offender group demonstrated lower victim empathy, greater pro-offending attitudes, an externalized locus of control, more assertiveness, a diminished ability to relate to fictional characters, and greater impulsivity. The mixed offender group showed higher levels of empathic concern for victims. They also demonstrated increased personal distress and perspective-taking ability than the Internet offender group. However, the main factor that distinguished the groups related to offense-supportive attitudes and identification with fictional characters. The second factor identified included higher levels of empathic concern and poorer self-management. These results are similar to earlier findings by Webb, Craissati, and Keen (2007), where Internet offenders exhibited lower levels of psychopathy, more control over their behavior, relatively higher levels of victim empathy, and fewer cognitive distortions. Similarly, Henry, Mandeville-Norden, Hayes, and Egan (2010), using a standard psychometric screening battery, were able to group their sample of Internet offenders into apparently normal, inadequate, and deviant. The inadequate group had clear socioaffective deficits and was not high in pro-offending measures. The deviant group was characterized by poor victim empathy. A further study by Marshall, O'Brien, Marshall, Booth, and Davis (2012) reported data from a preliminary study comparing Internet offenders with contact offenders on measures of social anxiety, loneliness, and obsessive-compulsive tendencies. They found support for obsessive-compulsive disorder and loneliness as features that differentiate these offenders.

Not all comparisons have been made solely with contact offenders. Graf and Dittman (2011) have noted that there may be a variety of differential diagnoses for Internet offenders, which include voyeurism. Jung, Ennis, Choy, & Hook (2013) have noted that it is plausible that some of the social and relational deficits observed in Internet offenders may have an influence on the indirect way in which they offend, similar to what is observed in voyeurs and exhibitionists. They suggest that Internet offenders may be sexually excited by the voyeuristic nature of viewing pornography and masturbating to fantasies while at home, and engage in maladaptive beliefs that they are not physically hurting a child. Their study compared 50 Internet offenders (image only), 45 exhibitionists or voyeurs, and 101 contact offenders. Their results suggested that the three groups were largely similar in terms of personality traits, psychiatric history, intimate relationships, and sexual and cultural history. There were differences between the groups in terms of academic achievement and elementary-school behavior. All three groups were likely to have been in cohabiting relationships, but the Internet offenders had fewer biological children and were more often single at the time of the index offense. This may suggest that low rates of contact abuse by Internet offenders may relate to lack of access to children. They also suggested that Internet offenders might report less interpersonal warmth, not due to a dislike of interpersonal relationships, but a lack of social skills that make these relationships uncomfortable and anxiety provoking.

Options for assessing Internet offenders are also limited. Outside of the Internet Behaviours and Attitudes Questionnaire (IBAQ), developed in 2007 by O'Brien and Webster, and the Children and Sexual Activities (C&SA) Scale (Howitt & Sheldon, 2007), there are no measures that have been developed specifically for an Internet offending population. Some have considered use of other existing measures, Magaletta, Faust, Bickart, and McLearen (2012), using the Personality Assessment Inventory (PAI), found differences between Internet offenders, contact offenders, and a normative sample from the PAI. Their results indicated that interpersonal deficits and depression featured most prominently in the profiles of Internet offenders, who also obtained lower scores on aggression and dominance than contact offenders or the normative sample. However, Tomak et al. (2009) suggested that personality scales such as the MMPI-2 have limited utility in differentiating between these different subtypes of sex offenders.

At present there are no assessment tools developed specifically for use with Internet offenders and this has raised issues about the applicability of existing measures. Wakeling, Howard, and Barnett (2011) compared the validity of a modified version of the Risk Matrix 2000 (RM2000) with the Offender Group Reconviction Scale 3 (OGRC3) on a sample of adult males convicted of an offense of possessing, manufacturing, or sharing IIOC, with the majority having at least 1 year of proven reoffending follow-up data. The sample was made up of two groups: 304 generalist sex offenders and 690 "Internet specialists." Their results indicated that those in the very-high-risk category sexually reoffended at a greater rate than the rest of the sample, but there was little difference between the rates in the other three risk categories, or alternatively the tool was not able to distinguish differences. Internet specialists as a group seemed less criminally inclined than the generalists group and had lower general reoffending and sexual reoffending risk. For the Internet specialists, almost all sexual reoffending was Internet related, whereas for the generalists, two thirds of all sexual reoffending was Internet related but a third was non-Internet related. This preliminary work suggests that modified actuarial measures may have some predictive utility, although low reconviction rates made comparisons challenging. Webb et al. (2007), using the RM2000 and Stable 2000, also saw this as problematic. Osborn, Elliott, Middleton, and Beech (2010) used the Static-99, the RM2000, as well as a revised RM2000. This version was changed in relation to Internet offenders and removed factors relating to "stranger victims" and "non-contact offenses." In their study, none of the offenders were convicted for a new offense in the follow-up period (1.5 to 4 years), so it was not possible to look at predictive accuracy, but the authors did examine risk categorizations using the original two scales and felt that both overestimated the risk for Internet offenders.

It has been argued that there are also no evidenced-based protocols to help guide practitioners with the assessment and treatment of Internet offenders, many of whom would have been convicted of the possession of indecent images of children (also known as child pornography and child abuse material; Jung et al., 2013). However, in the UK in 2006 one such accredited national treatment program was developed (i-SOTP) by the Home Office (the then National Justice Department) in response to the growth of Internet sex offenders in the UK criminal justice system (Middleton & Hayes, 2006). The development of this program was informed by the current evidence concerning potential treatment targets and was reflected in the "model of change," which included the following treatment goals: increase motivation and reduce discrepancies between perceived prosocial values and behavior; challenge offense-supportive attitudes and behaviors; build empathic responses; reduce the use of sex as a coping strategy; develop adequate relationship, intimacy, and coping skills; and develop realistic relapse-prevention strategies, which also address the development of new prosocial lifestyle goals. Also, the program included as a target ongoing assessment in order that a participant may be moved onto the existing accredited treatment programs for contact offenders as or when identification of greater risk and need indicated this to be required. The clinical impact of the program was assessed following completion of pre- and postpsychometric assessments by 264 convicted offenders (Middleton, Mandeville-Norden, & Hayes, 2009). Their results indicated improvements in socioaffective functioning and a decrease in pro-offending attitudes. Other treatment developments in the UK, such as Inform and Inform Plus, have been developed by The Lucy Faithful Foundation, and provide a structured psycho-education program for Internet offenders and significant others such as partners (see http://www .lucyfaithfull.org.uk/inform_plus.htm). Delmonico and Griffin (2008) outline additional assessment and treatment strategies. The latter includes basic Internet management, electronic management, and medication management.

One final area that is worthy of consideration is the role of forensic evidence and how this might inform assessment and intervention with Internet offenders. One aspect of this offending, not previously seen in contact offenses against children, is that these offenses leave behind a permanent product: images or text that relate to the offense. Glasgow (2010) has argued that such digital evidence provides insights into the preferred material that is used to generate augmented sexual and interpersonal fantasies, which may evolve over time and change the types of images sought. The pattern of images accessed and viewed over time may reflect evolving sexual interests, an escalation of instrumental behavior, and indications of growing compulsivity. They also provide an accurate record of what the offender was accessing, which can be compared with self-reports. The only tool that has been developed to systematically rate the content of images is the COPINE Scale (Taylor, Holland, & Quayle, 2001), which was adapted by the UK Sentencing Advisory Panel to provide a five point scale giving an objective estimation of the level of victimization in the images collected. This was used as a "multiplier" in relation to other aspects of the offense to determine possible sentencing. The content of the images, as measured by the Sentencing Advisory Panel guidelines, has also been used by Long, Alison, and McManus (2013) to examine the relationship between IIOC possession and contact offending. Their original sample included 30 dual offenders and 30 noncontact offenders examined in relation to the quantity and types of images collected and their relationship with offending behavior. It was possible to discriminate between groups by previous conviction, access to children and the number, proportion, and type of IIOC viewed. Within the dual offenders there was a close match between the type of offense (sexual touching, penetrative abuse, and sadism) and the content of the images in their possession.

Thus, a number of factors must be taken into consideration in working with offenders who have committed Internet related offenses. In particular, attention must be given to the assessment measures selected and the content of the digital material utilized by the offender in terms of how these can inform risk assessment and treatment in specific cases.

Case Introduction

Mr. M is a 51-year-old man who was arrested 3 years ago for the possession of child abuse images (under the Civic Government [Scotland] Act 1982 Sect 52A[1]). A second charge of distribution was pled away. He was given an 18-month custodial sentence with an additional 18 months extended sentence. There was evidence that he had used a file sharing program to access images but no indication that he had distributed images or been in contact with other offenders, or children, through any Internet platforms.

Forensic analysis indicated that in excess of 3,000 still images were located on the hard drive of his computer. There was no evidence of any video files. The images included children across all ages and corresponded to all levels of the Sentencing Panel Guidelines scale (2003). It was, however, noted that the majority of the images were of girls aged approximately between 8 and 12 years of age (prepubescent), and were largely at Levels 1 and 2 of the scale (sexual posing or sexual activity between children of both genders), with 152 images at Level 5, depicting sadism or bestiality. The images had been downloaded over a period of 6 years, had been sorted into folders, but in a very rudimentary way, and it was noted that few images appeared to have been deleted. Additionally, adult pornography was also found, although it was unclear as to the quantity or how recently it had been accessed. They were all saved to the hard drive on his personal laptop and there was no evidence of images on any of the other computers in the house. There was no use of encryption or erasing software, although the laptop was password protected. It was noted that there was one previous offense dating back to 1989 for drink driving for which he received a fine and lost his license for 12 months.

Presenting complaints

Mr. M's arrest was a devastating shock for the family; although he remained in the family home until shortly before the time of sentence, albeit in the spare bedroom. On being give a custodial sentence he lost his job and for a few months he also lost contact with his family. Contact was reestablished through phone calls and letters, but on his release from prison he was not allowed to reside in the family home. This appeared to reflect both his wife's wishes and the instructions from the statutory child support agencies. However, Mr. M and his wife continued to meet on a regular basis.

After approximately 6 months he was allowed back into the family home. He was assessed as no risk to his own children, although restrictions were placed on his level of contact with his son and his friends. While anxious to gain further employment he had not been successful and he was becoming increasingly pessimistic about this. In the interim he had developed an interest in gardening and was spending a lot of time landscaping the family garden. He was not allowed unsupervised access to the Internet.

Outside of family relations, Mr. M remains socially isolated. One of the neighbors has been openly supportive to him, but Mr. M now avoids local events. He remains in the guest bedroom, although he is more hopeful about his relationship with his wife and they have been out together socially. Mrs. M will not agree to see a marriage counselor with him. She refers to his offending as a massive mistake that she believes will not be repeated. She appears to have good relationships with the social workers regarding risk management around the couple's children. Mr. M believes the children have adjusted well to his return. Mrs. M is adamant that should she find him in possession of pornography, their relationship will be over.

History

Mr. M was born and raised in the UK and has an older sister. His father died when he was 7 years old and his mother remarried when he was 8.

He had a poor relationship with his stepfather who was a bully and very controlling, and who occasionally physically abused him. His relationship with his mother is reported to be good but lacking emotional closeness, and he keeps infrequent but regular contact with her and his sister. His stepfather died 10 years ago. He successfully completed a degree in accountancy and business studies and after graduation he started work with a building society. He did moderately well in his work and earned an average salary, although less than his wife.

He met his wife when they were at university and had had one earlier relationship before this. They married 2 years after graduation and have two children: a girl of 17 years and a boy who is 15. They have a comfortable house in a middle-class area of the city. Mr. M is a regular and quite heavy drinker, but there is no evidence of dependency and he has never abused drugs. His physical and psychological health is good.

Mr. M's introduction to sex was through finding his stepfather's pornography collection when he was aged 11 to 12. He gained popularity with his friends by sharing these. He attended an all-boys secondary school and described himself as "shy," particularly around women. Apart from some very brief explorations with fellow pupils, he had no romantic or sexual experiences at school.

Mr. M felt held back by his shyness when at university and his hopes of sexual adventures did not materialize. With the exception of one occasion, when he was drunk, he has remained faithful to his wife. He continued to use pornography (commercially available magazines and DVDs) throughout his life, apart from the first few years of his marriage, and has on occasion visited strip or lap dancing clubs. He views himself as sexually active, but not unusually so, and acknowledges an interest in various types of fetishistic pornography which has never been realized in his relationship.

Assessment

Mr. M describes relationship difficulties as a primary factor in his offending. He discussed a distancing in his relationship with his wife over time. He attributes this to her tiredness and gynecological difficulties, which led to a significant reduction in their sexual activity. At the time of the offending, Mr. M had got into the pattern of going into his "study" later in the evening after his wife had gone to bed. The children would either be in their rooms or out with friends. He would have a whisky (or two) and start accessing pornography. He states that he came across indecent images of children through pursuing an interest in school uniform images.

Although he says he was initially horrified, he admits to finding the images "thrilling" but he maintains that this was more to do with the illicitness than sexual interest. He denies any arousal to the more violent images and states that he "should have deleted them." However, he acknowledges using the other pictures for masturbation, which appears to have become more frequent over time and would be daily if he was feeling stressed.

On the Risk Matrix 2000 he scored low, with no aggravating factors. His STABLE assessment (i.e., a measure of dynamic risk) score was low, 6 in total: 1 as he was only able to identify his wife as a significant other; 1 because, though not lonely, he has little social contact following arrest; 1 for sexual preoccupation (long standing pornography use and slightly elevated masturbation of two to three times per week); 1 for sex as coping (use of pornography as a mood enhancer, way of dealing with boredom, or means of emotional regulation); and 2 for deviant sexual interests.

Psychometric assessment indicated a high score for impression management. The only other elevated (although not high scores) were for emotional loneliness and external locus of control. He scored very low on the deviancy questionnaires.

Case conceptualization

As previously noted, Mr. M's earlier developmental experiences were marked by the death of his father when he was aged 7 and his mother remarrying a year later. His relationship with his mother was experienced as emotionally distant and his relationship with his stepfather was punitive and at times physically violent. His stepfather was also a user of pornography, and Mr. M gained popularity with his friends through sharing these magazines. He attended a single-sex school where he felt shy and socially uncomfortable and this continued throughout his university life. There were very few romantic or sexual relationships in his life and his wife is the only person that he has had a sustained relationship with. Throughout his life he has used pornography as an aid to fantasy and masturbation, and has occasionally used strip clubs or lap dancing when not with his wife. He acknowledges having a sexual interest in school uniforms and this is described as his route into accessing IIOC. There may be other fetishistic interests that have not been disclosed. He always masturbated as a self-soothing way of dealing with painful feelings, and this appears to have increased over time. It is likely that alcohol has also been used in a similar way. There has also been a decrease in sexual and emotional intimacy with his wife, which he attributes to her illness and general levels of tiredness. Outside of his wife's family and friends he appears to be socially isolated and keeps something of a distance between himself and his mother and sister. Going online to access pornography and IIOC was associated with alcohol and being able to create a safe space (his study) in which to commit these offenses, while feeling secure and possibly reassuring himself that what he was doing was without harm to others.

Early experiences impacted on attachment relationships and undermined his self-confidence in social relationships. Exposure to pornography in early puberty facilitated relationships with peers, but was also later used to fuel masturbatory fantasies, provide emotional relief from anxiety, and largely substitute for real-life relationships in early adulthood. While he successfully negotiated a sexual relationship with his wife, this had been impacted on by her illness and general tiredness resulting in emotional distance and sexual disengagement. In contrast to him, she was more socially outgoing, had an extensive family with whom she was close, and a more successful career. With the availability of the Internet his response to social anxieties and emotional loneliness was to seek out a private space within his home to access both legal pornography and IIOC. It is possible that his fetishistic interest in school uniforms facilitated the progression from legal to illegal content, and the false sense of security that followed his access to images at home and the disinhibition that followed from his accompanying alcohol intake.

Course of treatment and assessment of progress

Mr. M attended a prison-based sex offender program during his sentence. While he was assessed as not having a high level of treatment need, it was recommended that he take part in a community program to reinforce what he had learnt. The group that Mr. M attended was a relapse-prevention 50-hour or 20-session provision adapted from an accredited UK Home Office program. The adaptations incorporated a good lives model emphasis, a more specific focus on Internet offending and Internet safety planning, mindfulness exercises for emotional regulation, and management of disclosure issues.

The group covered the following content areas: an analysis of antecedents, behavior, and consequences of offending with a specific focus on preoffense difficulties and maladaptive coping strategies; a focus on locus of control and positive coping strategies; consideration of attitudes and beliefs and how they were formed and influenced by internal and external influences; victim awareness; use of online abuse images, strategies for controlling risky sexual thoughts, and Internet safety planning; and disclosure issues and related skills practice.

Initially, Mr. M thought the community program was unnecessary but agreed to participate. During the group sessions Mr. M was cooperative, although his level of engagement was in question, as he required prompting to contribute. As the group continued he became increasingly enthusiastic and appeared to gain a lot from the support of the other men. Mr. M articulated that he felt that the most impactful part of the program were the victim-awareness exercises, which he used to reflect on how he would be able to talk to his children about his offending.

While the view of the group facilitators largely concurred with the value of the victim awareness exercise to Mr. M, concern was expressed as to whether the group work interventions were appropriately targeted, particularly in relation to his sexual behavior and interests. His status as low risk meant that he was not assigned to a longer, more comprehensive program that would have examined these in more depth. There were concerns, given his past history, that if circumstances deteriorated, he would return to Internet pornography use and potentially reoffend by accessing IIOC. There is further discussion of these areas later in this chapter in sections on "Treatment Implications" and "Recommendations to Clinicians and Students."

Complicating factors

Mr. M had no known psychological or physical illnesses. His use of alcohol was at times excessive, but there was no suggestion of dependence. However, there were concerns that he used alcohol in a similar way to his use of the Internet and IIOC: as a form of emotional avoidance. Marshall and Marshall (2000) proposed that sex offenders use sexual behaviors as a coping mechanism when in a state of negative affect, and Howells, Day and Wright (n.d.) suggested that this is reinforced because it is effective. McCoy and Fremouw (2010) contest this, arguing that methodological limitations preclude a causal relationship between negative affect and sexual offending. In addition, Wall, Pearce, and McGuire (2011) addressed some of the methodological limitations identified (for example, by using a nonoffending comparison group) but did not find any differences between Internet offenders, contact offenders, nonsexual offenders, and nonoffenders on scales of emotional avoidance. However, there has been support from Middleton, Elliott, Mandeville-Norden, and Beech (2006) and Wetterneck, Burgess, Short, Smith, and Cervantes (2012) in terms of both deficits in intimacy skills and emotional dysregulation being elevated in Internet offenders.

Access and barriers to care

At present, Mr. M has support from his immediate family and there is some suggestion that he is managing to rebuild his relationship with his wife, albeit there is no change in their sexual relationship. As previously identified, Mrs. M has decided that she will not seek any help with this. She is currently working, while Mr. M remains unemployed and, given his unwillingness to go outside his immediate environment, socially quite isolated. Throughout his life Mr. M has used pornography as a stimulus for sexual fantasy and behavior, and his wife has now presented this as a situation that she will not tolerate. While at present he has only supervised access to the Internet, there must be concerns that, given his limited self-soothing behavior, should he feel elevated levels of stress with regard to his marital relationship or his lack of employment, he may seek to alleviate this by going online to access sexual material, and possible IIOC. Eke, Seto, and Williams' (2011) research on the histories of Internet offenders and the likelihood of future offending would suggest that with a longer period postoffense more offenders are detected for new offenses, with recidivism for contact sexual offenses predicted by criminal history, and in particular violent offense history and the age of the offender at the time of their first conviction. However, importantly, they also examined failures on conditional release, and in particular where offenders put themselves in "risky" situations, such as being alone with children. Their analysis suggests that one-quarter of the extended sample were charged with failures, which is consistent with other sex offender groups. Failures included breaches of conditions about being alone with children, accessing the Internet and contacting children and downloading IIOC, as well as other violations which were nonsexual or indicated noncompliance.

Follow-up

Mr. M is known to have, thus far, attended one relapse prevention program in order to consolidate his progress. He reported that he felt supported in this. However, the outcomes of this follow-up program are unknown.

Treatment implications of the case

Some concern was felt by the group facilitators that the program did not directly target Mr. M's sexual behavior or sexual interests, and that the function of the offending for Mr. M was not fully explored or addressed. While he seemed to gain benefit from the empathy exercises that explored the relationship between the images and sexual victimization and exploitation of children, the origins of these interests and his fascination with school uniforms and/or any other offense-related fetishistic interests to be identified was not explored in any detail. As noted above, given the low risk/need status of Mr. M, he was not assigned to a longer, more comprehensive program in which some of these needs would have been addressed. This is due to both resource issues, which necessitate resources being directed to the highest risk/need offenders, but also concerns about over-treating Internet-only offenders.

It would have been desirable for Mr. M's treatment to be informed by reference to key criminogenic factors, a comprehensive individual formulation of his risk, needs, and strengths, and a menu-based approach where the intervention is tailored to this formulation. Such an approach is manifest in some newer sex offender treatment program design (such as the Moving Forward: Making Changes programme of the Scottish Government and Scottish Prison Service, accredited in 2013*). Mr. M's area of greatest need identified on the Stable 2000 was deviant sexual interest, thus the ideal treatment approach would have addressed this.

In addition, in common with many men who are convicted of Internet-related offenses, restrictions were placed on his use of the Internet. Berlin and Sawyer (2012) have commented on the compulsive use of the Internet by these offenders and the dramatic consequences for them of being caught accessing IIOC. The loss of the Internet has a profound impact on routine activities, such as seeking employment, paying bills, and accessing travel, serving to isolate such men further and increasingly set them apart from others. Yar (2013) has suggested that these prohibitions are intended not only to facilitate the punishment and incapacitation of Internet sex offenders, but also to prohibit people deemed as high risk from accessing Internet sites and services in the first place. This is seen as a precrime preventative logic of action (Zedner, 2007). de Almeida Neto et al. (2013b) argued that restricted access to Internet-enabled computers as a condition for serving a community sentence leaves offenders with no opportunity to practice skills acquired in treatment until their sentence has expired. This often coincides with withdrawal of psychological support at a time when there may be fewer incentives for the implementation of relapse-prevention skills. Importantly, the skills acquired in therapy may not have been practiced in ways that ensure generalizability into real life scenarios. They conclude that access restrictions may provide only a temporary reduction in Internet recidivism that may be restricted to the length of the sentence.

---

*   This response was provided by the lead author, Ethel Quayle, please contact her directly if necessary – email address Ethel.Quayle@ed.ac.uk

Recommendations to Clinicians and Students

Internet sex offenders represent a heterogeneous group of men who engage in sexual offenses against children that have a lot in common with voyeurism. While we have some understanding of which men pose the greatest risk to children in the offline environment (offending history, age at first arrest, substance use, and sexual interest in children), these do not apply to many of those convicted of Internet-only offenses. The challenge is whether they have a need for treatment at all, and if they do, whether these treatment needs can be met by existing programs and alongside other sexual offenders. Jung et al. (2013) have suggested that this may not be a cost-effective approach as many, but not all, of these men would benefit more from interventions that are tailored to maintaining their inhibitions (both internal and external) to the commission of contact offenses, and focusing more on decreasing their unique characteristics of emotional loneliness, interpersonal difficulties, and emotional regulation. Certainly, the case of Mr. M highlights difficulties with emotional and sexual relationships and a reluctance to form close interpersonal bonds. The case also illustrates how the Internet affords opportunities to meet sexual and emotional needs and facilitates access to deviant material which might otherwise never have been obtained, or not without considerable effort and greater risk of detection than via the Internet with its particular features of accessibility anonymity and affordability. Given the way that the Internet and online social media dominate our lives, it is likely that intervention with such offenders will by necessity have to consider how we can support them to engage with a technology-mediated world whilst meeting their needs in ways that will not result in the commission of further offenses.

Acknowledgement

The authors would like to thank our colleague, Susan Forsyth, Senior Social Worker, Community Intervention Service, Edinburgh, for her considerable help with this chapter.

References

Adler, A. (2001). The perverse law of child pornography. *The Columbia Law Review*, 101(2), 209–273.

Antoniou, A. (2013). Possession of prohibited images of children: Three years on. *The Journal of Criminal Law, 77*, 337–353.

Babchishin, K., Hanson, R. K., & Hermann, C. A. (2010). The characteristics of online sex offenders: A meta-analysis. *Sexual Abuse: A Journal of Research and Treatment, 23*, 93–123.

Berlin, F. S., & Sawyer, D. (2012). Potential consequences of accessing child pornography over the Internet and who is accessing it. *Sexual Addiction & Compulsivity, 19*, 30–40.

Bourke, M. L., & Hernandez, A. E. (2009). The "Butner Study" redux: A report of the incidence of hands-on child victimization by child pornography offenders. *Journal of Family Violence, 24*, 183–191.

Briggs, P., Simon, W. T., & Simonsen, S. (2011). An exploratory study of Internet-initiated sexual offenses and the chat room sex offender: Has the Internet enabled a new typology of sex offender? *Sexual Abuse: A Journal of Research and Treatment, 23*(1), 72–91.

Buschman, J., Wilcox, D., Krapohl, D., Oelrich, M., & Hackett, S. (2010). Cyber-sex offender risk assessment. An explorative study. *Journal of Sexual Aggression, 16*(2), 197–209.

Buttell, F. P., & Carney, M. M. (2001). Treatment provider awareness of the possible impact of the Internet on the treatment of sex offenders: An alert to a problem. *Journal of Child Sexual Abuse, 10*(3), 117–125.

de Almeida Neto, A. C., Eyland, S., Ware, J. Galouzis, J., & Kevin, M. (2013a). Internet sexual offending: Overview of potential contributing factors and intervention strategies. *Psychiatry, Psychology & Law, 20*(2), 168–181.

de Almeida Neto, A. C., Eyland, S., Ware, J. Galouzis, J., & Kevin, M. (2013b). Internet sexual offending: Overview of potential contributing factors and intervention strategies. *Psychiatry, Psychology & Law, 20*(2), 182–187.

Delmonico, D. L., & Griffin, E. J. (2008). Online sex offending. In D. R. Laws & W. T. O'Donohue (Eds.), *Sexual deviance: Theory, assessment and treatment*. New York: Guilford Press.

Eke, A. W., Seto, M. C., & Williams, J. (2011). Examining the criminal history and future offending of child pornography offenders: An extended prospective follow-up study. *Law & Human Behavior, 35*(6), 466–478.

Elliott, I. A., Beech, A. R., & Mandeville-Norden, R. (2013). The psychological profiles of Internet, contact, and mixed Internet/contact sex offenders. *Sexual Abuse: A Journal of Research and Treatment, 25*(1), 3–20.

Glasgow, D. (2010). The potential of digital evidence to contribute to risk assessment of Internet offenders. *Journal of Sexual Aggression, 16*(1), 87–106.

Graf, M., & Dittman, V. (2011). Forensic-psychiatric treatment of Internet offenders. In D. P. Boer, R. Eher, L. A. Craig, M. H. Miner, & F. Pfäfflin (Eds.), *International perspectives on the assessment and treatment of sexual offenders: Theory, practice and research*. Chichester, UK: Wiley-Blackwell.

Henry, O., Mandeville-Norden, R., Hayes, E., & Egan, V. (2010). Do internet-based sexual offenders reduce to normal, inadequate and deviant groups? *Journal of Sexual Aggression, 16*(1), 33–46.

Howells, K., Day, A., & Wright, S. (n.d). Affect, emotions and sex offending. *Psychology Crime & Law*, 10(2), 179–195.

Howitt, D., & Sheldon, K. (2007). The role of cognitive distortions in paedophilic offending: Internet and contact offenders compared. *Psychology Crime & Law*, 13(5), 469–486.

Hunton, J. (2011). A rigorous approach to formalising the technical investigation stages of cybercrime and criminality within a UK law enforcement environment. *Digital Investigation*, 7, 105–113.

Jung, S., Ennis, L., Choy, A. L., & Hook, T. (2013). Child pornography possessors: Comparisons and contrasts with contact and non-contact offenders. *Journal of Sexual Aggression*, 19(3), 295–310.

Long, M. L., Alison, L. A., &. McManus, M. A. (2013). Child pornography and likelihood of contact abuse: A comparison between contact child sexual offenders and noncontact offenders. *Sexual Abuse: A Journal of Research and Treatment*, 25(4), 370–395.

Magaletta, P. R., Faust, E., Bickart, W., & McLearen, A. M. (2012). Exploring clinical and personality characteristics of adult male Internet-only child pornography offenders. *International Journal of Offender Therapy and comparative Criminology*, 58(2), 137–153.

Marshall, W. L., & Marshall, L. E. (2000). The origins of sexual offending. *Trauma, Violence, and Abuse*, 1(3), 250–263.

Marshall, L. E., O'Brien, M. D., Marshall, W. L., Booth, B., & Davis, A. (2012). Obsessive-Compulsive Disorder, social phobia, and loneliness in incarcerated internet child pornography offenders. *Sexual Addiction & Compulsivity*, 19(1/2), 41–52.

McCoy, K., & Fremouw, W. (2010). The relation between negative affect and sexual offending: A critical review. *Clinical Psychology Review*, 30(3), 317–325.

Middleton, D., Elliott, I. A., Mandeville-Norden, R., & Beech, A. R. (2006). An investigation into the applicability of the Ward and Siegert pathways model of child sexual abuse with Internet offenders. *Psychology, Crime & Law*, 12, 589–603.

Middleton, D., & Hayes, E. (2006). *Internet sex offender treatment programme theory manual*. London: National Offender Management Service (NOMS) Interventions Unit, Ministry of Justice.

Middleton, D., Mandeville-Norden, R., & Hayes, E. (2009). Does treatment work with Internet sex offenders? Emerging findings from the Internet Sex Offender Treatment Programme (i-SOTP). *Journal of Sexual Aggression*, 15(1), 5–19.

Neutze, J., Grundmann, D., Scherner, G., & Beier, K. M. (2012). Undetected and detected child sexual abuse and child pornography offenders. *International Journal of Law and Psychiatry*, 35, 168–175.

O'Brien, M. D., & Webster, S. D. (2007). The construction and preliminary validation of the Internet Behaviours and Attitudes Questionnaire (IBAQ). *Sex Abuse*, 19, 237–256.

Osborn, J., Elliott, I. A., Middleton, D., & Beech, A. R. (2010). The use of actuarial risk assessment measures with UK Internet child pornography offenders. *Journal of Aggression, Conflict and Peace Research*, 2, 16–24.

Robilotta, S. A., Mercado, C. C., & De Gue, S. (2008). Application of the polygraph examination in the assessment and treatment of Internet sex offenders. *Journal of Forensic Psychiatry Practice*, 8(4), 383–393.

Sentencing Panel Guidelines scale (2003). Available online from http://sentencingcouncil.judiciary.gov.uk/sentencing-guidelines.htm?T=Cases&catID=5&subject=PORNOGRAPHY&SubSubject=Making%20and%20distributing%20indecent%20photographs%20of%20a%20child.

Seto, M., Karl Hanson, R., & Babchishin, K. (2011). Contact sexual offending by men with online sexual offenses. *Sexual Abuse: A Journal Of Research & Treatment*, 23(1), 124–145.

Taylor, M. M., Holland, G. G., & Quayle, E. E. (2001). Typology of Paedophile Picture Collections. *Police Journal*, 74, 97–107.

Taylor, M., & Quayle, E. (2003). *Child pornography: An Internet crime*. Brighton, UK: Routledge.

Tomak, S., Weschler, F., Ghahramanlou-Holloway, M., Virden, T., & Nademin, M. (2009). An empirical study of the personality characteristics of Internet sex offenders. *Journal Of Sexual Aggression*, 15(2), 139–148.

Wakeling, H. C., Howard, P., & Barnett, G. (2011). Comparing the validity of the RM2000 scales and OGRS$_3$ for predicting recidivism by Internet sexual offenders. *Sexual Abuse: A Journal of Research and Treatment*, 23(1), 146–168.

Wall, G., Pearce, E., & McGuire, J. (2011). Are Internet offenders emotionally avoidant? *Psychology, Crime & Law (UK)*, 17(5), 381–401.

Webb, L., Craissati, J., & Keen, S. (2007). Characteristics of Internet child pornography: A comparison with child molesters. *Sexual Abuse: A Journal of research and Treatment*, 19, 449–465.

Wetterneck, C. T., Burgess, A. J., Short, M. B., Smith, A. H., & Cervantes, M. E. (2012). The role of sexual compulsivity, impulsivity, and experiential avoidance in internet pornography use. *Psychological Record*, 62(1), 3–17.

Yar, M. (2013). The policing of Internet sex offences: pluralised governance versus hierarchies of standing. *Policing & Society*, 23(4), 482–497.

Zedner, L. (2007). Pre-crime and post-criminology? *Theoretical Criminology*, 11(2), 261–281.

11
Women Who Sexually Offend: A Case Study

Dawn Pflugradt and Franca Cortoni

Introduction

Although awareness of female sexual offenders has increased, information related to this group remains scarce. It is clear that the research being conducted on male sexual offenders does not necessarily generalize to their female counterparts (see Cortoni & Gannon, 2011, for a review). In general, women have a much lower risk of offending and reoffending. They also diverge in their responses to custody and community supervision, likely due to the differing nature of their risk and needs (Blanchette & Brown, 2006). As a result, a *gender-informed* as opposed to a *gender-neutral* approach to the assessment and treatment of female sexual offenders is warranted.

Numerous highly publicized cases of sexual abuse committed by females have resulted in an increased demand for information in this area (Center for Sex Offender Management, 2007). Unlike the study of male sexual offenders, research on female sexual offenders is inundated with difficulties, one of which is the small sample size. For example, it is estimated that female sexual offenders comprise only 5% of the entire adult sexual offender population (Cortoni, Hanson, & Coache, 2009). As a result, clinical studies involving large numbers of female sexual offenders are currently nonexistent. Despite these limitations, women

Sex Offender Treatment: A Case Study Approach to Issues and Interventions,
First Edition. Edited by Daniel T. Wilcox, Tanya Garrett, and Leigh Harkins.
© 2015 John Wiley & Sons, Ltd. Published 2015 by John Wiley & Sons, Ltd.

convicted for sexual offenses, just like men, are in need of evidence-based assessment and treatment practices. Using a case study approach, this chapter discusses current best clinical practices with female sexual offenders.

Who Are Female Sexual Offenders?

Female sexual offenders represent a diverse group of individuals with heterogeneous treatment needs (Gannon, Rose, & Ward, 2008; Sandler & Freeman, 2007; Vandiver & Kercher, 2004). In the following section, we outline current findings regarding the sociodemographic, developmental, and offense features of female sexual offenders.

Evidence suggests that female sexual offenders generally hold few educational or vocational qualifications (Matravers, 2005; Nathan & Ward, 2001; Tardif, Auclair, Jacob, & Carpentier, 2005), have less financial resources than male sexual offenders, and generally come from low or middle socioeconomic status categories (Allen, 1991; Lewis & Stanley, 2000; Travin, Cullen, & Protter, 1990). These findings suggest that one focus of a woman's rehabilitation is her overall socioeconomic functioning (Blanchette & Brown, 2006).

Female sexual offenders appear to have adverse developmental experiences characterized by physical, sexual, or emotional abuse and neglect (Fromuth & Conn, 1997; Gannon et al., 2008; Green & Kaplan, 1994; Hislop, 2001; Lewis & Stanley, 2000; McCarty, 1986; Nathan & Ward, 2001). It is unclear, however, how such abusive experiences may lead females to sexually offend. To date, the etiological pathways that would involve an association between childhood abuse and sexual abuse perpetrated by adult females are unspecified. Consequently, while attention should be paid to these issues when assessing and treating female sexual offenders, it is important to understand that there is no evidence of a direct causal link between childhood experiences and later offending. Rather, it is likely that it is the manner in which the woman has learned to cope with her difficulties that is linked to her offending (see Blanchette & Brown, 2006, for a review).

Many authors have reported that female sexual offenders exhibit emotional dependency and passivity (Green & Kaplan, 1994; Hislop, 2001), low self-esteem (Hunter & Mathews, 1997; Mathews, Matthews, & Speltz, 1989), inadequate social skills (Hislop, 2001), and poor self-identity (Green & Kaplan, 1994; Hislop, 2001; Mathews, Matthews, & Speltz, 1989). Some research also suggests that female sexual offenders have high rates of mental health disturbances (Faller, 1995; Green & Kaplan, 1994; Miller, Turner, & Henderson, 2009; O'Connor, 1987). However, the association between mental health issues and female sexual offending is a contentious issue, since it is possible that only the most pathological female sexual offenders have traditionally been apprehended by the authorities. As the research on female sexual offenders is limited, it is currently impossible to draw valid conclusions about the true relationship between mental illness and female sexual offending (see Rousseau & Cortoni, 2010, for a review).

Likely, the most unique feature of female sexual offenders, compared to their male counterparts, is their propensity to offend in the company of a co-offender (Grayston & De Luca, 1999; Green & Kaplan, 1994; Lewis & Stanley, 2000; Matravers, 2005; Nathan & Ward, 2001; Vandiver, 2006). For example, in her comparison of solo ($n = 123$) and co-offenders ($n = 104$), Vandiver (2006) found that while 71% of the co-offending women had male co-offenders, another 21% ($n = 22$) had both male and female co-offenders, and 8% ($n = 8$) had sexually offended only in the company of other females. Females who have co-offenders may offend of their own volition alongside the co-offender, or they may offend in the context of considerable coercion and physical threats of violence (Gannon et al., 2008; Vandiver, 2006).

Women who engage in sexually offending behavior typically know their victims (Faller, 1995; Vandiver & Kercher, 2004). Further, women who specifically offend against children typically hold caregiver responsibilities towards that child (e.g., mothers, relatives, or babysitters; Faller, 1987, 1995; Lewis & Stanley, 2000; Pflugradt & Allen, 2012). Females who sexually abuse children are also likely to target younger children than their male counterparts (Faller, 1987; Rudin, Zalweski, & Bodmer-Turner, 1995). Although results vary according to studies, it appears that solo offenders tend to assault a greater proportion of males, while those with male co-offenders tend to have more female victims (e.g., Vandiver, 2006). In terms of physical force and aggression used in the commission of the offense, some researchers have argued that females are less physically aggressive than males (see Grayston & De Luca, 1999); other researchers have not supported this contention (Mathews, Hunter, & Vuz, 1997). Finally, in comparison to male offenders, female sexual offenders tend to proportionally engage in less penetration of the victim (Peter, 2009).

Types of Female Sexual Offenders and Their Offense Process

Groups of female sexual offenders have been examined in order to identify typologies or offenders who have similar offense characteristics (Mathews et al., 1989; Sandler & Freeman, 2007; Vandiver & Kercher, 2004). Whereas the identification of typologies has been helpful in some regards, it has shown limited clinical utility (Pflugradt & Allen, 2010).

Typologies have also provided limited information about the etiology of sexually offending behavior among women. Gannon and her colleagues (Gannon et al., 2008, 2013) moved away from typologies and started to delineate the offense process for female sexual offending. These authors constructed an offense chain model; the descriptive model of the offense process for female sexual offenders (DMFSO). Their model not only highlighted *how* and *why* the offense process unfolded, but how particular *patterns* of sexual offending evolved.

Gannon et al.'s (2008, 2013) model describes the lifetime sequence of contextual, behavioral, cognitive, and affective events that facilitate and maintain female sexual offending. Further, it shows that women tend to follow one of two main pathways to offending, while a few follow a third pathway. The first pathway, *directed-avoidant*, describes an offense process characterized by sexual offense avoidance and negative affect. The women in this pathway offended either out of extreme fear for their lives or because they wanted to obtain intimacy with their male co-offender. These women were often oblivious to, or passive to the early planning of child sexual abuse initiated by the male co-offender.

The second pathway, called *explicit-approach*, describes women who appeared to explicitly plan their offense in order to achieve various goals such as sexual gratification, intimacy with victim, or financial reward (i.e., prostitution-related offending). These women tended to experience positive affect such as excitement in anticipation of their offense. The third pathway, called the *implicit-disorganized* pathway, describes women who offended against either children or adults. This offense pathway appears to be characterized by little organized planning and sudden disorganized offending associated with either negative or positive affect.

In addition, this model (Gannon et al., 2008, 2013) delineates how the elements addressed in this chapter (i.e., cognition, affect, behavioral, and contextual factors) contribute to the offense process. While the initial model was validated in an independent sample (i.e., Gannon et al., 2013), it is important to note that it still requires further investigation before its clinical utility can be confirmed. Nonetheless, the model provides interesting avenues to help guide the assessment of the offense pattern of female sexual offenders.

Assessment: Risk of Recidivism

When assessing sexual offenders, evaluators are first concerned with risk of sexual recidivism. In comparison to males, female sexual offenders have much lower rates of all types of recidivism. Specifically, in their meta-analysis of the recidivism rates of 2,490 female sexual offenders over a 6.5 year follow-up period, Cortoni, Hanson, and Coache (2010) found rates of recidivism of 1.5% for new sexual offenses, 6% for new violent offenses, and 20% for any new type of offense.

Because of the low base rate of sexual recidivism among female sexual offenders, it is extremely difficult to establish empirically validated risk factors for sexual recidivism, but there exists some research that can help guide the assessment of risk of recidivism. First, as with males, a prior criminal history is indicative of a *higher* risk (in comparison to other women and not men's risk) of general or violent (nonsexual) recidivism among women (Sandler & Freeman, 2009; Vandiver, 2007). Being younger at arrest for the index sexual offense also appears related to a rearrest for new general offenses (i.e., nonsexual and nonviolent). Age, however, does not appear related to sexual recidivism among hands-on female sexual offenders (Sandler & Freeman, 2009).

To date, only one study has identified a potential predictor for sexual recidivism in women. In their study of 1,400 women in New York State, Sandler & Freeman (2009) found that the number of prior child abuse (any type) offenses was related to later sexual recidivism. This finding is unique to women. Perhaps because women tend to be the primary caregivers, they are more likely than men to come to the attention of the criminal justice system for nonsexual abuse of children. Alternatively, it could be that the sexual abuse of children, for these women, is part of a broader pattern of abuse against children. Nevertheless, it suggests that there is at least one gender-specific factor for sexual recidivism among women.

There is currently no instrument validated to assess risk of sexual recidivism among women. Male-based tools, such as the Static-99, are not validated for women as they contain risk factors that are not validated for women. Evaluators must, therefore, rely on their clinical judgment, guided and structured by the research literature when tasked to assess this type of risk among women. The extremely low base rates of sexual recidivism among women indicate that unless blatant factors are present (e.g., the woman states she will commit a new sexual offense), most women will be at a low risk of committing a new sexual offense. Her risk for violent or general recidivism, however, could potentially be higher and should be assessed independently. To assess this type of risk, consideration should be given to the use of tools validated to assess risk of general and violent (nonsexual) recidivism among female offenders, such as the Level of Supervision Inventory – Revised (Andrews & Bonta, 1995). While this tool will not inform on the risk of sexual recidivism, it will provide an overall assessment of risk and identify areas of concern related to violent recidivism.

Clinical Factors to Consider Among Female Sexual Offenders

The goals of a specialized assessment of sexual offenders are to determine the likelihood of sexual reoffending and to ascertain areas for therapeutic intervention that will reduce that risk and provide offenders with alternative models of thinking and behavior. The assessment of risk factors should be based on a thorough analysis of the woman's offending behavior, including the presence of a co-offender, and an analysis of the elements that contributed to the offense. The assessment of treatment needs should be guided by current empirical knowledge of the factors that appear related to sexual offending in women. As identified by Cortoni and Gannon (2011), clinical factors associated with female sexual offending tend to group within five broad domains: intimacy and relationship issues; cognitive processes; emotional processes; sexual dynamics; and social functioning. Within this context, relationship problems, attitudes and cognitions that support the offending behavior, the use of sex to regulate emotional states, and emotional dysregulation problems are common among female sexual offenders (Eldridge & Saradjian, 2000; Grayston & De Luca, 1999; Nathan & Ward, 2002). Sexual gratification, a desire for intimacy (with either a victim or a codefendant), and instrumental goals such as revenge or humiliation are also associated with female sexual offending (Gannon et al., 2008). Finally, because female sexual offenders, just like their male counterparts, also engage in other criminal behavior, factors such as the presence and extent of antisocial attitudes, antisocial associates, and substance abuse as a precursor to the offending behavior should also be considered (Cortoni, 2010).

These areas are well described in the literature on the assessment and treatment of female sexual offenders (see Cortoni & Gannon, 2011, and Cortoni & Gannon, 2013, for a review). To summarize, clinical assessment and treatment practices should focus on the woman's relationship and parental status, her coping patterns, and her general psychosocial functioning, including the use of substances. As the woman's developmental and family history helps set the stage for the woman's current functioning, an understanding of her background factors is also important. This information provides clues to the elements that have likely contributed to the development of the offending behavior, and sets the context from which realistic goals for the future can be established.

The development and history of sexual behavior is another important area to address. Tied to this area is the meaning and role of sex in the woman's life. Her beliefs about sexual activity, and by extension sexual abuse, may be linked to her beliefs about gender roles, sense of entitlement, or refusal to acknowledge the harm caused by the abuse. In this context, the role that sex and sexuality play in the woman's life should be examined to establish their potential motivational role in the offending behavior. In addition, a careful examination of the coping patterns of women is required to determine the role sexual activity in general and sexual abuse in particular may play in alleviating negative emotional states. The presence and extent of deviant sexual fantasies and arousal will need to be considered within this context, although it must be remembered that it is as yet unclear whether deviant arousal and fantasies among females play the same role in offending as they do for males. General sexuality research indicates that women's sexual arousal patterns are very different than those of males: while men's physiological sexual arousal actually reflects their sexual preferences, women's arousal patterns are much more fluid and tend not to demonstrate such specificity (Basson, 2002; Chivers, Rieger, Latty, & Bailey, 2004; Suschinsky, Lalumière, & Chivers, 2009). Therefore, caution is warranted not to interpret female sexual issues in the same manner as those of males.

Finally, female sexual offenders tend to hold distorted beliefs about themselves and about children, as well as deny or minimize their involvement in the abuse (Beech, Parrett, Ward, & Fisher, 2009; Gannon, Hoare, Rose, & Parrett, 2012; see Gannon & Alleyne, 2013, for a review). Pro-offending attitudes and other distorted beliefs need to be examined and their likely contribution to the offending behavior established. Core beliefs about relationships, children, and gender roles also require examination as they are likely intertwined with pro-offending attitudes (Eldridge & Saradjian, 2000).

Case Example: Michelle

Case studies are a way to apply the current knowledge base to clinical work. Through case studies, theories can be tested in a way that cannot be done through empirical large-scale studies. The following is a case study of a female sexual offender. The case study is written to demonstrate a systematic assessment process. Specifically, recidivism risk will be addressed first, treatment needs second and unique characteristics will be assessed third.

Michelle is a 31-year-old, divorced, Caucasian female, convicted for repeated sexual assault of the same child. The victim was her 9-year-old stepson who had been living with Michelle and her husband, the boy's father, since her marriage. Michelle was responsible for the boy as well as their three biological children's day-to-day care. There were no allegations and there are no indications that Michelle perpetrated any sexual assaults on any of her biological children. The abuse started with fondling and eventually involved Michelle performing oral sex on the boy and having the boy perform oral sex on her. On one occasion, Michelle attempted to place the boy's penis in her vagina, but was unsuccessful. The abuse occurred multiple times per week and lasted for approximately 6 months. The abuse came to the attention of the authorities after her victim started talking to his teacher regarding his home life. Although the victim did not provide the teacher with direct information regarding the assaults, she contacted child protection services and the victim eventually disclosed the assaults to caseworkers. When Michelle was interviewed by caseworkers and the police, she did not deny the assaults. Michelle was arrested and eventually convicted for the assaults. She received a 5-year sentence followed by 10 years of community supervision.

While incarcerated, Michelle underwent an assessment to establish her risk of recidivism and her treatment needs. During the assessment, Michelle was generally open and willing to discuss the details of the offenses. While she acknowledged the offending behavior, Michelle stated that her actions never seemed to bother her victim. She also felt that the boy benefited from the closeness inherent in the abuse. She verbalized that, to her, sex equals love and that she enjoyed showing the boy how much she loved him. Michelle was able to recognize that what she did was wrong, although she could not understand why she was sentenced to prison, since she thought that her victim did not appear to be upset or impacted by her abusive sexual acts. She was also upset about her inability to see her biological children as a result of her assaultive behaviors with her stepson.

Michelle grew up in a two-parent home. She reported that she had a sister and described her family as "not close." Her mother and father were both emotionally abusive toward Michelle and her sister. A paternal uncle also sexually assaulted Michelle when she was 11 years old. Michelle did not receive emotional support from her family when she was assaulted, and often felt that her family believed the incident was her fault. Michelle has had no contact with her sister or her parents since she left home after high school at age 18, mostly because her significant other (now ex-husband) did not get along with her parents and would not allow her to contact them. Michelle's husband was also physically abusive to her during their relationship. At the time of the offenses, Michelle was married but unhappy. She was often alone for long periods of time with her victim (stepson) and her three biological children. Her husband was a truck driver and not involved in any aspect of Michelle's and the children's life. He was also not involved in Michelle's offending behavior. During the marriage, Michelle did not work despite the fact that her husband did not make enough to support the family. As a result, Michelle and her family received government assistance and utilized community programs to assist her with food costs. Although Michelle is a high school graduate, she has no employment skills. Her work history is almost nonexistent except for a position at a local fast food restaurant when she was in high school.

Looking closer at her relationship history, it became evident that Michelle was isolated and lacked any intimate relationships. She had no friends the same age and relatively few acquaintances. Prior to her marriage, Michelle had a number of one-night stands and short-term relationships. Her only significant relationship was with her husband, which started when she was 18 and ended in divorce at the age of 31 (due to her incarceration). As previously stated, this marriage lacked both physical and emotional intimacy and her ex-husband was most often on the road. Michelle was the primary caregiver to her three biological and one stepchild. Her primary caregiver obligations, as well as her limited financial resources, further isolated Michelle and prevented her from participating in activities outside of the home. Her ability to deal with her isolation was almost nonexistent. When stressed, Michelle turned to using alcohol in excess within her home. Over time, as Michelle lacked adult interactions, she started to place her 9-year-old stepson in an adult role to meet her needs for intimacy and social interaction, leading to the eventual sexually offending behavior.

Michelle's sexual orientation is heterosexual. She never, as a child, saw adults having sex and her first voluntary sexual contact was at the age of 16 with a same-age male peer. She has never had sexual experiences with females. In terms of her sexual history, Michelle has had nine male sexual partners (exclusive of her victim), and the longest she was involved with a continuous sexual or romantic partner was with her now ex-husband. Michelle reported that sex was a way for her to show that she loved her partner as well as a way for her to feel loved. Prior to being with her ex-husband, Michelle used sex as a way to "get attention" from male peers. While married, Michelle often used sex as a way to feel close to or cared for by her husband.

Risk assessment

In order to establish an adequate estimate of risk to recidivate, an assessment needs to focus on risk for sexual recidivism as well as risk for general criminal recidivism. Research tells us that Michelle is highly unlikely to commit another sexual offense. Specifically, given the low base rates of sexual recidivism among women and the lack of other documented history of child maltreatment (as per research, the only factor that appears related to risk of sexual recidivism), Michelle's risk to commit another sexual offense is low. The next step in the assessment process would be to assess general and/or violent criminal recidivism using an instrument such as the Level of Supervision Inventory – Revised (Andrews & Bonta, 1995). Michelle does not have a prior criminal history, antisocial attitudes or associates, or a significant substance abuse history. Prior to this conviction, Michelle lived a generally prosocial lifestyle. Therefore, it would appear that her risk of general and violent recidivism is also low.

Treatment needs assessment and identification of other elements related to offending

After assessing the recidivism risk, a comprehensive assessment focuses on the clinical factors associated with Michelle's sexual offending (see the earlier discussion on the five factors or domains). It is important to note that the factors or domains often overlap in female offenders. For this reason, it is important that female sexual offender assessment and treatment services take into account the gender specificity of female sexual offending and recognize that this behavior does not occur separate from the rest of the woman's life (Cortoni & Gannon, 2011). This part of the assessment will identify areas to target in treatment in order to help Michelle deal with the issues related to her offending behavior and develop a healthier life.

Cognitive processes domain Information related to cognitive distortions among female sexual offenders is only starting to emerge. Based on the systematic review conducted by Gannon and Alleyne (2013), the following cognitive distortions appear to be prevalent in female offenders: child abuse supportive beliefs, general sexual beliefs or gender stereotypes, rape myth acceptance, and difficulties with victim empathy. Although these cognitive distortions appear similar to the distortions that have been empirically validated for male sexual offenders, they contain important differences (Gannon & Alleyne, 2013). In addition, it appears that women who offend on their own often have more offense-supportive beliefs (Gannon & Alleyne, 2013). Hence, when assessing Michelle's cognitive distortions, one must keep in mind the differences between men and women as well as the fact that Michelle perpetrated her assaults without a co-offender.

One set of cognitive distortions that particularly distinguish female from male sexual offenders is the *child abuse supportive beliefs*. These differences are apparent in our case. During the assessment, it became clear that Michelle views males as dangerous. Given Michelle's past abusive relationship dynamic with her husband, this is not surprising, as female sexual offenders typically exhibit a pattern of violent victimization at the hand of their partners (Gannon et al., 2008). As a result, Michelle found contact with her child victim much less threatening. A related cognition is the fact that Michelle viewed sexual abuse perpetrated by males (on children) as more harmful than the abuse she (as a woman) perpetrated. In fact, she viewed the abuse she perpetrated as nonharmful, and helpful in some ways. In addition, although Michelle was sexually interested in her victim, she did not and could not generalize this sexual interest to all children or to any other child. This set of cognitions suggests that Michelle was able to rationalize her abuse on her victim while being clear that, in general, sexual abuse of children (by males) is harmful. In this case, treatment would need to explore and resolve the source of this type of cognition. Another set of cognitions exhibited by Michelle was the belief that sex is a way for people to show they care about the other person. Through her sexual abuse of her victim, Michelle believed that she was demonstrating how much she cared for her stepson. Further, she interpreted his lack of resistance as evidence that he was not harmed by the abuse and that he cared for her.

It is worthwhile to note here that this latter set of cognitions appears directly related to Michelle's difficulty with victim empathy and perspective taking (Gannon & Alleyne, 2013). Michelle struggled with being able to understand how she harmed her stepson when she really cared about him and felt that she was nurturing him while the assaults were occurring. In treatment, Michelle would benefit from psychosocial education regarding the impact of sexual abuse on victims by women. This education would, in turn, help Michelle better understand how her behavior would have impacted not only her victim, but also her other children.

Sexual issues   Even though research is almost nonexistent related to paraphilic interests in women, this is an area that needs to be assessed. As previously stated, research has demonstrated that men's physiological sexual arousal actually reflects their sexual preferences, while women's arousal patterns are much more fluid and tend not to demonstrate such specificity (Chivers et al., 2004; Suschinsky, Lalumière & Chivers, 2009). In our case, there is no evidence that Michelle has any child-specific sexual interest or any other paraphilic or deviant interests. For example, she had no patterns of behavior(s) related to diagnosable paraphilias (i.e., no pattern of interest in prepubescent children, and her offending dynamics were not indicative of sadism). As stated above, she saw her child victim as being sexual but did not generalize this to all children. This indicates that Michelle's sexually abusive behavior was likely more the result of a need for intimacy and closeness than the result of a specific sexual interest in children. Within the context of treatment, it will be useful to explore how Michelle came to associate sex with a child as a means to fulfill a need for intimacy and help her develop healthier patterns to meet those needs.

Knowledge of healthy sexuality is another area that warrants intervention. The assessment revealed that Michelle was naïve regarding female sexuality in general. Assessment results indicated that Michelle would benefit from education related to general female sexuality and healthy ways to meet her sexual needs.

Emotional processes and intimacy and relationship issues   In female sexual offenders, emotional processes and intimacy and relationship issues often go hand in hand. As previously stated, Michelle was rather emotionally and socially isolated. She described being extremely lonely as she did not have friends or family in whom to confide, nor was she able to connect emotionally with her husband, partly due to the abusive relationship dynamic. This desire to connect was pervasive and had been occurring in her life for over 10 years. In fact, it was a contributing factor that led her to move in and marry her husband so quickly. The assessment clearly showed that Michelle needed to work on relationship difficulties and intimacy deficits. In addition, Michelle never fully addressed issues related to her own sexual victimization at age 11. Treatment should explore if or how this victimization may have contributed to her distorted cognitions related to her offending behavior.

Michelle also struggled with her ability to cope with her life situation (being alone, raising her children alone, etc.). The assessment indicated that Michelle became depressed and starting using alcohol (at times) to try and deal with the stress of everyday life. This dysfunctional coping strategy, coupled with the distorted cognitions identified above, led Michelle to turn to her 9-year-old stepson to meet her needs for emotional intimacy. In fact, looking closer at her case, one can see that Michelle's needs for emotional intimacy were being met by her victim prior to the actual offending. Considering how Michelle inappropriately connects sex and caring, it is perhaps not surprising that Michelle eventually progressed to sexual activity with the child.

The assessment should also take into consideration the woman's current mental health status as well as her mental health history. At the time of the assessment, Michelle exhibited depressive symptoms that appeared related to being away from her children as well as being incarcerated. These symptoms warrant therapeutic attention. Further, Michelle's description of her emotional state at the time of her offense(s) indicated that she had been suffering from a mild form of depression at that time as well. As women in general need more social support in order to deal with stressors (Rumgay, 2004), the lack of such support in Michelle's life likely contributed to this depression. To help address these issues, education regarding symptoms indicative of depression as well as education related to appropriate treatment and monitoring would be helpful in this case. In addition, Michelle's alcohol use and her inability to appropriately cope with stress were additional areas that warranted treatment.

Social functioning   Michelle's main social interactional pattern consisted of her caregiver role to her victim and her other children. Despite her limited interaction with adults, she did not appear to lack appropriate social skills. She understood the nuances of social relationships, as well as how to maintain the relationships once formed. In fact, Michelle craved adult interaction. Michelle's issue in the area of social functioning was related to a lack of resources (financial, childcare, outside employment, etc.). Her lack of resources (social and financial) prevented her from having time away from her children and victim, and further isolated her and supported her offending. Michelle is in need of various sources of support to develop better financial and social resources that will help her effectively meet her social and emotional needs. It is likely that once those needs are met, Michelle's depression would also disappear.

Assessment of unique characteristics   As identified by the Center for Sex Offender Management (2007), there are areas that contribute to the offending behavior but cannot be directly addressed by treatment. These complicating factors need to be addressed in order for Michelle to achieve a successful reintegration in the community. For Michelle, these areas include her low socioeconomic status that results from her lack of job skills and her low educational attainment. Assisting and supporting Michelle in order to achieve additional education and/or job skills will better prepare her to live in the community and will directly reduce her need to rely on others for financial support. In turn, she would be better prepared to offer a stable and more financially secure environment to her children.

Michelle will also need assistance building an appropriate support system. Learning how to identify healthy relationships and boundaries in treatment is only half of the equation. Michelle needs to practice and demonstrate what she has learned in a safe environment with an appropriate group of people. This can be particularly difficult for people who have been convicted of sexual offenses. Connecting Michelle with relevant and supportive community groups will serve to prevent isolation. The use of mentors or circles of support to assist her should also be considered.

An area that is relatively unique to women is the fact that women continue to be the primary caregivers of children. This area becomes very complicated when a woman has been convicted of the sexual assault of a child. More often than not, women will wish either to return to or to continue parenting their children after being convicted of a sexual offense. (Note that Michelle did not abuse her own children.) With male sexual offenders, the issue is straightforward: the vast majority of male sexual offenders do not have primary responsibility for children. With female sexual offenders, however, child protection services are more likely than not to remove the children from the care of the woman, and may have great resistance to the idea that she should be allowed to reunite with her children. Therefore, in treatment there must be a focus on parenting issues, including the acknowledgement that female sexual offenders may not be able to resume the care of their own children. Female sexual offenders such as Michelle would benefit from continuing support in this area.

Recommendations for Students and Clinicians

As can be seen in this case, the assessment and treatment of female sexual offenders consists of a very individualized approach that examines the factors unique to the woman who has engaged in sexually offending behavior. Over the past few years, increased research efforts have been devoted to understanding the risk of recidivism of female sexual offenders, their offending processes, and, finally, the factors that contribute to sexually offending behavior among women. While much remains unknown, we now understand that female sexual offenders have assessment and treatment needs that are often quite different from those of males. As such, it is important not to apply the research related to male sexual offenders indiscriminately to female sexual offenders. Clinicians who offer assessment and treatment services to female sexual offenders need to familiarize themselves with the research in order to be able to provide gender-informed assessment and treatment services to this population. We owe the victims of these women nothing less.

References

Allen, C. M. (1991). *Women and men who sexually abuse children: A comparative analysis.* Orwell, VT: Safer Society Press.

Andrews, D. A., & Bonta, J. (1995). *Level of Service Inventory – Revised.* Toronto, Canada: Multi-Health Systems.

Basson, R. (2002). A model of women's sexual arousal. *Journal of Sex and Marital Therapy, 28,* 1–10.

Beech, A. R., Parrett, N., Ward, T., & Fisher, D. (2009). Assessing female sexual offenders' motivations and cognitions: An exploratory study. *Psychology, Crime, and Law, 15,* 201–216.

Blanchette, K., & Brown, S. L. (2006). *The assessment and treatment of women offenders: An integrated perspective.* Chichester, UK: John Wiley & Sons.

Center for Sex Offender Management. (2007). Female sex offenders (Web site). Retrieved April 8, 2014 from http://www.csom.org/pubs/female_sex_offenders_brief.pdf. Washington, DC: U.S. Department of Justice, Bureau of Prisons, National Institute of Corrections.

Chivers, M. L., Rieger, G., Latty, E., & Bailey, J. M. (2004). A sex difference in the specificity of sexual arousal. *Psychological Science, 15,* 736–744.

Cortoni, F. (2010). The assessment of female sexual offenders. In T. A. Gannon & F. Cortoni (Eds.), *Female sexual offenders: Theory, assessment, and treatment* (pp. 87–100). Chichester, UK: Wiley-Blackwell.

Cortoni, F., & Gannon, T. A. (2011). Female sexual offenders. In D. P. Boer, R. Eher, L. A. Craig, M. Miner, & F. Phafflin (Eds.), *International perspectives on the assessment and treatment of sex offenders: Theory, practice and research* (pp. 35–54). Chichester, UK: Wiley-Blackwell.

Cortoni, F., & Gannon, T. A. (2013). What works with female sexual offenders. In L. A. Craig, L. Dixon, & T. A. Gannon (Eds.), *What works in offender rehabilitation: An evidence based approach to assessment and treatment.* Chichester, UK: Wiley-Blackwell.

Cortoni, F., Hanson, R. K., & Coache, M. E. (2009). Les délinquantes sexuelles: Prévalence et récidive. *Revue internationale de criminologie et de police technique et scientifique, LXII,* 319–336.

Cortoni, F., Hanson, R. K., & Coache, M. E. (2010). The recidivism rates of female sexual offenders are low: A meta-analysis. *Sexual Abuse: A Journal of Research and Treatment, 22,* 387–401.

Eldridge, H., & Saradjian, J. (2000). Replacing the function of abusive behaviors for the offender: Remaking relapse prevention in working with women who sexually abuse children. In D. R. Laws, S. M. Hudson, & T. Ward (Eds.), *Remaking relapse prevention with sex offenders: A sourcebook* (pp. 402–426). Thousand Oaks, CA: Sage.

Faller, K. C. (1987). Women who sexually abuse children. *Violence and Victims, 2,* 263–276.

Faller, K. C. (1995). A clinical sample of women who have sexually abused children. *Journal of Child Sexual Abuse, 4,* 13–30.

Fromuth, M. E., & Conn, V. E. (1997). Hidden perpetrators: Sexual molestation in a nonclinical sample of college women. *Journal of Interpersonal Violence, 12,* 456–465.

Gannon, T. A., & Alleyne, E. K. A. (2013). Female sexual abusers' cognition: A systematic review. *Trauma, Violence, & Abuse, 14*(1), 67–79.

Gannon, T. A., Hoare, J., Rose, M. R., & Parrett, N. (2012). A re-examination of female child molesters' implicit theories: Evidence of female specificity? *Psychology, Crime and Law, 18,* 209–224.

Gannon, T. A., Rose, M. R., & Ward, T. (2008). A descriptive model of the offense process for female sexual offenders. *Sexual Abuse: A Journal of Research and Treatment, 20,* 352–374.

Gannon, T. A., Waugh, G., Taylor, K., Blanchette, K., O'Connor, A., Blake, E., et al. (2013). Women who sexually offend display three main offense styles: A re-examination of the descriptive model of female sexual offending. *Sexual Abuse: A Journal of Research and Treatment,* Published online before print May 15, 2013. doi: 10.1177/1079063213486835.

Grayston, A. D., & De Luca, R. V. (1999). Female perpetrators of child sexual abuse: A review of the clinical and empirical literature. *Aggression and Violent Behavior, 4,* 93–106.

Green, A. H., & Kaplan, M. S. (1994). Psychiatric impairment and childhood victimization experiences in female child molesters. *Journal of the American Academy of Child and Adolescent Psychiatry, 33,* 954–961.

Hislop, J. (2001). *Female sex offenders: What therapists, law enforcement and child protective services need to know*. Ravensdale, WA: Issues Press/Idyll Arbor.

Hunter, J. A., & Mathews, R. (1997). Sexual deviance in females. In R. D. Laws & W. O'Donohue (Eds.), *Sexual deviance: Theory, assessment, and treatment* (pp. 465–480). New York: Guilford Press.

Lewis, C. F., & Stanley, C. R. (2000). Women accused of sexual offenses. *Behavioral Sciences and the Law*, *18*, 73–81.

Mathews, R., Hunter, J. A., & Vuz, J. (1997). Juvenile female sexual offenders: Clinical characteristics and treatment issues. *Sexual Abuse: A Journal of Research and Treatment*, *9*, 187–199.

Mathews, R., Matthews, J. K., & Speltz, K. (1989). *Female sexual offenders: An exploratory study*. Orwell, VT: Safer Society Press.

Matravers, A. (2005). Understanding women sex offenders. *Criminology in Cambridge: Newsletter of the Institute of Criminology*, 10–13.

McCarty, L. M. (1986). Mother–child incest: Characteristics of the offender. *Child Welfare*, *65*, 447–458.

Miller, H. A., Turner, K., & Henderson, C. E. (2009). Psychopathology of sex offenders: A comparison of males and females using latent profile analysis. *Criminal Justice and Behavior*, *36*, 778–792.

Nathan, P., & Ward, T. (2001). Females who sexually abuse children: Assessment and treatment issues. *Psychiatry, Psychology and Law*, *8*, 44–45.

Nathan, P., & Ward, T. (2002). Female sex offenders: Clinical and demographic features. *Journal of Sexual Aggression*, *8*, 5–21.

O'Connor, A. A. (1987). Female sex offenders. *British Journal of Psychiatry*, *150*, 615–620.

Peter, T. (2009). Exploring taboos: Comparing male and female perpetrated child sexual abuse. *Journal of Interpersonal Violence*, *24*, 1111–1128.

Pflugradt, D. M., & Allen, B. P. (2010). An exploratory analysis of executive functioning for female sexual offenders: A comparison of characteristics across offense typologies. *Journal of Child Sexual Abuse*, *19*, 434–449.

Pflugradt, D. M., & Allen, B. P. (2012). A grounded theory analysis of sexual sadism in females. *Journal of Sexual Aggression*, *18*, 325–337.

Rousseau, M. M., & Cortoni, R. (2010). The mental health needs of female sexual offenders. In T. A. Gannon & F. Cortoni (Eds.), *Female sexual offenders: Theory, assessment, and treatment* (pp. 73–86). Chichester, UK: Wiley-Blackwell.

Rudin, M., Zalweski, C., & Bodmer-Turner, J. (1995). Characteristics of child sexual abuser victims according to perpetrator gender. *Child Abuse and Neglect*, *19*, 963–973.

Rumgay, J. (2004). Living with paradox: Community supervision of women offenders. In G. McIvor (Ed.), *Women who offend* (pp. 99–125). London: Jessica Kingsley.

Sandler, J. C., & Freeman, N. J. (2007). Typology of female sex offenders: A test of Vandiver and Kercher. *Sexual Abuse: A Journal of Research and Treatment*, *19*, 73–89.

Sandler, J. C., & Freeman, N. J. (2009). Female sex offender recidivism: A large-scale empirical analysis. *Sexual Abuse: A Journal of Research and Treatment*, *21*, 455–473.

Suschinsky, K. D., Lalumière, M. L., & Chivers, M. L. (2009). Sex differences in patterns of genital sexual arousal: Measurement artifacts or true phenomena? *Archives of Sexual Behavior*, *38*, 559–573.

Tardif, M., Auclair, N., Jacob, M., & Carpentier, J. (2005). Sexual abuse perpetrated by adult and juvenile females: An ultimate attempt to resolve a conflict associated with maternal identity. *Child Abuse & Neglect*, *29*, 153–167.

Travin, S., Cullen, K., & Protter, B. (1990). Female sex offenders: Severe victims and victimizers. *Journal of Forensic Sciences*, *35*, 140–150.

Vandiver, D. M. (2006). Female sex offenders: A comparison of solo offenders and co-offenders. *Violence and Victims*, *21*, 339–354.

Vandiver, D. M. (2007, March). *An examination of re-arrest rates of 942 male and 471 female registered sex offenders*. Academy of the Criminal Justice Sciences, Feature Panel on Sex Offenders: Seattle, WA.

Vandiver, D. M., & Kercher, G. (2004). Offender and victim characteristics of registered sexual offenders in Texas: A proposed typology of female sexual offenders. *Sexual Abuse: A Journal of Research and Treatment*, *16*, 121–137.

12

Working with a Sexual Offender with Bipolar Disorder

Tanya Garrett

Theoretical and Research Basis for Treatment

There is relatively little literature regarding psychological treatment of sexual offenders with severe mental health problems. In considering psychological treatment for this population, a sound psychological formulation (Gardner, 2005) is important in order to establish the connection, if any, between the mental illness and the offending behavior (Sahota & Chesterman, 1998), and hence to assist in determining appropriate treatment options and the individual offender's treatment needs. It is also important to ensure that individuals' mental disorders are appropriately treated in order that they are able to benefit from intervention relating to their offending behavior (Leversee & Ryan, 2010). Bipolar disorder is one such mental disorder, a mood disorder in which individuals experience episodes of a frenzied state known as mania, typically alternating with episodes of depression.

Bipolar Disorder and Offending

Bipolar disorder has been little researched among offender populations in general, and even less among sexual offenders (Ahlmeyer, Kleinsasser,

Sex Offender Treatment: A Case Study Approach to Issues and Interventions,
First Edition. Edited by Daniel T. Wilcox, Tanya Garrett, and Leigh Harkins.
© 2015 John Wiley & Sons, Ltd. Published 2015 by John Wiley & Sons, Ltd.

Stoner, & Retzlaff, 2003). Problems with limited research are compounded by the fact that, in some studies, those with bipolar disorder are not examined as a group but rather are included amongst groups of broader mental disorders. For example, in an international study of serious mental disorder among imprisoned populations undertaken by Fazel and Danesh (2002), those with bipolar disorder were not considered separately, but, presumably, were included in a "psychotic" population, mood disorders not having been included separately. In one of a limited number of studies looking specifically at bipolar disorder and offending, Good (1978) found that some 7–8% of individuals referred for psychiatric evaluation had bipolar disorder but notes that bipolar disorder tends to be under-diagnosed in prison populations, so the actual prevalence is likely higher. Good suggests that aggression and sexually inappropriate behavior are relatively common among those with a diagnosis of bipolar disorder generally, though he also noted that these types of behavior are relatively under-researched.

In spite of these behaviors being associated with bipolar disorder, it is suggested that other mental disorders represent greater risk for violence. Hansen and Schmidt (1999) suggest that those with schizophrenia and others with nonaffective psychosis are more likely to commit violent offenses than those with bipolar disorder. A more recent extensive study combining information from systematic review and population-based longitudinal studies (Fazel, Lichtenstein, Grann, Goodwin, & Langstrom, 2010) found that risk of violent crime in individuals with bipolar disorder was confined to those with comorbid substance use. In their study, sexual offenses were classified as violent offenses, and hence the study does not differentiate between the two types of offending. However, there are some studies that have looked specifically at bipolar disorder in sexual offenders.

Bipolar Disorder and Sexual Offending

Research relating to the detail of the psychopathology of sexual offenders has tended to concentrate more on personality factors (e.g., Ahlmeyer, Kleinsasser, Stoner, & Retzlaff, 2003; Leue, Borchard, & Hoyer, 2004) and research findings regarding the proportion of sexual offenders with bipolar disorder are often obscured due to the differing classification approaches used. More specifically, those with bipolar disorder are sometimes classified with psychotic disorders, and in other studies, with mood disorders. Thus, with inconsistencies in terms of how bipolar disorder is classified, it is difficult to draw any conclusions about the prevalence of bipolar disorder amongst sex offenders.

In spite of the above noted limitations, there are some studies that have specifically examined bipolar disorder amongst sex offenders. Galli et al. (1999), in a study of adolescent sexual offenders, found that more than half of their sample of 22 adolescents met diagnostic criteria for bipolar disorder. McElroy et al. (1999) similarly found that more than one-third of their sample of 36 male sexual offenders in a residential treatment facility had bipolar disorder. In a later study by the same research team (Dunsieth et al., 2004), using a larger sample of 113 men admitted to the same facility, a similar proportion (35%) was found to have bipolar disorder. DelBello et al. (1999) found that sexual offenders with bipolar disorder were more likely to have experienced a brain injury secondary to head trauma than sexual offenders without bipolar disorder or bipolar patients who had not committed sexual offenses, thus highlighting a possible link between brain trauma and bipolar disorder in sexual offenders. In spite of limitations in the research, and issues with classification, it is evident that bipolar disorder represents an important area for consideration in working with sexual offenders.

Psychological Treatment

Traditionally, psychological treatment for sexual offenders (e.g., Marshall, Anderson, & Fernandez, 1999) has focused on cognitive-behavioral methodology, in particular relapse-prevention techniques, and has been informed by certain models of offending, principally those of Finkelhor (1984, 1986) and Wolf (1984). Issues usually included in treatment are the discussion of denial, cognitive distortions, sexual fantasies, and victim empathy.

Clearly, psychological treatment for sexual offenders with bipolar disorder must consider, and incorporate where appropriate, principles of psychological treatment of severe mental health difficulties. George (1998) and Scott (1996) offer summaries of the major approaches in the field of psychological treatment of bipolar disorder. George suggests that an integrated treatment approach should incorporate cognitive and stress-vulnerability models, and should focus on engagement, psychoeducation, relapse prevention, and cognitive therapy. Scott notes that psychological approaches to treating bipolar disorder have some empirical support, and highlights the need for combining psychological interventions with pharmacotherapy. Indeed, the National Institute for Health and Clinical

Excellence, tasked in the UK with providing guidance to clinicians, recommends psychological intervention as well as pharmacological treatment for individuals with bipolar disorder (National Institute for Health and Clinical Excellence, 2006).

Thus, there is plenty of literature on the psychological treatment of sexual offenders and emerging literature in relation to the psychological treatment of severe mental illness. It could be argued that while treating sexual offenders who have a severe mental illness is not new to forensic mental health specialists, the implications of mental illness on treating sexual offending have not tended to be systematically considered. This is likely to be the result of the tendency of forensic mental health services in the UK to focus on mental health issues rather than the risk–needs paradigm (e.g., Gendreau, 1996) that has dominated offender management. Hence, it has, until relatively recently, been rare for staff, even in forensic mental health services, to have considered matters of offending and risk, to the extent of some arguing that it is not part of their concern.

Further, there has been insufficient examination of motivation in the offending of those with mental illness generally. Hodge and Renwick make this point when they argue the following:

> there has been a remarkable lack of consideration given to the factors underpinning mentally disordered offenders' motivation for engagement and participation in the treatment process ... this disregard of motivational matters occurs despite the fact that ... these factors often bear heavily on clinical decision-making regarding critical issues such as continuing detention and perceived dangerousness ... examination of motivational issues in this population is long overdue (2001, p. 221).

Consequently, relatively little attention has thus far been afforded to the question of what, if any, adaptations need to be made within mental health settings to the traditional interventions that have been offered to sexual offenders in prison or probation settings.

The present chapter details the individual treatment of a male sexual offender with a diagnosis of bipolar disorder. It was decided to offer him individual treatment focusing on both specific aspects of his mental illness and his sexual offending, which had been identified by the treating clinical team as areas of need. He was one of a number of mentally ill sexual offenders who resided in the facility who were considered unsuitable for group treatment or who declined such treatment. Additionally, there were concerns regarding the provision of group treatment for sexual offenders in a setting where delusions regarding child molesters were relatively common amongst other residents. These issues resulted in a decision that group treatment would not be offered as it was considered that to be identified as a sexual offender by virtue of attending a "sex offender group" might place participants at risk from other clients, and that demand for group treatment was low.

Case Introduction

Don[1] is a male African-Caribbean patient who was in his mid-40s at the time of the current intervention. He was detained in a National Health Service regional medium-secure mental health facility under the provisions of the Mental Health Act 1983. At the time of writing, Don was part way through his second admission, having been readmitted due to deterioration in his mental state following lack of compliance with his medication regime and suspicions that he may have been engaging in further sexually inappropriate behavior whilst living in the community. His first admission lasted for 19 months. The period between his discharge and readmission was 14 months.

Presenting complaints

Don is diagnosed with bipolar disorder. Prior to his admission to this facility he had a previous admission to a nonforensic mental health facility in another part of the country, and had also spent time in prison. He has been prescribed psychotropic medication to treat his mental illness, though his insight into the need for this and consequently his compliance have been problematic.

History

In terms of his personal history, Don's longstanding friend (who would visit him regularly and who, with his permission, I interviewed) describes him as possibly having been sexually abused as a child whilst residing in a children's home. Don himself has refused to discuss such matters. Don reported that he was subjected to violence by his stepfather, who hit him with a slipper, but states that this was not excessive. Don advises that his behavior was not problematic or disturbed as a child, not at home, at school, or in the community. He states that he did not truant from school, and was never suspended or expelled. He reports that he participated in school musical productions, made good academic progress, and enjoyed positive relationships with his teachers. He recalled only minor misbehavior as a child with friends, such as, "messing about on train tracks," for which he was not apprehended. It has not been possible to corroborate such information, as the only member of Don's family who might do so is his mother, whom he stated he did not wish the team to contact in the early stages of his admissions. He later advised that she was ill, but when she had recovered she did not respond to the author's attempt to make contact with her.

Don has held several different jobs. After leaving school Don trained as a silver service waiter for 2 years and worked full-time for a year in a hotel. He left this post to work in the music industry. He has since worked in the music industry, having been involved with various bands, and had considerable success in this field. His friend has said that when under pressure, he would leave the recording studio or be so rude that others would leave. He was working at one point with a production team, but they apparently all left due to his rudeness. His friend has advised that he has always left bands before they became successful, possibly because he was unable to cope with success, perhaps deliberately alienating himself from others. He has also busked. Don himself tends to minimize his employment difficulties, stating that he always enjoyed good relationships with colleagues. Prior to his current admission, he advises that he was working on "a project," but offered no further details in this regard.

Don's friend has said that Don took LSD and crack cocaine in the past. Don denies this, although he has stated that he has smoked marijuana and taken ecstasy. At other times, however, he has denied ever using illegal drugs. He has a conviction for possession of controlled drugs. He received a fine for this offense. In one of the witness statements relating to the index (sexual) offenses, it was noted that he smelled strongly of alcohol. When he was arrested, the police were so concerned about his intoxication that they considered a mental health assessment. Don denies that he was thus intoxicated at that time.

Don lived for 4 years with a partner, a time when he was, according to his friend, taking large quantities of cocaine. This was his longest relationship and is said to have ended due to his behavior, possibly argumentativeness. Don himself states that he tended to be "egotistical" in this relationship, refusing to share household tasks with his partner. He admitted that he could have done more in that relationship, but did not do so, as he was preoccupied with his career. He stated that the relationship ended because, "she couldn't take any more." He stated that he has not behaved similarly in other relationships. He has no children. One of his ex-partners has reported that he made her walk several paces behind him lest he be attacked for having a relationship with a white woman. He denied that he has a history of casual, brief relationships, saying that he has had only two significant relationships, one lasting 4 years, described above, and one which lasted for 2 years, with a woman some years his senior (he was 19, she was 35). He reports that the latter relationship was different because she was older and more experienced.

Case conceptualization

Don appeared to have suffered deterioration in his mental health over a period of time, resulting in his psychiatric hospitalization prior to his index offense. He was unable to hold down a job and his self-care was poor. At times, however, he became threatening and struggled to maintain appropriate social interactions. He experienced periods of euphoria and racing thoughts, used illegal drugs, and became sexually disinhibited.

Don's first conviction for a violent offense was assault, for which he received a 12-month conditional discharge. He was convicted a year later of threatening behavior and received a fine. Don has two cautions for assault, both of which occurred in the same year, 8 years after his conviction for threatening behavior. He was subsequently convicted of an offense of indecent assault and again received a fine. Two years later, he was convicted of kidnapping, indecent assault, and two counts of assault. Don pleaded not guilty to these offenses. Don was also convicted of harassment, after following a lone woman around a city center some months earlier. He was given a fine and was made subject to a restraining order.

One of Don's victims, a 15-year-old girl, alleged that he approached her at a bus stop. She reported that he started speaking to her and tried to kiss and cuddle her. She also alleged that when she ran away, he followed her and pulled her down a road, into a secluded spot. It was her account that he restrained her, slapped her across the face and tried to undo her trousers, but she escaped. In respect of the offenses of assault, Don is said to have stared at a woman on the bus in a threatening manner. The same woman alleged that she saw him again 2 weeks later when he followed her, swearing at her. Around the same time, a 14-year-old girl alleged that Don was walking along the road when he approached her and tried to grab her neck, but the girl ducked. Following his discharge prior to his second admission to the secure mental health facility, there were concerns that Don had attended a lap-dancing club and was accused of inappropriately touching one of the dancers there. He was not charged in respect of this alleged offense. It appeared that his sexual violence had increased in severity over time, as the most recent offenses involved more threats and physical violence than his previous sexual offenses.

It was considered that Don's offending had occurred in the context of his mental health issues and his success within the music industry, which both contributed to his sexual disinhibition and permissive attitude towards sexually coercive behavior. That is, he found himself in an environment in which, because of his success, he was regularly approached by women interested in him sexually, which perhaps contributed to a somewhat entitled attitude on the part of Don towards sexual activity, and, further, in which there was an atmosphere of casual sexual encounters. The inflated self-esteem, over-friendliness, casual sexual attitude, and increased libido which commonly occur during a manic state, in combination with these circumstances, resulted in Don forcing his sexual attentions on women who were unknown to him.

During the 33 months of his two admissions, the following components of psychological assessment and intervention were offered to Don:

1. Psychosocial history and risk assessment
2. Discussion of offending and intervention regarding eye contact (first admission)
3. Medication
4. Denial and relapse-prevention work (regarding sexual offending and mental health issues; second admission)

Assessment

On initial meeting, Don was somewhat hostile, but he subsequently presented as pleasant, polite, and co-operative. At times, Don himself requested additional appointments, indicating his level of engagement. There were some issues that he found too difficult or unpalatable to accept, though overall Don accepted the concerns of the professionals and the need to modify his behavior to ensure that he does not place himself at risk of reconviction for sexual offenses. Thus, his level of engagement was not expected to present a challenge in treatment.

Although Don never behaved inappropriately during sessions, there were some concerns regarding his presentation. On initial contact, he presented as somewhat intimidating. When he was first seen alone, he stood close to a female professional by the closed interview room door, and he was asked to sit down as the professional felt intimidated. Although he responded appropriately, she also found his way of looking at her to be somewhat intense. At times during these early stages, Don asked personal questions of professionals (e.g., he asked a female professional where she lived), but accepted advice that such questions were inappropriate. At times Don appeared to find sessions difficult and negative, and on one occasion requested some positive feedback.

Throughout the assessment phase, Don maintained that he did not perpetrate any sexual offenses. Initially he stated that the two complainants in the index offense worked together to fabricate the allegations. He stated that he does not know them. In respect of his previous conviction for indecent assault, he stated that this occurred when he was standing at a bus stop and asked a woman to allow him to stand under her umbrella. He said that she was unhappy with this and he tapped her on the bottom to indicate that he was joking. He accepted that perhaps his lifestyle as a singer and musician has resulted in him using less than subtle sociosexual cues with women. In addition, he accepted that his constant eye contact, combined with active symptoms of mental illness could in the future be "misinterpreted" by women and result in further accusations of sexual offending. He accepted that when mentally unwell, his risk of violence is also elevated.

In spite of denying his sexual offenses, Don was able to acknowledge that some of his behaviors had been of concern, namely an incident where he raised his shirt in the community whilst on escorted leave and rubbed his chest. He accepted that whilst no sexual intent was present on his part, such behavior was inappropriate in someone with his history of sexual offending, and could be misinterpreted by members of the public. He was unable, however, to understand why a female professional felt that he was staring at her flirtatiously, saying that he was not consciously flirting with her and did not find her sexually attractive. In another incident, escorting nursing staff felt that he was staring at three women and looking at a woman's bottom in a supermarket. Don denied this, saying that he felt that these staff had offered a "vindictive" account of the incident. In a further incident he stated to his female nurse escort when they sat on a bench outside the clinic "I can chat you up now." Don told me that he was "only joking" and could not see why this was inappropriate. Thus, working with Don to understand his inappropriate sexual behavior is an important treatment target.

Initially, although Don was co-operative with professional intervention, he had a tendency to minimize his past problematic behavior, for example, his alienation of others in the past due to his rudeness, and, perhaps, his offending behavior. It was considered likely that his interpersonal difficulties, including his sexual offending and, possibly, his occasional violence, had developed in the context of his mental illness, as his friend confirmed that, prior to this, he presented in a significantly different, and more positive, manner. Thus, it was considered essential that his compliance with intervention, including medication, be improved in order to prevent further reoffending.

Risk assessments were repeated on four occasions over the period of Don's two admissions, and involved completion of the HCR-20 (Webster, Douglas, Eaves, & Hart, 1997) and the Psychopathy Checklist – Revised (PCL-R; Hare, 1991), which highlighted the paucity of source data available in this case, such as information from Don's mother.

Several risk factors were identified for Don. These included his significant history of substance misuse, particularly at times when he was financially solvent. At the time of assessment, his insight required further development. He appeared to have thought realistically about the future, but there was little information about potential future destabilizers for this client. It was considered, however, that he is likely to be exposed to stress should he re-enter the music industry. The most significant factors in terms of future risk were the likely lack of personal support and his likely noncompliance with treatment due to his denial.

Don was considered to pose a low risk of violence whilst detained, as his behavior had not been a cause for concern in this respect since his detention, and as he was co-operative with treatment at that time. However, it was felt that should he be discharged into the community he would pose a moderate risk of violent reoffending. Based on his previous offenses, this would appear most likely to take the form of sexual violence against young female victims previously unknown to him. The nature of the risk was that of physical assault and behaving in a threatening manner towards them. He has also engaged in a degree of physical violence against people known to him (i.e. his former partner's father and his mother), therefore it was clear that in the community he would be at risk of possible physical violence towards individuals known to him.

As a result of his past successful career in the music industry, Don's interpersonal behavior with women was likely to have been objectively lacking in subtlety, and potentially abusive, but, in the context of the music industry, common at the time. An example of this was the nature of Don's eye contact, which posed considerable problems during his admissions, but which he showed the ability to moderate as a result of psychological intervention. Due to these factors, he is likely to have had little difficulty in forming relationships with, or in securing sexual contact with women. There was no evidence of deviant sexual drive, rather of normal sexual drive satisfied by deviant means. Thus, an area that required attention was how to negotiate appropriate interpersonal relationships.

Although Don had improved his co-operation with professional interventions after his first admission, he still tended to minimize and deny his past problematic behavior (e.g., his alienation of others in the past due to his rudeness, and his offending behavior). He continued to deny his substance misuse, and thus it was difficult to establish whether his substance use contributed to his offending, though it seems likely that he was intoxicated with alcohol at the time of committing the index offenses, at least. Don accepted that he posed a risk of reoffending both sexually and violently, particularly should he relapse in terms of his mental illness, and he was willing to engage in interventions aimed to reduce this risk. For example he understood that engaging in unbroken eye contact that focuses on women's bodies could result in further convictions, in conjunction with a relapse in his mental illness. Thus, it was noted that it would be essential to monitor his behavior for interpersonal hostility, threatening behavior, or intrusive eye contact.

In summary, a number of issues were identified as areas to be addressed in treatment. These included addressing Don's denial, understanding his offending, and improving his compliance. His intrusive eye contact, negotiating interpersonal relationships, including issues of hostility and threatening behavior, and formulating a relapse-prevention strategy, were all considered important for this client.

Course of treatment and assessment of progress

The psychological treatment provided to Don adopted a broadly cognitive-behavioral approach, with a particular focus on relapse-prevention issues. There were several phases of intervention, over the course of two admissions, beginning with the problematic eye contact used by Don, since this was causing difficulties amongst nursing staff working with him, and beginning to talk about his view of his behavior and of his mental health issues. The second phase tackled his denial of his offending, via specific work on denial and its functions. Following Don's subsequent admissions that he had sexually offended, it was possible to work on relapse prevention in respect of his sexual offending and his mental illness, and to engage him in further work on his eye contact and use of pornography.

First admission   The first phase of Don's treatment involved discussions regarding the nature of his eye contact with women in general. He dealt with difficult and sensitive issues by accepting advice immediately or after some reflection between sessions, and by complying with requests for him to modify his behavior. I used my own experience of him as offering intense, direct, unbroken eye contact, which can be intimidating in nature. Nursing staff also reported him as staring at both male and female members of staff. Don seemed surprised by this. It emerged that Don had concluded, following discussions with friends, that people who vary eye contact lack confidence in their position. However, he responded well to discussion of this, and subsequently moderated his eye contact appropriately, both with myself during appointments and with others outside of the sessions to the extent that towards the end of his first admission, his eye contact was no longer reported as inappropriate.

Following Don's attempt to modify his eye contact I noted that when he looked away from my eyes, he looked at various parts of my body. Whilst I did not feel uncomfortable with this or intimidated by it, I felt that others could easily misinterpret Don's gaze in this respect, and that in view of his history of sexual offending, it was appropriate to address this with him. To his credit, Don accepted the potential difficulties in his gaze, though he stated that he was not specifically looking at my body in a sexual manner, rather, he was attempting to vary his gaze. He further modified his eye contact, such that it could no longer be regarded as inappropriate.

It emerged that Don's view of his behavior and that of others differed significantly in a number of areas. Don stated that he has never been violent towards his mother and was unable to recall his violent offending. He denied that he has ever taken LSD or crack cocaine, or that he was intoxicated by alcohol on arrest for the index offenses, as alleged by the police. He was not prepared to accept that he might have forgotten some of the events surrounding his sexual offenses.

At the end of this first phase of treatment, I concluded that Don was co-operative with psychological intervention aimed to address most of the relevant issues (such as his eye contact and assessment of risk), with the exception of his denial of his sexual offenses. During this phase of intervention, he presented as increasingly accepting of his mental illness and of the need for medication. He expressed an interest in reading about bipolar disorder and was provided with an information booklet and a book written by a professional diagnosed with this condition. However, this information was somewhat counter-productive, as Don felt that the diagnosis did not apply to him because he does not experience depression. He became more positive with his medication regime and did not feel that it was having adverse side effects on his creativity and sleep pattern; however, this remains an area to be monitored in treatment. He recognized that he was mentally ill at the time of his index offenses, and that he would be at risk of further sexual or violent offenses were he to become mentally ill again, and particularly were he to stop taking his medication. Due to his position that he had not explicitly sexually or violently offended, it was my opinion during Don's first admission that little additional progress was likely.

Second admission The second phase of the intervention took place during Don's second admission and comprised eight sessions over a 7-month period. Due to Don's continuing unwillingness at that stage to admit that he had sexually offended, a number of sessions were offered addressing his denial. This approach to treating sexual offenders with mental health difficulties who are in denial has been described elsewhere (Garrett & Thomas-Peter, 2009). This involves discussing in detail the function and normality of denial with a view to facilitating a disclosure. This was successful and, thus, Don subsequently participated appropriately in individual sessions designed to address the issues of pornography, his sexual interest, his offending behavior, and to devise relapse-prevention plans in relation to his sexual offending and his mental health problems.

During these sessions, Don showed a good ability to plan for the future and to identify some appropriate short-term plans while he remained detained, (e.g., to re-establish contact with some of his old friends, as he recognized that isolation is unhelpful, and possibly to become involved in performing in a Christmas concert). He said that in the longer-term future he would like to undertake some college courses and associated reading across a variety of topics, and become involved in sport. He said that he felt that these initiatives would assist him in making his environment positive. He noted, "if I go out and do the same things I did last time I would be vulnerable," by which he seemed to mean that he did not want to be seen as vulnerable to a relapse in his mental illness in the future.

We discussed the alleged incident prior to his second admission when he was said to have inappropriately touched a dancer in a lap-dancing club. Don's account was that he called the police after a "bouncer" assaulted him. When the police attended, he claims they interviewed the dancer and told Don that unless he dropped the complaint against the bouncer, they would charge him with sexual assault against the dancer. Don stated that the bouncer took a dislike to him for no apparent reason, and that there was no reason for him to be ejected from the club. He said he did not know what the dancer said to the police. Don told me that he had "got on well" with the dancer, who he paid for a private dance. He said that he did not have any physical contact with her, or with any other dancer, commenting in this regard, "I know my limitations." Don said that if he had not called the police, then this allegation would not have come to light.

Don accepted the proposal to discuss denial issues, to educate him in the normal function of denial in general life, to identify his "denial profile," and to apply this material to his sexual offending. Although Don had some difficulty identifying examples of denial from his own experience, and initially said that he does not use denial because he is a "straight guy," he was able to accept that his smoking of cigarettes illustrated his use of denial, for example regarding health risks posed by such behavior. I asked Don to think of some further examples of his own use of denial in general life before our next session. We discussed these examples to develop his understanding of the role of cognitive distortions in maintaining self-esteem. He seemed to understand this, specifically the role of denial, minimization, and justification. Don identified that he tends to deny in order to feel positive about himself. In this context we discussed various aspects of cognitive distortion, including denial, minimization, and justification, and Don was able to think of exaggeration and fabrication as additional mechanisms for increasing one's self-esteem.

Don stated that he felt that the purpose of the discussion about denial was clear and he accepted that he needed to take greater responsibility for his sexual offending and noted that he was beginning to, "face up to" his offenses. We discussed that although initially he might feel worse about himself, in the longer term he may feel better about himself as he will have a strategy (relapse-prevention plan) to reduce his likelihood of future offending of this nature, and that undergoing this work may assist him in being discharged from hospital.

In this context, I asked Don to discuss his sexual offenses including the incident at the lap-dancing club and the indecent assault on the female under 16. Don accepted (for the first time) that he had perpetrated this offense, noting, "I didn't get dragged through the Courts for nothing." He stated, however, that he could not remember the incident, but accepts that it was of a sexual nature. He said perhaps this occurred because he was mentally unwell at the time. Hence, Don was able to accept that when mentally unwell, he can become sexually disinhibited. Don also accepted that he uses inappropriate eye contact when mentally unwell, but could not recall doing it. With regard to his second conviction (indecent assault at a bus stop), Don accepted that he "tapped" the victim on her bottom with a newspaper, though he denied any sexual intent behind this. In respect of the incident at the lap-dancing club, Don accepted for the first time that in fact he touched the lap dancer on her bottom. He stated that he considered that she encouraged him to do so by her nonverbal behavior. Accepting that his hypothesis that he is sexually disinhibited when unwell is a reasonable one, we began work on his relapse-prevention plan with this in mind.

Don's sexual offending relapse-prevention plan focused on "high-risk situations" (Figure 12.1). He was able to identify that it would be inappropriate for him to frequent lap-dancing clubs again, as this would offer him inappropriate "temptation" and he does not want to "get into trouble." We also agreed that Don should avoid physical contact with strangers and avoid looking at pornographic material of women dressed as children. Don was able to identify that he needs to think of the consequences, including his likely reincarceration, to avoid future offending. He also identified some positive activities he might engage in, including accessing appropriate pornography. We managed to think of some examples together in relation to sources of social support and emergency strategies. Don agreed with my suggestion that our next task should be to produce a relapse-prevention plan with respect to his mental illness.

We went on to discuss Don's recent repeated inappropriate eye contact. He denied that he had engaged in inappropriate eye contact of late, and appeared to feel that the feedback provided by nursing staff that he had, was unjustified. Don was advised to try to ensure that he did not look at women inappropriately in future, using strategies which we have previously discussed, for example, concentrating on looking at women's eyes rather than other parts of their bodies.

During this phase of intervention, it was agreed that Don would be provided with some of the pornographic magazines previously confiscated from him, to begin to monitor the impact of exposure to pornography. This was to see if allowing him access on a longer-term basis would help to fulfill his normal sexual needs in a secure setting and possibly prevent inappropriate sexual behavior. Don was happy with this, though he emphasized that he does not consider it to be important or urgent that he gain access to pornography. Don provided magazines that were still in his possession and I was happy to return one magazine, as this did not contain any controversial images and would not be regarded as pornographic by many people. However, the other magazine was not suitable as it contained images of models dressed as schoolgirls, models resembling children in their lack of physical development, and images of women's bodies having been injured (though not severely). We agreed that these images would be edited from the magazine and he would be allowed to have it back minus the controversial images. Don was advised that there would be a care plan to monitor the impact of this access to pornography. He stated that he did not believe that there would be any effect. He stated

High-Risk Situations
Environment:
Lap-dancing clubs.
Talking to people I don't know, for example, in a bar.
Standing at a bus stop.
Personal:
Physical contact with strangers.
Looking at pornography involving women dressed as schoolgirls.
When I am mentally unwell.

Cognitive Distortions
Things seemed relaxed between us.
Fantasy Management Strategies
If this did happen, stop masturbating, do something else (cooking, playing music) and when I next masturbate, use images that are not deviant.

Coping Strategies
I will avoid lap-dancing clubs in future.
When in public, especially at bus stops or around young women, I'll keep myself to myself and I'll avoid any physical contact.
I'll make sure I keep taking my medication.

Lifestyle Changes
(How my lifestyle will have to change to avoid reoffending)
Make sure that I use pornography that does not show women dressed as schoolgirls.
Keep in touch with my friends.
I will make sure I keep playing my music.
I will get involved in community activities, for example, football and basketball.
I want to educate myself more, for example, science, math.

Emergency Strategies
(If I am in a high-risk situation and am having problems coping or feel that I'm at a high risk of reoffending I can . . .)
Think! Of the consequences.
Get out of the situation if possible.

Social Support
(People I can talk to if I need support or advice)
Ring friends.
Ring mother.
Ring social worker or CPN.
Ring *Stop It Now* on 0808 1000 9000.

Reasons I Don't Want to Reoffend
I don't want to go back to hospital or to prison.
It would get in the way of my career.
If I was in prison or hospital I wouldn't be able to see as much of my friends as I would like.
If I reoffended, it could be irritating or distressing for the victim.

Figure 12.1   Relapse-prevention plan – sexual offending.

in subsequent sessions that providing him with access to pornography did not result in frequent use of it, or frequent masturbation, and hence had no impact on his behavior or risk. This perception was borne out by observations carried out by nursing staff, which indicated no impact on Don's behavior from his access to pornography.

Don's belief was that the pornographic magazines that had been confiscated from him were, "top shelf, not too bad." He said that he did not know why it had been decided that he should not be allowed access to this material. When it was explained to him that some of the models were dressed as schoolgirls and appeared extremely young, he understood. Don did not describe having had any particular interest in schoolgirl images. He said that he selected these magazines because he liked the images in general (e.g., women in miniskirts). Don said that he did find certain images within the magazines sexually exciting but had difficulty identifying which images, or the features of such images. However, it would not appear that these related to the schoolgirl images. He denied that he had any positive reaction to the schoolgirl images, or even that he particularly noticed them. He said that if he had noticed them he would not have been interested, as he does not particularly like schoolgirl outfits. He stated that he no longer had these magazines sent to him (they were "catalogues" of pornographic films, featuring still images from these films, sent free by the company).

When asked about his past use of pornographic videos, Don stated that these depicted, "dancing girls, normal stuff." He said that they were videos obtained by post from the same company as the magazines. He stated that the actors in the films were aged approximately 20, and that he did not spend inordinate amounts of time viewing the films when he was in the community. Similarly, he said that he did not frequent lap-dancing clubs regularly. He regarded lap-dancing clubs as an appropriate outlet for his normal sexual interest in the context of him not having relationships at that time, and not wanting a relationship.

Don stated that since the pornographic magazines were confiscated from him he had rarely masturbated because he preferred to do so when looking at visual material, preferably films. He stated that he rarely fantasized and that if he does, he thought of films that he has seen previously. He specifically denied that he ever fantasized about females whom he had seen in other situations. Don told me that he would like to have access to appropriate pornography whilst detained, preferably videos, but would settle for magazines if necessary.

With regard to his view of a possible connection between pornography use and his sexual offending, Don stated that he did not believe that there was any such link, but acknowledged that such a link can exist in some sexual offenders. He stated that he does not believe that he sexually offended because he has not been able to access a female partner, because he has never had any difficulty in his interactions with females or in forming relationships. He commented, "I'm a pretty good-looking guy." Don stated that he has more recently chosen not to engage in relationships, as he has been concentrating on his music and the future. He stated that he would like to become involved in a relationship in the future. He did not feel that he would have any difficulty in forming a relationship now, even in the light of his lack of recent practice.

Don said that he had used a prostitute on one occasion, in approximately 1998, when he received a sum of money in relation to his previous recordings, which he decided to use to go out and celebrate. Don stated that this was a positive experience as the prostitute was professional, and looked after his needs. Don told me that in the context of relationships and sexual contact, he never had any interest or involvement in sadomasochistic practices, nor any interest in or access to child pornography. He commented that children should be respected, noting that he has never had any sexual interest in children, nor has he ever asked any of his partners to dress up as a child. It is perhaps of significance that Don told me that one of his partners once suggested she dress up as a schoolgirl. Don said that it did not happen, as his partner had, "more exciting outfits."

We completed a relapse-prevention plan with regard to Don's mental illness (Figure 12.2). He made good contributions to this. Don emphasized that he intended to ensure that when he was discharged, he would never be readmitted to hospital, (i.e., he will ensure his compliance with medication and follow his relapse-prevention plans).

Access and barriers to care

During psychological involvement, totaling 15 sessions over the course of his two admissions lasting 33 months, the author spent time with this compulsorily detained client with bipolar disorder and convictions for sexual offending, forming a rapport and discussing matters related to inappropriate eye contact, denial, and relapse prevention to encourage him to accept his offending behavior and to work in a meaningful manner on preventing reoffending in the future. This intervention necessitated a dual approach focusing on both his offending behavior and his mental health problems using a relapse-prevention model (Marlatt & Gordon, 1985) and directly addressing the issue of denial in order to encourage disclosure.

High-Risk Situations
Not occupying my time.
Being under stress (e.g. other people seeing my vulnerability and targeting me because I don't fit in).
Not being in touch with my friends.
Being isolated.
Not taking my medication.

Coping Strategies
Be focused and constructive.
I'll try to avoid stress/stressful situations to avoid a relapse.

Lifestyle Changes
I'll keep myself clean and tidy.
Keep in touch with my friends
I will make sure I keep playing my music
I will get involved in community activities, e.g. football and basketball
I want to educate myself more, e.g. science, maths

Emergency Strategies
Ring Social Worker or CPN.
Go to my GP.
Ring NHS Direct or the Samaritans.

Social Support
Ring friends
Ring mother
Ring social worker or CPN

Reasons I Don't Want to Relapse
I don't want to be readmitted to hospital as I will lose my freedom and would not be able to see as much of my friends as I would like.
It wouldn't be good for me to keep relapsing at this stage in my life.
I want to build up my relationships with my friends and I couldn't do that if I relapsed.
I want to have a relationship with a woman and that would not be very likely if I relapsed.

Figure 12.2 Relapse-prevention plan – mental illness.

During these sessions, following work on his use of denial, the client was willing to admit for the first time that he had sexually offended on three occasions, which he had previously denied. As a consequence of these admissions, further work regarding eye contact and gaze was undertaken with him, followed by structured relapse-prevention work relating to his mental illness and his offending behavior. This aimed to assist him in avoiding reoffending by recognizing the various contributions of his mental health difficulties to his offending behavior and the importance of maintaining good mental health. Stress, isolation, and lack of occupation or focus were important risk factors for him to monitor, as these had in the past led him to become mentally unwell.

Allowing the client access to appropriate pornography did not appear to have any significant impact on his behavior. For example, it did not result in an increase in his inappropriate eye contact or any other inappropriate sexualized behavior. It was hoped that allowing him this access would enhance his appropriate sexual outlets and possibly reduce his inappropriate eye contact, though it was thought that his inappropriate eye contact might be connected with his mental illness rather than inappropriate sexual behavior.

Towards the end of this phase of treatment, there was good evidence that the client was able to derive enjoyment from songwriting, playing music, and planning a concert with other residents. He was also able to make reasonably appropriate plans for the future, including making contact with family members and friends, being aware of the need for such support to lower his risk, and the possibility of living near to his friend in the near future.

Follow-up

Unfortunately, Don was unwilling to complete any psychometric assessment measures and hence such objective evidence is not available regarding the outcome of intervention. However, professionals felt that there was a significant improvement in his engagement with the multiprofessional team over the course of his admission and that important progress had been made with regard to his willingness to admit and take responsibility for his offending behavior, and in respect of his insight and eye contact. Hence, the team working with Don had a guardedly optimistic view regarding his future prognosis and likelihood of reoffending. At the time of writing, Don continued to reside in conditions of medium security, though in view of his progress there were plans to discharge him for the second time in the near future as soon as an appropriate placement was identified.

Treatment implications of the case

There are obvious differences between treatment offered in a hospital setting, versus that provided in prison and similar settings. Primarily, these relate to the complications arising from mental health considerations that may require simultaneous therapeutic attention or are the focus before or after offense-related intervention. There are also concerns regarding delusional beliefs of patients in such settings, which may impact upon the type of treatment that can be provided to sexual offenders. Further, there may not always be sufficient numbers of sexual offenders to justify group treatment in hospital settings. Whilst the process of treatment in this case was extremely lengthy, it is suggested that in complex cases such as that of Don, where multiple issues require attention and matters of engagement and rapport are paramount, such lengthy treatment is necessary and hence justifiable.

Recommendations to Clinicians and Students

Working with offenders with mental illness requires specialist knowledge, flexibility and sensitivity. It is not enough to apply a "one model fits all" approach, for example, group treatment, and only group treatment, across institutions. We must, first and foremost, consider the formulation for each individual offender, and the type or "dose" of treatment required, allowing for tailored treatment suitable to the needs of the specific population. Whilst, ideally, psychometric evaluation of the impact of treatment is desirable, this cannot always be achieved, and creative approaches to outcome measurement need to be considered.

Endnotes

1 The client's name and some personal details have been changed to protect his confidentiality.

References

Ahlmeyer, S., Kleinsasser, D., Stoner, J., & Retzlaff, P. (2003). Psychopathology of incarcerated sex offenders. *Journal of Personality Disorders*, *17*(4), 306–318.

DelBello, M. P., Soutullo, C. A., Zimmerman, M. E., Sax, K. W., Williams, J. R., McElroy, S. L., et al. (1999). Traumatic brain injury in individuals convicted of sexual offenses with and without bipolar disorder. *Psychiatry Research*, *89*, 281–286.

Dunsieth, N. W., Jr, Nelson, E. B., Brusman-Louis, L. A., Holcomb, J. L., Beckman, D., Welge, J. A., et al. (2004). Psychiatric and legal features of 113 men convicted of sexual offences. *Journal of Clinical Psychiatry*, *65*(3), 293–300.

Fazel, S., & Danesh, J. (2002). Serious mental disorder in 23,000 prisoners: A systematic review of 62 surveys. *The Lancet*, *359*, 545–550.

Fazel, S., Lichtenstein, P., Grann, M., Goodwin, G. G., and Langstrom, N. (2010). Bipolar disorder and violent crime. *Archives of General Psychiatry*, 67(9), 931–938.

Finkelhor, D. (1984). *Child sexual abuse: New theory and research*. New York: Free Press.

Finkelhor, D. (1986). *A sourcebook on child sexual abuse*. London: Sage.

Galli, V., McElroy, S. L., Soutullo, C. A., Kizer, D., Raute, N., Keck, P. E., et al. (1999). The psychiatric diagnoses of twenty-two adolescents who have sexually molested other children. *Comprehensive Psychiatry*, 40(2), 85–88.

Gardner, D. (2005). Getting it together: Integrative approaches to formulation. *Clinical Psychology Forum*, 15, 10–15.

Garrett, T., & Thomas-Peter, B. A. (2009). Interventions with sexual offenders with mental illness. In A. R. Beech, L. Craig, & K. D. Browne (Eds.), *Assessment and treatment of sex offenders: A handbook*. Chichester, UK: Wiley.

Gendreau, P. (1996). Offender rehabilitation: What we know and what needs to be done. *Criminal Justice and Behaviour*, 23(1), 144–161.

George, S. (1998). Towards an integrated treatment approach for manic depression. *Journal of Mental Health*, 7(2), 145–156.

Good, M. I. (1978). Primary affective disorder, aggression and criminality. A review and clinical study. *Archives of General Psychiatry*, 35(8), 954–960.

Hansen, P. E., & Schmidt, J. E. (1999). [Psychiatric observations 1986–1993. Sygehus Fyn, Middelfart, the unit of forensic psychiatry]. [Danish]. *Ugeskrift for Laeger*, 161(12), 1770–1774.

Hare, R. D. (1991). *Manual for the Hare psychopathy checklist* (Rev. ed.). Toronto, Canada: Multi-Health Systems.

Hodge, J., & Renwick, S. J. (2002). Motivating mentally abnormal offenders. In M. McMurran (Ed.), *Motivating offenders to change: A guide to engagement in therapy*. Chichester, UK: John Wiley & Sons.

Leue, A., Borchard, B., & Hoyer, J. (2004). Mental disorders in a forensic sample of sexual offenders. *European Psychiatry*, 19, 123–130.

Leversee, T., & Ryan, G. (2010). Brain development and function: Neurology and psychiatry in the treatment of sexually abusive youth. In G. Ryan, T. Leversee, & S. Lane (2010). *Juvenile sexual offending: Causes, consequences, and correction*. Hoboken, NJ: Wiley.

Marlatt, G. A., & Gordon, J. R. (Eds.). (1985). *Relapse prevention: Maintenance strategies in the treatment of addictive behaviors*. New York: Guilford Press.

Marshall, W. L., Anderson, D., & Fernandez, Y. (1999). *Cognitive behavioural treatment of sexual offenders*. Chichester, UK: Wiley.

McElroy, S. L., Soutullo, C. A., Taylor, P., Jr., Nelson, E. B., Beckman, D. A., Brusman, L. A., et al. (1999). Psychiatric features of 36 convicted sexual offenses. *Journal of Clinical Psychiatry*, 60(6), 414–420.

National Institute for Health and Clinical Excellence (2006). *NICE Clinical Guidelines CG38. Bipolar Disorder: The management of bipolar disorder in adults, children and adolescents, in primary and secondary care*. London: NICE.

Sahota, K., & Chesterman, P. (1998). Sexual offending in the context of mental illness. *The Journal of Forensic Psychiatry*, 9(2), 267–280.

Scott, J. (1996). The role of cognitive behaviour therapy in bipolar disorder. *Behavioural and Cognitive Psychotherapy*, 24, 195–208.

Webster, C. D., Douglas, K. S., Eaves, D., & Hart, S. D. (1997). *HCR-20, Version 2 (Historical, Clinical, Risk-20)*. Psychological Assessment Resource, Inc.

Wolf, S. (1984, November). *A multifactor model of deviant sexuality*. Paper presented at Third International Conference on Victimology, Lisbon, Portugal.

13

Treating Professionals Who Are Sexually Involved with Their Clients

Funmilayo Rachal, Gene G. Abel, and Tanya Garrett

Theoretical and Research Basis for Treatment

It is clear that sexual contact with patients is an issue across the different helping professions, both within and outside psychotherapy (Wilbers, Veenstra, van de Wiel, & Schultz, 1992). Generally speaking, the research in the US has yielded no differences in any respect between the main statutory psychotherapy professions of psychology, psychiatry, and social work (Borys & Pope, 1989). The literature estimates the prevalence rates of professionals who have engaged in professional sexual misconduct to range from 1.6% to 7% (e.g., Garrett & Davies, 1998; Gechtman, 1989; Kardener, Fuller, & Mensh 1973; Pope, Keith-Spiegel, & Tabachnick, 1986; Sansone & Sansone, 2009). This gap in prevalence rates represents the greater number of physicians who report engaging in sexual boundary violations compared to the smaller number that are reported and receive disciplinary sanctions. The specialties of medical practice with the highest number of professionals who are reported to engage in professional sexual misconduct include psychiatry, family practice, and general practice (Brooks, Gendel, Early, Gunderson, & Shore, 2012; Dehlendorf & Wolfe, 1998; Sansone & Sansone, 2009). The etiology of why individuals who practice in certain specialties are more vulnerable to boundary violations is unknown. However, it is probable that one of the contributing factors is that these specialties have the potential for the development of more long-term

Sex Offender Treatment: A Case Study Approach to Issues and Interventions,
First Edition. Edited by Daniel T. Wilcox, Tanya Garrett, and Leigh Harkins.
© 2015 John Wiley & Sons, Ltd. Published 2015 by John Wiley & Sons, Ltd.

therapeutic relationships centered on an emotional connectedness and obtaining intimate historical details from the patient, which place the professional at a higher risk. This risk is higher compared to other professionals whose patient encounters are less emotionally intrusive (Brooks et al., 2012).

Professionals who cross sexual boundaries with patients are at risk of exploiting the inherent power differential that exists within this relationship in addition to creating irreparable damage to the therapeutic alliance and the victim. In fact, the Federation of State and Medical Boards in the US established guidelines for addressing sexual boundaries which outlined components of the evaluation and treatment to assist in determining disciplinary sanctions against the offending medical professional (Federation of State Medical Boards of The United States, n.d.). The Federation of State Medical Boards reported that from 1997 to 2006 1.77% of the total complaints filed to the medical boards nationally were for allegations of sexual misconduct (Federation of State Medical Boards of The United States, 2006). A retrospective analysis of the Oregon Board of Medical Examiners from 1998 to 2002 reported 3.1% of closed complaints were for allegations of sexual misconduct, which showed a decrease from a comparative study that found 5.9% from 1991 to 1995 (Enborn, Parshley, & Kollath 2004). Hence, medical associations and licensing boards recognize the importance of protecting the public from unethical sexual boundary violations and when a complaint is received individuals are referred for assessments tailored at the examination of the static and dynamic factors that contribute to that individual's sexual misconduct. More importantly, these assessments determine a professional's rehabilitative prognosis.

The focus in this chapter will be with the evaluation and treatment of a physician who engaged in sexual misconduct. Each evaluation center assessing professionals has developed its own system of assessment, but many do so in the form of a multidisciplinary team that extensively examines the professional over the course of approximately 3 days. This chapter explores the system developed by the first two authors at the Behavioral Medicine Institute of Atlanta over the last 20 years of assessing and treating professionals engaged in sexual misconduct.

Case Introduction

Presenting complaint and history

Dr. A, a married internist in his 40s, was referred by his medical licensing board after he was accused of the inappropriate touching of prepubescent boys outside of his medical office. He reported that he had no history of sexual or physical abuse and was happily married. He denied a sexual interest in prepubescent boys or girls and reported that the allegations were "misunderstandings." He attested that for many years he had cared for his two teenage daughters and one preteen son without incident. As a consequence of the criminal charges against him, the licensing board suspended his license and requested an independent medical evaluation with an emphasis on his risk to patients. The licensing board feared the possibility that the doctor could have touched children for sexual purposes during the course of providing medical care in addition to these criminal allegations. Dr. A denied a history of inappropriate touching of children.

The initial encounter

Most evaluees report that they have been inappropriately accused of professional sexual misconduct and want to immediately defend themselves against the injustice of the allegation. The initial task is to conduct a fitness for duty evaluation that is not prejudiced against the individual being assessed but evaluates the allegations brought against him or her by the professional licensing board. The initial encounter begins with a telephone consultation that facilitates the establishment of a therapeutic contact prior to the individual being seen in the office. This consultation includes obtaining the essentials of the allegations and is an opportunity for the evaluator to outline the upcoming days of the evaluation. At the end of this encounter, a request is made for a 10-page description of the allegations written by the professional that should include the following elements: what happened, with whom, when, where, and their interpretation of any misunderstandings. This description of the allegations gives the individual the opportunity to describe their side of the story without admitting errors but focusing instead on misunderstandings regarding the allegations. The evaluator should avoid accepting a 10-page description from the professional's attorney, since the goal for the evaluator is to compare the 10-page account of the alleged sexual misconduct with the professional's account of what happened when the professional is seen, in addition to the history provided by the various collaborative sources.

Explaining the fitness for duty evaluation to the professional

The evaluation begins after all releases are signed. The evaluator explains that anything reported by the evaluee might appear in the subsequent report, and there are no "off-the-record" comments. The evaluator must also inform the individual that with this evaluation their confidentiality is waived because the summary of the evaluation is forwarded to the referring source, such as a professional licensing board. We do not discuss the collateral information already received but instead allow the evaluee to describe their side of the story because it is this direct explanation from the evaluee that affords the opportunity to compare it with their 10-page description and with the collateral information already received from the referring source. In the initial stages of the evaluation, the term sexual harassment is less pejorative and people appear more familiar with it than professional sexual misconduct and thus it may be used initially when referring to the allegations.

Clinical presentation at the assessment

When professionals are confronted with their possible inappropriate behavior, they usually immediately become angered and take the position of defending themselves without a consideration of the tremendous power differential that exists between a patient and a professional and the consequence to a patient or staff member who has been sexually harassed. Male professionals commonly take the position that sexual encounters simply involve dating where consensual sexual activities sometimes develop. They view themselves as the same person they were prior to becoming a professional, rather than accepting the mark of the power differential that develops as soon as the professional becomes licensed. It is especially difficult for professionals in the midst of defending themselves to empathize with the consequences of their behavior for their victim. But if they continue to sustain a hostile attitude with the evaluator and with the licensing board or referring source, the referring source could potentially place greater restrictions on them, since the professional would appear to be in denial and lack insight.

A professional's reluctance and hostility towards an evaluation requires that the clinician conduct a comprehensive history including but not limited to the clinical, social, and sexual history, review of collateral information, psychological testing, and psychophysiological evaluations (Abel, Osborn, & Warberg, 1998). This comprehensive approach targets the assessment of personality psychopathology, psychological disorders, and substance use disorders that may have been contributing factors, and will be integral during the course of treatment.

Objective assessment of sexual interest and the validity of self-report

Most cases referred for assessment involve alleged behavior not observed by third parties; therefore, it is critical to gather information that can provide an objective assessment about the allegations. We have found it helpful to utilize the direct measurement of sexual interest and polygraphs in the evaluation of cases of professional sexual misconduct. The direct measurement of sexual interest is accomplished with visual reaction time (viewing time) and/or plethysmography. Such direct measurement is not helpful with allegations of sexual involvement that is "normal sexual behavior," but is more helpful in situations that include sexual involvement with patients, staff, or individuals unable to give consent, those under age or those allegedly assaulted during procedures where they were unconscious. When the evaluee is accused of sexual involvement with patients who are under age, child pornography, Internet chatting with underage individuals, or unusual sexual interests, an objective sexual evaluation is also useful.

In the case of Dr. A, the objective measure of his sexual interest is advantageous due to the nature of the allegations made against him. During his evaluation, an objective assessment of his sexual interest was conducted. Figure 13.1 shows the results of the objective assessment measure used in the case of Dr. A, which is visual reaction time (VRT™).

In interpreting the VRT™ in Figure 13.1, when the horizontal shaded bar exceeds the vertical line it indicates that the individual has a sexual

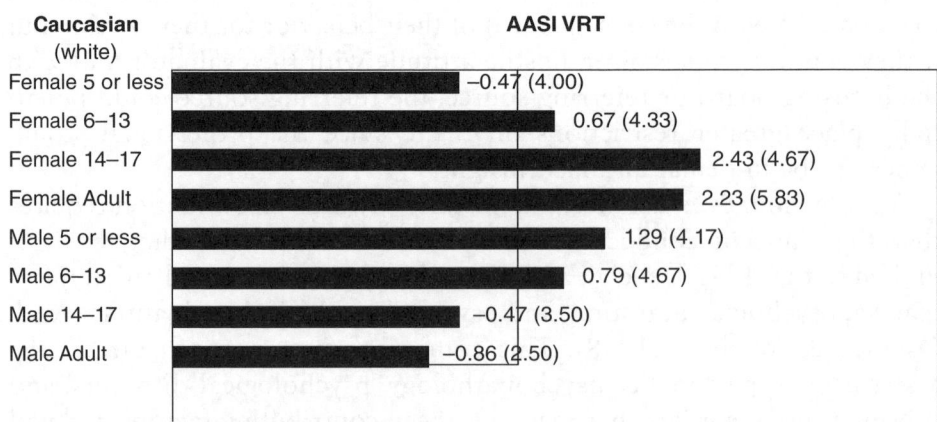

Figure 13.1   Objective assessment measure of sexual interest (visual reaction time (VRT™)). Adapted from Abel, Osborn, & Warberg, 1995, 1998.

interest in that category (Abel & Wiegel, 2009). Dr. A initially denied a sexual interest in prepubescent boys or girls. The objective measure above, however, indicated he had sexual interest in prepubescent boys and prepubescent girls. Specifically it demonstrates that Dr. A has a sexual interest in Caucasian females 6 to 13 years of age, adolescent females 14 to 17 years of age, and female adults. He also has a sexual interest in males 5 years or less, and males 6 to 13 years of age.

When shown these objective assessment results, Dr. A admitted to a sexual interest in prepubescent children of both genders and agreed to enter treatment. Dr. A further reported that his sexual interest began approximately 10 years prior to the allegations and began with his use of adult pornography which shifted to his viewing of teenage pornography. He reported that while he viewed the pornography he masturbated to these images and later began to notice that he became "curious" when having interactions with his children's friends. Despite this reported and measured sexual interest in prepubescent youth, Dr. A denied the allegations and denied touching minor patients for sexual purposes in his medical office.

The use of polygraphs in assessment

In addition to the direct assessment of sexual interest, we find polygraphs exceedingly helpful. Evaluees who have retained legal counsel immediately point out that polygraphs are inaccurate and subsequently are not accepted in legal proceedings. However, referral from the professional licensing boards usually does not involve a legal case, and licensing boards expect the evaluator to use whatever methods the evaluator has found effective in assessing cases of alleged professional sexual misconduct. Since most allegations do not involve the direct observation of genital contact between the professional and the patient, polygraphs serve as an adjunct to resolve issues regarding the disparities in the accounts of the incident.

By the end of the second day of a 3-day evaluation, the allegations and or admissions by the professional and collateral information have often clarified the potential issues that need further evaluation. Polygraph examinations, like any other assessment measure, have false positives and false negatives, but at Behavioral Medicine Institute of Atlanta we find them to be helpful in a number of different ways. During the fitness for duty evaluation regarding sexual misconduct it is a helpful adjunctive measure in determining whether there are additional victims. For example, an evaluee could be asked on a polygraph examination whether he has carried out sexual touching of patients or staff aside from the current allegation.

The following is data from an unpublished study conducted at the Behavioral Medicine Institute of Atlanta of 97 professionals accused of professional sexual misconduct who were referred for a polygraph examination. In this study, approximately 50% of professionals passed the polygraph and 43% of professionals failed the polygraph, 2% had indeterminate polygraph results, and 4% refused the polygraph. Of the individuals who failed the polygraph, approximately 33% admitted to additional victims of professional sexual misconduct after this failure. These results suggest that polygraphs may serve as an additional tool in seeking clarity in cases where an individual might be minimizing their professional sexual misconduct during the clinical interviews. The determination of whether an evaluee has carried out sexual touching of any patients or staff unknown to the board is important information to the referring source. This can be exceedingly helpful to boards since, although the professional may have touched patients or staff, a clear indication from the polygraph examination that there was no other inappropriate touching gives assurance to the board that other than what is known there is nothing else. Since the board and those treating the case of professional sexual misconduct are especially concerned about posttreatment reoffending, polygraphs can also be used to substantiate or not whether a treated individual has carried out any inappropriate touching since completing their assessment.

Treatment considerations and case conceptualization

Treatment for professional sexual misconduct takes a variety of forms, but we prefer the cognitive behavioral model with a strong relapse-prevention component (Abel et al., 1998). The treatment is divided into an acute phase and a maintenance phase, and each of these phases is dependent on multiple factors including the degree of the violation, the number of victims, and comorbid psychological or psychiatric factors.

Our practice has been using cognitive behavioral treatment for over 20 years because of its flexibility in dealing with almost all types of sexual misconduct between a professional and their patients and/or clients. The purpose of an assessment is to identify the factors or apparent factors that lead the professional into inappropriate contact. What follows are a few examples of attitudes, beliefs, and/or behaviors that stereotypically led to categories of professional sexual misconduct.

Professionals frequently become involved in sexual harassment as they rise in the power structure of an organization and their flirting, inappropriate touching, or inappropriate comments are initially ignored by ancillary staff. Treatment involves teaching the professional what constitutes sexual harassment, mobilizing the organization to have a written harassment-free policy, organizing the staff to retrain the organization periodically about how to avoid allegations of sexual harassment, and feedback to the professional when sexual harassment is suspected or alleged. Physicians' treatment of chronic pain patients, many of whom use addictive narcotics and some of whom are addicted to narcotics, frequently leads to the allegation of "sex for drugs," that is the professional gives excessive drugs for sexual favors from patients. These cases frequently involve the patient tolerating inappropriate comments, kisses, dating, and intercourse to ensure they obtain their narcotics. After treatment for sexual offending, the professional is frequently not allowed to treat patients with chronic pain, not allowed to work in a solo practice, and required to always have an informed chaperone present any time they see female patients where physical examinations are required.

Professionals with a breast fetish (severe fixation on women's breasts) who undertake examinations that traditionally require close contact with the patient's breasts area (breast examinations for cancer, cardiac evaluations, lung disease, echocardiograms, etc.) have extensive and severe attachments to women's breasts. These professionals undergo covert sensitization or odor aversion treatment to block or reduce their attachment to women's breasts. These cases are particularly difficult if, in the course of medical care, contact with a breast area traditionally occurs. In these cases, the recommendation may have to be made that they remove pelvic examinations and breast examinations from their practice and refer those cases to another professional. Some are required to conduct breast examinations in a very specific, rigid sequence so that any variations from those guidelines are reported.

We have treated children's dentists who abuse mothers of indigent children, which frequently is not reported by the mother since the mother of the child finds it nearly impossible to afford a dentist for their child, and thus tolerates such abuse by the dentist. Chaperones or dental assistants are subsequently fully informed about the allegations against the dentist, and the dentist, his staff, and the therapist hold periodic conferences to clarify proper boundaries between the dentists and the child's mother. Attorneys accused of establishing sexual relationships with their clients in the midst of litigation once again are educated regarding sexual harassment, protocols for having a sexual harassment free office, and supervision by more mature lawyers.

All of these cases profit by more open discussion with staff working with the professional regarding the allegations against them and or the realities of those allegations. Staff members, in the presence of the professional and the therapist, are trained in the importance of honest feedback to the therapist. The establishment of professional boundaries, the mechanism of frequent reporting of the professionals behavior to the therapist (which is provided on a quarterly basis to the licensing bureaus), as well as the integral part that polygraphs play to assure that inappropriate behavior does not occur after acute treatment is completed. Often, since the inappropriate behavior is alleged to have occurred with no one around, organizing treatment does not demand admission of inappropriate behavior, but instead organizes the professional's work life to remove situations that might give the appearance of the opportunity for inappropriate sexual behavior.

There are situations in which the licensing agency may have significant concerns related to the treatability and access to vulnerable patients if inappropriate sexual behavior has occurred in the workplace. Therefore, the treatment center must ensure that stringent recommendations and monitoring mechanisms are in place. For example, once Dr. A completed treatment, the medical board was initially hesitant to allow him to transition back to work, despite being deemed fit to return to practice. Since our recommendations included that he was not allowed to have anyone under 18 years of age in the office, his staff were agreeable to follow these recommendations, and he was polygraphed periodically regarding this issue, the board was agreeable to these stringent follow-up recommendations and allowed him to return to practice.

Course of treatment and assessment of progress

The duration of treatment and the sequencing of the treatment vary considerably from one program to another, especially with acute treatment. For the most difficult cases, the individual receives cognitive behavioral treatment for 5 hours a day, 5 days per week, for 8 weeks. However, in some cases treatment may take 1 to 3 weeks followed by the individual returning to practice for a week or 2, then returning for a week or 2 of treatment, and continuing back-and-forth between treatment and their professional duties. This alternation of treatment is only a possibility assuming that the patient is compliant, and checks and balances have been put in place to confirm that no further inappropriate behavior has happened.

In the case of Dr. A, he was not allowed to practice until he completed the cognitive behavioral treatment, and cases similar to this which involve pedophilia often require a completion of treatment or finishing a good portion of treatment before transitioning back to practice. Therefore, intensive treatment 5 days a week is very acceptable to the professional and the licensing board. With completion of the intensive treatment and ongoing maintenance treatment, the recidivism rate is approximately 1% at Behavioral Medicine of Atlanta (Abel et al., 1998).

The approach to acute treatment comprises individual and group psychotherapy and includes the following components: odor aversion, covert sensitization, victim empathy, cognitive restructuring, anger management, assertiveness training, intimacy training, relapse prevention, and addressing personality conflicts and characteristics.

1. Odor aversion: The professional is taught how to associate his deviant fantasies and behaviors with the negative consequences of offensive odor inhalation such as through the use of ammonia capsules (Abel & Osborn, 1999). In the case of Dr. A, odor aversion therapy is critical in reducing his sexual interest in children.

2. Covert sensitization: The professional learns the full impact of the consequences of his deviant behaviors and how to remind himself of those consequences continually so as to control his deviant behaviors (Abel, Osborn, Anthony, & Gardos, 1992). In the case of Dr. A, covert sensitization is also critical in reducing his sexual interest in children.

3. Victim empathy: The lack of empathy arises as the professional develops cognitive distortions to rationalize his behavior (Abel & Osborn, 1999). The professional examines his inappropriate sexual behavior from the standpoint of his victim and examines the negative impact of his behavior on the life of his victim. Victim empathy is also critical to treatment because sometimes offenders who molest children or who engage in a professional sexual boundary violation do not see the victim again. Therefore, the offender does not see the consequences of their victimization.

4. Cognitive restructuring: The professional confronts the incorrect beliefs and rationalizations that have supported his involvement in deviant sexual behaviors in the past through the use of cognitive restructuring (Abel, Osborn, & Warberg, 1995).

5. Anger management: The professional learns to identify inappropriate anger patterns in his behavior as well as developing appropriate anger management skills.

6. Assertiveness training: The professional learns to more effectively deal with others without aggression but, at the same time, still being able to express themselves.

7. Intimacy training: The professional learns the elements of an intimate relationship and how to develop closer intimacy in their relationships. They also learn to improve communication and better resolve problems within relationships. In addition, any sexually deviant behavior will also be addressed during this component of treatment.

8. Relapse prevention: The professional examines his motivation and identifies thought patterns and situations that put him at risk of acting out in order to develop more appropriate coping skills to deal with stress and to make appropriate changes in his behavior.

9. Personality characteristics and conflicts: In individual and group therapy, the professional examines his personality characteristics that create conflicts in his personal life. Individuals are given teaching materials on the different personality features and disorders and are assisted in improving insight into their personality characteristics and how it impacts their relational style with others. In particular, an individual learns how their personality characteristics may have contributed to the sexual misconduct.

10. Sexual harassment and boundaries: In this therapy module, the professionals are taught the definition of sexual harassment, its various forms, its impact on victims, and why many victims do not report it. Additionally, they learn how to establish and maintain a sexual harassment free workplace. The professionals are also taught about various types of boundaries that must be maintained, such as avoiding physical contact, flirtatious language, money, gifts and services, their role as a clinical provider, time, place, space, and how victims are impacted when these boundaries are violated.

The above treatment modules are a standard example of treatment offered to all professionals being treated for sexual misconduct. However, cognitive behavioral treatment can be adjusted to accommodate the specific treatment needs of the offending professional. With regards to Dr. A, he engaged in the above treatment and we added specific treatment related to his pedophilia to address this sexual interest (Abel, Osborn, & Phipps, 2001). He was very compliant with the treatment and he hired someone else to manage his medical practice while he was in treatment.

Complicating factors

A complicating factor to the assessment and treatment of a professional may be that the specifics of an unreported incident of child abuse are determined during the course of the evaluation or treatment. Prior to the assessment the professional must be thoroughly informed regarding the mandatory reporting laws and the consequences of the evaluator learning of unreported child molestation. This was an especially important factor during the assessment and treatment of Dr. A given the nature of his pedophilic interest and prior allegations of child molestation.

It is very common that offending professionals within the course of treatment begin appreciating the totality of the consequences of their engaging in sexual misconduct. Specifically, an individual may have significant negative consequences to their practice and family, and extreme financial loss. Depression is a very common result and, therefore, the treatment provider has to be attentive to intervening immediately especially in assessing the risk of suicidality in the offending professional. The offending professional must be given a sense of hope and informed that treatment has been effective with other professionals who have been treated with cognitive behavioral therapy and it is very probable that they will be returning to work.

Access and barriers to care

Treatment centers for professional sexual misconduct are limited and thus an individual's geographical location is one factor that is a barrier to maintenance treatment. With the development of technology those professionals who are in rural areas or in geographically distant areas can receive individual therapy via telemedicine. Another alternative for these individuals is to have ongoing psychotherapy with a local therapist who is familiar with the unique practice and psychological factors of the professional and can provide more intensive psychotherapy once the professional returns to their local area. This treatment is especially important when an individual has a personality disorder and will require long-term psychotherapy to address personality psychopathology. The major problem that individual therapists have in treating cases of professional sexual misconduct is that they must keep in mind what is best for the patient, but, at the same time, what is safe for potential patients in the future. Some therapists are reluctant to take on this dual responsibility in treating professional sexual misconduct and, therefore, should avoid it.

Licensing agencies are frequently unfamiliar with how effective treatment can be and, therefore, they need to be informed. It is helpful for the therapist to appear with the offending professional (if requested by the professional) at the time they must appear before the professional licensing agency or board. Thus, it is important for the treatment provider to educate the licensing board about the components of treatment, effectiveness of treatment, and recidivism rates posttreatment, when appearing before a professional licensing agency.

In the case of Dr. A, the barrier for him was his living in a rural area. Therefore, he received intensive acute therapy at Behavioral Medicine Institute of Atlanta, and once he entered into maintenance treatment, a local therapist followed him in addition to frequent contact with our treatment center. In addition, his wife was incorporated into the maintenance treatment to assure that he was compliant with treatment and address the familial dynamics of his behavior outside of the practice.

Follow-up

After the completion of the maintenance phase of treatment, the referring source is informed of the completion of treatment and the recommendation on whether the professional is fit to return to practice with external monitoring measures. If the licensing board or referral agent agrees to the return of the professional into practice, the monitoring by this source may be for 3 to 5 subsequent years. One longitudinal study conducted by Brooks and colleagues evaluating individuals who presented to the Colorado Physician Health Program found the length of monitoring ranged from 547 days to 1460 days for sexual misconduct (Brooks et al., 2012). Commonly, the licensing boards will enter into a consent order in which the individual signs an agreement with the licensing board that they will comply with certain restrictions for a certain period of time. In the case of Dr. A, he also signed a consent agreement which outlines that child molestation will be reported to authorities, as is mandated throughout the United States.

A system of checks and balances posttreatment is integral in minimizing the risk of reoffense. These include the following monitoring measures: the use of chaperones, staff surveillance forms, patient surveillance forms, polygraphs, a professional mentor, and the involvement in a psychotherapy group for professionals. Since the professional is having regular contact with patients after treatment and the duty of the professional licensing boards is to protect the safety of patients, it is essential that checks and balances be put in place to protect the public. The treatment provider of the offending professional will collect information from all the monitoring measures and assess whether the professional is compliant with the recommendations and then forward this information to the licensing board on a quarterly basis.

The use of a chaperone by offending professionals is greatly supported by licensing boards and involves the direct observation of the performance of the professional with patients. The polygraph and surveillance forms that are utilized in maintenance treatment are a mechanism to monitor that the professional is being compliant with the use of a chaperone.

Staff surveillance forms are self-report forms developed for staff working closely with the offending professional who are then asked for direct observation of their behavior and the professionals interactions with others during the course of their clinical work. The self-report forms are advanced to the treatment provider on a monthly basis and completed by the staff, but not observed by the professional. These forms are reviewed by the treatment provider to identify any suggestions of inappropriate behavior or noncompliance with the treatment plan. Items that are frequently included for some cases would be inquiring if the professional has a chaperone present for all physical examinations of patients, if the professional has a sexual harassment free office, if the chaperone has initialed all treatment notes reflecting that they were present during any physical examinations, and if the professional has avoided seeing patients of a specific gender or age if that were the recommendation of the treatment team.

Some professionals are not allowed to work over 40 hours per week or during certain times of day such as seeing patients or clients after hours. Thus, the staff working with the offending professional will be asked if the individual is being compliant with the treatment recommendations. It is obvious that the individuals filling out these staff surveillance forms may be paid by the offending professional and thus may either be intimidated or not report certain deviations as a result of a fear of the loss of employment. Hence, prior to beginning such staff surveillance forms, meetings are held with the offending professional's staff and the treatment team or provider to clarify the importance of honesty on the staff surveillance forms. The confirmation of compliance of such forms can be incorporated into polygraphs posttreatment. In the case of Dr. A, the staff surveillance form included monitoring that he was not treating underage patients and had no unsupervised contact with minors. Please see Table 13.1 for the form used to gather information from Dr. A's staff.

Patient satisfaction forms are the opportunity to receive feedback from the patient. Since the patient is a professional's "customer," it is appropriate for the professional and his treatment provider to have feedback from the patient regarding the professional's behavior. In the case of clergy, the form would be the opportunity for church members to provide feedback, and this form specifically addresses the professionalism of contact with church members (Warberg, Abel, & Osborn, 1996). Patient satisfaction

Table 13.1 Staff Surveillance Form. (Adapted from Abel, Osborn & Warberg, 1995, 1998.)

STAFF SURVEILLANCE FORM

Rater's Name (Please Print)_____

Date_____

Rater's Signature:_____

Dr. _____ strictly adheres to an adult only practice. He needs your assistance in providing him feedback regarding his interaction with patients and their family members. Please evaluate each area of performance by circling the appropriate answer (Yes, No, Don't Know).

1. Sees no patients under age 18.	Yes	No	Don't Know
2. If children under 18 are in the treatment area with relatives, he is <u>always</u> accompanied by a staff member.	Yes	No	Don't Know
3. Deals with patients and their family members in an ethical manner.	Yes	No	Don't Know
4. Interacts professionally with patients, patient's family members and staff and shows no evidence of sexual harassment.	Yes	No	Don't Know
5. Avoids revealing details about his personal life to patients, their families and his staff.	Yes	No	Don't Know

Please add any specific comments below. _____

_____

Dr. _____'s signature below indicates his awareness and approval of your surveillance of him and that he agrees to your advancing these reports, irrespective of their consequences, to his supervisor or therapist. Please advance your report directly to:

_____

Doctor Signature

forms are completed every 3 months, and are completed by all patients seen in a 1-week interval. The forms include questions about the professional's practice that would normally be requested by any practice, but also includes items such as does the professional have a sexual harassment free office, the presence of a chaperone, and specific treatment recommendations that the offending professional must follow. For example, Dr. A's patient satisfaction forms included questioning about whether he treats individuals less than 18 years of age and conducts examinations in a professional manner. Please see Table 13.2 below for the form used to gather information from Dr. A's patients.

Table 13.2   Patient Satisfaction Survey. (Adapted from Abel, Osborn & Warberg, 1995, 1998.)

Patient Satisfaction Survey

It is our desire to offer good quality care in a comfortable atmosphere. We value your opinion about how we are doing and would like to have you rate us in a number of areas. Please circle the answer which best describes your opinion about your care and treatment at our office. Please include any comments that you feel would help us improve the service we provide you.

Your Doctor's Name:_____

Today's Date:_____

Does your doctor,

1.	Sees me at my scheduled time?	Yes	No	Don't Know
2.	Conduct medical exams in a professional manner?	Yes	No	Don't Know
3.	Have a sexual harassment free office?	Yes	No	Don't Know
4.	Only treat individuals 18 or older?	Yes	No	Don't Know
5.	Explain anticipated examinations, diagnoses and treatment?	Yes	No	Don't Know

Please add any comments that you think would help us improve your care or make you feel more comfortable.

_____

_____

_____

Please circle your gender   Female   Male

_____

Please initial (no full name please)   (Today's date)

Please return to the business manager when completed

The satisfaction forms are passed out by the staff and are not shown to the offending professional, but advanced to the therapist and incorporated into the quarterly reports that are provided by the therapist to the board or referring agency. If the therapist reviewing the forms identifies patterns of replies that indicate concern with regard to noncompliance, the therapist may contact the physician or staff for further clarification (Abel & Osborn, 1999).

Polygraphs can be a useful adjunct to supervising the professional who has returned to practice. Boards are familiar with urine or blood screens to rule out relapse from substance abuse, since it provides fairly objective evidence about relapse. Polygraphs are used to confirm that in the case of professional sexual misconduct the professional has not touched patients or staff for sexual gratification since entering treatment, and has been compliant with the elements of the consent decree they have signed from the licensing board. Our use of polygraphs at Behavioral Medicine Institute of Atlanta is not meant to imply their validity, but simply to point out that they are a vital element of assessing the validity of the evaluee's report, the extent of inappropriate behavior, and confirmation that inappropriate behavior has stopped posttreatment.

Polygraphs for an individual accused of the inappropriate touching of patients or staff members may be conducted at 3-, 6-, and 12-month intervals following treatment, and every 12 months thereafter. Dr. A was asked the following polygraph questions in such a fashion:

1. Since completing your previous polygraph, have you touched a patient or former patient, or staff member or former staff member, for sexual gratification?
2. Since completing your previous polygraph, have you had oral, vaginal, or anal sex with any patient or former patient, or any staff person or former staff person?
3. Since completing your previous polygraph, have you masturbated to thoughts of children less than 18 years of age?
4. Since your last polygraph, have you been alone with a patient under 18 years of age?

The outcome of the polygraph results were then incorporated into the quarterly reports advanced to the licensing board. It is especially important to point out to licensing boards that there are false positives and false negatives with polygraphs and they are not what are called "ground truth." If an individual fails a polygraph examination, it does not automatically mean that they should not practice. In the event that an individual should fail a polygraph, then the treatment agent examines factors that potentially contributed to the failure. Interventions that may be implemented after the failure of a polygraph include increasing the frequency of supervision and reporting, repeating the polygraph by a different polygrapher, and/or further examination and investigation of the professional and the professional's staff regarding this specific allegation. These interventions can assist the treatment provider in further determining the possibility of the polygraph results as true positive or false positive.

Another element of maintenance treatment is having the offending professional identify a mentor who can provide a level of supervision regarding the proper maintenance of professional boundaries. The mentor should have the same clinical training as the offending professional so that they may have a better knowledge about the practice setting and needs of the offending professional. The mentor should also be informed of the issues surrounding the professional sexual misconduct, especially through reading the professional's evaluation summary that includes the details of their inappropriate behavior.

A final component of external monitoring is having the offending professional involved in a psychotherapy group specifically for offending professionals. There is a considerable anxiety when professionals are accused of inappropriate sexual behavior and when transitioning back into practice. It is especially helpful to develop groups of such professionals in treatment or posttreatment so that the experiences of other professionals can be shared between group members. This is helpful because some group members are in the midst of treatment, some have completed the intensive portion of treatment recently, some have been followed for 6 months to a year, and others may have been followed for 5 years or more. Despite this heterogeneity amongst all group members in their treatment, the group members can share their experiences of how they dealt with specific problems that came up during their follow-up, including but not limited to further interactions with the referring source, daily professional interactions with patients and staff, the retraining of staff, legal issues, and high risk situations (Abel et al., 1995). In essence, some group members are usually on a different timeline of treatment compared to other group members and they can be of considerable assistance to one another. The frequency of these meetings depends upon where the member stands in the treatment process and this ranges from attending monthly to at least every 3 months. As with any psychotherapeutic group, the issues of confidentiality are discussed to make it clear that breaches of confidentiality within the context of the group would lead to an individual's dismissal. More importantly, the veil of confidentiality allows individuals that participate within these professional groups a venue to openly discuss the issues that arise personally and professionally without the fear of being exposed publicly.

Treatment implications of the case

The case of Dr. A demonstrates to the reader that it is possible to treat an individual who has sexual interest in children on an outpatient basis. The inclusion of Dr. A's case in this chapter demonstrates that even physicians with a sexual interest in children can return to practice posttreatment, although of course not to treat individuals under 18 years of age. However, professional sexual misconduct treatment more commonly involves professionals having sex with adult patients or former patients or staff, and this too includes the elements of treatment discussed in this chapter.

The follow-up over 5 years in duration with Dr. A's licensing board with continued polygraphs showed no evidence of any type of inappropriate sexual contact with children. He continues in treatment well beyond his licensing board monitoring contract.

Recommendations to Clinicians and Students

We recommend that an individual who has no experience in this area work closely with a treatment program that has experience and is well established in this area. Dr. A's case is also not appropriate for treatment that is primarily provided by a student or trainee, owing to the nature of the allegations and since an individual's license and the public's safety are at risk. The reason this is important is that the failure of treatment can be catastrophic for victimized patients and the professional may lose their license. Furthermore, it is important that the professional licensing board feel comfortable with the checks and balance systems that are instituted so that they feel the offending professional is adequately supervised and the public is protected.

References

Abel, G. G., & Osborn, C. (1999). Cognitive-behavioral treatment of sexual misconduct. In J. Bloom, C. Nadelson, & M. Notman (Eds.), *Physician sexual misconduct* (pp. 225–246). Arlington, VA: American Psychiatric Press.

Abel, G. G., Osborn, C., Anthony, D., & Gardos, P. (1992). Current treatments of paraphiliacs. *Annual Review of Sex Research*, 3, 255–290.

Abel, G. G., Osborn, C., & Phipps, A. (2001). Pedophilia. In G. Gabbard and S. Levin (Eds.), *Treatments of psychiatric disorders* (3rd ed., Vol. 2, pp. 1981–2005). Arlington, VA: American Psychiatric Press.

Abel, G. G., Osborn, C., & Warberg, B. (1995). Cognitive-behavioral treatment for professional sexual misconduct. *Psychiatric Annals*, 25(2), 106–112.

Abel, G. G., Osborn, C., & Warberg, B. (1998). Professionals. In W. Marshall, Y. Fernandez, S. Hudson, & T. Ward (Eds.), *Sourcebook of treatment programs for sexual offenders* (1st ed., pp. 319–335). New York: Springer-Verlag.

Abel, G. G., & Wiegel, M. (2009). Visual reaction time: Development, theory, empirical evidence, and beyond. In F. Saleh, J. M. Bradford, A. J. Grudzinskas, & D. Brodsky (Eds.), *Sex offenders: Identification, risk assessment, treatment, and legal issues* (pp. 101–118). New York: Oxford University Press.

Borys, D. S., & Pope, K. S. (1989). Dual relationships between therapist and client: A national study of psychologists, psychiatrists and social workers. *Professional Psychology: Research and Practice, 20,* 283–293.

Brooks, E., Gendel, M., Early, S., Gunderson, D., & Shore, J. (2012). Physician boundary violations in a physician's health program: A 19-year review. *Journal of American Academy of Psychiatry and The Law, 40,* 59–66.

Dehlendorf, C., and Wolfe, S. (1998). Physicians disciplined for sex-related offenses. *Journal of the American Medical Association, 279*(23), 1883–1888.

Enborn, J., Parshley, P., & Kollath, J. (2004). A follow-up evaluation of sexual misconduct complaints: the Oregon Board of Medical Examiners, 1998 through 2002. *American Journal of Obstetrics and Gynecology, 190*(6), 1642–1650.

Federation of State Medical Boards of The United States. (n.d.). *The discipline module and overview of the board's discipline process.* Retrieved April 14, 2014 from http://www.fsmb.org/pdf/foundation-mpp-discipline-module.pdf

Federation of State Medical Boards of The United States. (2006). *Addressing sexual boundaries: Guidelines for state medical boards.* Retrieved April 14, 2014 from http://www.fsmb.org/pdf/GRPOL_Sexual%20Boundaries.pdf

Garrett, T., & Davis, J. (1998). The prevalence of sexual contact between British clinical psychologists and their patients. *Clinical Psychology and Psychotherapy, 5,* 253–263.

Gechtman, L. (1989). Sexual contact between social workers and their clients. In G. O. Gabbard (Ed.), *Sexual exploitation in professional relationships* (pp. 27–38). Washington, DC: American Psychiatric Press.

Kardener, S., Fuller, M., & Mensh, I. (1973). A survey of physicians' attitudes and practices regarding erotic and nonerotic contact with patients. *American Journal of Psychiatry, 130,* 1077–1081.

Pope, K. S., Keith-Spiegel, P., & Tabachnick, B. G. (1986). Sexual attraction to clients: The human therapist and the (sometimes) inhuman training system. *American Psychologist, 41*(2), 147–158.

Sansone, R., & Sansone, L. (2009). Crossing the line. *Psychiatry (Edgmont), 6*(6), 45–48.

Warberg, B., Abel, G., & Osborn, C. (1996). Cognitive-behavioral treatment for professional sexual misconduct among the clergy. *Pastoral Psychology, 45*(1), 49–63.

Wilbers, D., Veenstra, G., van de Wiel, H. B. M., & Schultz, W. C. M. (1992). Sexual contact in the doctor–patient relationship in the Netherlands. *British Medical Journal, 304,* 1531–1534.

14

Working with Zoosexual Offenders (Addressing High Levels of Deviance)

Daniel T. Wilcox, Caroline M. Foss,
and Marguerite L. Donathy

Introduction

The authors of this chapter produced an article in relation to a male sexual offender with zoosexual interests some time ago (Wilcox, Foss, & Donathy, 2005). In the intervening period, there has been very little published in relation to these kinds of issues, possibly as a result of the stigma associated with sexual activity with animals. The current chapter provides an overview of the existing literature together with a focus on this individual and another two individuals who have engaged in zoosexual offenses, highlighting the levels of deviance and crossover associated with this subgroup of sexual offenders.

Theoretical and Research Basis for Treatment

Considerably more is known about most human sexual aberrations and abusive acts than about sexual activities with animals. Indeed, for most individuals, even experienced professionals, such cases give rise to discomfort, feelings of incredulity, and perhaps accompanying (and psychologically distancing) nervous laughter (Wilcox et al., 2005). There is also a perception that professionals writing about human sexual contact with animals may be "frowned upon by colleagues" (Beetz & Podberscek,

Sex Offender Treatment: A Case Study Approach to Issues and Interventions,
First Edition. Edited by Daniel T. Wilcox, Tanya Garrett, and Leigh Harkins.
© 2015 John Wiley & Sons, Ltd. Published 2015 by John Wiley & Sons, Ltd.

2009, p. vii). However, human sexual contact with animals is something that dates back many thousands of years (Rosenberger, 1968). Beetz and Podberscek provide a historical overview of bestiality traversing time, culture, religion, and class. They discuss changes to the law in various countries around the world and note an array of animals that have been targeted by humans for sexual exploitation, from domestic pets and farm animals, including sheep, horses, and cattle, to crocodiles, snakes, and bees. Cleopatra was reputed to have used a sealed box containing agitated bees as a sexual stimulant (Love, 1992).

There has been some disagreement about the overall prevalence of zoophilia and bestiality. For example, Money (1986) and Earls and Lalumiére (2002) asserted that true clinical zoophilia (or preferential bestiality) is likely to be quite rare, while Kinsey, Pomeroy, and Martin (1948) reported that approximately 1 in 13 men engage in sexual contact with animals. Unfortunately, Kinsey et al.'s (1948) research provided little clarification as to whether this engagement was preferential (zoophilic) or in some way reflected a compensatory sexual outlet more associated with bestialists. However, Miletski (2001) reported prevalence rates provided by Hunt (1974) wherein 4.9% of the men and 1.9% of the women in the study reported having engaged in bestiality. This contrasted with a study by Kinsey, Pomeroy, Martin, and Gebhard (1953) involving 5,792 women, where they reported that approximately 5% of these women had engaged in some form of sexual contact with animals.

Within criminal justice settings, individuals convicted of sexual offenses involving animals were found to be the most deviant and indiscriminate of sex offenders, with the greatest degree of crossover offending (Abel, Becker, Mittelman, Cunningham-Rathner, Rouleau, & Murphy, 1987; Abel & Rouleau, 1990). Crossover is identified when an individual moves from a specific pattern of offending into other areas: for example, from intrafamilial to extrafamilial abuse; from abuse of children to abuse of adults; from noncontact to contact offenses; and when individuals demonstrate other sexual behaviors that are distinctly different from their index offense, including, for example, fetish behaviors, sadomasochism, or sexual activity with animals. Abel (1999) strongly advises that professionals should be mindful of the potential level of dangerousness in individuals convicted of zoophilic offenses. Indeed, a study by Abel, Becker, Cunningham-Rathner, Mittelman, and Rouleau (1988) revealed that 100% of their zoophilic subgroup (n = 14) had more than one paraphilia, with 50% having more than five additional paraphilias.

Perhaps it is because of the high deviance (e.g., zoophiles frequently present with other, more "routine" or societally concerning, paraphilic involvements) that sexual activity with animals is not diagnosed specifically in either of the two principal diagnostic manuals for mental disorders, namely the *International Classification of Diseases* (10th ed.; ICD-10; World Health Organization, 1992) and the *Diagnostic and Statistical Manual of Mental Disorders* (5th ed.; DSM-5; American Psychiatric Association, 2013). Indeed, it has been asserted that, "zoophilia is virtually never a clinically significant problem by itself" (American Psychiatric Association, 1987, p. 405). Rather, sexual activity with animals is noted among "Other Disorders of Sexual Preference" and "Paraphilia Not Otherwise Specified" respectively. The ICD-10 refers to patterns of sexual preference and activity and includes a reference to sexual activity with animals. The DSM-5 refers to zoophilia among other paraphilic interests and activities, and describes insufficient evidence to warrant its inclusion as other than "Paraphilia Not Otherwise Specified."

Within the field of sex offender work, zoophilia has become the prevalent term for criminal sexual acts involving humans and animals (Abel & Rouleau, 1990), largely replacing the previously used term, bestiality. However, there has been much debate in relation to this issue (Master, 1966; Matthews, 1994; Miletski, 2002; Neufeldt & Guralnik, 1989), such that some researchers (Earls & Lalumiére, 2002) have set out to identify typologies for individuals who engage in sexual activity with animals with a view to distinguishing offender characteristics and motivations. This kind of typology is similar to the model put forward by Knight and Prentky (1990) in relation to rapists and by Wright et al. (1996) for stalking behavior. However, it is our view that Aggrawal (2011) offers a useful classification system based on his earlier model for necrophilia (Aggrawal, 2009) in an effort to "end this confusion" (p. 73). Aggrawal's ten-category classification system is on a continuum, allowing for a much broader definition of bestiality and zoophilia as well as multiple categorizations as appropriate.

Importantly, however, none of the studies the present authors have reviewed in their thorough literature search have directed specific attention to the high-deviancy and significant crossover sexual behaviors that have been observed. Indeed, individuals convicted of zoophilic behaviors have been reported to have the highest crossover rates for deviant sexual acts (Abel & Rouleau, 1990) and practitioners should not assume on the basis of a sexual offender's index offense that they would not commit other sexual offenses (Heil, Ahlmeyer, & Simons, 2003; Wilcox & Sosnowski, 2005). Other areas of concern with zoophilic offenders relate to higher levels of cognitive or intellectual impairment and greater evidence of past sexual victimization (Duffield, Hassiotis, & Vizard, 1998).

For these reasons, the way in which we treat individuals involved in sexual contact with animals is extremely important if we are to maintain an appropriate focus on public protection. However, we consider that, along with further research, the development of intervention tools will be essential in achieving and maintaining therapeutic gains.

Case Study 1: Mr. Z

Our first case study relates to Mr. Z, a man who, at the time of referral, was in his mid 40s and who was referred via probation services at pre-sentence stage for assessment of risk, amenability to treatment, and prognosis for successful change. Mr. Z is a man of British nationality and Caucasian ethnicity who has a longstanding history of sexually deviant and violent behaviors. The referral related to his conviction for two counts of attempted buggery of horses. At the time of Mr. Z's arrest, he denied the allegations. However, he was convicted and received a 3 year Probation Order with a requirement to attend the Community-Sex Offender Groupwork Programme (West Midlands Probation Service, 2000).

Presenting complaints

Mr. Z's sexual offending began in his early adolescence or childhood, and during polygraph examination (discussed later) he reported a wide range of sexually deviant behaviors. There are suggestions that Mr. Z's interest in zoosexual activities intensified in adulthood. Overall, Mr. Z presented as a sexually disinhibited individual with a variety of deviant interests. It may be asserted that Mr. Z's lack of appropriate sexual outlets, combined with inadequate social and intimacy skills (Marshall, Anderson, & Fernandez, 1999), contributed to the development of sexual interest in animals. Nonetheless, there were indications that Mr. Z had acquired a genuine and specific sexual attraction to horses, as exemplified by his self-reporting of occasional preferential masturbatory fantasies about horses.

History

Mr. Z presented as a heavily built man with low self-esteem and poor hygiene and grooming. Affectively, he was rather flat, cautious, and defensive. While he was co-operative, he demonstrated poor eye contact and there was evidence of social awkwardness. Mr. Z described a difficult childhood wherein he was socially isolated and bullied. Indeed, his perception was that he had been ridiculed and persecuted for most of his life. He reported that his father, in particular, was very critical of him from a young age and that this had affected his ability to form reciprocal relationships. As a result of these early experiences, Mr. Z presented with some frustration and anger and he acknowledged fantasizing about sexually aggressing as a form of "getting even." Employment difficulties were also in evidence, as were intellectual limitations.

Mr. Z had a longstanding history of sexual and violent offending. He had convictions for seven sexual assaults, two of which were for rape and were described in police reports as "callous acts of sexual violence." Other offenses included indecent assaults and exposure. He had a conviction for actual bodily harm and for threatening and abusive behavior, together with a conviction for breaching his Probation Order. Mr. Z spent approximately 5 years in custody.

Assessment

Mr. Z was administered the Shipley Institute of Living Scale (SILS; Zachary, 1996). While he demonstrated vocabulary skills at the twenty-fifth percentile (25%), his abstract reasoning abilities were below the tenth percentile (<10%). Mr. Z was deemed to function within the borderline range of intelligence (American Psychiatric Association, 2013).

Actuarial risk assessment employing the RM2000 (Thornton et al., 2003) revealed Mr. Z to be in the high-risk category. There was also evidence of high deviance (Beckett, Beech, Fisher, & Fordham, 1994). In our opinion, Mr. Z fits the profile of a sexually obsessed and largely indiscriminate offender. This type of sexual offender seems likely to experiment with many kinds of sexual behavior. Employing the "pathways model" of relapse prevention developed by Ward and Hudson (2000), Mr. Z would probably be best described as an approach-automatic offender whose behavior can be characterized as impulsive, situational, and under-regulated. There are indications that his offending behavior is very entrenched and that he is always in cycle (Wolf, 1988), i.e. he is always waiting to offend and has a broad range of sexual interests, such that the presentation of offense opportunities is the key stimulus factor associated with risk of future offending, because he is characterologically drawn towards abuse opportunities. As such, while sexual fantasy is likely to play a secondary role as a precipitant to offending, it may at times give shape to the expression of a sexually abusive outlet. Mr. Z is amoral and ego syntonic with regard to capitalizing on sexual outlets. Further, due to a heightened sex drive and an externalized locus of

Table 14.1 Estimated Additional Offenses Disclosed during Pre-test Interview

Victims of indecent assault	700
Stalking incidents (as an adult)	400
Victims of frottage	300
Victims of indecent exposure (as an adult)	30–50
Victims of indecent exposure (as a child)	50–80
Public masturbation (as an adult)	20–30
Public masturbation (as a child)	10
Victims of obscene telephone calls	2

Note: Reproduced with permission from Wilcox, D. T., Foss, C. M., & Donathy, M. L. (2005). A case study of a male sex offender with zoosexual interests and behaviors. *Journal of Sexual Aggression*, *11(3)*, 305–317.

control, his offending behavior appeared to often involve limited organization and planning.

Mr. Z was not open to fully disclosing his sexual history and interests, leading to a request for polygraph examination. To determine the extent of Mr. Z's offending behaviors for which he was not convicted, a Sexual History Disclosure Examination was undertaken (Wilcox & Sosnowski, 2005; Wilcox, Sosnowski, Warberg, & Beech, 2005). Table 14.1 provides a summary of estimated additional offenses disclosed by Mr. Z during pretest interview.

In addition, Mr. Z acknowledged masturbating to images and fantasies about victims' physical features and their reactions to his offending, as well as fantasizing about women accepting him both socially and sexually. Despite these numerous additional disclosures, unfortunately, full disclosure may not have been achieved as the examination was prematurely terminated due to feelings of distress and anger on the part of Mr. Z, much of which related to the disclosures about his sexually abusive acts during his childhood.

Case conceptualization

Levels of deviance are an important factor in determining treatment needs, as those with high levels of deviance are known to recidivate at a higher rate (Allam, 2000; Andrews & Bonta, 2010; Beech, 1997/1998). While the primary focus of Mr. Z's sexual fantasies is adult females, his most recent sexual offending was against animals. This demonstrates highly deviant sexualized thinking associated with a heightened risk of further sexual offending.

On the basis of Aggrawal's (2011) classification system, we would posit that Mr. Z would fit into categories III and VII, Zoophilic Fantasizers and Opportunistic Zoophiles. Individuals who are classified as Zoophilic Fantasizers engage in zoophilic fantasies of intercourse with animals and may masturbate in the presence of animals. Mr. Z fantasized about intercourse with animals and masturbated in their presence, though he denied this latter issue. In any event, he acknowledged masturbating to pictures of horses in prison with the rationale that it was "safer" than to "take out sexual aggression on a woman." Such self-serving distortions about sexual behavior with animals are not unusual in our experience. For example, an offender with a history of sexually abusing children informed the first author that he had decided to have sex with dogs in a local parkland area, rather than pursuing his interest in children. Notably, he was apprehended for this because police found him in possession of a hunting knife and he informed them that this related to his sexual interest in dogs as he described, "sometimes they don't like it."

Aggrawal (2011) suggests that individuals who are Opportunistic Zoophiles normally engage in sexual behaviors with animals but would also be content to engage in sexual activities with humans. With regard to Mr. Z, while he is content to have sexual intercourse with a human, if the opportunity arose for sexual activity with an animal, he would not refrain from doing so. However, it is unlikely that he "loves the animal at an emotional level" as is asserted with many bestialists.

Course of treatment and assessment of progress

Based on Mr. Z's assessment results, it was initially deemed appropriate for him to engage in the mainstream Community-Sex Offender Group-work Programme (C-SOGP). However, it quickly became apparent that he experienced difficulties in this setting, largely as a result of his awkward social presentation and his problem solving difficulties. Indeed, the other group members began to "scapegoat" Mr. Z and, as his progress was insufficient, it was considered appropriate to transfer him to the Adapted SOGP. While this group was primarily established to provide a groupwork setting for individuals with diagnosable intellectual disabilities, it was subsequently extended for those with borderline intellectual functioning

(Allam, Middleton, & Browne, 1997; Wilcox, 2004a, b). The rationale for this was that individuals with borderline functioning have difficulty acquiring new skills and competencies and the adapted group reinforced learning through a range of mediums including drama, art, role play, relaxation, and imaginative work. Facilitators employed a multisensory approach to engaging offenders and there was a strong reliance on homework to confirm that positive changes were being made and maintained (Blacker, Beech, Wilcox, & Boer, 2011; Wilcox, Beech, Markall, & Blacker, 2009; Wilcox et al., 2005).

A multicomponent approach (Cerrone, 1991) was employed, with family therapy being modified to include therapists, probation officers, and hostel staff in a co-ordinated and structured manner in order to understand and manage Mr. Z's behavior. In working with him, the primary focus was one of public protection using the containment approach (English, 1998). Mr. Z was also subject to scrutiny by the Multi Agency Public Protection Arrangements (MAPPA) board (Home Office, 2003) with the involvement of police, probation, social services, and the local primary care trust. The groupwork therapeutic process included the development of broad relapse prevention skills, including assisting offenders to understand, predict, and control sexually abusive behaviors, sexually deviant interests, pro-offending cognitive distortions, and socio-affective functioning. The program also directed attention to improving self-management skills (Marshall et al., 1999; West Midlands Probation Service, 2000). Group and individual sessions included social assertiveness training and sex education as part of the adapted program, which are considered an effective means of reducing risk (Cerrone, 1991). Individual sessions were also conducted to gain a better understanding of Mr. Z's wide-ranging deviant interests. Therapeutic intervention incorporated the behavioral method of stimulus control procedures (Tarrier, Wells, & Haddock, 1998) to assist Mr. Z in recognizing situations and feelings that might elicit zoosexual and other deviant responses, together with early identification to determine alternative courses of action. There was also an element of covert sensitization (Marshall et al., 1999) to assist him in identifying and stopping pro-offending thoughts.

Quite early on in the program, Mr. Z disclosed sexually abusive fantasies about a woman at a further education course he attended. It was clear to facilitators that Mr. Z was quite imminently at risk of perpetrating a further sexual offense, as he acknowledged having followed this woman to a less-used building exit, with explicit thoughts of assaulting her. Mr. Z's probation officer was informed of this disclosure and a decision was taken to terminate Mr. Z's involvement in this course. However, Mr. Z required support from peers to come to terms with this decision and to accept that it was the responsible and "less risky" thing to do.

Notably, Mr. Z's offenses were a source of notable discomfort for him in groupwork. For example, initially he referenced his conviction in vague terms such as "offenses against livestock." Further, at the outset of treatment and for a significant period of therapeutic intervention, Mr. Z wholly denied any interest in or arousal to sexual activity with animals.

Complicating factors

During treatment, Mr. Z reported significant emotional abuse during his childhood, as well as additional paraphilic interests. While he made gains in the adapted group, he continued to have interpersonal difficulties within the hostel where he resided, such that treatment facilitators had to intervene on Mr. Z's behalf. Further work was undertaken with Mr. Z to increase his coping abilities, including anxiety management skills, relaxation training, and cognitive reframing. Mr. Z reported that this sometimes helped him to control his anger.

Access and barriers to care

Throughout treatment, Mr. Z continued to deny any prior planning for his offenses. However, it was clear to all concerned that it was not a purely spontaneous act insofar as Mr. Z had considered the difficulties associated with penetrating a full size horse, judging this during interview to be "physically impossible." Rather, he chose to target Shetland ponies. In addition, Mr. Z's offenses occurred in a rural area where he would not have had such ready access to his usual targets, on the basis of his known history of stalking and frottage. It also transpired over time that Mr. Z had developed a paraphilic interest in horses while previously incarcerated as he was noted to masturbate to images of them, increasing his motivation and intention to engage in these activities should the opportunity arise postrelease (Finkelhor, 1986; Ward & Hudson, 2000). Mr. Z subsequently reported that on the day of his offense he was experiencing a variety of feelings that would have placed him at a high risk of reoffending. These emotions included anger, depression, rejection, loneliness, and sexual frustration.

Mr. Z was also known to have a leather fetish and he enjoyed attending "country fairs," though when this was discussed with him he accepted that he would be placing himself in risky situations if he did so. Importantly, Mr. Z may have had some difficulty discriminating between fantasy and reality and certainly appeared to confabulate. He fabricated stories about his interactions with women and when questioned about this in group became defensive. Indeed, the reference to a "girlfriend" he described seemed likely to have been about someone in whom he became interested, likely through following, but with whom he never established a relationship. Mr. Z attributed his offending to being in a "very depressed state – very out of it," stating that this had been the result of "a relationship breakdown." Mr. Z said that he had dated a woman for 5 months and the relationship ended when he disclosed his offending history to her. Mr. Z also reported that she "put him down" because he was "unable to get an erection." During the individual sessions and further to discussions with his hostel keyworker, Mr. Z later acknowledged that this "relationship" was almost entirely fanciful as the young woman did not reciprocate his feelings and regarded him as an unwelcome stranger with whom she periodically came into contact.

Also during the therapeutic process, there were two incidences of stalking, one victim was a stranger and the other was a staff member at the hostel where Mr. Z resided. Mr. Z was challenged about these issues and although he initially denied engaging in these behaviors, he subsequently acknowledged doing so. However, he had also been observed masturbating in a field while watching farm animals, though he continued to deny this offense throughout, claiming that he had been urinating.

Follow-up

Within the adapted group, Mr. Z made some motivational gains and appeared to feel less isolated than when attending the mainstream group. Attendance improved and through this slower more tailored approach a better contribution to the groupwork was achieved. His polygraph disclosure also served to increase his openness within the group and although he required reminders and encouragement, he showed improvements in terms of hygiene, appearance, and self-esteem. The latter improvements had a helpful impact, as Mr. Z was then not targeted as much by his peers in the group. Further, the consequent better participation by Mr. Z resulted in some apparent improvements in his ability to manage deviant sexual urges. Relatedly, there were indications of his offending behavior being better contained through improved collaboration with therapists, probation officers, and residential keyworkers, such that offense cycles may have been averted and further offending interrupted.

Multiagency arrangements were in place for Mr. Z over the course of his 3-year Probation Order. At the conclusion of Mr. Z's order, despite some gains, he continued to pose a significant potential threat to the public (in particular adult females) and, as such, ongoing monitoring was recommended. There were also serious concerns about his potential arousal to children, exacerbated by his unwillingness to be open in respect of this issue. With encouragement, Mr. Z agreed to continue to engage in one-to-one monthly sessions for a further 17 months at the conclusion of his order. During this time, his attendance was generally good, though he did miss two sessions, at which time his appearance and hygiene were observed to have deteriorated. These kinds of issues are considered important risk factors (Craig, Browne, Stringer, & Beech, 2005; Hanson & Harris, 1999). Nonetheless, when challenged about these issues, Mr. Z responded positively. In addition, Mr. Z maintained regular contact with the manager of the hostel where he had resided and with the local community police officer. Having these various professionals involved in an ongoing capacity served to improve community safety through ongoing observation and assessment.

While it is not known whether Mr. Z has reoffended sexually since his convictions in 1993, he has not been arrested or convicted of any further sexual offenses since that time. He was, however, arrested for failing to notify the authorities of a change in residence and for carrying an offensive weapon. Overall, it was judged that Mr. Z's noncompulsory extended involvement directly impacted upon risk factors. He evidenced adequate responsiveness to voluntary supervision and continuing therapeutic assistance. He also achieved greater continuity and support in terms of lifestyle management and quality of life. Mr. Z benefited from extensive interagency involvement with an emphasis on public protection. Interventions interrupted a pattern of serious criminal convictions and provided tentative support, despite ongoing concerns, that such cases can demonstrate treatment potential and produce observable gains.

There continued to be concerns about Mr. Z concealing important aspects of his offense cycle and deviant arousal. He has since declined further supportive work and it is not known what his current status is, though he is not involved with the local probation service. He continues to be high risk and he is not registered on the Sex Offenders' Register (Her Majesty's Stationery Office, 1997) because his conviction predated the Act. Mr. Z is no longer subject to formal supervision and his whereabouts are unknown. This is concerning in view of his multiple paraphilias, his assessed level of dangerousness, and the seemingly beneficial impact of his probation and postprobation treatment and supervision.

Case Study 2: Mr. A

Case introduction

Mr. A was a tall, stocky 23-year-old homosexual man who presented as very well-groomed, neat, and orderly. Mr. A was convicted of the possession of child pornography, for which he received a 5-year probation sentence with the condition to successfully complete the Sex Offender Treatment Programme. Officers retrieved images from his computer of a prepubescent female performing fellatio on prepubescent boys, an image of a female under the age of 10 performing cunnilingus on an adult female, an image of prepubescent boys engaging in anal sex, and other adult sexual activity.

Mr. A reported regularly to a probation officer and he was mandated to undergo annual polygraph examination. He was required to register as a sexual offender. He was referred for outpatient sexual offender treatment as a result of a suspended imposition of sentence (SIS). The merit of completing treatment under an SIS was that the offenses would not remain on Mr. A's record if he successfully completed his probation within the allocated time.

Presenting complaints

Mr. A's deviant sexual interests began in late childhood or early adolescence. Mr. A reported having experimented sexually with his younger brother, the family dog, and farm horses. His use of pornography intensified in his teenage years and early adulthood, leading up to his arrest for possession of child pornography. Overall, Mr. A presented as sexually compulsive, and this included fetish paraphilia disclosures throughout the course of treatment. Mr. A reported social isolation and anxiety about approaching possible partners. Over the course of treatment, Mr. A admitted an addiction to adult pornography as well as engaging in a wide range of sexually deviant behaviors and fetishes.

History

Mr. A had no prior criminal history. He reported discovering pornography at the age of 11 while at school, reportedly viewing a gay website in the library with other students. Mr. A claimed that he did not know how the site appeared, though he recalled seeing a nude male on the site. However, it should be noted that Mr. A's treatment provider questioned the veracity of his reported childhood sexual experiences. Shortly after his first exposure to pornography, he began secretly viewing adult pornographic images on the family computer. Mr. A became aroused by the images and began masturbating daily beginning at age 12. His interest transferred to viewing mostly gay male pornographic images at around the age of 13.

Mr. A began masturbating the family dog at the age of 12, rationalizing his behavior as "experimentation," though contradictorily describing having masturbated to specific fantasies of masturbating the dog. He engaged in sexual acts with the family dog for a period of 6 months before becoming involved sexually with his brother. During this time, Mr. A began having sexual relations with a horse on the property. He admitted that his zoosexual behavior was the most difficult topic of discussion. Mr. A reported the sexual penetration of a horse on six or seven occasions before discontinuing. Despite his assertion of feeling shame afterwards, Mr. A acknowledged experiencing sexual excitement when offending against animals. Mr. A continued to engage in sexually deviant acts throughout high school, though he denied any current fantasies or desires to offend against animals. Mr. A denied viewing animal pornography, though he stated he might have downloaded it "unintentionally."

Mr. A disclosed fetishes in relation to men's underwear, boots, chaps, and hats. He reported masturbating while wearing cowboy boots as this caused him to feel like a masculine cowboy. Mr. A reported that he has a large penis, which caused his brother pain when he tried to penetrate him. Mr. A masturbated to images of jock straps to enhance a visual image of the size of his penis.

While Mr. A regularly denied masturbating altogether when a polygraph examination was undertaken, he consistently reported daily masturbation to his therapist.

Mr. A viewed searches of "cock rings, jock straps, and cowboys" on EBay, with most images depicting the male's underwear midsection. He recently admitted masturbating while watching a TV rodeo event because he was attracted to the cowboys. Mr. A admitted inserting objects into his rectum for pleasure and continuing to "sex text" an older male whom he met online when he was 16. It is believed that this older man approached Mr. A via a chat room.

Mr. A denied any history of sexual abuse. Further, he has not had sexual intercourse with anyone other than his brother. He adamantly denied any attraction to minors and reported that he "accidentally" downloaded child pornography because he was downloading so much material through a sharing site called LimeWire. Mr. A reported viewing pornography to relieve stress. At the age of 18, Mr. A engaged in oral sex on one occasion with another gay male who was known to him and of appropriate age. This is Mr. A's only reported age-appropriate sexual encounter.

Assessment

While Mr. A's intellectual functioning was not formally assessed, he was judged to function within the high average to above average range based on his academic success. Mr. A graduated with top honors from a well-established university. On the RM2000, Mr. A's results were within the high-risk category in relation to sexual reoffending.

Case conceptualization

Mr. A was fearful of approaching possible partners and it appeared that the Internet served to "connect" Mr. A with the outside world. Mr. A appeared to fit into an avoidant active pathway (Ward & Hudson, 2000) and tended to use retroflection as a primary process style. Retroflection is a process in which he does to himself what he wishes others would do to him. It could be argued that Mr. A's fetish behaviors are retroflective. For example, he fantasized of "bear" (gay term for burly man) cowboys performing oral sex on him. He wears cowboy boots when masturbating to enhance the fantasy and the boots give Mr. A the perception that he is the cowboy he desires.

Course of treatment and assessment of progress

The Sexual Offender Treatment Programme is designed to address denial, thinking errors, victim empathy, and relapse prevention, but also includes components of the good lives model (GLM). Some researchers argue that the traditional relapse-prevention model and the GLM should unite together to combine risk management and recognition of future goals and life successes (Harkins, Flak, Beech, & Woodhams, 2012; Ward, Mann, & Gannon, 2007). This combination unites risk management and addresses underlying core issues that have blocked offenders from moving forward. The GLM also helps offenders work on shame reduction and personal accountability when looking to the future of risk reduction.

During the course of treatment, Mr. A disclosed that at the age of 12, he became involved in a sexual relationship with his 10-year-old brother. Sexual behaviors almost always included anal intercourse and oral sex. The sex continued with his brother for 6 years until Mr. A was 18 years of age. Mr. A reported that the sexual behaviors were "consensual" and they stopped just prior to his move out of the family home to attend college. Mr. A denied any sexual attraction to his brother, stating that it was simply a sexual outlet. He reported a close relationship with his parents, noting that he subsequently returned to live at home together with his brother and sister.

The therapeutic process involved a multidisciplinary team approach to involve Mr. A's parents and probation, to include Internet monitoring software installed on his computer, and frequent use of the polygraph to monitor behaviors.

Complicating factors

Mr. A reported no history of victimization or abuse. However, he perceived himself as introverted and anxious when meeting new people stating, "I was always this way." Mr. A reported an unremarkable childhood, noting that he began to feel "different" during puberty. He said that he became increasingly aware of a sexual attraction towards males. He reported that he became openly homosexual at the age of 19.

Access and barriers to care

Mr. A was co-operative and polite but extremely guarded. Initially, he lacked insight about zoosexual offending behavior. For example, he did not report to the group about his zoosexual offenses until 3 years into treatment. Mr. A minimized the offending by blaming it on childhood experimentation. He reported that the abuse did not harm the animals and the family dog appeared to enjoy the abuse. He did not acknowledge any pre-existing fantasies leading to his zoosexual offenses, nor did he acknowledge planning or "seemingly irrelevant decisions" that placed him one-step closer to offending. He appeared to be in denial about any attraction to animals or minors. In addition, he made minimal progress following a healthy sexual behavior plan on a consistent basis. Mr. A often relapsed and viewed images that were consistent with fetish paraphilias and images that could be identified as pornographic.

Polygraph disclosures suggested that Mr. A was currently in his offending cycle but he expressed great difficulty recognizing similar patterns of behavior.

Follow-up

At the time of writing, Mr. A had been engaged in treatment for approximately 3 years, and had made minimal progress. He recently requested individual counseling. He was fearful of approaching other homosexual males and he isolated himself. Mr. A is working on reducing anxiety, increasing ego strength, and is working on a strategy to approach possible partners without using the Internet. Individualized treatment goals include work with Mr. A to recognize deviant sexual arousal, making healthier sexual choices, challenging denial, arousal restructuring, and relapse-prevention planning.

Since the start of individual therapy, as well as continuing with group therapy, Mr. A has become more social in group settings and recently went on his first date with a man. However, Mr. A appears to continue to engage in secretive sexual behaviors without acknowledging his offending chain and has great difficulty accepting responsibility for his offending. It is clear that Mr. A has an extensive sexual history with pornography and fetish behaviors to include sexual behaviors with animals. His history indicates that he was an "opportunistic zoosexual" according to Aggrawal's (2011) classification system, but he denies any sexual desires to act out against animals at this time. It is unclear as to whether he would act out sexually against an animal if no other sexual outlets were available to him.

Mr. A is a moderate-risk offender. At the time of writing this chapter, he appears to be in the beginning stages of acknowledging deviant sexual arousal patterns and does not consistently use a viable relapse prevention plan, which will likely increase his risk of reoffending. Mr. A will continue with individual and group treatment. Group treatment will aim to help break down denial to include acknowledgment of addiction components to his offending behaviors and incorporating the GLM to future goals.

Case Study 3: Mr. B

Case introduction

Mr. B was a 24-year-old Caucasian male referred for sexual offender treatment as a result of committing incest against his 13-year-old sister. He was approximately 22 at the time of arrest but he disclosed that he had been sodomizing his sister since she was 7 years of age and began having intercourse with her when she was 13. Mr. B was 16 when he began offending against his sister but he had been offending against other victims since the age of 13.

Presenting complaints

Mr. B had a severe history of abuse and neglect beginning in early childhood. He began sexually offending against his adopted sisters and community members into adulthood until his arrest. He had engaged in sexual contact with farm animals, including cats, chickens, and cows, up until his recent incarceration. It was clear that Mr. B presented with deviant sexual arousal patterns from an early age, including zoophilic sexual interests and desires.

Throughout the course of treatment, Mr. B continued to engage in zoosexual behaviors with animals until he was discharged unsuccessfully from his treatment program as a result of failing to attend group therapy and lack of progress in treatment.

History

Mr. B had no prior criminal history but was placed in and out of foster homes until the age of 7. His parents were low functioning and did not appear to have the capability to adequately care for him and his six siblings. Mr. B had a conviction for speeding but no other forensic history. However, there were allegations of sexual abuse against other victims, though legally this remained unsubstantiated.

A Mennonite family adopted Mr. B at the age of 7. He was brought into a home where there were multiple children and stepchildren. Boundaries were limited at best. All children worked on the family farm and were often left unsupervised. The Mennonite community is closely related to the Amish. He attended Mennonite school and completed the eighth grade before dropping out.

Mr. B had a detailed history of early abuse and neglect. He was physically abused and neglected by his parents. He originally denied any sexual abuse victimization but later reported that a boy in his teens raped him when he was 5. He reported feeling loved but lonely. Mr. B often talked about his adoptive father in a positive light, but never talked about his mother.

Mr. B had never engaged in an appropriate sexual relationship. He denied the use of pornography.

Assessment

Mr. B's intellectual functioning was in a range suggestive of mild learning disability and borderline intelligence. He had an expressive language disorder and a diagnosis of articulation deficit, which adversely impacted upon his education and his involvement with sexual offender treatment. On the RM2000, Mr. B was within the medium-risk category.

Case conceptualization

Mr. B can be classified as an approach automatic offender (Ward & Hudson, 2000). He disclosed seven victims through the course of treatment, all female adopted siblings or girls who were part of the Mennonite community. Mr. B appeared to blame the girls for his offending believing "they wanted it" or led him on.

The youngest victim was 5 when Mr. B was 13. Most of his victims ranged from 5 to 13 years of age. Mr. B told all the victims not to tell, which indicated acknowledgement of the behavior as illegal and morally wrong. His distortions appeared entrenched. He reported that he believed all his victims enjoyed the abuse because they never told him to stop.

Mr. B disclosed attempting sex with chickens, cats, and cows. He reported that he felt lonely and "sexed." He committed acts against animals in his early teens up until he was terminated from group. He reported he would rather offend against animals than people. He was open about his attraction to animals, specifically cows. He knew certain "heifers" would kick so he would choose cows that "liked it." This suggested a planning process or "setting up" to offend.

Although he was never successful with intercourse with cats or chickens (he tried many times to the point of injury), the animals' fur and feathers served as arousal for masturbation. According to the classification research from Aggrawal (2011), Mr. B meets the criteria for class IV: tactile zoophiles; interest in animals increased to the level of touching them to receive sexual stimulation. Mr. B also meets the criteria for class VII: opportunistic zoosexuals. He denied any traditional definition of zoophilia where he was in love with animals. His acting out was to satisfy his sexual arousal.

Course of treatment and assessment of progress

Mr. B met requirements to attend a treatment group for offenders with learning disabilities. He was the lowest-functioning member of the group. Often, members had difficulty understanding him due to his pervasive speech disorder. Repetition was used to reinforce learning, and Mr. B needed assistance with all written work.

The therapeutic process focused mostly on relapse-prevention components of sexual offender treatment as these have been proven to be effective with those with limited intellectual capacity. Elements of the GLM were also inherent within the treatment approach, for example, aiming to enhance quality of life (please see chapter 8).

Family therapy was requested but denied by the family. Family members minimized Mr. B's risk. Probation officers were active in monitoring his whereabouts but often monitoring was difficult due to the closed rural community and geographical landscape.

Complicating factors

Mr. B presented with disorganized thought patterns and distorted beliefs. He often responded with anger or took up a defensive position. Further, the group attempted to use him as a scapegoat as his intellectual limitations were obvious and his sexual behavior appeared to stand out from the average offender. In these regards, Mr. B was very similar to Mr. Z.

Access and barriers to care

Mr. B was not following any safety plan to avoid reoffending. He was discovered riding tractors with minors on his lap, and he was left to work alone on a farm with farm animals. His adoptive parents refused to participate in a supervisor group and he had very little support. He was found violating on numerous occasions for high-risk behaviors and was placed on GPS monitoring as a result.

Mr. B's plan consisted of asking the "little children" to leave the farm so he could work. His religious community did not believe Mr. B was a risk. His plan to stay away from animals failed many times. He reported that just being in the presence of animals made him want to have sex with them. He would find opportunities to be alone with animals (ignoring components of his safety plan to never be alone) and attempt sexual activity, knowing that someone would be arriving within 5 minutes. He claimed that he was never caught but when he was kicked in the face by a cow and received bruising, the farmers questioned his motives. Unfortunately, there were no other readily available work positions for him that did not include farming.

Mr. B did not appear to have any internal structures in place to stop offending against animals.

Follow-up

Mr. B attended treatment for approximately 8 months. However, his attendance was sporadic and, as noted above, he was discharged from treatment as a result. He was an indiscriminate, high-risk, intellectually disabled offender who, if given the opportunity, would offend against potential human victims and animals. His victims will most likely be vulnerable and known to him. At the time of publication, Mr. B was attending treatment with another provider, though it is unknown whether he has made any progress in terms of reducing his risk.

Treatment Implications of the Case Studies

The current trend of research suggests incorporating both relapse-prevention and GLM components into treatment. Ward et al. (2007) and Harkins et al. (2012) are in favor of balancing both models for treatment of sexual offenders but as Harkins et al. report, "too much focus on promoting goods could result in a happy, but still dangerous offender" (p. 536).

As demonstrated by the above case studies, often individuals convicted of sexual offenses against animals are high risk and high deviancy. They demonstrate a greater amount of indiscriminate offending and higher rates of crossover. As such, we would argue that among all sexual offenders, these individuals require the most treatment. While existing treatment models can assist in reducing risk, the intensity and duration of interventions of most standard treatment programs does not appear to be sufficient to fully address such high-risk and high-deviance offenders' needs. We would suggest that further research is needed with a view to developing more structured and robust therapeutic models for working with individuals who have zoophilic interests.

Such high-risk and high-deviance offenders would benefit from more intensive community monitoring, frequent polygraphs, and lifetime registration (Harkins, Ware, & Mann, 2013). Therapy aimed to include mindfulness-centered dialectical behavioral therapy (DBT) would be beneficial, as components of DBT teach distress tolerance skills. Indiscriminate patterns of abuse noted in these offenders suggest that improved emotional resilience is likely to be crucial to disrupt engrained offense-related cognitive behavioral response chains.

Recommendations to Clinicians and Students

Best practice guidance would suggest a broad base of therapeutic and psychoeducational support availability for these individuals, together with the development of good offender–professional support relationships with a view to maintaining longitudinal involvement. As referenced above, focusing on acute risk issues is important, and regular supervision enables early intervention with regard to these factors. This necessitates finding a balance between process and content oriented intervention work as these offenders are more likely to manifestly bring current risk issues into the treatment sessions. Therefore, providing intervention work that is too structured and scripted may result in a lost opportunity to address acute relapse concerns. As such, conventional, accredited groupwork programs may be helpful but they should be run conjointly with individual sessions targeting these issues on an ongoing basis.

Gaining the co-operation of high-deviance offenders such as zoophilics is, in our opinion, often aided by including an element of "acceptance therapy" to assist clients whose sexual orientation is, and likely always will be, towards markedly sexually deviant behaviors. In relation to this, developing victim empathy is unlikely to be of any significant assistance with this group of offenders. However, fantasy modification work with a self-regulation emphasis and an underpinning focus on conceptualizing shame as a meaningful emotional component to attach to the behavioral consequences of further offending has shown therapeutic benefits (Brown, 2011). As such, tailored and supportive treatment programs are important and should include components on sexual addiction, modules addressing compulsive sexual behavior, and significant surveillance and monitoring efforts, including regular polygraph examinations. Notably, more deviant and indiscriminate offenders benefit from attending groups with individuals who have similar criminogenic backgrounds. This allows more intensive work to be undertaken and importantly will likely reduce harm that might be caused to low-risk offenders by engaging in treatment with high-deviance men.

In conclusion, intensive therapeutic input, surveillance and containment of deviant sexual behavior are key aims in the treatment and management of high-deviance and high-risk offenders. However, the aims of internalizing control, a co-operative orientation, and personal accountability must be overriding concerns, both in terms of providing ethical treatment (Wilcox, 2013) and in affording these offenders an opportunity to experience the respect of professionals and a sense of progress in life.

Acknowledgements

Some of the content of this chapter was first published in 2005 in the *Journal of Sexual Aggression* published by Taylor and Francis (doi: 10.1080/13552600500333804) entitled "A case study of a male sex offender with zoosexual interests and behaviors." The authors have modified some of the content, adding further case studies and conducting an updated literature review.

References

Abel, G. (1999, August). *Assessing and treating sex offenders*. Paper presented at the Specialized Services Conference Presentation on Assessing and Treating Sex Offenders. Chicago, IL.

Abel, G., Becker, J., Mittelman, M., Cunningham-Rathner, J., Rouleau, J., & Murphy, W. (1987). Self-reported sex crimes of nonincarcerated paraphiliacs. *Journal of Interpersonal Violence, 2*(3), 3–25. doi: 10.1177/088626087002001001.

Abel, G. G., Becker, J. V., Cunningham-Rathner, J., Mittelman, M. S., & Rouleau, J. L. (1988). Multiple paraphilic diagnoses among sex offenders. *Bulletin of the American Academy of Psychiatry and the Law, 16*, 153–168.

Abel, G., & Rouleau, J. (1990). The nature and extent of sexual assault. In W. L. Marshall, R. Laws, & H. Barbaree (Eds.), *Handbook of Sexual Assault: Issues, Theories, and Treatment of the Offender* (pp. 9–21). New York: Plenum Press.

Aggrawal, A. (2009). A new classification of necrophilia. *Journal of Forensic and Legal Medicine, 16*(6), 316–320. doi: 10.1016/j.jflm.2008.12.023.

Aggrawal, A. (2011). A new classification of zoophilia. *Journal of Forensic and Legal Medicine, 18*(2), 73–78. doi: 10.1016/j.jflm.2011.01.004.

Allam, J. (2000). *Sex offender groupwork programme: Evaluation manual accredited programme*. Birmingham: West Midlands Probation Service (accredited by the Home Office).

Allam, J., Middleton, D., & Browne, K. (1997). Different clients, different needs? Practice issues in community-based treatment for sex offenders. *Criminal Behavior and Mental Health, 7*, 69–84. doi: 10.1002/cbm.145.

American Psychiatric Association. (1987). *Diagnostic and statistical manual of mental disorders* (3rd ed.). Washington, DC: American Psychiatric Publishing.

American Psychiatric Association. (2013). *Diagnostic and statistical manual of mental disorders* (5th ed.). Arlington, VA: American Psychiatric Publishing.

Andrews, D., & Bonta, J. (2010). *The psychology of criminal conduct* (5th ed.). Cincinnati, OH: Anderson.

Beckett, R., Beech, A. R., Fisher, D., & Fordham, S. (1994). *Community-based treatment for sex offenders: An evaluation of seven treatment programmes*. Crown Copyright. Available from Home Office Library, 59 Queen Anne's Gate, London W1H 9AT.

Beech, A. (1997/1998). Towards a psychometric typology for assessing pre-treatment level of problems in child abusers. *Journal of Sexual Aggression, 3*(2), 87–100. doi: 10.1080/1355260978413272.

Beetz, A., & Podberscek, A. (2009). *Bestiality and zoophilia: Sexual relations with animals*. Oxford, UK: Berg.

Blacker, J., Beech, A. R., Wilcox, D. T., & Boer, D. (2011). The assessment of dynamic risk and recidivism in a sample of special needs sexual offenders. *Psychology, Crime and Law, 17*(1), 75–92. doi: 10.1080/10683160903392376.

Brown, S. (2011) *Treating sex offenders: An introduction to sex offender treatment programmes*. Didcot, UK: Routledge.

Cerrone, G. (1991). Zoophilia in a rural population: Two case studies. *Journal of Rural Community Psychology, 12*(1), 29–39.

Craig, L., Browne, K., Stringer, I., & Beech, A. R. (2005). Sexual recidivism: A review of static, dynamic and actuarial predictors. *Journal of Sexual Aggression, 11*(1), 65–84. doi: 10.1080/13552600410001667733.

Duffield, G., Hassiotis, A., & Vizard, E. (1998). Zoophilia in young sexual abusers. *Journal of Forensic Psychiatry, 9*(2), 294–304. doi: 10.1080/09585189808402198.

Earls, C., & Lalumière, M. (2002). A case study of preferential bestiality (zoophilia). *Sexual Abuse: A Journal of Research and Treatment, 14*(1), 83–88. doi: 10.1177/107906320201400106.

English, K. (1998). The containment approach: An aggressive strategy for the community management of adult sex offenders. *Psychology, Public Policy and Law, 4*(1/2), 218–235. doi: 1076-8971/98.

Finkelhor, D. (1986). *A sourcebook on child sexual abuse*. Beverly Hills, CA: Sage.

Hanson, K., & Harris, A. (1999). *Dynamic predictors of sexual recidivism*. Canada: Corrections Research, Department of the Solicitor General.

Harkins, L., Flak, V., Beech, A. R., & Woodhams, J. (2012). Evaluation of a community-based sex offender treatment program using a good lives model approach. *Sexual Abuse: A Journal of Research and Treatment, 24*(6), 519–543. doi: 10/1177/1079063211429469.

Harkins, L., Ware, J., & Mann, R. (2013). Interventions with dangerous offenders. In G. Davies & A. R. Beech (Eds.), *Forensic psychology: Crime, justice, law, interventions* (2nd ed., pp. 349–368). Chichester, UK: Wiley-Blackwell.

Heil, P., Ahlmeyer, S., & Simons, D. (2003). Crossover sexual offenses. *Sexual Abuse: A Journal of Research and Treatment, 15*(4), 221–236. doi: 10.1177/107906320301500401.

Her Majesty's Stationery Office. (1997). *Sex Offenders Act 1997*. Crown Copyright, London: The Stationery Office.

Home Office. (2003). MAPPA guidance. Retrieved May 8, 2008 from http://www.probation.homeoffice.gov.uk/files/pdf/MAPPA%20Guidance%20Update%202004.pdf.

Hunt, M. (1974). *Sexual behavior in the 1970s*. Chicago, IL: Playboy Press.

Kinsey, A., Pomeroy, W., & Martin, C. (1948). *Sexual behavior in the human male*. Philadelphia, PA: W. B. Saunders.

Kinsey, A., Pomeroy, W., Martin, C., & Gebhard, P. (1953). *Sexual behavior in the human female*. Philadelphia, PA: W. B. Saunders.

Knight, R., & Prentky, R. (1990). Classifying sexual offenders: The development and corroboration of taxonomic models. In W. L. Marshall, R. Laws, & H. Barbaree (Eds.), *Handbook of sexual assault: Issues, theories, and treatment of the offender* (pp. 23–49). New York: Plenum Press.

Love, B. (1992). *Encyclopedia of unusual sexual practices*. Fort Lee, NJ: Barricade Books.

Marshall, W. L., Anderson, D., & Fernandez, Y. (1999). *Cognitive behavioral treatment of sexual offenders*. Chichester, UK: John Wiley & Sons.

Master, R. (1966). *Sex-driven people*. Los Angeles, CA: Sherbourne Press.

Matthews, M. (1994). *The horseman: Obsessions of a zoophile*. Amherst, NY: Prometheus Books.

Miletski, H. (2001). Zoophilia: Implications for therapy. *Journal of Sex Education and Therapy, 26,* 85–89.

Miletski, H. (2002). *Understanding bestiality and zoophilia*. Bethesda, MD: East-West.

Money, J. (1986). *Lovemaps: Clinical concepts of sexual/erotic health and pathology, paraphilia and gender transposition in childhood, adolescence, and maturity*. New York: Irvington.

Neufeldt, V., & Guralnik, D. (1989). *Webster's new world dictionary: Third college edition*. New York: Webster's New World Dictionaries.

Rosenberger, J. (1968). *Bestiality*. Los Angeles, CA: Medco Books.

Tarrier, N., Wells, A., & Haddock, G. (1998). *Treating complex cases: Cognitive behavioral therapy approach*. Chichester, UK: John Wiley & Sons.

Thornton, D., Mann, R. E., Webster, S. D., Blud, L., Travers, R., Friendship, C., et al. (2003). Distinguishing and combining risks for sexual and violent recidivism. *Annals of New York Academy of Science, 989,* 225–235.

Ward, T., & Hudson, S. (2000). A self-regulation model of relapse prevention. In R. Laws, S. Hudson, & T. Ward (Eds.), *Remaking relapse prevention with sex offenders. A sourcebook.* (pp. 79–101). Thousand Oaks, CA: Sage.

Ward, T., Mann, R., & Gannon, T. (2007). The good lives model of rehabilitation: Clinical implications. *Aggression and Violent Behavior, 12,* 87–107. doi: 10.1016/j.avb.2006.03.004.

West Midlands Probation Service, Sex Offender Unit. (2000). *Community sex offender groupwork programme/manual*. Birmingham, UK: West Midlands Probation Service (accredited by the Home Office).

Wilcox, D. T. (2004a). Treatment of intellectual disabled individuals who have committed sexual offenses: A review of the literature. *Journal of Sexual Aggression, 10,* 85–100.

Wilcox, D. T. (2004b, September). *Treatment of developmentally disabled men who have committed sexual offenses: A review of the progress to date*. Keynote Presentation at the Scottish National Organisation for the Treatment of Abusers (NOTA) Annual Conference, Stirling, Scotland.

Wilcox, D. T. (2013). Ethical practice in the use of the polygraph in working with sex offenders. In K. Harrison & B. Rainey (Eds.), *Legal and ethical aspects of sex offender treatment and management.* Chichester, UK: John Wiley & Sons.

Wilcox, D. T., Beech, A. R., Markall, H., & Blacker, J. (2009). Actuarial risk assessment and recidivism in a sample of UK intellectually disabled sexual offenders. *Journal of Sexual Aggression, 15*(1), 97–106. doi: 10.1080/13552600802578577.

Wilcox, D. T., Foss, C. M., & Donathy, M. L. (2005). A case study of a male sex offender with zoosexual interests and behaviors. *Journal of Sexual Aggression, 11*(3), 305–317. doi: 10.1080/13552600500333804.

Wilcox, D. T., & Sosnowski, D. (2005). Polygraph examination of British sexual offenders: A pilot study on sexual history disclosure testing. *Journal of Sexual Aggression, 11*, 3–25. doi: 10.1080/1355260041000667797.

Wilcox, D. T., Sosnowski, D., Warberg, B., & Beech, A. R. (2005). Sexual history disclosure using the polygraph in a sample of British sex offenders in treatment. *Polygraph Journal, 34*(3), 171–181.

Wolf, S. (1988). A model of sexual aggression/addiction. *Journal of Social Work and Human Sexuality, 7*(1), 131–147. doi: 10.1300/J291v07n01_10.

World Health Organization. (1992). *The ICD-10 classification of mental and behavioral disorders.* Geneva, Switzerland: WHO.

Wright, J., Burgess, A., Burgess, A., Laszlo, A., McCrary, G., & Douglas, J. (1996). A typology of interpersonal stalking. *Journal of Interpersonal Violence, 11*(4), 487–502. doi: 10.1177/088626096011004003.

Zachary, R. (1996). *Shipley institute of living scale: Revised manual* (8th ed.). Available from: Western Psychological Services, 12031 Wiltshire Blvd, Los Angeles, CA 90025-1251.

15

Psychopathy and Sexual Offending

Caroline Logan and Julie Hird

Introduction

Psychopathy is a severe disorder of personality, incorporating key traits of pathological narcissism in addition to antisocial, histrionic, and paranoid presentations (Blackburn, 2006). This broad conceptualization of the construct, as well as developments in its measurement, provide two of the most important and influential advances in the forensic field in the twentieth century. From this work, there emerged a critical role for assessments of psychopathic traits in the understanding of violent and sexually violent behavior and in the evaluation and management of risk of harm to others (e.g., Hare, 1999). The importance of this development persists into the twenty-first century with a wealth of further research and discussion ongoing on the subject on the manifestation of psychopathy in practice (e.g., Skeem & Cooke, 2010), and on its relevance to treatment interventions for a variety of needs (e.g., Logan, Rypdal, & Hoff, 2012).

This chapter addresses the relevance of psychopathic traits to treatment, specifically treatment related to harmful sexual behavior. The chapter will examine what we know about sexual offenders who are psychopathic, and how the treatment and management of such sexual offenders is and should be different from that for those who are not psychopathic. Relevant literature will be reviewed to these ends. However, a

Sex Offender Treatment: A Case Study Approach to Issues and Interventions,
First Edition. Edited by Daniel T. Wilcox, Tanya Garrett, and Leigh Harkins.
© 2015 John Wiley & Sons, Ltd. Published 2015 by John Wiley & Sons, Ltd.

fictional case study will be used to communicate the most relevant guidance about clinical practice with this client group.

Theoretical and Evidence-Base for Treatment

Psychopathy, sexual offending, and treatment

There is a link between personality pathology and rule-breaking and harmful behavior (e.g., Yu, Geddes, & Fazel, 2012). Some of the evidence for this link has examined the construct of psychopathy, measured using the Psychopathy Checklist – Revised (PCL-R; Hare, 2003) or its derivatives (the Psychopathy Checklist: Screening Version; PCL: SV; Hart, Cox, & Hare, 1995; or the Psychopathy Checklist – Youth Version; PCL-YV; Forth, Kosson, & Hare, 2003). Studies using these instruments have repeatedly demonstrated a strong link between psychopathic traits and rule-breaking and harmful behavior; men, women, and young people with high levels of psychopathic traits are noted to commit more acts of violence compared to those without psychopathic traits (e.g., Douglas, Vincent, & Edens, 2006), and they reoffend more seriously and more quickly than nonpsychopaths (e.g., Hare, 1999).

However, the precise nature of the relationship between measures of psychopathic traits and conduct is not at all clear. Debate exists about just how well the PCL-R actually captures the psychopathy construct and about the role of antisocial conduct as either a symptom of psychopathy or a "mere downstream correlate" of its presence (Skeem & Cooke, 2010, p. 433). Consequently, while statistical associations exist between measures of psychopathy and harmful behavior, the functional link between the two variables remains subject to debate (Duggan & Howard, 2009). In this chapter, we will focus on research and guidance that emphasizes the personality pathology central to what we understand psychopathy to be, namely deficits in the individual's sense of self (e.g., they are self-centered, self-justifying, and entitled), their emotional experience and expression (e.g., they lack emotional range and depth), their relationships with others (e.g., they are status-oriented, unempathic, and uncaring), and their behavior (e.g., they are disruptive, reckless, and unreliable; Cooke, Hart, Logan, & Michie, 2012). This broader definition of psychopathy is used here because many sexual offenders are not psychopathic as defined by high scores on the PCL-R, yet their conduct is reminiscent of such pathology.

Sexually harmful behavior is driven by a range of factors, including deviant sexual interests and arousal, criminal orientation, adverse and dysfunctional relationship experiences and skills, experience and history of sexual and nonsexual violence, attitudes and beliefs that minimize or condone sexual violence, problems with self-awareness and stress management, mental health problems and substance misuse, problems with planning and treatment response, and personality pathology characterized by empathy deficits (e.g., Hart et al., 2003). Although usually taken into consideration, personality pathology has a less central role in sexual violence risk assessment and management compared to nonsexual violence risk – because of the relevance of so many other variables across the range of harmful sexual behavior (Ward & Beech, 2008). However, when personality pathology is present and relevant to an individual's sexually harmful behavior and future risk of the same, psychopathic personality traits are invariably a critical consideration. Why?

Individuals who both have psychopathic traits and are sexually harmful are, on the whole, perpetrators of severe forms of sexual violence (e.g., Hart et al., 2003). The sexual offenses of psychopaths tend to involve a diverse range of victims and activities and serious physical violence, often driven by anger, often opportunistic and against strangers, driven by nonsexual motivations such as opportunism and instrumentality (e.g., revenge), using weapons, and/or protracted though not always competent grooming activity (Porter, Woodworth, Earle, Drugge, & Boer, 2003). Psychopathic traits are found at high levels in those who are responsible for offenses of rape (Porter, Birt, & Boer, 2001) and sexual sadism is a common occurrence in psychopathic sexual offenders compared to nonpsychopathic sexual offenders (Porter et al., 2003). Symptoms of psychopathy, including sense of entitlement, recklessness and poor impulse control, and poor planning ability, have a strong and direct association with the risk of antisocial conduct and violence (Hart, 1998), including sexual violence (Krug, Dahlberg, Mercy, Zwi, & Lozano, 2002). Such symptoms function either to increase the perceived benefits of harmful behavior, and/or decrease their perceived costs (Hart & Logan, 2011). Recidivism rates, especially sexual recidivism, are high where psychopathy (as measured by PCL-R scores) is present in combination with deviant sexual arousal (Hawes, Boccaccini, & Murrie, 2013).

Treating sexual offenders with psychopathic traits

The evidence base is modest at best and not especially optimistic about the treatment of sexual offending behavior in individuals who are also psychopathic (Doren & Yates, 2008). However, drawing from this literature, and from the psychopathy treatment literature more generally, a number of issues can be delineated with a view to their being managed if not directly addressed in treatment interventions. The underlying driver in the points that follow, and in the remainder of this chapter, is to try to address the question "What treatment, by whom, is most effective for this individual, with what specific problems, under which set of circumstances, and how does it come about?" (Paul, 1967, quoted in Laws & O'Donohue, 2008, p. 7).

1. **Assessment** is critical. First, practitioners – and researchers – must be mindful of the influence of other mental disorders on personality presentation. Practitioners must evaluate personality disorder *in addition to* taking into account the influence of other conditions on clinical presentation. Second, practitioners should measure personality pathology generally and not just psychopathy, and measure psychopathic traits using more than just the PCL-R. Third, utilize multiple measures and methods of assessment – interviews, collateral sources, self-report, structured observations, applied repeatedly – to identify and measure the strength of traits or symptoms and the functional impairment they cause, as well as the link between impairment and sexual (and other) offending behavior. Fourth, do not neglect to measure protective factors or strengths – the "primary human goods" of the Ward and Stewart (2003) good lives model.

2. **Formulation** should be used to draw together assessment findings ahead of treatment planning – it is the essential bridge between assessments and proportionate and fair interventions (Hart & Logan, 2011). Formulation is the opportunity for the practitioner to demonstrate their understanding, ideally gained collaboratively with the client, about *why* he or she is sexually harmful – what were the key drivers, destabilizers, and disinhibitors that explain their harmful conduct in the past and are likely to be relevant to the potential for harmful sexual conduct in the future?

3. Decide on the most appropriate **treatment targets and outcomes.** Desistance from sexual offending is an obvious outcome, but other appropriate, achievable, and desirable goals (e.g., improving the individual's psychological wellbeing and developing his or her control over their behavior, feelings, attitudes, and thinking processes) should also be set. Also, how will the achievement of these outcomes be monitored and measured over time? A decision will be required as to whether the primary – or priority – treatment should be for the individual's sexual offending behavior or for his or her personality pathol-

ogy. Assessment findings and the outcome of the attention to the client's formulation will help to decide on the answer to this fundamental question.

4. Decide on the most appropriate **treatment modalities** (e.g., group intervention or individual). What is the individual's learning style and how best should treatment be tailored to have maximum and enduring impact? Following assessment and formulation, treatment providers will be in a good position to determine what form of intervention has the potential to generate the most lasting positive effect on the client whilst, in the case of a psychopathic offender, minimizing the negative effects of his or her participation in treatment on their peers and on the treatment providers (Atkinson & Tew, 2012; Tew, Harkins, & Dixon, 2013).

5. Identify the **therapist variables** most conducive to generating change in this individual. Working with offenders who are psychopathic places considerable demands on treatment providers and their selection, training and support is as essential a consideration as is the engagement of the client in treatment (Atkinson & Tew, 2012).

6. Identify and prepare to manage **treatment-interfering issues** likely to arise (e.g., dropout is a perennial problem in treating clients with psychopathic traits; Olver & Wong, 2009).

7. Determine what circumstances are required to **maintain positive treatment effect** over time and manage risk in the long term (Harrison, 2010). Invariably, and in order for there to be some confidence in its success, the risk management of a sexual offender with psychopathic traits will require a co-ordinated approach across agencies (such as the multiagency public protection arrangements available in the UK) and over a lengthy period of time (Logan, 2011). It is now routine for this persistent risk management requirement to be organized around license or registration conditions of many years duration.

Concluding comments

Sexual offenders who have psychopathic personality traits are a small but demanding cohort of clients. They are demanding because of the nature and severity of the offenses they have committed and might go on to commit, because of the time and resources required to assess, formulate, treat, and manage them, and because of the significant impact they have on treatment providers, their peers in treatment, and their victims. The following case study will illustrate these issues in a more detailed way.

An Illustrative Case

Mr. G is a 47-year-old Caucasian male living in a domestic dwelling in Manchester, UK. He has cohabited with women for 6 or more months a total of nine times since he was 16-years of age, and he has eight children by six women. His children range in age from 5 to 32 years and he has not been involved in the care of any of them beyond the first year of their lives – Mr. G generally leaves the family home, asks the woman and their child to leave, or the children are taken into care. At the time of referral, Mr. G was living with a 19-year-old woman, Pauline, whom he identified as his current partner and who is known to have learning difficulties, was previously a looked-after child, and to whom he is related (she is the daughter of Mr. G's first cousin). Mr. G has undertaken work as a laborer in the past but, after suffering a fall on a building site in his early 20s and damaging his back, he has been unemployed (when at liberty) and in receipt of disability and other state benefits.

Presenting complaints

Mr. G was referred to the adult forensic service within Manchester mental health services by his offender manager – the probation officer responsible for co-ordinating the risk management efforts relating to an individual offender. Mr. G was released from prison 1 month prior to the referral after serving 5 years of a 7-year sentence for rape, his seventh conviction for a sexual offense during a prolific criminal career featuring multiple offenses of sexual and nonsexual violence, including with weapons and against intimate partners. The offender manager made the referral to request the assistance of a forensic clinical psychologist while supervising Mr. G during the remainder of his time on license. The offender manager felt that Mr. G's case was complicated, wanted assistance with a risk assessment and formulation, and proposed to ensure Mr. G's management was psychologically informed in order to make it consistent, relevant, and effective. The offender manager had discussed this referral with Mr. G and, although he expressed concern about the implications of the involvement of a forensic mental health service in his management, he agreed to work with the offender manager as directed by the psychologist and to meet with the psychologist too if required. The offender manager's referral was accepted by the psychology department in the adult forensic service and allocated to one of the senior clinical psychologists in the team. The psychologist made contact with the offender manager and collected together relevant historical information about Mr. G prior to commencing work in earnest.

History

Mr. G was born and raised in Manchester. He was the eighth child of 13 born to a mother who worked as a prostitute. The identity of his father is unknown to him – and to his mother. Mr. G's mother died when he was 17 years of age. He is in contact with two of his siblings who continue to live in the Manchester area. He has no knowledge of the remainder of his siblings.

Mr. G underwent his early schooling without much incident. He left school when he was incarcerated for his first serious offense (at age 15 years) – he attended some classes in the young offenders institution to which he was sent, but sat no exams and, on his release, did not return to school in his home area. Mr. G has not undergone any education or training since this time. He has no qualifications. Nonetheless, he regards himself as very competent if not an expert in several areas and the intellectual superior of most of the people, including professionals, he encounters.

Mr. G has experienced no head injuries in his lifetime – he has been hit and punched on the head a few times in fights but has never lost consciousness. He is not known to have experienced any birth traumas or learning difficulties. His lack of qualifications appears due to poor motivation rather than learning deficits. Mr. G has a history of alcohol abuse – it has been a factor in several, though not all, of the offenses of which he has been convicted – although it does not appear that he has ever been dependent on alcohol. He is overweight and has type two diabetes, and he has a heart condition for which he receives regular medication. The back injury he sustained as a young man has been subject to extensive treatment, including surgery, and he is maintained currently on a program of medication to treat its effects.

Mr. G received his first conviction when he was 11-years of age, for theft. He received his first custodial sentence when he was 15, for assault. He received his first conviction for a sexual offense when he was 17-years of age, for indecent assault. He has a total of 56 convictions for 63 offenses. The majority are acquisitive offenses (16) but he also has 14 for offenses against the courts (e.g., breach of conditions, failure to appear), nine convictions for nonsexual violent offenses, seven convictions for sexual offenses, three convictions for weapons offenses, three convictions for kidnapping, and a number of driving offenses. He has received custodial sentences on eight occasions, with the last sentence – for rape, sentenced to 7 years – being the longest. He has spent a total of 17 years in custody since he was 15-years of age.

Mr. G's nine convictions for nonsexual violent offenses have been against peers (two), police officers whilst being arrested (two), and against three of his intimate partners. The latter assaults occurred in the content of brief but abusive relationships with women all of whom made multiple complaints to the police about Mr. G but who refused to proceed with charges due, it is thought, to a realistic fear of retribution. One woman alleged that he stalked her for a year after she ended their relationship and threatened her and their child with violence unless she returned to him. She did not and instead left the area without pressing charges. One of his victims was pregnant at the time she was assaulted.

Mr. G's seven convictions for sexual violence all involved women and young people with whom he was having or attempting to have a relationship; all the victims were known to him prior to their assault, and the context of the offenses was usually a dispute about the relationship (e.g., the victim wishing to end the relationship or to terminate an unplanned pregnancy or when the victim was suspected of being intimate with another man). His youngest victim was 13-years of age (the victim of his first conviction for sexual violence, when he was aged 17 years), and his oldest victim was 24 (the victim of his 2008 conviction for rape, when he was aged 42 years). Two of his victims were pregnant with his children at the time of their sexual assault.

On three occasions, Mr. G has kidnapped his victims and detained them unlawfully prior to assault. And his preferred weapon of choice on these and other occasions has been a knife, which he has used to threaten his victims and force their compliance and also to cut his victim's faces in order to leave permanent and highly visible scars. Nonsexual and sexual assaults following kidnapping have generally been protracted, lasting at least 1 hour and as long as 36 hours.

Whilst in custody, Mr. G has participated in several programs including reasoning and rehabilitation, a course for the perpetrators of intimate partner violence, and the sexual offender treatment program, which he has done twice.

Assessment

Following a detailed discussion about the case, the psychologist proposed to meet with Mr. G during his next appointment with his offender manager. It was thought that a familiar setting and the known face of his offender manager would create the context for a more positive discussion about the assessment requested. The offender manager spoke with Mr. G and, though still reluctant, he consented to the three-way meeting. That meeting took place 2 weeks later.

The offender manager started the meeting by introducing the psychologist. The psychologist outlined what had been requested of her and asked Mr. G to express his views. It was his view that he was not in need of assessment or any further treatment. He had done the treatment he was required to do when he was in prison, and now he was free and he wanted to put it behind him. He did not see the point in any interference in his life by mental health services. He was clear that he did not have a mental health problem, he was not going to reoffend and his past offenses "such as they were" were overstated if not completely unjustified, and he did not have time for this, all expressed with eloquence and quite politely but with an emphasis that bordered on dominating.

The psychologist's objective in this first encounter with Mr. G was to get him to consent to some degree of assessment, on the basis of which a collaborative formulation would be derived and a risk management plan prepared. This was her bottom line. She hoped that Mr. G would consent to the assessment *and* to any further treatment thought necessary, but she thought this outcome less likely than the former and this was clear to her from quite early on in the meeting. So, she focused on helping him to identify some of the problems his behavior had generated for him – time spent in custody when he would rather have been free, problematic relationships when he would rather have had peaceful ones, and so on. And she did this patiently and quietly whilst being responsive and empathic to Mr. G's voiced and implied concerns – his feelings about having been "stitched up" by risk assessments in the past and by psychologists too.

After 45 minutes, Mr. G agreed that while he had done his treatment in prison, and he still wasn't going to do any more, he was willing to talk a little further about himself and the problems that recur in his life, which he couldn't seem to get on top of. So together they made a list of the things Mr. G valued in his life, with the psychologist shaping this list in terms of the "primary goods" discussed by Ward and Stewart (2003; e.g., achievement, intimacy, power). At the end of the allotted time, Mr. G appeared to want to carry on. So it was put to him that they could do so but the following week. He was wary. The psychologist suggested that understanding more about what Mr. G wanted and how those desires were frustrated might help him to take more control of his life and not reoffend. Mr. G agreed that this was a reasonable objective, and he consented to meet with the psychologist again. The psychologist also agreed that any report that emerged from their discussions together would be discussed with him before it was shown to anyone else, so that he would get a chance to comment on it and to have his comments incorporated into the report. She said she didn't promise to change her views about Mr. G following his feedback, but she wanted to ensure that they were balanced with his view and that the report was as free from factual errors as possible. She expressed the hope that such a collaborative way of working would meet with his approval, and he informed her that he had not worked in this way before and that it was acceptable to him so far.

On the morning it was due to take place, Mr. G canceled the appointment that had been arranged the previous week. However, the offender manager called Mr. G and, using the same motivational approach, encouraged him to attend the appointment after all. From that afternoon onwards, during the course of four assessment sessions, the psychologist gathered more and more information about Mr. G to supplement that obtained from other sources.

Mr. G was subject to two extensive assessments while he was in prison relating to his participation in the sexual offender treatment program. He had also been subject to two PCL-R assessments while in prison. As these reports had been disclosed to Mr. G at the time they were completed, the psychologist was able to discuss them with him once again, especially as both assessments indicated the presence of a clinically significant level of psychopathy. Taking the stance of curious observer, she was able to supplement these assessments with more up-to-date information about Mr. G's personality presentation more generally, his ability to tolerate stress and the often unhelpful means by which he tries to cope with it, his relationship skills and what he does to protect himself from perceived threat, both physical and emotional, and his sexual interests.

The psychologist noted during the course of the assessment that Mr. G did not always provide information that was consistent with that recorded in his files, and that the pattern of discrepancy was such that his self-report presented him in a better and more blameless light than did the reports about him by others. When asked about his offenses, he invariably blamed his victim and was unable to describe any of his victims in a way that suggested he had a real understanding of their feelings or of the effects of his conduct on them. Also, the psychologist noted that when he wanted to be persuasive, such as when he was emphasizing how much his ex-partner was in fact to blame for his assault on her, Mr. G talked forcefully at her and his eye contact was intense and unblinking. He regularly sought reassurance from the psychologist that she both understood his point of view and that she accepted and believed it – and that her report would endorse what he said. He flattered her, crediting the psychologist with great wisdom. The psychologist remained neutral during such phases in their work, and deflected questions about her conclusions by asking him about the fears that seemed to underpin his insistence on her belief in his point of view.

Following their fourth meeting, the psychologist asked Mr. G if she could take some time to draft a statement that would communicate her understanding of him and the behaviors that have brought him into conflict with the law and distressed him and those around him. When they met again 2 weeks later, the psychologist presented her formulation to Mr. G in a document watermarked "DRAFT," making it clear that this was a work in progress rather than her finalized point of view. The psychologist went through the formulation, engaging Mr. G in its elaboration, whilst gathering yet more information about his self-awareness, motivations, and personality style. The following section contains the formulation finally agreed with Mr. G.

Case formulation

Mr. G finds some parts of his life a great challenge. Relationships with women with whom he is or wants to be intimate are particularly challenging for him. This is because he worries about being out of control of these relationships, being disrespected by these women, being cheated, rejected, and let down. He worries that when he realizes that these things are or may be happening, he has to respond to "save face" and that his response is always forceful and often violent, in order to make them not do it again and to punish them for their disloyalty and for making him feel so distressed, vulnerable, and foolish. Mr. G uses sexual violence when he feels most threatened and vulnerable, or when he wants his victim to feel some of the pain he thinks she has caused him by rejecting or dishonoring him. Therefore, it is sometimes very difficult for Mr. G to take full responsibility for his actions and, instead, he will blame his victim for being the cause of his assault on her.

It seems also to be the case that Mr. G's motivation for assaulting women and girls sexually is driven more by his personality than by deviant sexual arousal, although he acknowledges that he thinks a lot about sex, regards his sexuality as a source of pride as well as pleasure, and prizes a high level of sexual activity regardless of the cost or inconvenience to others. As a child, Mr. G was well aware of his mother's employment and he has vivid memories of her undertaking this work, being exposed to a high level of impersonal sexual activity, and being aroused to much of what he saw. However, as a child he was also emotionally neglected by his family and physically abused, and fantasies of being powerful, in control, and of violent revenge against those who hurt and diminished him, were vital to his wellbeing and survival.

It has been difficult in the past for Mr. G to acknowledge that he has played an important role in bringing about the kind of relationships in which violence and sexual violence are used as a way of being assertive and coping with his fears. This is because of his pride. But it may also be because he has not given himself the opportunity to try to learn the skills that would help him develop deeper and more meaningful intimate relationships with women and because closeness itself can make people feel quite vulnerable, which is the feeling he most wants to avoid. Therefore, Mr. G is at risk of being harmful sexually again in the future because he is still lacking the skills to manage relationships well and without conflict, and because of his continuing fear of closeness with others and trust. He is broadly sympathetic to this point of view – he could acknowledge that when he and the psychologist reviewed this formulation together. However, he does still feel inclined to believe that his victims, especially those whom he regarded himself to be in a relationship with at the time, were much more responsible for the offenses of which he has been convicted than is communicated here. Clearly there is still some work to be done to manage Mr. G's risk of sexual violence while he continues to minimize his role in its occurrence.

Relationships more generally are a challenge for Mr. G. He is a very competitive man and constantly challenges other men in an attempt to prove that he is higher in status, power, control, and influence. He can exhaust himself with the effort it takes for him to be vigilant all the time for signs that male acquaintances are trying to thwart, diminish, and overwhelm him. It is as if being diminished in the eyes of other men is a kind of death for him and he has to defend his position of power as if his life depended on it. These stakes make it easier to understand why Mr. G has used extreme violence in response to what to outsiders appeared to be quite minor provocation. Therefore, Mr. G is at risk of being physically (nonsexually) harmful again in the future because he is still a very competitive man who cannot stand to lose whatever it is he wants or wants to retain.

Also, Mr. G finds it quite easy to break the law – to take action because he thinks it is justified regardless of what anyone else thinks, to steal because he wants something and does not want to pay for it, to damage property because he feels like it. He feels entitled to do what he wants because it helps him to feel in control and powerful. To obey the law would diminish him and it is this feeling of weakness that he is most motivated to avoid. Therefore, Mr. G will continue to be at risk of breaking the law and rules more generally for as long as doing so makes him feel powerful, and for as long as he needs to have such tangible forms of evidence of his effect – his influence – on the world.

The treatments Mr. G has received to date have not really touched on these underlying drivers of his offending behavior. This is why it is the opinion of the author of this report that Mr. G remains at risk of being sexually harmful towards women, physically harmful towards men and women, and criminally oriented more generally. However, and most importantly, it appears that Mr. G has enough understanding of these motivating factors and a growing desire to stay out of prison, which together could make it sufficiently worth his while to work together with his offender manager and others to help them to help him control the excesses of his conduct. In the course of reviewing this formulation, and although it has been painful for him to do so, Mr. G acknowledges that this is the case.

Course of treatment and assessment of progress

Once the formulation was agreed with Mr. G, the psychologist met with the offender manager to prepare a treatment plan that would address both his outstanding treatment needs and manage his risk of harm to others. They agreed that the person they were most concerned about was his current partner, and her safety was to be a central point of focus for them in their work. The psychologist was not in a position to deliver that work to Mr. G, but she proposed to help the offender manager prepare the treatment plan and offer regular supervision during the course of its implementation.

The psychologist's treatment plan for Mr. G was essentially that of structured case management (see Bateman & Krawitz, 2013), organized critically around the meaning of harmful behavior to Mr. G as described in the formulation above and agreed with him as the starting point for his risk management. The principles of structured case management are as follows:

- **Careful assessment** is critical. The psychologist prepared all of her observations on Mr. G, including her understanding of the findings of the assessments previously carried out on him, in a report, which underpinned the formulation agreed. However, it was this formulation, which the offender manager would take responsibility for updating

following supervision sessions with the psychologist, that was to be
and remain the basis for all the work undertaken with Mr. G and how
that work would be communicated with relevant others.

- Mr. G's **collaboration** would be sought through prioritizing the quality
of the offender manager's working relationship with him. The offender
manager understood that her engagement with Mr. G should prioritize
openness, transparency, consistency, and trust. She agreed, therefore,
to keep Mr. G informed about any observations she made, including
concerns that she had about him, and that his motivation to continue
to engage with her would be maintained by reminding him about his
desire to improve his life. She also understood that to help Mr. G see
that he had a degree of control over the nature and pace of work
would help with his engagement in the process. The offender manager
agreed that she would work with Mr. G for as long as she could, use
supervision to cope with the personal demands such a working relationship might impose on her, and if a change of personnel were
required, this would be done in a planned and organized way.

- During the last meeting between the psychologist and Mr. G, and after
reviewing the formulation, they discussed possible **treatment targets**.
Mr. G was able to identify and agree with some, although not as many
as the psychologist had identified. However, it was thought more
important that Mr. G commit to engagement and collaborative risk
management than that the psychologist force her view on him. She
agreed to the treatment needs he identified, therefore, with the expecta-
tion that the outstanding treatment needs would be added in due
course. Treatment needs identified and agreed were as follows: using
alternatives to violence when he is in disagreement with his partner,
relationship skills generally, and coping with stress (and avoiding
maladaptive strategies, such as alcohol abuse). The psychologist additionally identified maintaining motivation and engagement as a long-
term requirement of the work that the offender manager and Mr. G
would do together, crisis scenario planning, developing his resilience
to and ability to handle conflict with others, and greater cognitive
flexibility. It was agreed with Mr. G that evidence of a positive
outcome of this work would be: (a) a reduction in the number of
accusations of aggression and violence made by others against him,
(b) no accusations of aggression or violence – or sexual violence –
made against him by his partner, (c) a general improvement in his
wellbeing, and (d) evidence that he is keeping as active as he can
manage, undertaking activities that give him some enjoyment and do
not bring him into conflict with the law.

- A variety of **modalities** were planned to address the treatment needs identified. Regular meetings with the offender manager were to be prioritized, the focus for which was to be his problem-solving skills, crisis planning and management, and review. In addition, Mr. G would be asked to attend a probation-led intervention for men with a history of domestic violence. Subsequent to this, he would be asked to join a thinking skills group. The offender manager would co-ordinate these interventions and collate feedback from course facilitators. In addition, the offender manager would meet with Mr. G's partner occasionally to discuss with her any concerns she might have about her safety or about Mr. G, sessions that would help the offender manager further understand the reasons for conflict and violence in his relationships. He was also subject to management through local multiagency public protection arrangements (MAPPA), which meant that practitioners and managers from multiple relevant services were interested in him desisting from violence – and were prepared to collaborate in doing so. Mr. G was rated a MAPPA level 2 offender. The risk management plans of such offenders require the active involvement of several agencies (e.g., probation, police, mental health) through regular meetings (Harrison, 2010).

- The offender manager pledged to use **supervision and peer support** in order to maintain an objective and agreeable stance with Mr. G, regardless of his manner towards her. She would prepare for meetings with him so that she was herself psychologically ready to deal with problems that he would bring to their meetings. She would utilize coworking with the psychologist and a fellow (male) probation officer if she felt that this would be required because of the nature or stage of their work together. The offender manager's key priority was to maintain Mr. G's engagement with her and her service, and these various processes were intended as safeguards to ensure that this was achieved.

- The most likely **treatment interfering activities** that were anticipated by the offender manager and the psychologist were Mr. G's disengagement from supervision/interventions and his efforts to sabotage the work under way. He had a long-term supervision order, which would keep him attending meetings with his probation officer on pain of recall to prison – this was a powerful motivator for him. Therefore, he was unlikely not to turn up for scheduled appointments. But the concern was that he would turn up and not engage fully in discussions, or actively disrupt sessions by being challenging or confrontational, or aggressive and intimidating. By planning for these possibilities in advance, and by understanding that their purpose would be to protect Mr. G from unpleasant feelings (such as taking responsibility for his unacceptable conduct), it was hypothesized that they would be better managed and without incurring lasting damage to their work. This scenario planning activity is vital to risk management (Hart & Logan, 2011).

• Finally, it was agreed that **reviews** would take place every 3 months, to include Mr. G, in order to determine the extent of any improvements made and any unanticipated barriers to managed risk.

Follow-up

Mr. G met with his offender manager every fortnight, and his progress was reviewed approximately every 3 months from the implementation of the plan described above. He was subject to close supervision for 2 years following his release from prison, and the plan for this time was to have him invest sufficiently in a future free from violence that he would continue some form of intervention voluntarily thereafter. The option of a sexual offenses prevention order was kept in reserve, and in fact never utilized. Ongoing engagement with him allowed the offender manager to monitor and manage his relationships with others, and the opportunity to prevent violence towards Mr. G's partner.

Multiple difficulties arose during those 2 years. Mr. G's relationship with his partner, Pauline, deteriorated and they split up. However, there is no information to suggest that he assaulted Pauline during the course of their separation, and Pauline herself denies that he did so although he was verbally abusive to her and destroyed her property at their previously shared home. Subsequently, he drank heavily and there was a noticeable change – deterioration – in his attitudes towards women; he was angry with Pauline and distressed at the ending of their relationship, and he projected his anger onto all women, making them collectively to blame for his sadness. In response, meetings with his offender manager were arranged weekly, with telephone contact in between meetings. However, although his situation was difficult for several months, he did not disengage from his offender manager and he attended all of the appointments made.

In addition, during and in the immediate aftermath of his split from Pauline, when the offender manager tried to work with Mr. G to help him reflect on the part he played in their break up, he became very angry and threatened his offender manager with legal action. She accepted his need to express himself in this way, she responded to what she assumed to have been the underlying drivers of this proposed action (fear), and helped him towards a way of reflecting on his role in the breakup that avoided him losing face in acknowledging it. This was a very challenging time for the offender manager and she utilized the support of the psychologist and her colleagues throughout. However, her focus did not waver. Mr. G became more amenable to discussion and there was no further mention of the litigation threatened.

At the time of writing, Mr. G is coming to the end of his supervision order and has expressed his willingness to commit to voluntary supervision for a continued period of time. His care continues to be co-ordinated around the points raised above and he continues to demonstrate a capacity to modify his behavior to stay within the law. He remains a troubled man with severe problems in his attachments to others and in his emotional experience and expression. However, his disorder does not express itself in terms of violent and sexually violent behavior in the way it once did. Having had a comparatively calm 2 years or so, Mr. G is more committed than ever to staying out of prison. Nonetheless, at their regular reviews, the offender manager continues to discuss with him how things could go wrong and what more they need to put in place to ensure that such difficulties can be averted.

Conclusions and practice recommendations

Mr. G was subject to a range of interventions designed both to address his psychological needs and manage his risk. The primary objective of this work was to maintain his engagement with it, given the very high risk that he would attempt to disengage with the process of risk management and sabotage this work or his relationship with the offender manager. The secondary objective was to focus on the effects of his disorder on his behavior, to change the way his disorder was expressed and managed by him more so than to address the core disorder itself. By making it in Mr. G's own interests to change his behavior he was more motivated to stay engaged. And staying engaged with a wide-ranging process of risk management made it more likely that future harm would be prevented or limited. The offender manager and the psychologist tried to be realistic about what they could achieve with Mr. G given the amount and type of treatment tried with him previously, and judged that a structured case management approach was most likely to be effective with this case at this time. By committing themselves to long-term engagement with Mr. G, utilizing the resources of multiple agencies in a co-ordinated way, they have been able to make progress towards the objectives identified with Mr. G.

References

Atkinson, R., & Tew, J. (2012). Working with psychopathic offenders: Lessons from the Chromis Program. *International Journal of Forensic Mental Health*, *11*, 299–311.

Bateman, A. W., & Krawitz, R. (2013). *Borderline personality disorder: An evidence-based guide for generalist mental health professionals*. Oxford, UK: Oxford University Press.

Blackburn, R. (2006). Other theoretical models of psychopathy. In C. J. Patrick (Ed.), *Handbook of psychopathy* (pp. 35–57). New York: Guilford Press.

Cooke, D. J., Hart, S. D., Logan, C., & Michie, C. (2012). Explicating the construct of psychopathy: Development and validation of a conceptual model, the comprehensive assessment of psychopathic personality (CAPP). *International Journal of Forensic Mental Health*, *11*, 242–252.

Doren, D. M., & Yates, P. M. (2008). Effectiveness of sex offender treatment for psychopathic sexual offenders. *International Journal of Offender Therapy and Comparative Criminology*, *52*, 234–245.

Douglas, K. S., Vincent, G. M., & Edens, J. F. (2006). Risk for criminal recidivism: The role of psychopathy. In C. J. Patrick (Ed.), *Handbook of psychopathy* (pp. 533–554). New York: Guilford Press.

Duggan, C., & Howard, R. (2009). The "functional link" between personality disorder and violence: A critical approach. In M. McMurran & R. Howard (Eds.), *Personality, personality disorder and violence* (pp. 19–37). Chichester, UK: Wiley-Blackwell.

Forth, A. E., Kosson, D. S., & Hare, R. D. (2003). *Hare psychopathy checklist: Youth version (PCL:YV)*. Tonawanda, NY: Multi-Health Systems.

Hare, R. D. (1999). Psychopathy as a risk factor for violence. *Psychiatric Quarterly*, *70*, 181–197.

Hare, R. D. (2003). *The Hare psychopathy checklist – revised* (2nd ed.). Toronto, OH: Multi-Health Systems.

Harrison, K., (Ed.). (2010). *Managing high-risk sex offenders in the community: Risk management, treatment and social responsibility*. Cullompton, UK: Willan.

Hart, S. D. (1998). The role of psychopathy in assessing risk for violence: Conceptual and methodological issues. *Legal and Criminological Psychology*, *3*, 123–140.

Hart, S. C., Cox, D. N., & Hare, R. D. (1995). *Manual for the Hare psychopathy checklist – revised: Screening version*. Toronto, OH: Multi-Health Systems.

Hart, S. D., & Logan, C. (2011). Formulation of violence risk using evidence-based assessments: The structured professional judgment approach. In P. Sturmey & M. McMurran (Eds.), *Forensic case formulation* (pp. 83–106). Chichester, UK: Wiley-Blackwell.

Hart, S. D., Kropp, P. K., Laws, D. R. Klaver, J., Logan, C., & Watt, K. A. (2003). *The risk for sexual violence protocol: Structured professional guidelines for assessing risk of sexual violence*. Mental Health, Law and Policy Institute. Vancouver, Canada: Simon Fraser University.

Hawes, S. W., Boccaccini, M. T., & Murrie, D. C. (2013). Psychopathy and the combination of psychopathy and sexual deviance as predictors of sexual recidivism: Meta-analytic findings using the psychopathy checklist – revised. *Psychological Assessment, 25*, 233–243.

Krug, E. G., Dahlberg, L. L., Mercy, J. A., Zwi, A. B., & Lozano, R., (Eds.). (2002). *World report on violence and health*. Geneva, Switzerland: World Health Organization.

Laws, D. R., & O'Donohue, W. (2008). *Sexual deviance: Theory, assessment, and treatment* (2nd ed.). New York: Guilford Press.

Logan, C. (2011). Managing high risk personality disordered offenders: Lessons learned to date. In B. McSherry & P. Keyser (Eds.), *"Dangerous" people: Policy, prediction and practice*. Oxford, UK: Routledge.

Logan, C., Rypdal, K., & Hoff, H. A. (2012). Understanding, treating and managing psychopathy: Moving on. *International Journal of Forensic Mental Health, 11*, 239–241.

Olver, M. E., & Wong, S. C. P. (2009). Therapeutic responses of psychopathic sexual offenders: Treatment attrition, therapeutic change, and long-term recidivism. *Journal of Consulting and Clinical Psychology, 77*, 328–336.

Paul, G. (1967). Strategy of outcome research in psychotherapy. *Journal of Consulting and Clinical Psychology, 31*, 109–118.

Porter, S., Birt, A., & Boer, D. (2001). Investigation of the criminal and conditional release profiles of Canadian federal offenders as a function of psychopathy. *Law and Human Behavior, 25*, 647–661.

Porter, S., Woodworth, M., Earle, J., Drugge, J., & Boer, D. (2003). Characteristics of sexual homicides committed by psychopathic and non-psychopathic offenders. *Law and Human Behavior, 27*, 459–470.

Skeem, J. L., & Cooke, D. J. (2010). Is criminal behavior a central component of psychopathy? Conceptual directions for resolving the debate. *Psychological Assessment, 22*, 433–445.

Tew, J., Harkins, L., & Dixon, L. (2013). What works in reducing violent reoffending in psychopathic offenders. In L. Craig, L. Dixon, & T. Gannon (Eds.), *What works in offender rehabilitation: An evidence based approach to assessment and treatment*. Chichester, UK: Wiley-Blackwell.

Ward, T., & Beech, A. R. (2008). An integrated theory of sexual offending. In D. R. Laws & W. O'Donohue (Eds.), *Sexual Deviance: Theory, assessment, and treatment* (2nd ed., pp. 21–36). New York: Guilford Press.

Ward, T., & Stewart, C. A. (2003). Good lives and the rehabilitation of sexual offenders. In T. Ward, D. R. Laws, & S. M. Hudson (Eds.), *Sexual Deviance: Issues and controversies* (pp. 21–44). Thousand Oaks, CA: Sage.

Yu, R., Geddes, J. R., & Fazel, S. (2012). Personality disorders, violence, and antisocial behavior: A systematic review and meta-regression analysis. *Journal of Personality Disorders, 26*, 775–792.

16

Assessment and Treatment When Sex Is Attached to a Killing: A Case Study

Adam J. Carter and Clive R. Hollin

Introduction

It is clear that some murders have a sexual element and that some sexual crimes culminate in murder. However, the term "sexual murder" is not a legal term and therefore lacks a legal definition. Nevertheless, the term is used in both research and practice to describe cases in which a murder appears to have a strong sexual element (e.g., Proulx, Cusson, & Beauregard, 2007). For example, within the National Offender Management Service in England and Wales, a sexual murder is seen as where there is an identifiable sexual element to the killing. In the UK, the term "sexual killing" is arguably more appropriate than "sexual murder" as the act of killing includes murder, manslaughter, and manslaughter with diminished responsibility. The absence of a legal definition also sets problems in estimating numbers; as Schlesinger notes, "Given the multiple complex problems with definition, it is easy to understand why accurate statistics on the incidence of sexual murder would be difficult to calculate" (2004, p. 7). The rate of sexual killings in the UK in 2003 was estimated to be approximately 6% of the total number of homicides (Beech, Fisher, & Ward, 2005); in Canada during 1974 to 1986 the same estimate was 4% (Roberts & Grossman, 1993). The process of sentence management for such offenders relies in part on accurate risk assessment; for example, the

Sex Offender Treatment: A Case Study Approach to Issues and Interventions, First Edition. Edited by Daniel T. Wilcox, Tanya Garrett, and Leigh Harkins.
© 2015 John Wiley & Sons, Ltd. Published 2015 by John Wiley & Sons, Ltd.

parole board in England and Wales would wish to know about any changes in risk level over a prison sentence and current level of risk of reconviction.

In attempting to describe sexual killing, Oliver, Beech, Fisher, and Beckett (2007) proposed that sexual killers are rapists who have killed because of their excessive anger, to try and avoid detection, or because the victim was physically vulnerable and hence likely to die from injuries sustained during the attack. There appears to be more similarities than differences in the characteristics of sexual killers and other sexual aggressors (e.g., Grubin, 1994; Oliver et al., 2007) and so it remains to be established that sexual killers are a separate group of sexual offenders (Cusson, 2007). Thus, the challenges which practitioners face in carrying out risk assessments with sexual offenders, such as identifying whether particular sexual interests or paraphilias contributed to offending, are also applicable to sexual killers. However, there are several specific issues associated with identifying the risk factors relevant to risk assessments with sexual killers. The first point to consider is the basic issue of deciding what constitutes a sexual killing.

Classifying a Killing as Sexual

As Schlesinger noted, "Many seemingly sexual murders are not sexually motivated" (2004, p. 3) and the reverse is as likely to be true. Thus, the first issue is to classify a killing as sexual, a task made more difficult by the different ways in which killing and sex can be attached. There may be *direct* attachment where the killing is integral to the perpetrator's pursuit of sexual gratification and the sexual aspect of the offense can be demonstrably connected to the death: such cases include those where the act of killing is itself sexually gratifying, or where the purpose is to enable sexual acts to be carried out with the victim's body. In *indirect* attachment the killing is not a source of sexual stimulation, rather the offense occurs in a sexual context: the context may be the elimination of a victim, and hence witness, of a sexual assault, or where the victim is killed as they try to escape from a sexual attack. There are cases with a mixture of direct and indirect types of sexual killing as, for example, when the victim dies while trying to escape and the perpetrator carries out a sexual assault after death. The process of determining whether an offense was sexually motivated may be complicated by the presence of other potentially contributory factors such as alcohol, paraphilia, and drugs (Folino, 2000).

The issue of offense classification has been addressed in the literature. Revitch (1965) proposed a classification of sexual killing and assaults on women in which the perpetrator's motivation for killing and assault is *impulsive*, where the killing and assault are not pursued for sexual gratification, *compulsive*, where the opposite is the case, and *catathymic*, where the attack is triggered by tension and an outburst of anger. The FBI devised a classification based on *organized* or *disorganized* crime scene behavior, intended to point to perpetrator characteristics and therefore discriminating sexual from other killers (Ressler, Burgess, Douglas, Hartman, & D'Agostino, 1986). Beech et al. (2005) reported that their sample of sexual killers could be classified according to the presence or absence of implicit theories – dangerous world, the male sex drive is uncontrollable, entitlement, women as sex objects, and women are unknowable or dangerous – previously identified as likely to be prevalent among rapists. Beech et al. were able to divide a sample of sexual killers into three groups using combinations of these implicit theories. There are various other classifications which categorize the killing as sexually motivated, resulting from anger, or instrumental in the sense of enforcing submission or silencing the victim (Beauregard, Proulx, & St-Yves, 2007; Beech et al., 2005; Clarke & Carter, 2000; Keppel & Walter, 1999).

Subgroups of sexual murder

The classification of murders as sexual allows several subgroups to emerge, each defined by particular characteristics. The first subgroup is where the killing is *sexually arousing* such that it enables the perpetrator to enact their sexual fantasies. These offenses are characterized by the murder being highly planned, the victim being highly controlled, perhaps with the use of restraints, and may involve prolonged torture to heighten the offender's sexual arousal (Beech et al., 2005; Clarke & Carter, 2000; Keppel & Walter, 1999; Ressler, Burgess, & Douglas, 1988). The other subgroups of sexual killers described in the literature include: *sexual killings triggered by anger*, which may follow a victim's words or actions, result from a grievance against women, or from a wish to gain revenge against women (Beech et al., 2005; Clarke & Carter, 2000; Keppel & Walter, 1999); and *instrumental sexual killing*, where the death is not planned but serves to silence or control the victim (Beech et al., 2005; Clarke & Carter, 2000; Keppel & Walter, 1999).

Yet further, Beauregard and Proulx (2002) describe *sadistic* and *anger* profiles for sexual killers, which share some similarities with the organized and disorganized sexual killer types. After analyses of crime-phase variables, Beauregard et al. (2007) classified their sample of sexual murderers as *angry* or *sadistic*: While both groups mainly raped their victims, the angry perpetrators had significantly greater levels of precrime anger, were more likely to have experienced loneliness, and were less likely than the sadistic killers to plan the offense and to torture their victim. However, "anger" highlights the characteristics of offenders and the offense rather than accounting for the sexual aspects of the crime. Finally, several studies of sexual killers have used Ressler et al.'s (1988) description, which, along with supporting information and some disclosure from the perpetrator, can be applied to classify cases as sexual killings (e.g., Beauregard & Proulx, 2002; Briken, Habermann, Kafka, Berner, & Hill, 2006). Ressler et al. state that the evidence indicating that a murder was sexual includes "victim attire or lack of attire; exposure of the sexual parts of the victim's body; sexual positioning of the victim's body; insertion of foreign objects into the victim's body cavities; evidence of sexual intercourse (oral, anal, vaginal); and evidence of substitute sexual activity, interest or sadistic fantasy" (p. xiii).

Assessing Risk

Context

In most risk assessments with sexual offenders the offense is defined with established recidivism base-rates, risk criteria, and a valid and reliable risk assessment instrument (e.g., Risk Matrix 2000; Thornton, 2010). In the case of sexual murder, however, the assessor is working with an offense involving an unknown, but probably low, base-rate of recidivism for sexual killing. Based on studies carried out in Germany, Hill, Habermann, Klusmann, Berner, and Briken (2008) reported the only published study on the recidivism of sexual killers. From a sample of 90 sexual killers, identified using Ressler et al.'s (1988) definition, who had been released from detention, Hill et al. reported recidivism rates of 23.1% for sexual offenses and 18.3% for nonsexual offenses over a 20-year "at risk" period. In terms of attempted or actual homicide, Hill et al. reported a recidivism rate of 3.3%, which is comparable to homicide generally. Additionally, while violent recidivism was most common around 5 years after release, sexual offenses could occur after much longer periods. Hill et al. suggest that "it might be necessary to extend post-release relapse prevention strategies, treatment, support, and parole supervision over longer periods to reduce risk of sexual reoffending" (p. 12). Carter, Mann, and

Wakeling (2008) reported that in England and Wales between 2000 and 2007 none of the sexual killers released on license were known to have committed another killing.

The lack of empirical research means that risk assessment with sexual murderers faces all the difficulties associated with assessing a low-frequency, highly-serious offense, without established risk criteria and a valid risk assessment tool, relying on case material and interview (Beech, 2001). Nonetheless, practitioners can still apply the basic principles of risk assessment, drawing with due caution on the wider literature addressing violent and sexual offending.

In order to assess a sexual killer, a case formulation should be made with a focus on the perpetrator's demographic and psychological characteristics, their behavior immediately prior to the offense, what happened during the offense, including all violent and sexual acts, and what happened after the crime (Gresswell & Hollin, 1992). The practice of taking a history is useful in setting the context for developmental processes and antecedents to the offense that may inform areas such as schemas, fantasy, and alcohol or substance dependency, which may be part of a risk management plan (Perkins, 2008; Schlesinger, 2004).

The assessment of the perpetrator should include background details along with psychological factors, such as the use of fantasy, loneliness, experience of negative moods states, attitudes towards women, and ability to solve problems, that are all potentially relevant to understanding the offense. The available crime scene information should be carefully reviewed, including the pathologist's report and any witness statements. In placing the offense within a situational context, information about the victim and their circumstances should also be considered. A wide-ranging consideration of the situation may well provide more useful initial information than a narrow focus on whether the offense was motivated by the perpetrator's anger or sadistic pleasure.

When turning to the question of motivation, the main question is whether there is a sexual element to the killing and, if so, is it a direct or indirect form of sexual killing and is there a sadistic element? Thus, based on the case material and an awareness of the literature, hypotheses for a potential sexual element to the killing may be formulated (Beech et al., 2005; Perkins, 2008; Schlesinger, 2004). However, identifying the perpetrator who killed principally in the pursuit of sexual arousal as opposed to those who killed for another purpose can be problematic. There are sexual murderers of the type described by Oliver et al. (2007) who could be considered rapists who have killed with indirect attachment, for example, out of excessive anger, but their identification depends on reliable disclosure from the perpetrator, hence the need to interview the perpetrator.

Interview

It is often necessary to acquire information from the perpetrator to determine if sex was attached to their killing (Folino, 2000). This type of interview is not a neutral exchange of information: Perkins refers to the "context and contingencies that apply in the situation where the assessment is being carried out" (2008, p. 95), highlighting that the perpetrator has a vested interest in the outcome of the assessment. There is an array of possible consequences for the perpetrator in making disclosures about his offense, which may vary if made at the time of prosecution, or during incarceration, or when being considered for parole or release (Perkins, 2008). The perpetrator may also have personal or pragmatic reasons for preferring to give another explanation for their actions. In England and Wales a conviction for rape linked to murder would lead to classification as a "sex offender" under The Sexual Offences Act 2003, which would be likely to lead to assessment and possibly treatment as part of their sentence plan (Crown Prosecution Service, 2013). A classification of "sexual offender" can also present difficulties in serving a sentence in a mainstream prison location, and may necessitate a move to a vulnerable prisoner unit to avoid violence. The first author has experience of perpetrators feeling great shame in talking about their offense or taking exception to being asked to consider a sexual aspect to their offense when their conviction is not for a sexual offense. A familiarity with the literature on sexual killing may assist in reassuring the offender regarding the practitioner's competence.

The crime scene evidence may show that the victim was raped and strangled but an interview with the offender is the only way to determine motivation. The perpetrator may have killed because he finds the act of strangulation sexually stimulating but there is a range of other possible explanations. Clarke and Carter (2000) reported the case of a man who killed because he was sexually aroused by the sight of blood. However, as Myers, Husted, Safarik, and O'Toole (2006) noted with reference to anger-based theories of sexual killing, explanations of the offense based on perpetrators' accounts must consider the perpetrator's reasons for their explanation of their actions. With reference to serial killers, although this point is also applicable to nonserial sexual killers, Myers et al. propose that offenders will favor endorsing or providing an anger motivation for the killing in order to avoid being labeled as a sex offender. It may be preferable both in prison and after release to be seen as a "hot head" rather than a "sexual deviant." It is also possible that factors such as brain injury, epilepsy, PTSD, or memory disturbance may present a genuine obstacle to the perpetrator in talking about the offense, in which case a specialist assessment may be required.

A case study will now be used to illustrate some of the above issues in the assessment and treatment of sexual killers.

Case Study Where Sex Attached to a Killing

Introduction

Mr. Y is serving a life sentence following a conviction for manslaughter with diminished responsibility. He was in his 20s at the time of the offense and his female victim was in her late teens. Mr. Y was seen by the first author to determine if there was a sexual motivation to his offense. There was no suggestion at the time of prosecution that a sexual offense had been committed alongside his index offense. Mr. Y's account was that on the night of the offense, he had consenting sex with the victim, after they had both been drinking, in the grounds of a golf course. He said that during sex, his victim ridiculed him about his performance; she laughed and he lost his temper and "hit the roof." Mr. Y said he then began to hit his victim, punching her "until she wasn't moving." The cause of death was an injury to the head and there was evidence that the victim had been strangled. The pathologist's report suggested that the head trauma resulted from blows from a fist or foot. While the pathologist reported evidence that sexual intercourse had taken place, it was not suggested either at the time of arrest and upon conviction that the sex was nonconsenting. However, there were various pieces of information known at the time of prosecution that were contrary to Mr. Y's account. First, the victim's friends did not believe that he had been her long-term boyfriend. In particular, her closest friend said that the victim told her everything and so she would have known if she had a boyfriend for several months, as Mr. Y claimed. Second, an 8-inch knife was found very close to the crime scene and was traced to the meat-packing factory where Mr. Y sometimes worked. Third, there was evidence that Mr. Y had ejaculated twice, once inside a condom and once inside the victim's vagina, countering his claim of being unable to perform sexually.

Mr. Y pleaded guilty to manslaughter on the grounds of diminished responsibility on the basis that both the prosecution and defense psychiatrists agreed that he had a psychopathic personality disorder. During Mr. Y's sentence, several prison staff raised the issue concerning the victim status as a girlfriend and further suggested that the offense was premeditated. At the direction of a parole board hearing, Mr. Y was assessed to attempt to determine the motivation for the offense.

Presenting complaints

At the time of the assessment, Mr. Y was in his late 40s, had spent a considerable time in prison, and had passed his tariff (the minimum period that a life-sentence prisoner must serve before being considered for parole). He presented as a suspicious and uncooperative man: a heavy smoker, he complained of migraines and back pain, for which he took painkillers. He did not see himself as a sexual offender and was aggrieved at not progressing more quickly towards release. Rather than solving problems himself, Mr. Y was quick to resort to his legal advisors to represent him on matters, even quite trivial ones, which he disagreed with. His reputation in prison was that he was antiauthority and he had a tendency to be petulant. In more recent years Mr. Y had presented as despondent and could be withdrawn, believing he was never going to be released and so would die in prison.

History

The following information is taken largely from the presentence report completed for the court by a probation officer. Mr. Y came from what was recorded as a stable and caring family. As a child, Mr. Y was spoiled by his parents, particularly his mother, who was described as very protective and overindulging. He had injured his back as a child falling from a tree and had missed several months of school. He was described as delicate, easily prone to tantrums or getting upset and at first running off to his room or the garden but later, from around age 9 or 10 he left the house to see relatives who overindulged and spoilt him.

Mr. Y reported a history of problems with relationships, which had started in his early teens when he often fell out with his father and ran away from home. He said that he spent time with mates but he was never that close to anyone. In terms of sexual relationships, he said that he had problems maintaining relationships with women and aged about 14 had casual sexual relationships with a number of females. He regularly truanted and his criminal career began in his early teens: at age 14 he was cautioned for shoplifting and also received a 12-month probation order for stealing a bicycle. He had later convictions for indecent assaults, the first of which was for grabbing a shopkeeper's breast. His account was that he did this for a dare when buying some alcohol from a shop with his friends, he said the woman involved had laughed at the time but later reported him to appease her boyfriend, whom Mr. Y said he did not get on with. On another occasion, for which he served a borstal sentence, Mr. Y grabbed a woman's breast when she was sunbathing at a local beauty spot: once again he explained this away as a prank, a "bit of fun" taken the wrong way. Finally, two years before the index offense, he served a 6-month custodial sentence for a completely unprovoked attack in which he stabbed, with a screwdriver, a woman standing at a bus stop. The woman, who he did not know, said that before the stabbing he had tried to grab her around the neck.

In the months leading up to the index offense, Mr. Y's relationship with his family was strained, particularly with his father with whom he often fought, sometimes physically. He had been thrown out of the house several times and stayed with relatives, his friends, and sometimes slept in his uncle's garage. He drank until he was drunk when he could afford it, used drugs, and spent his free time playing darts in local pubs.

Assessment

Mr. Y completed several psychometric assessments and semistructured interviews, which were used alongside file information to triangulate evidence both to identify treatment needs related to risk of future sexual offending and to inform case formulation. IQ assessment indicated he was above average intelligence. During interview with the first author, Mr. Y said that he killed the victim after an argument over sex, adding that on the day of the offense he had been drinking and using drugs. When he met the victim, who he said was his girlfriend, they drank more as they did not have their own home and they went to the grounds of the golf club to have sex because it was quiet and they would not be disturbed. Mr. Y said that because of his intoxicated state he found it hard to get an erection, although they did have sex he could not perform when his victim asked for sex again, which led to her ridiculing him. He said that he lost his temper and killed her: he said that he did not plan the offense; rather "it just happened." Mr. Y was asked to consider what questions his offending history and index offense might pose those, such as the parole board, involved in his progression through his sentence? While he took the stance that his offense was the result of losing his temper under the influence, he recognized that people may be concerned there was a sexual motivation to the offense if they believed that the victim did not consent to sex. Mr. Y was asked to consider, hypothetically, what the consequences could be if the offense was not triggered by an argument between a girlfriend and boyfriend about sex and, rather than just "happening," it was anger that had led to him being forceful and violent in the sexual encounter? He replied that it would mean he needed other help than just with drugs and alcohol problems.

Mr. Y also undertook a penile plethysmograph (PPG) assessment: although PPG assessment does not routinely identify an individual's offense-related sexual interests, it does have value in the assessment of sexual killers (Perkins, 2008). The PPG assessment indicated that Mr. Y was equally aroused by scenes of consenting sex between an adult male and an adult female, rape, and nonsexual aggression against an adult female. Mr. Y could not offer an explanation for the profile but said that he "preferred rough sex, involving some slapping."

Case conceptualization

The crime scene information provided evidence consistent with a sexual killing as described by Ressler et al. (1988): there was a lack of attire, fully exposing the lower half of the victim's body, and evidence of sexual intercourse. Mr. Y's account of the offense was inconsistent with crime scene evidence and what was known about the victim at the time of the investigation. In the build-up to the offense, Mr. Y had difficulties solving problems, he was drinking heavily, and he was frustrated by his failed attempts to form relationships. His life was unstable and he had been thrown out of home necessitating staying with work colleagues or sleeping in his uncle's garage. He had no daily routine, his employment was irregular, working the odd day or week in a meat-packing factory or doing laboring work to make money for drink and drugs.

Perkins outlined the merits of referring to models of sexual murder as "a useful framework in which to gather data and formulate a hypothesis" (2008, p. 96). Mr. Y's case met many of the characteristics of the crime profile of an angry sexual murderer proposed by Beauregard et al. (2007). In addition, he shared offense characteristics with sexual murderers with a "dangerous world" implicit theory, whose reported motivation is grievance with a high likelihood of resentment and anger towards women rather than sexual fantasies prior to the killing. Mr. Y accepted that he had been drinking and lost control and, following the PPG assessment, said that he enjoyed rough sex and slapping. His disclosures pointed to likely treatment targets (Mann & Marshall, 2009). Mr. Y accepted that he had difficulties managing problems in the time leading up to the offense and during his prison sentence. He finally consented to undertake an accredited sexual offending treatment program.

Course of treatment

Given the similarity in treatment needs between sexual killers and sexual aggressors, cognitive skills programs that address the attitudes that support offending, victim empathy, and relapse prevention, together with a secondary schema-focused program, have shown to be of benefit to offenders deemed to be sexual killers (Beech et al., 2005), although it has been suggested that adjustments should be made to make treatment responsive to this offender group (see Carter et al. 2008).

Mr. Y undertook both core and extended sexual offender accredited treatment programs that were delivered to groups of men serving a life sentence for a crime where there was a clear or possible sexual element or motivation to their killing. The core program aims to help participants understand why they offended, restructure thinking that contributed to their offending, develop victim empathy, improve problem solving skills, learn to recognize risk factors, and develop coping strategies. Mr. Y made progress on all of the key treatment targets on this course.

While on the core program, Mr. Y completed a decision chain where he considered his thinking, decisions, moods, and behavior leading up to the offense. During this exercise, which involved him discussing his chain in the group, Mr. Y disclosed that he had planned to kill the victim prior to meeting her and that he was going to have sex with her first whether she consented or not. He also disclosed that he was gay but was unable to have relationships with men as he thought his friends and family would disown him. This dilemma was a contributing factor to his grievance towards women. Mr. Y's low self-esteem and sense of despair meant that his motivation fluctuated. On occasion he believed he was unable to meet the goals of treatment. At other times he took issue when challenged. If he did take issue when challenged he sometimes threatened to leave the treatment group, rip up work, or said he would not speak until he had contacted his solicitor. It took some time to talk him around and encourage him to re-engage. The practitioners (including the first author) developed methods to work responsively with Mr. Y, using exercises that did not require him to answer questions about himself directly but encouraged him to describe what someone would have seen if they saw a video clip of an interaction in the build-up to the offense or the crime scene. This strategy helped him to talk about matters that he found difficult or shameful.

During the core program, it became apparent that he held a grievance towards women. He talked about how his previous sexual offenses had been about a grievance towards women and an escalation of wanting to hurt them. He said the rapes in his current offense were not preceded by sexual thoughts or fantasies about rape but were triggered by anger and resentment about having to have sex with women when he really wanted to be with a man. In the crime phase, his decision chain described thoughts indicating a desire to humiliate and control his victim. Mr. Y said that in fact his victim did not want sex and he had not been ridiculed: he made up this story because he thought his father would stand by him if he had been provoked by a girlfriend during consenting sex but would disown him if he knew he had committed rape and killed someone who was really just an acquaintance. Although he had been drinking, he said he had exaggerated the quantity to support his account at the time of his arrest, he added that he probably had not taken drugs, although he did afterwards when he took an overdose in a suicide attempt.

Following completion of the core program, Mr. Y undertook the extended program, which helps participants address dysfunctional and entrenched schemas and to develop emotional regulation and intimacy through improving their relationships skills, including coping when relationships are difficult. Thus, Mr. Y worked on learning to control, manage and challenge a number of schemas that he labeled *entitlement*, *grievance*, and *worthlessness*, and he developed techniques such as alternative self-talk for challenging his schemas. For example, with reference to his worthlessness schema, Mr. Y recognized that despite not always finding it easy, he had completed exercises and the treatment. In terms of challenging his worthlessness schema he developed alternative self-talk such as "at least I'll have a go. I may struggle at first but my life will be better for trying." He also recognized how his unhelpful schemas were interlinked and used this understanding to develop skills to manage his emotions. Mr. Y recognized that when he started to feel he was not doing anything right and that he was different from other men, this triggered feeling worthless, depressed, and lonely, which led to rumination and activation of his grievance schema where he wanted to make people suffer because he was suffering. He also developed skills and techniques for communicating and managing difficulties in relationships such as identifying warning signs that both he and people in his support network could recognize and act upon, for example, getting into a pattern of feeling worthless and depressed signaled that "things could be starting to go wrong for me."

Complicating factors

Although Mr. Y made positive treatment gains on both programs, he continued to find it difficult to discuss his feelings. It was recommended that he keep a comprehensive diary of his feelings, noting when he had shared them and the experience of doing so to help to reinforce the benefits when he recognized them and to communicate how he felt. It was also recommended that Mr. Y continue to manage his schemas and to solve problems without simply relying on enlisting the services of his solicitor. He also understood the benefits of developing his support network to share problems and avoid loneliness.

The possibility of offense-related sexual interests, such as an interest in rape, remained after completion of the programs given his previous convictions for sexual assault, the PPG results, that the murder and rape were premeditated, and that strangulation was employed, a common method among sexual killers (Carter & Hollin, 2010), and the indications of an attempt to grab a victim around the neck in a previous violent assault on a female. (A second PPG assessment was not interpretable due to the very low arousal levels, which may have been due to the medication for his bad back.) In addition, he was with the victim for 2 hours, which gave him ample time to carry out a prolonged and sexually arousing offense, and he was able to ejaculate when raping the victim and knowing he was going to kill her. Evidence against offense-related sexual interests was that he had been open and had engaged with treatment, so it is possible that he would have self-reported had there been an issue, and he had disclosed fantasies to rape to sate his feelings of anger and not to gain sexual gratification. Mr. Y also appeared more comfortable generally about himself and his sexual orientation, he spoke openly about being gay and had told his family.

Access and barriers to care

Although there remained questions over his sexual interests, it was recommended and endorsed by the parole board that Mr. Y move to open prison conditions to help generalize the learning from treatment in an environment with less security conditions and so prepare for release. His offender manager would be located some distance from the open prison to which he was transferred, which made it difficult to build a relationship with them. In addition, as he had committed manslaughter and accepted a sexual offense, it could be more difficult to find work in the community in preparation for release. He also had to take part in further work on alcohol and drug use.

Follow-up

Mr. Y transferred to open conditions and was undertaking work on managing his drug and alcohol use when the first author last had contact with his offender manager. He also had a work placement arranged at an industrial laundry company.

Treatment implications

While Mr. Y's case illustrates the challenges involved in the assessment and treatment of sexual killers, it should also serve to encourage and help practitioners working with such perpetrators. While it was not the goal of treatment to encourage Mr. Y to confess to his offense, the reassurance that he could disclose problems and difficulties that led him to commit the crime, along with help to address these difficulties and strengthen protective factors with people who had knowledge of his type of offense, helped him to disclose. The opportunity to talk about possible motivations and hypotheses in a group of men in a similar situation also allowed him to "try out" different ways of thinking and to talk about difficult, possibly shameful, topics. He was able to develop coping strategies and new skills to help with improving intimacy and managing his emotions, and practice these skills in a safe and supportive environment to use outside of treatment. Mr. Y's case also aptly represents the difficulties in determining the relevance of offense-related sexual interests when assessing sexual killers. While his offense was premeditated, which is more common for sadistic killers, his case followed the path of the "angry sexual murderer," as summarized by Proulx:

> In terms of development, they are seriously socially maladapted, which is manifested during childhood and adolescence by conflicts with authority, difficulties adjusting to school, and violent and impulsive crimes. As adults, angry sexual murderers maintain an inappropriate mode of social functioning. They abuse alcohol and drugs and are unable to keep a job. Nevertheless, they are not socially isolated, despite the fact that their romantic relationships are marked by occasional acts of violence. They consume little pornography and do not report deviant sexual fantasies (2008, p. 225).

While Mr. Y provided a motivation for his offense that did not involve sadistic sexual fantasizing or fantasies about rape, there is the possibility that he was not truly open about his motivation. Thus, there was a careful balancing of the progress Mr. Y had made in addressing his criminogenic risk factors, the strengthening of his protective factors, his behavior in prison, and his age when recommending his progression through his sentence.

Recommendations to Clinicians and Students

Managing risk with sexual murderers

Risk management strategies have been developed based on the premise of intervention to reduce the risk factors associated with sexual killing (Beauregard et al., 2007; Carter et al., 2008). The focus of such interventions, some of which are similar to those found in the wider sex offender literature (Beech et al., 2005), include any enduring criminogenic factors such as problem drinking, the perpetrator's attitudes towards women, lifestyle factors such as social and emotional isolation, and sexual preferences such as sadism and paraphilias.

There is a body of research with sex offenders which shows that criminogenic risk factors can be modified to reduce risk using psychological methods, most effectively through cognitive-behavioral (e.g., Lösel & Schmucker, 2005) and biomedical approaches (Bradford, 2008; Grubin, 2008). In addition, protective factors such as a constructive occupation and healthy social support (Rehabilitation Services Group & Maruna, 2010) can be strengthened to ameliorate risk (Hart, 2008). There is no reason to suppose that sexual killers would not similarly respond to appropriately targeted interventions, as the case of Mr. Y illustrates. Of course, practitioners will necessarily have familiarity with individual perpetrators in order to specify case-specific risk factors and their management, balancing risk reduction with the risk of harm should the perpetrator reoffend.

Information sharing

The communication of information in cases such as Mr. Y is critical. This communication should include information regarding the basis on which the sex is attached to the killing and should be shared with other parties such as the courts, prison and probation staff, and the parole board. The written assessment should be jargon-free to ensure its accessibility to nonspecialists, with a clear statement regarding the limitations of any structured risk assessment tools. The assessment report should also state where the practitioner and perpetrator agree and disagree as, for example, regarding paraphilic interests. A clear offense formulation should inform the identification of dynamic risk factors, along with suggestions for changing and managing these factors; any protective factors should be identified and strategies suggested for their continued support. The potential warning signs that risk has increased or there is a need for increased support or monitoring should be noted, particularly with respect to decisions regarding release from custody or a return to secure conditions. Advice may be offered on employment opportunities to be avoided, such as a necrophiliac working in a mortuary or cemetery (Hart, 2008). Where possible, advice should be given on how best to engage with the perpetrator including the most effective way to talk about issues they find awkward or shameful, or the approach to take if there is a lack of openness or willingness to talk. There may be helpful information gleaned during the interview about engagement and responsivity factors that make risk assessment and management particularly challenging. If such information is not recorded it can easily be lost.

Security options and release from custody

Informed by their knowledge of the criteria for transfer to different levels of security and release from custody, practitioners may give safe and workable recommendations for risk management. Necessarily, practitioners should have knowledge of the kind of establishment and regime that an offender will experience in a prison or, say, in a community hostel: discussions with other practitioners are necessary to ensure that recommendations for further work and support are realistic and practical. Hart has outlined the principles for the management of risk of further sexual violence:

> First, the strategy should reflect overall judgements regarding the risk posed by the offender. Second it should focus on risk management activities or tactics that are relevant in the case at hand, so each relevant risk factor is addressed (i.e., neutralised or contained) by one or more activities. Third, it should be personalised in a way that maximises robustness and effectiveness for the offender (2008, p. 149).

Conclusion

This chapter has outlined some of the challenges and issues for assessment and treatment when sex is attached to killing, particularly concerning paraphilia and offense-related sexual interests. The case is presented for familiarity with research on sexual killers to develop motivational hypotheses to assist case formulation with suggestions on the sharing of information and construction of considered management plans for the safe progression of these perpetrators through their sentence.

References

Beech, A. R. (2001). Case material and interview. In C. R. Hollin (Ed.), *Handbook of offender assessment and treatment* (pp. 123–136). Chichester, UK: Wiley.

Beech, A. R., Fisher, D., & Ward, T. (2005). Sexual murderers' implicit theories. *Journal of Interpersonal Violence, 20*, 1366–1389.

Beauregard, E., & Proulx, J. (2002). Profiles in the offending process of nonserial sexual murderers. *International Journal of Offender Therapy and Comparative Criminology, 46*, 386–399.

Beauregard, E., Proulx, J., & St-Yves, M. (2007). Angry or sadistic: Two types of sexual murderers. In J. Proulx, E. Beauregard, M. Cusson, & A. Nicole (Eds.), *Sexual murderers: A comparative analysis and new perspectives* (pp. 107–122). Chichester, UK: Wiley.

Bradford, J. M. W. (2008). The biomedical treatment of sexual sadism and associated conditions. In A. Harris & C. Pagé (Eds.), *Sexual homicide and paraphilias (pp. 109–125)*. Correctional Service of Canada.

Briken, P., Habermann, N., Kafka, M. P., Berner, W., & Hill, A. (2006). The paraphilia-related disorders: An investigation of the relevance of the concept in sexual murderers. *Journal of Forensic Sciences, 5*, 683–688.

Carter, A. J., & Hollin, C. R. (2010). Characteristics of non-serial sexual homicide offenders: A review. *Psychology, Crime & Law, 16*, 25–45.

Carter, A. J., Mann, R. E., & Wakeling, H. C. (2008). Sexual killers and post mortem interference offenders: Assessment treatment and risk management. In J. R. Harris & C. Pagé (Eds.), *Sexual homicide and paraphilias: The correctional service of Canada's experts forum 2007 (pp. 167–208)*. Correctional Services Canada.

Clarke, J., & Carter, A. J. (2000). Relapse prevention with sexual murderers. In D. R. Laws, S. M. Hudson, & T. Ward (Eds.), *Remaking relapse prevention with sex offenders: A sourcebook* (pp. 389–401). Thousand Oaks, CA: Sage.

Crown Prosecution Service. (2013). *Rape counts, linked to murder, left to lie on file*. Retrieved July 14, 2013, from http://www.cps.gov.uk/legal/p_to_r/rape _counts_linked_to_murder/#a04

Cusson, M. (2007). Sexual murderers: Myth and reality. In J. Proulx, E. Beauregard, M. Cusson, & A. Nicole (Eds.), *Sexual murderers: A comparative analysis and new perspectives* (pp. 1–5). Chichester, UK: Wiley.

Folino, J. O. (2000). Sexual homicides and their classification according to motivation: A report from Argentina. *International Journal of Offender Therapy and Comparative Criminology, 44,* 470–750.

Gresswell, D. M., & Hollin, C. R. (1992). Towards a new methodology for making sense of case material: An illustrative case involving attempted multiple murder. *Criminal Behavior and Mental Health, 2,* 329–341.

Grubin, D. (1994). Sexual murder. *British Journal of Psychiatry, 165,* 624–629.

Grubin, D. (2008). The use of medication in the treatment of sex offenders. *Prison Service Journal, 178,* 37–43.

Hart, S. D. (2008). Risk assessment: Sexual violence and the role of paraphilia. In A. Harris & C. Page (Eds.), *Sexual homicide and paraphilias (pp. 131–160).* Correctional Service of Canada.

Hill, A., Habermann, N., Klusmann, D., Berner, W., & Briken, P. (2008). Criminal recidivism in sexual homicide perpetrators. *International Journal of Offender Therapy and Comparative Criminology, 52*(1), 5–20.

Keppel, R. D., & Walter, R. (1999). Profiling killers: A revised classification model for understanding sexual murder. *International Journal of Offender Therapy and Comparative Criminology, 43,* 417–437.

Lösel, F., & Schmucker, M. (2005). The effectiveness of treatment for sexual offenders: a comprehensive meta-analysis. *Journal of Experimental Criminology, 1,* 117–146.

Mann, R. E., & Marshall, W. L. (2009). Advances in the treatment of adult sexual offenders. In A. R. Beech, L. A. Craig, & K. D. Browne (Eds.), *Assessment and treatment of sexual offenders: A handbook (pp. 329–348).* Chichester, UK: John Wiley & Sons.

Myers, W. C., Husted, D. S., Safarik, M. E., & O'Toole, M. E. (2006). The motivation behind serial sexual homicide: Is it sex, power, and control, or anger? *Journal of Forensic Sciences, 51,* 900–907.

Oliver, C. J., Beech, A. R., Fisher, D., & Beckett, R. (2007). A comparison of rapists and sexual murderers on demographic and selected psychometric measures. In J. Proulx, E. Beauregard, M. Cusson, & A. Nicole (Eds.), *Sexual murderers: A comparative analysis and new perspectives* (pp. 159–173). Chichester, UK: John Wiley & Sons.

Perkins, D. E. (2008). Diagnosis, assessment and identification of severe paraphilic disorders. In A. Harris & C. Page (Eds.), *Sexual homicide and paraphilias (pp. 77–104).* Correctional Service of Canada.

Proulx, J. (2008). Sexual murderers: Theories, assessment and treatment. In A. Harris & C. Page (Eds.), *Sexual homicide and paraphilias (pp. 225–252).* Correctional Service of Canada.

Proulx, J., Cusson, M., & Beauregard, E. (2007). Sexual murder: Definitions, epidemiology and theories. In J. Proulx, E. Beauregard, M. Cusson, &

A. Nicole (Eds.), *Sexual murderers: A comparative analysis and new perspectives* (pp. 9–28). Chichester, UK: John Wiley & Sons.

Rehabilitation Services Group & Maruna, S. (2010). *Understanding desistance from crime*. National Offender Management Service Factsheet. Available from NOMS.

Ressler, R. K., Burgess, A. W., & Douglas, J. E. (1988). *Sexual homicide: Patterns and motives*. New York: Lexington.

Ressler, R. K., Burgess, A. W., Douglas, J. E., Hartman, C. R., & D'Agostino, R. B. (1986). Sexual killers and their victims: Identifying patterns through crime scene analysis. *Journal of Interpersonal Violence, 1,* 288–308.

Revitch, E. (1965). Sex murder and the potential sex murderer. *Diseases of the Nervous System, 26,* 640–648.

Roberts, J. V., & Grossman, M. G. (1993). Sexual homicide in Canada: A descriptive analysis. *Annals of Sex Research, 6,* 5–25.

Schlesinger, L. B. (2004). *Sexual murder: Cathathymic and compulsive homicides.* Boca Raton, FL: CRC Press.

Thornton, D. (2010). *Scoring guide for Risk Matrix 2000.10/SVC.* National Offender Management Service.

Part IV

Specialized Interventions

17
Addressing Denial

Jayson Ware and Leigh Harkins

Theoretical and Research Basis for Treatment

No one should be surprised that an individual accused of sexual offenses will minimize the offense, externalize blame, or deny culpability. Initially, up to 87% of sex offenders have been found to partially or categorically deny responsibility for the sexual crimes they have been accused of committing (Maletzky, 1991). Whereas researchers have identified up to 14 different types of denial (Wright & Schneider, 2004), this is not necessarily of assistance to clinicians tasked with treating the offender. Ware and Mann (2012) argued that, from a clinical perspective, many sex offenders are either categorically or completely denying responsibility (denying), or omitting or underplaying certain aspects of the offending or its consequences (making excuses). Others will acknowledge that sexual contact occurred but claim that it was consensual or claim complete memory loss.

Those that offer excuses for their offending represent the vast majority of offenders commonly identified as deniers. A small number of sex offenders will, however, steadfastly maintain that they have been falsely accused, mistakenly identified, or were not present when the sexual abuse occurred. These men will often maintain their innocence even when the denial may result in negative consequences such as a longer prison term or tougher supervision conditions. These sex offenders pose particular management and treatment dilemmas (Ware & Marshall, 2014). They

Sex Offender Treatment: A Case Study Approach to Issues and Interventions,
First Edition. Edited by Daniel T. Wilcox, Tanya Garrett, and Leigh Harkins.
© 2015 John Wiley & Sons, Ltd. Published 2015 by John Wiley & Sons, Ltd.

rarely volunteer for treatment, are often deemed ineligible or unsuitable even if they were to volunteer, and in the event that they were able to commence treatment are often discharged for lack of treatment progress (Blagden, Winder, Thorne, & Gregson, 2011).

Consequently, sex offenders who categorically deny responsibility often remain untreated, even when assessed as an ongoing risk to the public. The issue, eloquently summarized by Laws (2002, p. 197) is how "the therapists engage the clients [*deniers*] in a program [*treatment*] they say they do not need, for a problem they say they do not have, to prevent another offense that they say they did not commit in the first place." There remains disagreement and debate over how to respond to categorical deniers, with some therapists believing it is simply unethical or fruitless to provide treatment to someone who states that they have no problem. Others maintain that allowing a sex offender to maintain their denial is morally wrong and will, therefore, aggressively strive for full acceptance of responsibility (Blagden et al., 2011; Levenson, 2011; Ware & Mann, 2012).

Whilst categorical denial has traditionally been viewed as a risk factor or treatment target (Schneider & Wright, 2004), research evidence seems to suggest otherwise. No consistent relationship has been found between denial and sexual recidivism (Hanson & Bussière, 1998; Hanson & Morton-Bourgon, 2005; Mann, Hanson, & Thornton, 2010). More recently, a number of studies have attempted to examine the issue in greater detail and have examined the moderating effects of other factors, such as assessed recidivism risk. Both Harkins et al. (2010) and Nunes et al. (2007) found that low-risk sex offenders who denied their offenses were more likely to reoffend than those low-risk offenders who admitted. Langton et al. (2008) reported the opposite. They found that higher levels of minimization and denial predicted sexual recidivism among higher-risk offenders and decreased the threat for low-risk offenders.

There remains a lack of clarity as to the importance of denial and recidivism (Ware & Marshall, 2014), with many therapists still maintaining that denial results in increased recidivism (Blagden et al., 2011). It appears that whilst the majority of sex offenders who maintain that they have not committed any sexual crimes will not reoffend, some will, and the denial for these offenders may be an important issue to address. Ware and Mann (2012) suggest that the function or purpose of the denial is the key issue to understanding when denial needs to be overcome. Lord and Willmot (2004), for example, asked sex offenders who had previously denied responsibility, but then admitted, why it was that they denied. They found that the majority of sex offenders who had previously categorically denied did so because of the fear of negative consequences and, in particular, fear of losing the support of their families. Only a small minority of offenders within the Lord and Willmot study reported maintaining their categorical denial in order to continue committing sexual crimes or maintain their sexual fantasies.

Denial appears to have been targeted extensively in treatment, as it was assumed that it related to beliefs or attitudes about sexual offending (Salter, 1988), however, it is not empirically clear to what degree they are in fact linked. Dean, Mann, Milner, and Maruna (2008), for example, noted that statements of attitude or belief about sexual offending (e.g., "children are sexually provocative") are distinctly different from statements that give reason to why the offense occurred (e.g., "she asked me to touch her"). Ware and Mann (2012) further noted that denial occurs after the offense and therefore is unlikely to be a causal fact but rather a strategy for minimizing consequences.

Ware and Marshall (2014) have outlined four different strategies for treating a sex offender who categorically denies responsibility. The first option is to simply do nothing and the offender is excluded from treatment. Ware and Marshall argued that this approach is neither palatable to the community (particularly if the offender is assessed as higher risk) nor is it based on sound evidence. The second option is to explicitly target the denial as part of a pretreatment intervention, either in a one-to-one or group format. Ware and Marshall noted that the evidence appears mixed with less than half of all sex offenders taking responsibility after these interventions (see Brake & Shannon, 1997; Murphy & Barry, 1995; Schlank & Shaw, 1996). The third and most common option is to allow these deniers to enter treatment along with those who admit and then attempt to overcome the denial within the broader context of the program. The final option, encouraged by Ware and Marshall for the small number of steadfast categorical deniers, is where treatment is provided but there is no attempt to overcome denial. In this approach, the denial is not challenged and instead the goal is to help the offender identify problems in his life that led him to be in a position where he could be *accused* of sexual offending and to focus on reducing the risk of being accused again (Marshall, Thornton, Marshall, Fernandez, & Mann, 2001).

This case study reflects a successful attempt to overcome categorical denial in a sex offender whereby a combination of the third and fourth options above are used within a group therapy context. In this instance, there was an initial treatment approach of not seeking to overcome denial but instead to focus on reducing the chances of the offender being "accused" of further allegations. Subsequently, however, the offender started to accept some, albeit limited, responsibility and at this time, there was a more active attempt to overcome the denial.

Case Introduction

Brian (not his real name) was a Caucasian 22-year-old male who was convicted of molesting a 12-year-old girl, unknown to him, at a playground. The victim was approached from behind while walking home after playing with friends. The park was in darkness. She was forced into nearby secluded bushes and subjected to a prolonged sexual assault while being forcefully held down and gagged. The sexual assault only ceased when Brian was disturbed by a passerby who had heard a struggle and crying. Brian fled from the scene without being seen by the passerby but was arrested later that evening. The victim had recognized Brian from other occasions where he had frequented the park whilst intoxicated. Although Brian had maintained his innocence, he received a 7-year custodial sentence.

Brian had previously been convicted of indecent assault of an 18-year-old adult female whom he was "dating" at the time. He forcibly engaged her in sexual intercourse in the back of a motor vehicle after attending a party with the victim. Whilst not using explicit violence, the victim maintained that she feared that he would physically assault her. At that time, when Brian was himself 19 years old, he acknowledged having sex with the victim but denied that it was a crime. He claimed instead that the victim had given her explicit consent to full sexual intercourse. He served 12 months in custody. Brian also had two previous convictions for wilful damage against his mother's property and for resisting police arrest.

Presenting complaints

Whilst incarcerated Brian was approached by a number of prison staff and encouraged to attend the sex offender treatment program. Brian refused, instead maintaining that he was, in fact, innocent and was being falsely accused. He reported that he was not in the vicinity of the park the evening when the sexual assault took place. Brian further claimed that he was "being set up" because of a drug deal that had "gone bad."

Given Brian's steadfast denial of sexual assault of the 12-year-old girl, the prison staff suggested that he could attend treatment and instead work on the issues relating to his previous sexual offense, and that this would allow Brian to complete treatment before his earliest possible release date.

They assumed that this would be sufficiently motivating for Brian. He remained adamant, however, that he was neither a "child molester" nor a "sex offender" (given that he reported that the sex was consensual) and did not want to be identified as such within the prison wing.

Importantly, however, Brian did state repeatedly that he "wanted help" and did not want to be accused of any sexual crime again. Prison staff reported that he appeared to lack self-esteem and did not readily mix with other offenders within the designated sex offender wing of the prison. Prison staff were also able to deduce that Brian's mother and sister appeared to strongly believe in his innocence. They were regular visitors to the prison, had arranged for further legal counsel to consider an appeal against his sentence, openly questioned many aspects of the police facts, and maintained that Brian would not "do such a thing." Notwithstanding their belief in Brian's innocence, his mother and sister appeared to be very supportive and prosocial, and offered accommodation, financial support, and ongoing stability upon Brian's eventual release from prison. They were also adamant that they would do whatever it took to ensure that their son would not be accused of further sexual crimes upon his release. This said, Brian had told many of the prison staff that his mother and sister were the "only things left in his life" and he was very fearful of losing their support.

History

There were a number of critical instances within Brian's background that are likely to have contributed to his sexual offending and, arguably, his categorical denial of responsibility. Many of these facts were not known until after Brian commenced treatment and developed a trusting relationship with his therapist.

His childhood was clearly very difficult. His parents separated when he was an infant and he had only sporadic contact with his father throughout his childhood. What contact he did have with his father appeared to be marked by emotional and physical abuse. These abusive experiences were to significantly disrupt Brian's emotional and social development and his ability to trust others. As a result of his father's abuse toward him, Brian reported strong feelings of anger and resentment towards his mother, who he felt should have protected him from the abuse, and towards his sister, who he believed did not have to suffer as he did (he was subsequently physically violent towards them, although never convicted of this). Notwithstanding this, his mother and sister remained the most important people in Brian's life.

Throughout his adolescence Brian reported feeling lonely and desiring of friendships with those who would not "ignore" him. Brian appears to have lacked social skills and spent most of his time with a small number of friends. He reported that all they did was "hang out at someone's house" and drink alcohol and smoke cannabis. Brian also spoke of a number of casual sexual encounters with females beginning when he was 18 years of age. These appear to have been instigated by Brian when both he and the females were heavily intoxicated. He reported that he had not had an intimate relationship with a female other than these incidences, although maintained that these were proof of his sexual adequacy. He did, however, report that he desired a girlfriend but simply feared being rejected by everyone.

Brian reported being unhappy and feeling "low" all of the time. It appears that he had low self-esteem and a belief that there was little he could do to improve his circumstances. Brian's main strategy for coping with these negative emotions since he was 15 years of age was alcohol. He reported drinking to excess whenever he felt unhappy, which appeared to be almost daily. Towards the end of his treatment, Brian also reported that he had spent "a lot of down time" watching pornography and masturbating to fantasies involving consenting adults. However, late in his treatment he did admit to occasional sexual thoughts of school-age girls.

Brian reported similar circumstances occurring immediately prior to both sexual offenses. He reported "liking a girl" but feeling unable to initiate any meaningful conversations or contact with them. This resulted in him feeling "at his lowest" and his use of alcohol and sexual fantasy increased significantly at these times. He also reported fighting with his mother and sister at the time and believing that they were no longer supporting him.

Assessment

Brian was assessed on the Static-99 (Hanson & Thornton, 2000) and STABLE-2007 (Hanson, Harris, Scott, & Helmus, 2007) as a high-risk sex offender. A comprehensive battery of standardized tests was administered as part of the sex offender treatment program assessment stage. Consistent with his presentation, and not surprisingly given his denial at time of assessment, Brian's psychometric assessment results indicated a tendency to present himself favorably. This is a common finding with those who categorically deny, as they will often minimize all problems in their lives in order to show that they did not have any reasons for sexual offending (see Cooper, 2005; Ware & Marshall, 2014). Notwithstanding this tendency, and importantly, Brian's responses still indicated an acceptance of inappropriate sexual myths, high levels of sexual fantasy, and a belief that external factors control events. High levels of anxiety were also evident, together with low self-esteem, fear of intimacy, and experiences and emotions associated with loneliness.

Case conceptualization

Brian's case created a significant case-management dilemma. He had been assessed as a high-risk sex offender with a number of clearly identified treatment targets. He was, however, refusing all offers of treatment whilst maintaining his innocence.

Unless an innovative strategy was developed, Brian was to remain an untreated high-risk sex offender. In this case, he was, therefore, unlikely to be released by the parole authority and might even have to serve the majority of his sentence in custody (see Hood et al., 2002, for discussion of parole authorities and their views on denial). Whilst this might have had the short-term advantage of protecting the community, he would then be released with limited or nonexistent supervision and restrictive conditions, and remain untreated. Clearly these outcomes were not ideal and an effective solution to this dilemma had to be found.

Two immediate case-management goals were generated. The first goal was to somehow encourage Brian into treatment. In this particular prison, there simply were not the resources to provide anything other than very limited individual treatment. The aim was to encourage Brian to commence a group based sex offender treatment program even if he still maintained his denial. While many treatment programs do not consider sex offenders who maintain their categorical denial as eligible or suitable for treatment (Levenson, 2011), in this particular instance, the treatment program did not exclude deniers. As Schneider and Wright (2004) have noted, restricting treatment to those who are already accepting responsibility is, in effect, expecting many sex offenders who are denying their offense to then admit this of their own accord without treatment. Whilst this does happen, the majority of deniers who subsequently admit appear to do so within a therapeutic context (Blagden et al., 2011; Lord & Willmot 2004). Further, continued denial does not appear to necessarily prevent ongoing treatment gains (Beckett, Beech, Fisher, & Fordham, 1994; Maletzky & Steinhauser, 1998). This suggests that categorical denial need not interfere with treatment gains on other important topics. This said, in most instances where a sex offender maintains his categorical denial for a recent offense but accepts responsibility for previous sexual offending then the therapist should accept this individual into treatment and focus initially on his previous sex offending (see Ware & Marshall, 2014). Brian was, however, denying being a sex offender altogether and was stating emphatically that he would not accept treatment for crimes he did not commit.

The second goal was to engage Brian sufficiently so that he would complete the program and in doing so have worked on all of the factors assessed to relate to his ongoing risk of committing further sexual crimes. Once Brian was sufficiently engaged in treatment, the therapist needed to decide if the denial was to be challenged and overcome. Ware and Marshall (2014) argue that there are two distinct options for the therapist. The first and most common approach is to seek to overcome the categorical denial. However, this approach, in Ware and Marshall's view, has some distinct risks and requires some flexibility and consideration.

Therapists will often report that problems soon arise after a categorical denier commences treatment alongside admitters, as he is likely to be considered disruptive or resistant by both the therapist and the other group members. His denial can elicit frustration and agitation from others. In turn, this may result in even greater defensiveness from the denier. This may ultimately result in the denier being discharged from, or voluntarily dropping out of, treatment (Beyko & Wong, 2005; Ware & Bright, 2008). This is not a positive result. Marshall, Marshall, and Ware (2009) caution that it may not be the offender's denial per se but rather some therapist's persistent, if not aggressive, attempts to overcome denial, or the rigidity of the treatment program's content and structure, that leads the denying offender to be discharged or to drop out. Ware and Mann (2012) also noted that most treatment programs have acceptance of responsibility as an initial treatment target. The difficulty, as demonstrated by Lord and Willmot (2004), is that deniers will usually require time within a therapeutic environment before being able to admit responsibility. Requiring deniers to accept responsibility, particularly *full* responsibility, within the first 4 to 6 weeks of treatment is fraught with difficulty. Additionally, Ware and Mann argue that if therapists are seeking to overcome denial relatively quickly then they (and other group members) will invariably become more confrontational or hostile in their approach. Confrontational approaches to sex offender treatment have been shown to reduce the overall effectiveness of sexual offender treatment (Marshall, 2005). These issues can be overcome by the therapist delaying when he or she will seek to overcome the denial and by ensuring that the therapeutic engagement remains the core focus irrespective of whether or not the offender remains in denial. Ware, Mann, and Wakeling (2009) also argued that this is much easier within individual treatment or when a rolling open group format is used.

An alternative approach to treating sex offenders in categorical denial was developed by Marshall et al. (2001) in which there is no attempt to overcome the denial but instead the focus is on reducing the likelihood of further *allegations*. The program is presented to offenders as an opportunity to identify problems in their lives that led them to be in a position where they could be accused and convicted of a sexual crime and to focus on making sure that they cannot be accused in the future. In this approach it is suggested to the offenders that it must have been something about their behaviors, attitudes, thoughts, and feelings within certain situations that led to the allegations, and may, therefore, lead to more allegations in the future unless they are able to manage themselves better than in the past. Once the offender has agreed to treatment then the therapist can focus on treatment targets in the same way that he or she would with admitters, with the exception of sexual deviancy. Marshall and colleagues suggested approaching this particular issue under the guise of healthy sexuality and in so doing still providing skills and knowledge that could be used to manage sexual arousal. A preliminary appraisal of this approach to treating categorical deniers showed that the long-term reoffense rate after release from prison was significantly lower (2.5%) than expected (13.5%) and approximately the same as for treated admitters (Marshall, Marshall, Serran, & O'Brien, 2011). It is suggested that this approach be used with those sex offenders who maintain their denial irrespective of all attempts to overcome this. In this sense, it provides an additional, seemingly effective, option for treating offenders who would otherwise remain untreated.

In this case, a combination of these approaches was used. The alternative approach where denial is not confronted was used initially as a treatment option for Brian. This engaged him into treatment using the approach of seeking to reduce the likelihood of further *allegations*, and, therefore, not seeking to challenge the denial was followed by the therapist until such time that it appeared that Brian was ready to accept responsibility of his own accord. At that stage, it was decided to positively challenge the denial. If Brian had not been ready to accept responsibility, the therapist would have simply continued with the strategy of assisting him to focus on making sure that there could be no further allegations.

Course of treatment and assessment of progress

The following describes the key components of initial motivation sessions to encourage Brian into treatment and specific strategies used within treatment to both work with the denial initially and maintain Brian's engagement. Some of the key principles used with Brian are also described to highlight the therapist's flexibility, initial sidestepping of the denial, and ultimate overcoming of denial later in the treatment program.

Individual motivational intervention   Brian completed four individual 1-hour sessions over the course of 4 weeks to motivate him to attend a sex offender treatment program. Brian was initially very reluctant to consent to treatment. He maintained his innocence at every opportunity and was evasive and defensive. Brian stated that he was expecting the therapist to try to "trick" him into discussing things about his convictions as a way of gaining a confession about his current offenses. Whilst clearly very wary of the therapist's intentions, Brian did agree that he had a number of problems in his life that he would like assistance with. He was also curious as to the benefits (to him) of treatment – even knowing this was a sex offender treatment program. The therapist took this as a good sign and as an indication that Brian might be considering accepting responsibility.

Using motivational interviewing techniques (see Prescott & Porter 2011 for a description of the use of motivational interviewing with sex offenders), the therapist offered Brian the opportunity to agree to commence treatment where he would be working towards reducing the likelihood of his being *accused* of a sexual crime again. The therapist agreed that he would not discuss the (alleged) sexual crimes unless Brian wanted to. It was also suggested that this treatment option might help him work on other aspects of his life in which he was actually asking for help – such as his self-esteem, problems coping with low mood, and alcohol abuse. At this point, the therapist was very mindful that sex offenders often also refuse treatment due to their beliefs that the goals of treatment do not match their own pressing life issues (Mann, Webster, Wakeling, & Keylock, 2013). In other words, Brian had an opportunity to develop some skills that would lead to a more positive and satisfying life, which would thereby reduce his risk of being falsely accused again.

The therapist further focused on some of the issues relating to Brian's denial. He asked Brian to consider "What would your mother and sister think of your efforts to make sure no one accused you of this again?" "How might you use the opportunity to feel better about yourself?" "How would you make sure that you aren't accused of this again – either by an adult or child?" and "How can you take some control over this?" It was repeatedly made clear to Brian that he could discontinue treatment at any point without negative consequence. The therapist encouraged Brian to consider the advantages of this treatment option. These included that he could demonstrate a commitment to change, work on some issues he wanted help with, show his mother and sister how serious he was in making sure he couldn't be accused again, and possibly even get released by the parole authority.

The therapist also had the opportunity to meet with Brian's sister. The therapist answered all of her questions regarding the proposed treatment approach. She was also very wary of any attempts to coerce Brian into admitting to something they (she and her mother) still believed he did not do, but at least saw the usefulness of helping Brian develop strategies to make sure that he could not be accused of anything again. She was adamant that she and her mother would make sure Brian couldn't be accused of further sexual crimes. However, the therapist was able to point out that Brian was unlikely to spend all of his time in the future in the presence of his mother or sister, thus he needed to take responsibility for ensuring he could not be accused again himself. She agreed to help get Brian into the treatment program but wanted a guarantee that he could discontinue at any time.

At the conclusion of four motivational sessions, Brian very cautiously agreed to commence treatment as long as it was agreed that he would only be working towards reducing the likelihood of his being *accused* of a sexual crime again.

Group based treatment – general approach and course of treatment   Immediately upon agreeing to participate, Brian commenced a group based treatment program alongside nine other sex offenders, all of whom were accepting some degree of responsibility for their sexual crimes. This was a rolling or open-ended group and, therefore, five of the nine offenders had actually completed a significant proportion of their treatment. The therapist was very clear with the treatment group that, in Brian's case, he maintained his innocence and agreed to participate only in that he wanted to make sure he could not be accused of any further sexual crimes. The group members were encouraged to focus on Brian's involvement as a positive step and to assist him in his goals.

The therapist hypothesized that the key reasons for Brian's denial were his fear of losing his family support and his low self-esteem, rather than an explicit desire to continue offending. Brian's statements during the motivation sessions suggested that he desired help but would not admit responsibility due to what he perceived to be the catastrophic consequences of losing his mother and sister's support. The therapist further hypothesized, using information from the Police Record of Facts, psychometric assessment results, and Brian's initial descriptions of his life at the time of the offending, that his self-esteem was low and that one of his strategies to cope with this was to avoid the reality of accepting responsibility for the sexual crimes. The therapist also knew that Brian had problems coping with negative emotions, an acceptance of inappropriate sexual myths and appeared to use sex to cope, had alcohol abuse issues, and had difficulties building satisfying relationships.

With these hypotheses in mind, the therapist decided to work on self-esteem and the support of Brian's mother and sister as a priority. This would be followed by therapeutic work regarding his coping with emotions and alcohol abuse issues. The therapist was in no hurry to target the denial and, in fact, intentionally worked with Brian on nonthreatening, nonoffense-specific, yet important, treatment targets first. This had the advantage of ensuring that Brian did not feel too confronted (which could have led to discontinuation of treatment). Brian appeared somewhat surprised by this approach and, although initially guarded, appeared to genuinely value the opportunity to explore his self-esteem and coping issues that had caused him some longstanding problems.

Group based treatment – initial understanding (disclosure) component
After 6 weeks of treatment, the therapist chose to have Brian complete an understanding (or "disclosure") exercise. This is usually one of the first tasks of sex offender treatment and is a way in which offenders can join a treatment group, accept some responsibility for their offending, and commence a process of identifying important treatment foci.

At this time, Brian was an active participant in many group discussions and appeared to trust and respect most of the other group members and, most importantly, the therapist. Nevertheless, he instantly became defensive and withdrawn when forewarned that he would soon be asked to complete this exercise. Of note, Ware and Mann (2012) have raised concerns over the sequencing of this module, arguing that it should only be used when the offender has engaged with treatment and developed a therapeutic alliance with his therapist. They further note that many sex offenders appear to drop out of treatment when completing such exercises early in treatment.

The understanding exercise, in this instance, was similar to the typical "disclosure" type exercise in which offenders are asked to describe what happened immediately preceding the offense (Marshall et al., 2011).

However, this "disclosure" did not involve presenting the details of the offense but rather only the factors that led to the *allegation*. Whereas an offender is usually asked to tell the treatment group about his offense, Brian was asked to discuss what had happened on the day when the offense was alleged to have taken place with a view to understanding how he could have been falsely accused of sexual abuse.

The therapist gently encouraged Brian to consider how it was that *he* was accused of the offense, pointing out that it may have been because of the ways in which he had acted. Brian agreed to discuss his behaviors on the day of the offense. He disclosed that on the day in question he had fought with his mother. He had left the house agitated and feeling "shitty." Brian stated that these were really strong emotions. Brian then went to a friend's house but they were not there so he decided to buy alcohol and go to a local park to "chill out." He said that, at that point, he was thinking about all of the "crap in his life." He was not able to elaborate on why he wanted to go to that particular park but did note that it was a stupid idea although when asked why this was so, he was not able to explain. The therapist gently encouraged Brian to discuss seeing the victim on the day in question. He cautiously acknowledged seeing the victim, and even talking to her. Importantly, Brian also acknowledged that he had commented to the girl about her nice clothes, but then became defensive as he realized what he was saying. The therapist was able to steer Brian away from this defensiveness by continuing to focus on how the things Brian may have said or done could have prompted the victim to "falsely" accuse him.

In an encouraging and supportive manner, the therapist continued to ask further questions, each designed to elicit details regarding the thoughts, feelings, and behaviors that preceded the alleged offense. The therapist actively rewarded each detail of this disclosure and maintained a collaborative stance. Throughout this process the therapist repeatedly indicated to Brian that he could see how his behaviors could have led to an allegation. As a result Brian began to acknowledge this and in so doing began to take responsibility for behaving in problematic ways on the day of the offense. This was an important first step towards acceptance of responsibility.

After understanding component   Whilst continuing to work on the non-threatening aspects of Brian's treatment plan, the therapist also encouraged Brian to continue to actively seek to understand why he was accused of committing a sexual crime and how he would have to live his life in the future to make sure he was not accused of anything further. Brian appeared genuinely interested in this.

The therapist also continued to meet with Brian's mother and sister on several occasions. Whilst careful not to suggest explicitly that Brian was in fact responsible for the sexual assault, the therapist cautiously started to ask what would happen if Brian were to say that he had committed the crime. Initially the family members were, like Brian, adamant of his innocence and not willing to accept otherwise, but over time they started to soften their stance.

Overcoming of denial   Brian asked to speak to the therapist after 9 weeks of treatment. At this point, he had completed a number of individual treatment tasks relating to self-esteem and coping, and had participated in most other treatment exercises and discussions, including another offender's understanding (disclosure), in which Brian gave excellent and positive feedback regarding the individual's issues that culminated in a sexual crime.

Brian described feeling much better about himself, that he felt really supported by the therapist and the group members, and how, in particular, he was very respectful of the therapist keeping his promise not to make him "confess." Brian stated that he had now had the chance to think "long and hard" about his circumstances and that he had spent time with his mother and sister, both of whom had started to encourage him to take greater responsibility and control over his life. Moreover, Brian spoke very candidly about his friendship with one of the group members and admiration for this man. Perhaps due to all of these reasons, Brian stated that he was now willing to admit to some of "what they said I did."

Brian subsequently accepted responsibility for "having sex with the woman when she didn't want to," and "for molesting that girl." At this time, Brian was no longer, according to Ware and Mann (2012), denying his crimes but was now looking to make excuses for his actions. The therapist would subsequently work on these minimizations and externalization of responsibility over time, as well as all other treatment targets identified for Brian, including his use of sex to cope and his sexual preoccupations.

Summary   The therapist in this instance hypothesized that the denial was understandable or used by Brian as a strategy to minimize consequences. It was not considered a dynamic risk factor but rather an issue that could potentially have stopped Brian from benefitting from treatment. The innovative and positive approach to overcoming the denial overcame the case management dilemmas. In contrast, if he had been considered ineligible for treatment, or the denial had been targeted aggressively or within the first 6 weeks prior to his being engaged, then he would not have completed treatment. The therapist initially worked on nonthreatening yet important treatment targets and used a strategy of assisting Brian to work on the factors that led to his being *accused* of a sexual crime. This both engaged him into treatment and allowed him to complete tasks, including identifying background factors, without being confronted. Importantly, the therapist focused on issues that he hypothesized to be the cause of the denial – notably Brian's fears of losing his mother and sister and his low self-esteem.

Complicating factors

Within their review of acceptance of responsibility (overcoming denial and excuses) as a treatment target, Ware and Mann (2012) argued that the primary reason clinicians seek to overcome denial is that "it seems the right things to do." Levenson also notes that apologies and accountability are considered "the right thing to do" within our societal values (2011, p. 3). Categorical denial itself does not, however, appear to be an established risk factor and nor does it represent an obstacle to treatment engagement and benefit (see Ware & Mann, 2012).

There also appear to be very understandable reasons why someone accused of a sexual crime will maintain their innocence. Importantly, some individuals accused of sexual crimes will categorically deny some offenses and admit to others. Or, they may admit to previous offenses but categorically deny responsibility for the one they are now accused of committing. Ware and Marshall (2014) argue that categorical denial should be considered a strategy that is both contextual and situational. Understanding how to treat a sex offender who is denying requires some understanding of the function or purpose of denial for that offender. In Brian's case, his fear of losing the support of his mother and sister coupled with his sense of shame and self-loathing appear to be the main reasons for his denial.

Without due consideration of these issues, therapists may inadvertently be contributing to difficulties presented by sex offenders in denial. Rendering deniers ineligible or unsuitable for treatment, targeting denial early in treatment, using confrontational or hostile approaches, proceeding with treatment content in a nonflexible way, and refusing to accept that denial might not even need to be challenged are all issues for therapists that may complicate any approach to treating a categorical denier.

Treatment implications of the case

The option of excluding categorical deniers from treatment does not appear to be soundly based. Cohen (1995) noted that excluding deniers from treatment was neither legally nor therapeutically appropriate, particularly as courts have consistently ruled that sex offenders cannot be punished on the basis of denial alone.

Therapists need to be flexible in their approach to treating categorical deniers. As Ware and Marshall (2014) have noted, there is only limited evidence for the effectiveness of pretreatment interventions designed to overcome denial. It appears that the best treatment approach is to both include deniers in groups with admitters and apply a positive flexible therapeutic approach in which there is no hurry to overcome the denial and/or to use an approach in which there is no attempt to overcome denial but rather a focus on reducing further allegations.

In this particular case, a combination of the two approaches was used. The therapist encouraged Brian into treatment with the goal of reducing further allegations and not seeking to overcome the denial. Whilst maintaining this approach for a period of time to ensure adequate therapeutic engagement, it was then deemed appropriate to gently challenge the denial, particularly when it became evident that Brian was ready to accept some responsibility.

Recommendations to Clinicians and Students

It should come as no surprise that sex offenders will deny or minimize responsibility to some extent. A smaller number will maintain their complete or categorical denial irrespective of all initial attempts to overcome this denial. Clinicians should not naturally assume, however, that sex offenders who categorically deny are not amenable to treatment. What appears critical is an understanding of the function or purpose of the denial for each individual offender (Ware & Mann, 2012; Ware & Marshall, 2014). For some, it may be intention to reoffend, but for the majority it seems to be a strategy to minimize consequences for the offender, such as shame or loss of family. These are understandable reasons and it is perhaps surprising that so few sex offenders actually categorically deny (Marshall et al., 2009).

Sexual offenders who categorically deny having committed sexual abuse can be motivated to engage in effective treatment. Most clinicians will explicitly seek to overcome the denial, however there is an alternative approach in which the denial is not challenged and instead the goal is to help the offender identify problems in his life that led him to be in a position where he could be accused of sexual offending and to address these (see Marshall et al., 2001; Ware & Marshall, 2008). There is some preliminary evidence that indicates that this approach is as successful in reducing reoffending as conventional programs (Marshall, O'Brien, Marshall, & Serran, 2008). This innovative approach gives clinicians an alternative option for those sex offenders maintaining their categorical denial who are otherwise going to be left untreated.

This case study illustrated an approach to overcoming denial that commenced with the strategy of helping the offender identify problems in his life that led him to be in a position where he could be accused of sexual offending. This engaged the offender in treatment in the first instance and provided the therapist with the opportunity to develop a therapeutic alliance and trust. It also provided the therapist with the opportunity to understand the function of the denial for the offender and to develop strategies to address the actual issues that maintained the denial – without the therapist having to actually seek to challenge the denial. In so doing, this prevents the therapist from becoming overly confrontational or inflexible to the needs of the offender.

References

Beckett, R., Beech, A., Fisher, D., & Fordham, A. S. (1994). Community-based treatment of sex offenders: An evaluation of seven treatment programs. Home Office Occasional paper. London: Home Office.

Beyko, M. J., & Wong, S. C. P. (2005). Predictors of treatment attrition as indicators for program improvement not offender shortcomings: A study of sex offender treatment attrition. *Sexual Abuse: Journal of Research and Treatment*, 17, 375–389. DOI: 10.1177/107906320501700403.

Blagden, N. J., Winder, B., Thorne, K., & Gregson, M. (2011). No-one in the world would ever wanna speak to me again: An interpretative phenomenological analysis into convicted sexual offenders' accounts and experiences of maintaining and leaving denial. *Psychology, Crime, & Law*, 17, 563–585. DOI: 10.1080/10683160903397532.

Brake, S. C., & Shannon, D. (1997). Using pretreatment to increase admission in sex offenders. in B. K. Schwartz & H. Cellini (Eds.), *The sex offender: New insights, treatment innovations and legal developments* (Vol. II, pp. 5.1–5.16). Kingston, NJ: Civic Research Institute.

Cohen, F. (1995). Right to treatment. In B. K. Schwartz & H. R. Celline (Eds.), *The sexual offender: Corrections, treatment, and legal practice* (pp. 24.1–24.18). Kingston, NJ: Civic Research Institute.

Cooper, S. (2005). Understanding, treating, and managing sex offenders who deny their offence. *Journal of Sexual Aggression*, 11, 85–94. DOI: 10.1080/13552600412331272337.

Dean, C., Mann, R. E., Milner, R., & Maruna, S. (2008). Changing child sexual abusers' cognition. In T. A. Gannon, A. R. Beech, T. Ward, & D. Fisher (Eds.), *Aggressive offenders' cognitions: Theory, research and practice* (pp. 117–134). Chichester, UK: John Wiley & Sons.

Hanson, R. K., & Bussière, M. T. (1998). Predicting relapse: A meta-analysis of sexual offender recidivism studies. *Journal of Consulting and Clinical Psychology, 66*, 348–362.

Hanson, R. K., Harris, A. J. R., Scott, T.-L., & Helmus, L. (2007). *assessing the risk of sexual offenders on community supervision: The dynamic supervision project.* Corrections Research User Report 2007-05. Ottawa, Canada: Public Safety Canada.

Hanson, R. K., & Morton-Bourgon, K. (2005). The characteristics of persistent sexual offenders: A meta-analysis of recidivism studies. *Journal of Consulting and Clinical Psychology, 73*, 1154–1163.

Hanson, R. K., & Thornton, D. (2000). Improving risk assessment for sex offenders: A comparison of three actuarial scales. *Law and Human Behavior, 24*, 119–136. DOI: 10.1023/A:1005482921333.

Harkins, L., Beech, A. R., & Goodwill, A. M. (2010). Examining the influence of denial, motivation, and risk on sexual recidivism. *Sexual Abuse: A Journal of Research & Treatment, 22*, 78–94.

Hood, R., Shute, S., Feilzer, M., & Wilcox, A. (2002). Sex offenders emerging from long-term imprisonment: A study of their long-term reconviction rates and of parole board members' judgements of their risk. *British Journal of Criminology, 42*, 371–394.

Langton, C. M., Barbaree, H. E., Harkins, L., Arenovich, T., McNamee, J., Peacock, E. J., et al. (2008). Denial and minimization among sexual offenders: Post treatment presentation and association with sexual recidivism. *Criminal Justice and Behavior, 35*, 69–98.

Laws, D. R. (2002). Owning your own data: The management of denial. In M. McMurran (Ed.), *Motivating offenders to change: A guide to enhancing engagement in therapy* (pp. 173–191). Chichester, UK: John Wiley & Sons.

Levenson, J. S. (2011). "But I didn't do it!": Ethical treatment of sex offenders in denial. *Sexual Abuse: A Journal of Research and Treatment, 23*, 346–364.

Lord, A., and Willmot, P. (2004). The process of overcoming denial in sexual offenders. *Journal of Sexual Aggression, 10*, 51–61. DOI: 10.1080/135526 00410001670937.

Maletzky, B. M. (1991). *Treating the sexual offender.* Newbury Park, CA: Sage.

Maletzky, B. M., & Steinhauser, C. (1998). The Portland Sexual Abuse Clinic. In W. L. Marshall, Y. M. Fernandez, S. M. Hudson, & T. Ward (Eds.), *Sourcebook of treatment programs for sexual offenders* (pp. 105–116). New York: Plenum Press.

Mann, R. E., Hanson, R. K., & Thornton, D. (2010). Assessing risk for sexual recidivism: Some proposals on the nature of psychologically meaningful risk factors. *Sexual Abuse: A Journal of Research and Treatment, 22*, 191–217.

Mann, R. E., Webster, S. D., Wakeling, H. C., & Keylock, H. (2013). Why do sexual offenders refuse treatment? *Journal of Sexual Aggression*, *19*, 191–206. DOI: 10.1080/13552600.2012.703701.

Marshall, W. L. (2005). Therapist style in sexual offender treatment: Influence on indices of change. *Sexual Abuse: A Journal of Research and Treatment*, *17*, 109–116. DOI: 10.1177/107906320501700202.

Marshall, W. L., Marshall, L. E., Serran, G. A., & O'Brien (2011). *Rehabilitating sexual offenders: A strength-based approach*. Washington, DC: American Psychological Association.

Marshall, W. L., Marshall, L. E, & Ware, J. (2009). Cognitive distortions in sexual offenders: Should they all be treatment targets? *Sexual Abuse in Australia and New Zealand*, *2*, 21–33. DOI: 10.1080/10683160802190947.

Marshall, L. E., O'Brien, M. D., Marshall, W. L., & Serran, G. A. (2008, August). *The Treatment of Categorical Denial in Sexual Offenders*. Paper presented at the 10th International Conference of the International Association for the Treatment of Sexual Offenders, Cape Town, South Africa.

Marshall, W. L., Thornton, D., Marshall, L. E., Fernandez, Y. M., & Mann, R. E. (2001). Treatment of sex offenders who are in categorical denial: A pilot project. *Sexual Abuse: A Journal of Research and Treatment*, *14*, 205–215.

Nunes, K. L., Hanson, R. K., Firestone, P., Moulden, H. M., Greenberg, D. M., & Bradford, J. M. (2007). Denial predicts recidivism for some sexual offenders. *Sexual Abuse: A Journal of Research and Treatment*, *19*, 91–106. DOI: 10.1177/107906320701900202.

Prescott, D. S., & Porter, J. (2011). Motivational interviewing in the treatment of sexual offenders. In D. P. Boer, R. Eher, L. A. Craig, M. H. Miner, and F. Pfäfflin (Eds.), *International Perspectives on the Assessment and Treatment of Sexual Offenders. Theory, Practice and Research* (pp. 355–372). Chichester, UK: John Wiley & Sons.

Salter, A. C. (1988). *Treating child sex offenders and victims? Assessment and treatment of child sex offenders: A practice guide*. Beverly Hills, CA: Sage.

Schlank, A. M., & Shaw, T. (1996). Treating sexual offenders who deny their guilt: A pilot study. *Sexual Abuse: A Journal of Research and Treatment*, *8*, 17–23. DOI: 10.1007/BF02258013.

Schneider, S. L., & Wright, R. C. (2004). Understanding denial in sexual offenders: A review of cognitive and motivational processes to avoid responsibility. *Trauma, Violence and Abuse*, *5*, 3–20. DOI: 10.1177/1524838003259320.

Ware, J., & Bright, D. A. (2008). Evolution of a treatment program for sex offenders: Changes to the NSW custody based intensive treatment (CUBIT). *Psychiatry, Psychology, and Law*, *15*, 340–349. DOI: 10.1080/1321871 0802014543.

Ware, J., & Mann, R. E. (2012). How should "acceptance of responsibility" be addressed in sexual offending treatment programs? *Aggression and Violent Behavior*, *17*, 279–288. DOI: 10.1080/13218710802014543.

Ware, J., Mann, R. E., & Wakeling, H. (2009). Group versus individual treatment: What is the best modality for treating sexual offenders? *Sexual Abuse in Australia and New Zealand*, 2, 2–13.

Ware, J., & Marshall, W. L. (2008). Treatment engagement with a sexual offender who denies committing the offense. *Clinical Case Studies*, 7, 592–603. DOI: 10.1177/1534650108319913.

Ware, J., & Marshall, W. L. (2014). *Categorical denial in convicted sex offenders: The concept, its meaning, and its implications for risk and treatment*. Manuscript submitted for publication.

18

Changing Deviant Sexual Interests: Masturbatory Reconditioning with a Child Molester

William L. Marshall

Theoretical and Research Basis

Using masturbation as a vehicle to alter deviant sexual interests derives from conditioning accounts of the origin of such interests (Abel & Blanchard, 1974; Laws & Marshall, 1990; McGuire, Carlisle, & Young, 1965). These conditioning theories suggest that it is the repeated practice of masturbating to deviant images that entrenches a preference for such behaviors. If these notions are correct then masturbation could also provide a vehicle for changing these unacceptable interests and thereby eliminate the undesirable consequent behaviors. In this chapter, two procedures utilizing masturbation and its consequences to alter sexual interests will be outlined and applied to a persistent child molester. These two procedures have been described respectively as "directed masturbation" and "satiation therapy."

Directed masturbation

Since Marquis' (1970) original description of what he called "orgasmic reconditioning," there have been numerous reports of variations on this procedure for enhancing appropriate sexual interests in sexual offenders (Campbell-Fuller & Craig, 2009; Kremsdorf, Holmen, & Laws, 1980; Laws & Marshall, 1991; Maletzky, 1980, 1985, 1991; Marshall, 1974,

Sex Offender Treatment: A Case Study Approach to Issues and Interventions,
First Edition. Edited by Daniel T. Wilcox, Tanya Garrett, and Leigh Harkins.
© 2015 John Wiley & Sons, Ltd. Published 2015 by John Wiley & Sons, Ltd.

2006a). Most of these subsequent reports have used the descriptor "directed masturbation" at least in part to avoid implying that orgasm is the critical experience that must be associated with rehearsing appropriate fantasies. Orgasm is a significantly altered state during which heart rate increases to near or above 150 bpm (Rosen & Beck, 1988). As a resut, it seems unlikely that anything can be learned by association with the orgasmic stage. Even if learning did occur it would be surprising if it transferred to the normal state. The crucial pairing for directed masturbation to be effective appears to involve associating appropriate sexual fantasies with the "plateau stage" of sexual arousal (Masters & Johnson, 1966). The plateau stage is a heightened state of arousal. Heart rate among males during the plateau stage reaches 120 to 125 bpm (Rosen & Beck, 1988). This state of heightened arousal is, nevertheless, not so intense as to prevent learning from occurring; indeed it appears to be the optimal state of arousal for forming new sexually based associations.

In this technique, the therapist assists the client in developing several scenarios involving consenting sex with a peer-aged adult. These scenarios are sexually explicit and include descriptions of activities that are commonly practiced by intimate couples (e.g., vaginal intercourse in the case of heterosexuals, anal intercourse for homosexual males, oral–genital sex, fondling, caressing, sex in various positions). The client is instructed to initiate masturbation by whatever means necessary. For significantly deviant individuals this may require beginning with deviant fantasies but once fully aroused, the client is to switch to one of the appropriate images. The client is told that should he begin to lose arousal he should switch back to deviant thoughts until rearoused, at which point he should reimagine one of the appropriate fantasies. This switching sometimes has to be repeated several times until orgasm is achieved.

Satiation therapy

Masters and Johnson's (1966) observations of male sexual functioning revealed that within 2 minutes of the ejaculatory response, men enter what they called the "refractory period." In this state men are unresponsive to sexual stimulation that would otherwise be exciting to them. Marshall (1975, 1977) suggested that since the refractory period was essentially a period of nonreward (i.e., no sexual pleasure) for sexual thoughts, it could be utilized as a way of eliminating deviant interests. Marshall proposed activating deviant thoughts during the refractory period, which he suggested would lead to the extinction of their provocative capacity.

In Marshall's initial papers on the development of what he called "satiation therapy" (Marshall, 1975, 1977, 1979; Marshall & Barbaree, 1978; Marshall & Lippens, 1977) the client was instructed to continue to masturbate after orgasm while rehearsing every variation on his deviant fantasies for up to 1 hour. While the results of the early applications of the procedure revealed substantial reductions in deviant interests, as indexed by phallometric assessments, it proved to be such an arduous and uncomfortable procedure that many clients either refused to do it, or quickly found it too aversive.

As a result of these observations, satiation therapy was modified, primarily as a result of discussions with and suggestions made by Laws and his colleagues (Laws, 1995; Laws, Osborne, Avery-Clark, O'Neil, & Crawford, 1987), to make it both more effective and more palatable to clients. In particular, Laws suggested eliminating the need to masturbate after orgasm and to rehearse deviant thoughts for just 10 minutes in order to minimize the possibility of rearousal. In addition the sensible way to induce the essential refractory state is to utilize directed masturbation as the first step, and then have the client clean himself before initiating satiation. Since the refractory period does not onset until approximately two minutes after orgasm, having the client clean himself should exhaust this time. These changes have made satiation more palatable to clients.

Case Introduction

Graham was a 42-year-old schoolteacher who had been convicted of the sexual assaults of seven young girls in the age range 9 to 11 years. These girls were either in Graham's class or they were participants in after-school activities that he supervised. The offenses occurred over a period of several years. Graham had, rather surprisingly, served 12 months of a 23-month prison sentence and was referred to our outpatient clinic for treatment after release on parole. Graham did not receive treatment in prison but was eager to address his problems, which he said had plagued him since he first entered the teaching profession.

Interviews revealed that although he was married for most of the time the offenses took place, Graham said he had not been motivated to have sex with his wife for the past 10 to 15 years; she resented this and had asked him several times to seek sexual counseling. Graham said he did not pursue counseling because he was sure it would not be helpful unless he admitted to his strong sexual interest in young girls. He said he had now come to realize that he had nothing further to lose by facing his

problem and dealing with it. Graham readily admitted to regularly masturbating to sexual fantasies involving young girls since his late teens. He
admitted to having more victims than had been identified but he did not
provide sufficient details to have required reporting.

Graham's deviant sexual interest was explored through examining the
features of females that he found arousing, as well as considering his
previous relationships with women. Graham was asked if he had any
sexual interest in early-teenage girls. He indicated that he was aroused by
some of the teenage girls in his colleague's classes but only if they were
relatively physically undeveloped. A discussion followed that was aimed
at identifying a possible aversion to the appearance of secondary sexual
features in females, since this might account for his preferences. Graham
said that in fact he found developed breasts and the presence of pubic
hair to be attractive features of females so an acquired aversion to these
characteristics seemed unlikely. This discussion revealed that Graham had
found his mother to be quite threatening, both physically and emotionally,
and his first girlfriend at age 18 years was domineering and persistently
made derogatory remarks about Graham's physical features and his intellectual awareness. He said his wife was nicer than this woman but was
nevertheless somewhat aloof. Graham said the prepubescent girls in his
classes were nice, although some of the early teenagers at the school were
boisterous and rude which he found threatening. In addition to the masturbatory conditioning procedures, it was therefore necessary to both
desensitize Graham to criticism from females and assist him in developing
better skills in both seeking out an appropriate adult partner and in
maintaining an effective intimate relationship. These latter features
were addressed in a full treatment program that Graham entered after
the procedures aimed at changing his deviant sexual interests were
completed.

Graham said that his wife was his first and only adult sexual partner.
He did not attempt sexual contact with his previous girlfriend. Initially
in their marriage Graham and his wife had sex two or three times each
week, during which he sometimes found it necessary to fantasize young
girls in order to maintain arousal. Graham indicated that on several occasions early in his marriage, he was able to become aroused to his wife
during their precoital activities. However, this capacity began to wane
within the first year of the marriage; thereafter he had to fantasize young
girls during sex with his wife.

Graham said he began to form friendships with some of the girls in his
class who also participated in official after-school activities that he supervised. He said he carefully and slowly began to groom them and look for

things he could offer them as incentives to win their affection. Once Graham was confident the girls would not resist, and would be unlikely to report him, he said he would then initiate nonsexual touching to see how they would respond. If they seemed at ease he would gradually progress to more explicit sexual touching. Graham declared that he had never attempted penile penetration, but he did perform oral sex on the girls and inserted his finger into the vagina of several girls. The victims' reports matched Graham's claims.

Presenting complaints

Graham clearly met the *Diagnostic and Statistical Manual of Mental Disorders* (4th ed.; DSM-IV-TR);American Psychiatric Association, 2000) criteria for pedophilia, and had very limited capacity for sexual arousal to adult females. There was no evidence of any interest in males. Graham was determined to overcome his interest in young girls not only because of his fear of further apprehension and a consequent longer jail term, but also because he was deeply remorseful for having caused the victims such clear distress. The victims and their parents presented statements in court during Graham's sentencing hearing that outlined the problems he had caused, and this significantly distressed and surprised him. This information added to his motivation to change. His wife had initiated divorce proceedings immediately upon Graham's conviction and his admission to her of his guilt. He said he wished to seek another relationship but not until he was satisfied that he had conquered his problem. Rather surprisingly, Graham appeared to not harbor any resentment toward his wife or toward adult women in general.

Given Graham's presentation it was clear that he was well motivated to change. Both Graham's description of the offenses and that of the victims, revealed no evidence that he had been at all physically coercive. He appears to have used persuasion and incentives (small gifts and attention) to overcome whatever resistance the victims offered.

The likely targets for treatment included not only Graham's deviant sexual interests and apparent lack of enthusiasm for sex with adults, but also his problems in adult relationships. An assessment battery was designed to evaluate these potential targets.

History

Graham grew up in a family that appears to have had few problems. He said his parents did not show affection but nevertheless effectively provided for him and his two older sisters. As noted, Graham perceived his mother's behavior toward him as physically and emotionally abusive, and his two older sisters copied their mother's behavior toward him. His sisters constantly teased Graham and made fun of him, particularly when they saw him naked as a young boy. However, he said once they became adults they were quite nice to him and maintained good relations with him until he was sent to prison. His parents both died when Graham was a teenager, which he said did not particularly distress him. He seemed distant when discussing his family and admitted having little affection for any of them. Graham said he wanted to start new life, with a new job, new friends, and hopefully a new adult female partner.

In Graham's early days as a teacher, although he was attracted to several of the girls in his class, he made no attempt to be alone with them. Graham thought this was probably due to his fear of being discovered but he also attributed it to the fact that his sexual relationship with his wife was reasonably satisfactory during the early part of their marriage. However, the feelings of sexual attraction to young girls that had characterized his late-teenage years began to return as a result of the diminution of his sexual pleasure with his wife and the constant proximity of young girls in his class. Sex with his wife became routine, and both of them lost enthusiasm. Graham began to think about the girls in his classes in a sexual way and this heightened interest led him to start after-school activities (e.g., library reading, discussions of classroom topics, as well as discussions of likely test questions). These extracurricular activities were presented to the girls as opportunities to improve their grades in an enjoyable way. Initially, four girls, whom Graham paid special attention to in each of his classes, eagerly volunteered to participate in these activities. He said he would sit closely beside each of the girls during these activities and take the opportunity to touch them nonsexually. If they responded in the way he wanted, Graham would arrange for one-on-one sessions with them during which he would initiate overt sexual contact. Over time the number of girls from Graham's classes who attended the after-school sessions increased. He estimated that he had at least minimally molested (i.e., sexually touched them over their clothing) more than 20 young girls over a period of 16 years.

Assessment

In terms of dynamic risk factors, Graham's most significant feature was his long-time sexual interest in female children. While the primary focus of Graham's deviant interests were preteen girls, he admitted to some sexual interest in early teenagers but only if they seemed nonthreatening. Graham's next most important risk factor was the poor quality of his adult intimate relationships, associated with some degree of apprehension, if not fear, of adult females. However, while these features were all assessed, the treatment targeting Graham's deviant interests was conducted prior to any attempts to modify the other targets in order that the effects of the specific procedures aimed at changing sexual interests could be evaluated. Subsequent to the treatment aimed at deviant interests, Graham entered a full treatment program that addressed his other issues.

Two measures were used to assess Graham's sexual interest: phallometry and a diary detailing his sexual fantasies. Phallometric testing of Graham involved measuring his erectile responses to three sets of sexually explicit stimuli recorded on audiotapes, one of which described an adult male having consenting sex with an adult female while the others described an adult male sexually molesting either pubescent or prepubescent female children. Marshall and Fernandez (2003) reviewed evidence indicating that these sets of audio stimuli provided the best discrimination between men who had molested children who were known to them and all other types of sexual offenders, as well as nonoffending males. Graham was also asked to keep daily diaries over a 3-week pretreatment period, and throughout treatment and follow-up. These diaries recorded the daily frequency, intensity, and duration of appropriate and deviant sexual fantasies that occurred in three time periods: morning, afternoon, and evening. A composite score reflected an integration of the three indices.

The pretreatment results from phallometric testing and the daily diaries are presented in Figures 18.1 and 18.2. As can be seen, during pretreatment baseline recordings Graham showed considerable and significant arousal to prepubescent girls, some degree of arousal to teenage girls, and little or no arousal to adult females. His daily diaries essentially matched these data.

In addition to these measures of deviance, Graham also completed five self-report tests: Social Self-Esteem Inventory (Lawson, Marshall, & McGrath, 1979); Miller's Social Intimacy Scale (Miller & Lefcourt, 1982); UCLA Loneliness Scale – Revised (Russell, Peplau, & Cutrona, 1980); Abel's Cognition Scale (Abel et al., 1989); and the Marlowe-Crowne Social Desirability Scale (Crowne & Marlowe, 1960). The results on the Marlowe-Crowne test did not reveal any attempts at dissimulation, suggesting that Graham was being honest in his responses. He did not show more than mild levels of cognitive distortions; for example, Graham displayed a tendency to view some young girls as somewhat interested in sex with an adult and as somewhat sexually provocative, but otherwise he

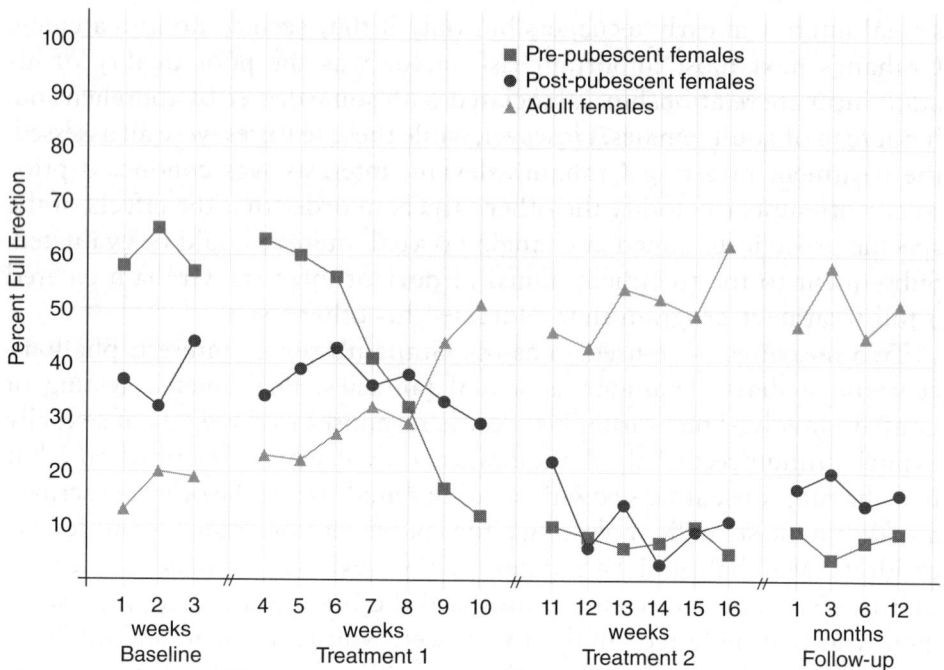

Figure 18.1 Arousal data from phallometric testing.

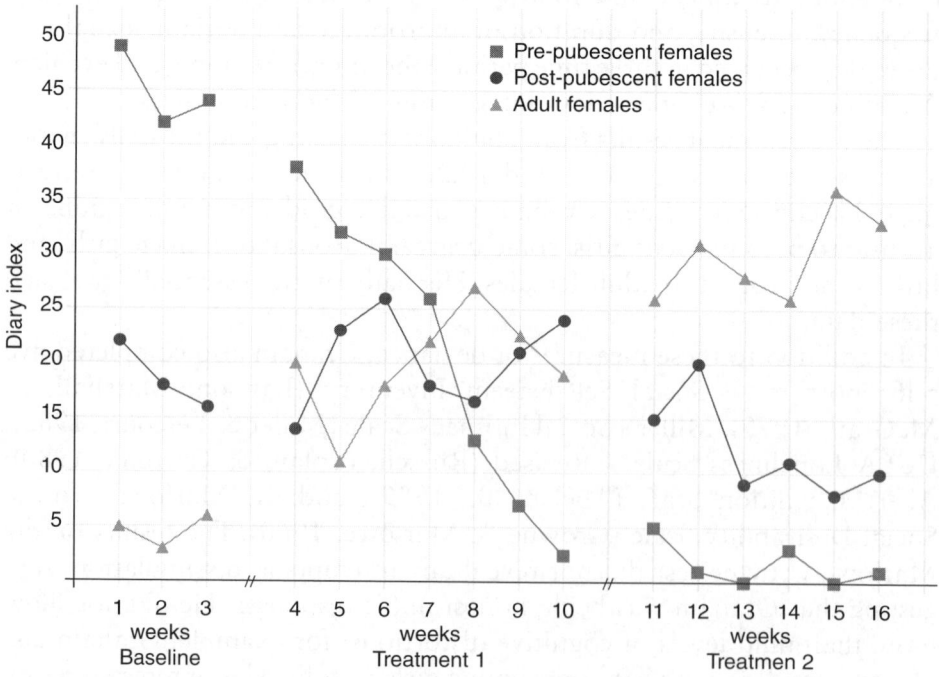

Figure 18.2 Arousal data from daily diaries.

did not endorse other distortions. Graham's responses revealed a degree of low self-esteem (115 against a norm of 132), low levels of intimacy (92 against a norm of 126), and high degrees of emotional loneliness (48 against a norm of 36). These various problems were successfully addressed in a later comprehensive program that represented an early version of our approach (Marshall, Earls, Segal, & Darke, 1983).

Case conceptualization

Since Graham was in the community when he presented at our clinic, his deviant sexual interests were targeted as a first step in order to diminish the risk that he might reoffend. This was also demanded by the referring agency. Graham also requested that we address this issue first as he was distressed by the rate of his deviant fantasies which, he said, increased in frequency when he was under stress. Graham agreed to enter our more comprehensive program once sufficient progress had been made on diminishing his deviant thoughts and urges. He felt he could not attend to other issues until this was dealt with. We agreed.

The goal of these initial interventions was, therefore, to decrease Graham's attraction to prepubescent and postpubescent girls and to increase his attraction to adult females.

Course of treatment and assessment

As noted, the initial treatment targets were Graham's sexual interests, which we will describe in detail here. Graham did subsequently complete a full program addressing most of the targets that are now considered criminogenic as well as his low self-esteem and associated feelings of shame. Throughout all aspects of treatment, whenever Graham expressed inappropriate thoughts about the sexuality of young girls, these distortions were challenged. At the time of this intervention (early 1980s) it was widely accepted that cognitive distortions should be targeted in the treatment of sexual offenders, a point of view that we (Marshall, Marshall, & Kingston, 2011; Marshall, Marshall, & Ware, 2009) have recently challenged. The follow-up evaluations at 6 months and 12 months occurred during and after the full treatment program. Thus, the later stability of the changes in phallometric and diary data are somewhat confounded by this subsequent intervention. Nevertheless, the phallometric and diary data should, if these specific interventions were effective, clearly demonstrate immediate and at least short-term effects of the fantasy-specific interventions.

After the data for the 3-week pretreatment baseline were collected, the interventions specifically aimed at changing Graham's sexual interests were introduced. In order to prepare for the directed masturbation procedure, Graham was assisted in identifying a set of appropriate fantasies. He selected, but did not name, four women he had known whom he identified as attractive and nonthreatening. Graham said he believed these women would likely elicit some degree of sexual arousal in him. Together the therapist and Graham produced eight scenarios that he was able to vividly imagine. These scenarios involved sexual activity with these women where the sexual activity progressed from mutual caressing, to touching of each other's genitals, to fellatio and cunnilingus, and finally to vaginal intercourse. In each of these scenarios the woman was depicted as consenting, affectionate, and actively engaged. These scenarios were written down so that Graham could rehearse them before each masturbatory session.

Graham was instructed to utilize directed masturbation procedures each time he normally masturbated under his usual conditions of privacy at home. He indicated that he typically masturbated two or three times per week. Graham was advised to initiate arousal by whatever method he typically used (e.g., self-stimulation while imagining young girls). Graham was told that once he was aroused to the level of a full erection, he was to switch to one of the appropriate scenarios and continue masturbating. If he began to lose arousal, he was told to switch back to his deviant images until he had regained full arousal at which point he was to return to imagining one of the appropriate sexual fantasies. Graham was told that after he ejaculated he was to clean himself and then initiate rehearsing every variation he could generate on his deviant fantasies for the following 8 to 10 minutes.

Associating appropriate sexual fantasies with preorgasmic arousal was meant to enhance the sexual attractiveness of appropriate images, while associating deviant fantasies with the period of sexual unresponsiveness (i.e., the refractory period) was intended to initiate extinction processes concerning these images. Extinction occurs when a previously entrenched habit is associated with a nonrewarding state (Falls, 1998).

These procedures were explained in detail to Graham and he was asked, in return, to repeat the procedures back to the therapist. This was done to ensure he fully understood what was required. At each subsequent weekly session, Graham was again asked to describe the procedure and to report on his practice. He was a bright and very attentive client who appeared to have diligently practiced the combined procedure. As can be seen in Figures 18.1 and 18.2, the combined procedure began to have a noticeable effect on interests and deviant fantasies about prepubescent girls after the third week of the first block of treatment (i.e., between weeks 6 and 7 on the figures).

The second block of treatment targeted Graham's interests in teenage girls and, as can be seen in Figures 18.1 and 18.2, the combined procedure produced rapid reductions in arousal to, and fantasies about, teenage girls. The relative stability of these responses during the first block of treatment that was aimed at reducing arousal to, and fantasies about, prepubescent girls, and the reduction of arousal to, and fantasies about, teenage girls in the second block, strongly suggest that it was the introduction of satiation therapy that produced the positive changes. In fact, the overall intervention strategy that was employed is a slight variation on the single-case experimental design that is described as "multiple-baseline across behaviors" (Hersen & Barlow, 1976). This design allows researchers to make confident assertions about the effects of particular procedures, independent of the effect expected from simply attending to the problem. Graham's responses to the adult stimuli were, prior to treatment, barely above 10% full erection, which we count as the minimum level for a true erectile response (see Marshall & Fernandez, 2003 for a detailed discussion of this issue). Fortunately, these responses showed a slow improvement reaching satisfactory, although not dramatic, levels by week 7, after which arousal to adult women remained stable.

At posttreatment and follow-up, Graham displayed normative responses, with the posttreatment and 3-month assessments revealing the uncontaminated effects of the behavioral procedures alone. Figures 18.1 and 18.2 reveal that these benefits were maintained at the later assessments (6 months and 12 months) after Graham entered and completed the full treatment program. A long-term (28 years posttreatment) check on official criminal records revealed no further involvement with the criminal justice system. Unfortunately, shortly after the 12-month assessment, Graham moved to a distant part of the country to, as he said, "start a new and better life." This meant that further assessments were not possible.

Complicating factors

There were no apparent complications in this case except for the fact that there is no direct evidence that the changes in deviant and appropriate sexual interests and fantasies were maintained beyond 12 months. However, the fact that Graham has remained offense-free for 28 years does suggest that the masturbatory procedures had effects that were complemented by his involvement in the subsequent full treatment program.

Before Graham left the town where he received treatment, he met a similarly aged woman with whom he developed a relationship. This, in fact, was a significant part of his reason for moving, as she obtained a job in another province.

Follow-up

As noted, follow-up contacts involved Graham's participation in the full program as well as repeated evaluations up to 12 months after these specific interventions. He very effectively participated in the full program, partly due to his delight at what he perceived as the benefits of the masturbatory conditioning procedures. Graham reported during the full program and at follow-up assessments, that whenever he felt any transitory sexual urges or thoughts about young girls he would reinitiate the masturbatory procedures, just as he had been advised to do.

Treatment implications

In an earlier single-case report (Marshall, 2006a) it was found that a nonmasturbation-based procedure (olfactory aversion) produced marked reductions in deviant interests but no effects at all on appropriate interests. In that study the subsequent application of directed masturbation produced increases in arousal to adults up to satisfactory levels. Thus, if a client displays high deviant and low appropriate responses, then the application of the combination of directed masturbation and satiation appears to be the strategy of choice, as was demonstrated in the present case.

Recommendations to Clinicians

While there is an obvious advantage in terms of experimental control to conducting treatment under conditions where the client's adherence can be directly monitored, the use of the present procedures would cause obvious privacy concerns if conducted under observable conditions. Therefore, masturbatory-based treatment procedures are best done under natural conditions, but efforts should be made to ensure the client is practicing the interventions in the appropriate manner. Ensuring the client understands the procedures both before and during their implementation has difficulties, but repeatedly asking the client to describe them and to indicate when, where, and how often he practices them can be helpful and is, perhaps, the only way in which we can check on clients.

The accumulation of data testifying to the efficacy of this combination of directed masturbation and satiation therapy (see Marshall, O'Brien, & Marshall, 2009) should encourage clinicians to see this strategy as their first choice in attempting to modify sexual interests. Utilizing such naturally occurring processes (i.e., masturbation and the postorgasm refractory period) should maximize treatment benefits, and the evidence appears to support this.

Alternative behavioral interventions to reduce deviant interests have also been shown to be effective (Marshall et al., 2009) but most of them involve some form of aversive conditioning, which can interfere with good therapist–client relationships. As a result, we recommend the combined masturbatory reconditioning procedures described in the present report, at least as the first step. If the satiation procedure fails to reduce deviant arousal, then olfactory aversion (see Marshall, 2006a) appears to be the best alternative for most sexual offenders, although ammonium aversion is perhaps the procedure of choice with exhibitionists (see Marshall, 2006b).

Clinicians should note that modifying deviant sexual interests should normally be done in the context of a full treatment program; however, there are instances, such as the present case, where there are sound reasons to target these interests as a first step in order to enable the client to better focus during the remainder of treatment.

References

Abel, G. G., & Blanchard, E. B. (1974). The role of fantasy in the treatment of sexual deviation. *Archives of General Psychiatry, 30*, 467–475.

Abel, G. G., Gore, D. K., Holland, C. L., Camp, N., Becker, J. V., & Rathner, J. (1989). The measurement of the cognitive distortions of child molesters. *Annals of Sex Research, 2*, 135–152.

American Psychiatric Association. (2000). *Diagnostic and statistical manual of mental disorders* (4th ed., Text revision). Washington, DC: American Psychiatric Publishing.

Campbell-Fuller, N., & Craig, L. A. (2009). The use of olfactory aversion and directed masturbation in modifying deviant sexual interest: A case study. *Journal of Sexual Aggression, 15*, 179–191.

Crowne, D. P., & Marlowe, D. (1960). A new scale of social desirability independent of psychopathology. *Journal of Consulting Psychology, 24*, 349–354.

Falls, W. A. (1998). Extinction: A review of theory and evidence suggesting that memories are not erased with nonreinforcement. In W. O'Donohue (Ed.), *Learning and behavior therapy* (pp. 205–229). Boston: Allyn and Bacon.

Hersen, M., & Barlow, D. H. (1976). *Single-case experimental designs: Strategies for studying behavior change.* New York: Pergamon.

Kremsdorf, R., Holmen, M., & Laws, D. R. (1980). Orgasmic reconditioning without deviant imagery: A case report with a pedophile. *Behaviour Research and Therapy, 18,* 203–207.

Laws, D. R. (1995). Verbal satiation: Notes on procedure, with speculations on its mechanism of effect. *Sexual Abuse: A Journal of Research and Treatment, 7,* 155–166.

Laws, D. R., & Marshall, W. L. (1990). A conditioning theory of the etiology and maintenance of deviant sexual preference and behavior. In W. L. Marshall, D. R. Laws, & H. E. Barbaree (Eds.), *Handbook of sexual assault: Issues, theories and treatment of the offender* (pp. 209–229). New York: Plenum Press.

Laws, D. R., & Marshall, W. L. (1991). Masturbatory reconditioning with sexual deviates: An evaluative review. *Advances in Behaviour Research and Therapy, 13,* 13–25.

Laws, D. R., Osborn, C. A., Avery-Clark, C., O'Neil, J. A., & Crawford, D. A. (1987). *Masturbatory satiation with sexual deviates.* Unpublished manuscript. University of South Florida, Florida Mental Health Institute, Tampa.

Lawson, J. S., Marshall, W. L., & McGrath, P. (1979). The Social Self-Esteem Inventory. *Educational and Psychological Measurement, 39,* 803–811.

Maletzky, B. M. (1980). Assisted covert sensitization. In D. J. Cox & R. J. Daitzman (Eds.), *Exhibitionism: Description, assessment, and treatment* (pp. 187–251). New York: Garland STPM Press.

Maletzky, B. M. (1985). Orgasmic reconditioning. In A. S. Bellack & M. Hersen (Eds.), *Dictionary of behavior therapy techniques* (pp. 157–158). New York: Pergamon Press.

Maletzky, B. M. (1991). *Treating the sexual offender.* Newbury Park, CA: Sage.

Marquis, J. N. (1970). Orgasmic reconditioning: Changing sexual object choice through controlling masturbation fantasies. *Journal of Behaviour Therapy and Experimental Psychiatry, 1,* 263–271.

Marshall, W. L. (1974). A combined treatment approach to the reduction of multiple fetish-related behaviors. *Journal of Consulting and Clinical Psychology, 42,* 613–616.

Marshall, W. L. (1975, August). *Satiation therapy for deviant sexual preferences.* Paper presented at the first Meeting of Sexual Offender Researchers, Memphis, TN.

Marshall, W. L. (1977, December). *Satiation therapy: Two case studies.* Paper presented at the 11th Annual Convention, Association for Advancement of Behavior Therapy, Atlanta, GA.

Marshall, W. L. (1979). Satiation therapy: A procedure for reducing deviant sexual arousal. *Journal of Applied Behavioral Analysis, 12,* 377–389.

Marshall, W. L. (2006a). Olfactory aversion and directed masturbation in the modification of deviant preferences: A case study of a child molester. *Clinical Case Studies, 5,* 3–14.

Marshall, W. L. (2006b). Ammonia aversion with an exhibitionist: A case study. *Clinical Case Studies, 5*, 15–24.

Marshall, W. L., & Barbaree, H. E. (1978). The reduction of deviant arousal. *Criminal Justice and Behavior, 5*, 294–303.

Marshall, W. L., Earls, C. M. Segal, Z. V., & Darke, J. (1983). A behavioral program for the assessment and treatment of sexual aggressors. In K. Craig & R. McMahon (Eds.), *Advances in clinical behavior therapy* (pp. 148–174). New York: Brunner/Mazel.

Marshall, W. L., & Fernandez, Y. M. (2003). *Phallometric testing with sexual offenders: Theory, research, and practice.* Brandon, VT: Safer Society Press.

Marshall, W. L., & Lippens, K. (1977). The clinical value of boredom: A procedure for reducing inappropriate sexual interests. *Journal of Nervous and Mental Disorders, 165*, 283–287.

Marshall, W. L., Marshall, L. E., & Kingston, D. A. (2011). Are the cognitive distortions of child molesters in need of treatment? *Journal of Sexual Aggression, 17*, 118–129.

Marshall, W. L., Marshall, L. E., & Ware, J. (2009). Cognitive distortions in sexual offenders: Should they all be treatment targets? *Sexual Abuse in Australia and New Zealand, 2*, 70–78.

Marshall, W. L., O'Brien, M. D., & Marshall, L. E. (2009). Modifying sexual preferences. In A. Beech, L. Craig, & K. Browne (Eds.), *Assessment and treatment of sex offenders: A handbook* (pp. 311–327). Chichester, UK: John Wiley & Sons.

Masters, W., & Johnson, V. (1966). *Human sexual response.* Boston: Little, Brown.

McGuire, R. J., Carlisle, J. M., & Young, B. G. (1965). Sexual deviations as conditioned behavior: A hypothesis. *Behaviour Research and Therapy, 2*, 185–190.

Miller, R. S., & Lefcourt, H. M. (1982). The assessment of social intimacy. *Journal of Personality Assessment, 46*, 514–518.

Rosen, R. C., & Beck, J. G. (1988). *Patterns of sexual arousal: Psychophysiological processes and clinical applications.* New York: Guilford Press.

Russell, D., Peplau, L. A., & Cutrona, C. E. (1980). The Revised UCLA Loneliness Scale. *Journal of Personality and Social Psychology, 39*, 472–480.

19

Understanding the Journeys of High-Risk Male Sex Offenders Voluntarily Receiving Medication to Reduce Their Sexual Preoccupation and/or Hypersexuality

Belinda Winder, Rebecca Lievesley, Helen Jane Elliott, Christine Norman, and Adarsh Kaul

Theoretical and Research Basis for Treatment

Sexual preoccupation is a significant predictor for sexual, violent, and general recidivism (Hanson, Harris, Scott, & Helmus, 2007; Hanson & Morton-Bourgon, 2004). It refers to "an abnormally intense interest in sex that dominates psychological functioning" (Mann, Hanson, & Thornton, 2010, p. 198), potentially resulting in individuals engaging in a high frequency of sexual behaviors. A high frequency of sexual behaviors is often defined as hypersexual disorder or hypersexuality, as measured by the number of total sexual outlets (number of outlets to orgasm; Kafka, 1997; Kinsey, Pomeroy, & Martin, 1948), a definition that later expanded to include only those sexual behaviors of an impersonal or solitary nature (Langström & Hanson, 2006).

Within the UK, psychological therapy (the Sex Offender Treatment Programme; SOTP) exists as the standard method of treatment for sexual

Sex Offender Treatment: A Case Study Approach to Issues and Interventions,
First Edition. Edited by Daniel T. Wilcox, Tanya Garrett, and Leigh Harkins.
© 2015 John Wiley & Sons, Ltd. Published 2015 by John Wiley & Sons, Ltd.

offenders (Ho & Ross, 2012). However, these programs cannot target specific deviant sexual interests present in some sexual offenders (Adi, Ashcroft, Browne, Beech, Fry-Smith, & Hyde, 2002), and frequent or intense sexual urges or thoughts can also impact upon engagement within the programs (Marshall, Marshall, & Serran, 2006; Saleh, Grudzinskas, Malin, & Dwyer, 2010). In such circumstances, the use of pharmacological interventions is supported. They have been used since the 1940s to reduce deviant sexual thoughts, fantasies, and behaviors (Bourget & Bradford, 2008) and aid engagement within psychological treatment programs (Saleh et al., 2010). As such, in 2007, the voluntary pharmacological treatment of sexual offenders within the UK (under the care of the prison or probation service) was established, allowing this to be used as a supplement to psychological treatment for those individuals who require it.

This chapter examines the pharmacological (anti-libidinal) treatment of sexual offenders, and considers both the group of individuals referred for this treatment and four case studies of individuals undergoing treatment.

The two main types of medication used within this UK prison establishment are the selective serotonin reuptake inhibitor (SSRI) Fluoxetine hydrochloride and the antiandrogen cyproterone acetate (CPA). CPA has its anti-libidinal effect by directly reducing testosterone levels. Testosterone is the primary sex hormone in males that binds to androgen receptors in the penis and testes to produce erection, tactile sensation, ejaculation, and sperm production, and in the brain, to affect sexual interest, thoughts, motivation, and desires (Bancroft, 2005; Jordan, Fromberger, Stolpmann, & Müller, 2011). There are large individual differences in testosterone levels that do not relate straightforwardly to intensity of sexual thoughts or behavior, either deviant or nondeviant (see Krueger & Kaplan, 2001, for review), but it is well established that there is a threshold level of testosterone (approximately 30 to 40% reduction) below which sexual arousal is substantially reduced (Bancroft, 1989). Antiandrogens such as CPA reduce testosterone levels below this threshold in order to reduce sexual preoccupation and behavior.

CPA reduces testosterone primarily by acting as a direct antagonist at androgen receptors (where testosterone binds), resulting ultimately in reduced testosterone production and release from the testes. It also has progestogenic effects (Brotherton, 1974), so that the overall effect is to reduce testosterone to prepubescent but not castration levels (Guay, 2009). The resultant (targeted) effects are reduced erection, ejaculation, and masturbation, as well as psychological changes in sexual interest, fantasy, and arousal. Its effects are generally thought to be reversible within 1 to

2 months (Garcia & Thibaut, 2011) with regeneration of testicular Leydig cells (that produce testosterone) taking longer (Brotherton, 1974). Regarding side effects, evidence is predominantly based on the use of CPA in medical conditions such as prostate cancer and there is no quantitative data for sex offenders (Guay, 2009). Possible side effects include (but are not limited to) gynecomastia, tiredness, depression of mood, osteoporosis, and weakness.

SSRIs such as Fluoxetine increase levels of serotonin in the neuronal synapse by blocking the transporter molecules that normally take serotonin back up into the presynaptic neurone resulting in serotonin remaining in the synapse for longer. This has the initial transitory effect of reducing serotonin production, but once this feedback mechanism becomes insensitive, serotonin production is no longer inhibited and the effect of SSRIs in blocking reuptake of serotonin leads to a functional increase in serotonin in the synapse.

So how does this increase in serotonin act as an anti-libidinal? Biopsychological models of sexual function (e.g., Bancroft & Janssen, 2000; Pfaus, 2009) propose that dopamine has an excitatory role and serotonin an inhibitory role in sexual function (although this depends on the subtype of serotonin receptor). Evidence demonstrates that serotonin inhibits sexual desire and psychological arousal, physiological arousal/erection, and orgasm (Jordan et al., 2011; Meston & Frohlich, 2000).

Protocols released by the UK National Offender Management Service suggest that SSRIs reduce compulsivity and impulsivity, but there is also robust evidence that serotonin has a direct role in increasing sexual satiety and inhibiting erection and ejaculation (Lorrain, Matuszewich, Friedman, & Hull, 1997; Pfaus, 2009). These well-evidenced "side effects" of SSRIs here become targeted effects. That said, a role of SSRIs in reducing compulsivity and impulsivity has been evidenced (Coleman, Gratzer, Nesvacil, & Raymond, 2000) and sexual disorders have been characterized by some as part of the obsessive compulsive spectrum (Bradford, 1999), although this categorization is still hypothetical (Bradford, 2001). Possible side effects of Fluoxetine include (but are not limited to) nausea, insomnia, hypersomnia, anorexia, and tremors.

Case Introduction

The case studies in this chapter document the journeys of four individuals within a UK prison serving custodial sentences for sexual offenses who have been referred for anti-libidinal medication. The establishment has been prescribing this medication since November 2009, with 69 individuals referred for the service as of May 2013.

Presenting complaints

All individuals referred for anti-libidinal medication have demonstrated one or more of the following:

- Hyperarousal (e.g., sexual rumination, sexual preoccupation, difficulties controlling sexual arousal, and high levels of sexual behavior).
- Intrusive sexual fantasies or urges.
- Sexual urges that are difficult to control.
- Sexual sadism or other dangerous paraphilias, or repetitive paraphilic offending such as voyeurism or exhibitionism (National Offender Management Service, 2007).

In addition, the hyperarousal and intrusive, deviant and/or uncontrollable urges will have impacted upon individuals' daily functioning, affecting areas of their life such as work and relationships.

Demographics and offense history

The following data describe the group of individuals referred for anti-libidinal medication to date ($n = 69$, May 2013).

IQ   The referral group had a mean IQ of 83.74 (SD = 14.97) that ranged from 59 to 114. IQ was typically measured by the Weschler Abbreviated Scale of Intelligence (WASI), and, where the IQ was below 80 or if there were significant indicators of either intellectual problems or adaptive functioning, by the Wechsler Adult Intelligence Scale (WAIS; v3/v4). The average IQ for the referral group was lower than that of the general population at this prison.

Age   The mean age of referrals was 43.64 years (SD = 14.69), ranging from 25 to 74. The average age for the referral group is equivalent to that of the general population at this prison.

Offense histories   Offense histories were predominantly of contact offenses against children, with a mean of 4.4 previous contact sexual offenses and 2.1 noncontact sexual offenses. The offense histories of the referral group are skewed towards child contact offenders, relative to the general population at this prison.

Assessment of risk

Static risk   The Risk Matrix 2000 (RM2000) is one of the most robust static risk tools used to predict sexual and violent offending. The measure is used within 8 weeks of an offender entering the prison in order to direct offenders towards appropriate cognitive behavioral therapy (CBT) treatments, such as the SOTP, the Healthy Relationship Programme (HRP), or the Healthy Sexual Functioning Programme (HSF).

The group of 69 individuals currently referred for anti-libidinal medication had a modal risk score placing them in the high risk of sexual reoffending category, with 2% assessed in the low, 26% medium, 42% high, and 30% in the very high risk categories. This indicates the referral group is at a higher risk level than the general population at this prison.

Dynamic risk   The Structured Assessment of Risk and Need (SARN-SO; Webster et al., 2006) is the dynamic risk tool used to understand offenders' treatment needs at this prison. Offenders who have been classified as suitable for one of the treatment programs available are assessed using the SARN-SO. Only offenders who are serving too short a sentence to enable them to complete a CBT intervention, are deemed unsuitable for treatment, or are at an early point in the system, will not have been assessed for dynamic risk. The majority of individuals will have at least the Treatment Needs Analysis (TNA) grid that accompanies a full SARN.

The individuals referred for anti-libidinal medication typically scored highly on the following SARN risk factors: inadequacy; sexual preoccupation or obsession with sex; impulsivity; lack of emotionally intimate relationships; poor problem solving; and child abuse supportive beliefs. See Figure 19.1 for a comparison against a general UK sex offender population.

Case conceptualization

Individuals referred for medication have typically completed or are completing CBT interventions, and referrals often arise when they are struggling to manage their sexual preoccupation during sessions where sexual offenses are discussed. Alternatively, individuals may be identified as potential candidates for medication during the first stage of the SARN (TNA). A third route into medication may be as a result of adjudications against, or security concerns about, the individual, which appear to be driven by hypersexuality and/or sexual preoccupation. For example, an individual exposing themselves to staff, disclosing fantasies that involve

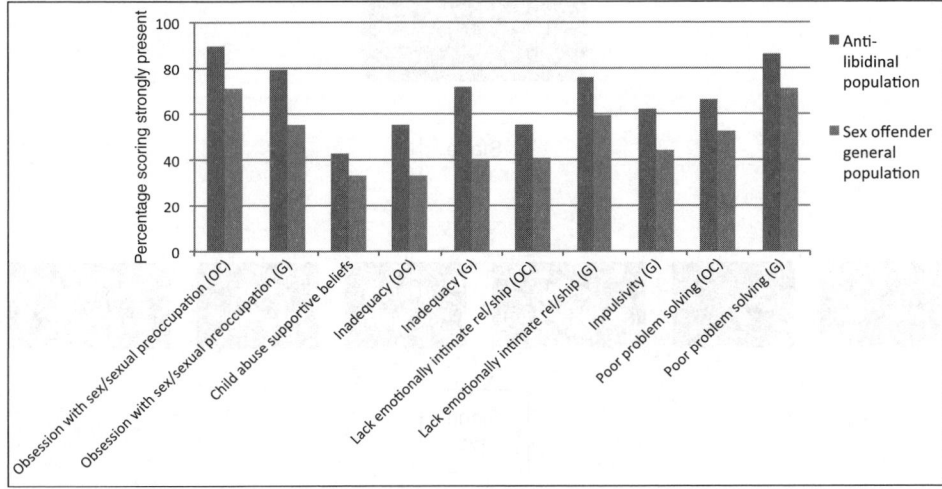

Figure 19.1 The SARN risk factors most frequently rated a 2 (strongly characteristic) for a UK sex offender population and anti-libidinal referral sex offenders.

sexual assault or rape of staff or fellow offenders, or the finding of inappropriate sexual material during a cell search. In such instances, any member of prison staff may refer a consenting offender for anti-libidinal medication.

The cases referred for anti-libidinal medication comprise individuals who cannot manage their sexual preoccupation and hypersexuality to the extent that it is causing them problems in everyday life. A proportion of men additionally feel their sexual preoccupation is a burden to them; they may find it difficult to engage in treatment or interact socially with others.

Referrals All individuals are assessed onsite for suitability by a forensic psychiatrist. Of the 69 referrals to date, eight are taking CPA, 38 are taking SSRIs, seven are taking a combination of CPA and SSRIs, one had a depot injection of triptorelin (gonadotropin-releasing hormone agonist), 11 are not taking medication, and four are under assessment for medication.

Course of treatment and assessment of progress

Individuals deemed suitable for medication following referral are typically started on 20 mg Fluoxetine, taken daily as a tablet, with dosage increased

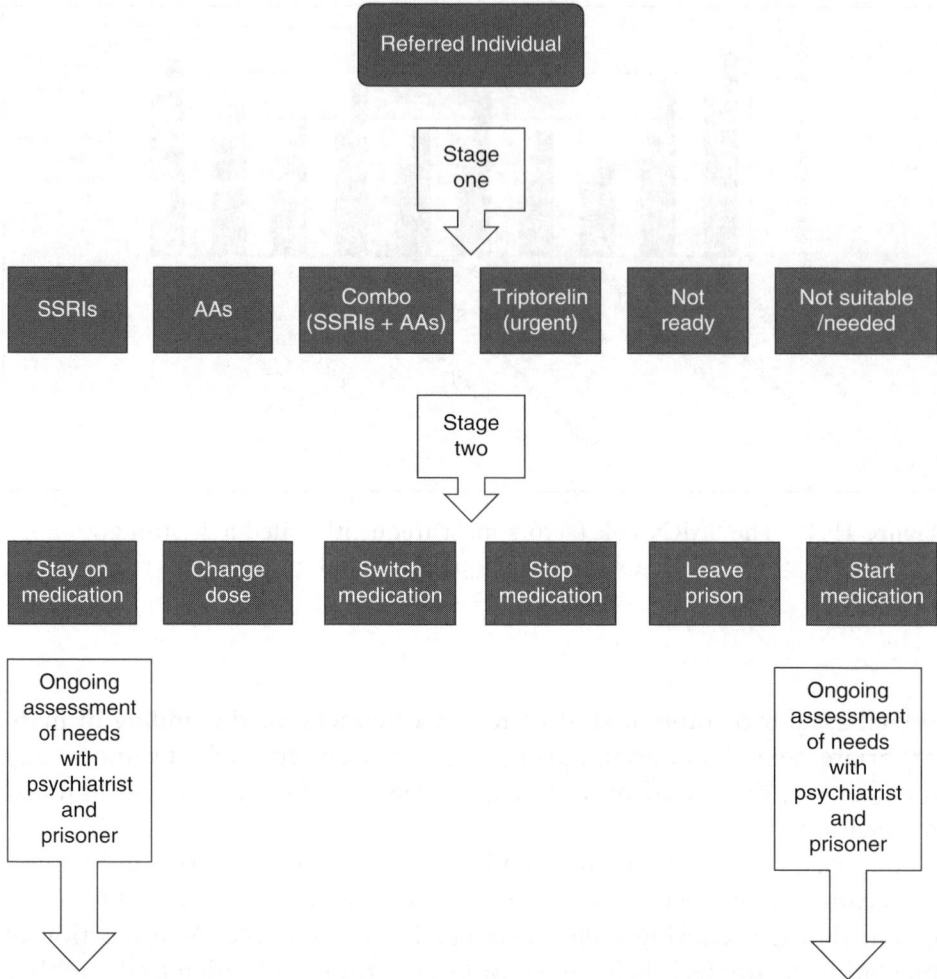

Figure 19.2 A flow chart of all the possible options for an offender following an antilibidinal referral.

to 40/60 mg where the consulting psychiatrist deems necessary. Where SSRIs do not appear to work, CPA is prescribed. Starting and typical dosage for CPA are 50 mg daily by tablet, increased to 100 mg where individuals are still reporting difficulties in managing deviant sexual fantasies, hypersexuality, and/or sexual preoccupation. Figure 19.2 demonstrates all the possible options for an offender who is referred for anti-libidinal medication.

The forensic psychiatrist sees individuals on a regular basis (instigated either by offender or psychiatrist) and at each appointment measures of

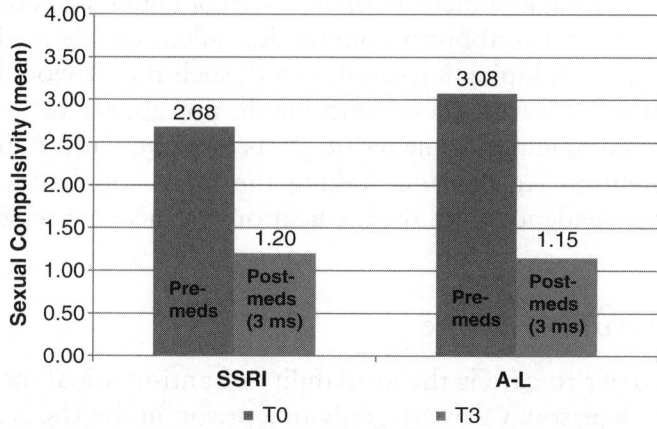

Figure 19.3   Mean sexual compulsivity scores for participants taking (i) SSRIs and (ii) Antiandrogens (A-L) to reduce sexual preoccupation premedication (T0) and 3 months postmedication (T3). From Winder, Lievesley, Kaul, Elliott, Thorne and Hocken, 2014. Reproduced with permission of Taylor & Francis.

hypersexuality and sexual preoccupation are collated. Psychometric measures (sexual compulsivity, anxiety, depression) are collated prior to individuals taking the medication (to establish baseline data) and every 3 months subsequently.

Figure 19.3 provides an indication of the reduction in sexual compulsivity among the group taking anti-libidinals.

Complicating factors (including medical management)

There are a number of complicating factors with anti-libidinal medication, including the compliance and engagement of offenders and the ongoing prescription of the medication. Generally, the level of compliance demonstrated by the offenders appears high, with individuals presenting as engaged and motivated to take the medication. This is to be expected given the medication is voluntary. Nevertheless, some noncompliance was apparent within the sample, either deliberate or as a consequence of forgetting to take the medication.

Deliberate noncompliance was reported by individuals on the grounds of experienced side effects (such as nausea or tiredness) and concerns raised about misinformation circulating around the prison (such as permanent loss of sexual ability). Concerns typically related to the potential impact on future sexual relationships and worries that the parole board would view the taking of medication as a sign of high risk. Some individuals expressed concerns about becoming dependent on the medication, or alternatively to developing a tolerance to it, such that it would no longer work for them. Although these concerns do not appear to be impacting upon current compliance, some participants displayed uncertainty regarding their intentions to continue taking the medication after release. A desire for independence from the medication was also expressed at times.

Access and barriers to care

An initial barrier to care is the availability of anti-libidinal medication at an individual's prison. Currently, only one prison in the UK is prescribing anti-libidinal medication, and this is limiting access to treatment.

A second barrier appears to be the difficulties involved in publicizing the availability of the medication to both offenders and staff; misconceptions about the medication and potential side effects abound, and one challenge is to ensure accurate knowledge about the medication is circulating around the establishment.

Another key issue when considering a potential barrier to care is that, with voluntary medication in particular, a good therapeutic relationship appears vital in providing individuals with a safe environment to voice and discuss their concerns about the medication and to have the opportunity to ask questions and make informed decisions about their treatment.

A final concern is around the availability of the medication for offenders who have been released back into the community. It is known that an offender's risk increases on release due to the amount of destabilizers within the community, particularly for child sexual offenders. However, we are concerned that many General Practitioners (GPs) are unaware of, or would not agree to prescribe, anti-libidinal medication for ex-offenders.

Follow-up

Short term The psychiatrist has regular meetings with all individuals taking anti-libidinals. Within these sessions, measures of hypersexuality and sexual preoccupation are collected. In addition, the research and project team meet every 3 months to monitor progress.

Data are currently being collected on adjudications and other indications of "offending behavior" while in prison as a method to determine the impact on behavior on a more short-term basis.

Long term Research with these individuals is already exploring the experiences of receiving the medication while in prison and, based on the challenges faced after release, it will be important to explore how this expands to the community, given the additional challenges of managing hypersexuality and sexual preoccupation in a less controlled environment. A reconviction study, with matched control group, is planned to evaluate the effectiveness of anti-libidinal medication 2 and 5 years postrelease.

Treatment implications of the cases

The aim of pharmacological treatment is to reduce or suppress deviant sexual interests and behaviors while maintaining those that are appropriate (Bradford, 2001). However, some individuals do not hold any appropriate sexual interests and, although the medication may still be used to reduce deviant sexual interests, this would result in an absence of sexual thoughts (and consequently sexual expression), reducing the likelihood of this being a long-term viable treatment option. Having healthy sexual relationships and satisfaction is a key "human good" and thus eliminating all sexual arousal is detrimental to a person's quality of life (good lives model; Ward & Marshall, 2004). This supports the view that psychological treatment is important alongside medication (Guay, 2009) to facilitate the development of healthy sexual interests.

For some individuals within this sample, including those receiving solely the SSRIs, the medication appears to be impacting upon their ability to become physically aroused or reach ejaculation. This creates concern for many with regards to their ability to achieve an intimate relationship on release and may affect their decision to continue medication in the community. Moreover, for some individuals, the lack of sexual outlets can cause offenders to stop taking medication, or may lead them to resort to more deviant fantasies to achieve orgasm.

Case Studies

The next section of this chapter outlines four case studies of individuals who were referred for anti-libidinal medication, detailing their "journeys" and the complicated nature of prescribing this medication:

1. Malcolm demonstrates a typical journey, taking the medication and showing significant reductions in hypersexuality and sexual preoccupation.

2. Earl demonstrates the journey of a small number of individuals who agree to take the medication, but then stop.
3. Stuart demonstrates another typical journey of an individual who requires the frequent adjustment of their medication type and dosage.
4. Derek's journey is less typical in that he has not received any CBT treatment, but agreed to take the medication. Derek was released from prison, but has now been returned following a license breach.

The information outlined within the following case studies was obtained from a number of sources including healthcare records, the Offender Assessment System (assesses risk and need), psychology and program reports, interviews with offenders, and psychometric data collected for the evaluation.

Case 1: Malcolm

Malcolm is a high-risk sexual offender who was convicted of his first offense aged 15. He is currently serving an indeterminate sentence for public protection for sexual offenses against a child under 13. Malcolm was referred for anti-libidinal medication in 2011.

Demographics and personal history

Malcolm is in his late 40s and of Caucasian British ethnicity. Growing up he lived with his parents and two siblings. Malcolm alleges his step-father sexually abused him from the age of 4 years onwards. He has a borderline intellectual disability (WAIS score 73) and reports being bullied at school.

Malcolm's first sexual encounter occurred when he was 8 years old involving his brother, sister, and school friends. He reports having over 20 partners, with only one significant relationship with a woman whom Malcolm married soon after she fell pregnant in his late 20s. He has been married for 16 years but the relationship ended as a result of his offending.

Malcolm has had contact with the mental health team during his prison sentence with issues of anxiety and poor emotional control (said to be linked to his learning difficulties). Malcolm suffers with pseudohallucinations and has self-harmed in the past. He reports hitting and punching himself when angry and frustrated. Malcolm also reports using drugs in the past, including crack and cannabis.

Offending history

Malcolm has a total of 19 offenses, 12 of which were sexual. His first conviction of two counts of indecent assault (against female children aged 8 to 11 years) was at the age of 15. His second conviction, aged 33, was for various driving offenses (involving alcohol) for which he received community service and a driving ban. Soon after, he was convicted of two offenses of indecent assault on a female under 14 and breach of community service. Malcolm's fourth conviction was for further driving offenses and his current conviction was for eight offenses against a male child under 13 (his son). These were: sexual assault on a child under 13 ($\times 2$); assault on a child under 13 by penetration ($\times 2$); and causing or inciting a child to engage in sexual activity ($\times 4$).

Malcolm is very open when discussing his entrenched offense-related beliefs that sex between children and adults is acceptable. Malcolm also recognizes his attraction to children, lack of intimate adult relationships, and loneliness as significant factors contributing to his offending.

Evidence of sexual preoccupation and hypersexuality

Malcolm has a preference for sexual interaction with children aged 8 to 11. He reports he first had sex at the age of 10 and then began having sex with his sister aged 11 for a prolonged period. Malcolm also discloses having sex at school five to eight times a day (including with an 8 year old when he was aged 16) and regularly using pornography.

In custody, Malcolm has reported becoming sexually aroused while watching TV and masturbating once or twice a day. He has disclosed that his sexual thoughts are becoming unmanageable.

Assessments

According to the RM2000, Malcolm is in the high-risk category for sexual offending and low-risk category for violent offending.

Malcolm was also assessed with the Psychopathy Checklist and although the report concluded that he does not have sufficient traits to suggest a diagnosis of psychopathy, he scored in the moderate range and a number of traits were highlighted as problematic factors: lack of remorse, callousness or lack of empathy, and failure to accept responsibility.

Malcolm's SARN indicated outstanding areas of need: obsession with sex, sexual preference for children, entrenched beliefs that sex between adults and children is okay, emotional congruence with children, impulsivity, and unstable lifestyle. Inadequacy was also seen as a key factor in terms of his ability and confidence when managing other risk areas.

Treatment journey

Psychological treatment programs   Malcolm has completed Enhanced Thinking Skills, Adapted SOTP, and Adapted Better Lives Booster. Overall, these programs have helped Malcolm to develop his confidence, self-esteem, social skills, and problem solving. Reports suggest that Malcolm remains open and honest about his offending and his still prevalent sexual attraction towards children; he has been advised that he should continue to work on managing his sexual thoughts with the help of medication and the skills he has learned in programs.

Anti-libidinal treatment   Malcolm was referred for anti-libidinal medication due to reports that his sexual urges and thoughts were becoming unmanageable. He was prescribed CPA at a dose of 50 mg daily as recommended by the psychiatrist. After 3 months, Malcolm wanted his medication dose increased as he was still having intrusive sexual thoughts and becoming easily aroused, which he found embarrassing. His dose was increased to 100 mg of CPA and he has now been taking this for over a year. Malcolm has reported that the medication is helping to reduce his sexual preoccupation, and this can be seen in Figure 19.5; time spent thinking about sex has decreased from a relatively high amount to extremely low. Figure 19.4 also demonstrates a reduction in Malcolm's

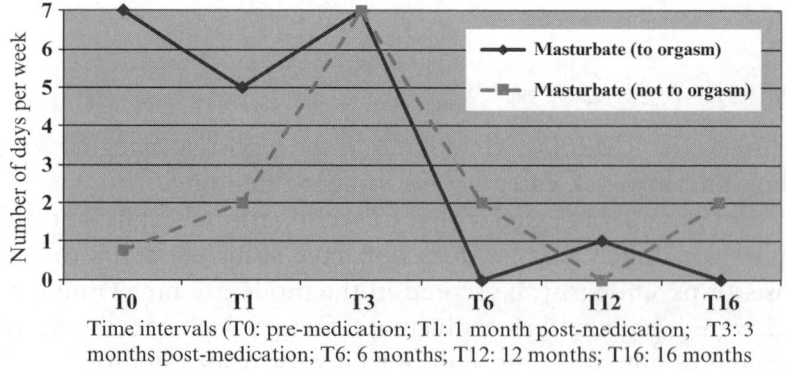

Time intervals (T0: pre-medication; T1: 1 month post-medication; T3: 3 months post-medication; T6: 6 months; T12: 12 months; T16: 16 months

Figure 19.4   Malcolm's self-reported of number of days in previous week masturbated.

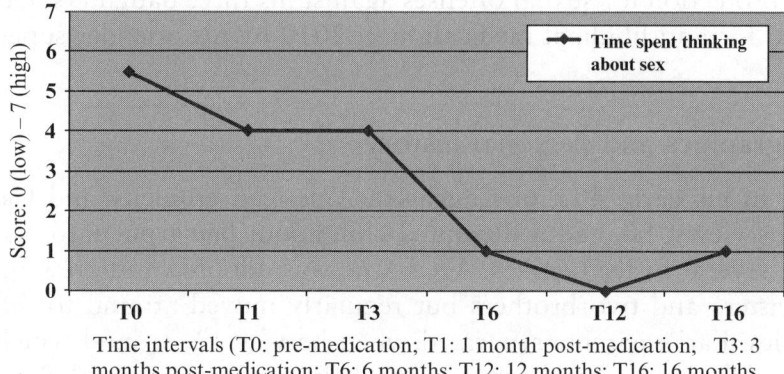

Figure 19.5 Malcolm's self-reported of amount of sexual preoccupation (time currently spent thinking about sex).

masturbation frequency from the 3-month mark onwards (T3) when he was prescribed CPA (100 mg).

Discussion

Malcolm has some very entrenched beliefs about sex with children, likely associated with the long-term sexual abuse he suffered as a child. He still reports having flashbacks to the abuse, and his sexual attraction towards children is intense and intrusive. The strength of his sexual preoccupation and deviancy is evident in the required high dose of CPA (100 mg), which is rarely prescribed. Reports suggest Malcolm's distorted cognitions concerning children and sexuality have prevented him from feeling empathy for his own victims. Malcolm also suffers with low self-esteem and the embarrassment he feels about his sexual preoccupation likely adds to this.

However, despite these difficulties, Malcolm has welcomed the anti-libidinal treatment, evident in his request for an increase in dosage. He wants to be relieved of the intrusive sexual thoughts and reports that the medication is helping to do this. Malcolm has expressed his desire to continue on the medication to help him manage his level of sexual thinking.

Case 2: Earl

Earl is a medium-risk sexual offender who was convicted of his first offense aged 18. He is currently serving an indeterminate sentence for public protection for sexual offenses against his three daughters. Earl was referred for anti-libidinal medication in 2010 by his offender supervisor.

Demographics and personal history

Earl is in his early 40 s, of Caucasian American ethnicity and Catholic religious views. He had a disrupted childhood; being put into care and having several foster families. Aged 5 he was adopted and grew up with three sisters and two brothers but regularly moved around to different countries. Earl's parents separated when he was 12, around which time he began displaying problematic sexual behaviors (e.g., exposure) and was again placed in care. Earl reports finding childhood difficult and self-reports having learning difficulties despite having an average IQ (WASI score 95).

Earl discloses having over 100 sexual partners, with his first sexual encounter occurring when he was 13. He reports knowing he was homo-sexual from the age of 14 but continuing to engage in sexual relations with both females and males. Earl married at 23 and had three daughters and one son. The marriage lasted 17 years (until current conviction) but Earl reports a distant relationship with repeated unfaithfulness on his part. There are also accounts of domestic abuse within the relationship.

Earl has previously been diagnosed with depression and mild ADHD. He also reports regularly using amphetamines and cannabis since the age of 14 and cocaine around the age of 38. Earl is described as a binge drinker.

Offending history

Earl has a total of six convictions for a range of offenses. Between the ages of 18 and 24 he received four convictions for burglary, theft, possessing a weapon, and assault with intent to resist arrest, for which he received probation and community service orders.

Aged 29, Earl was convicted of his first sexual offense, indecent assault against a 13-year-old girl, and received a community sentence. Earl was convicted of his current offenses aged 41, a total of 19 counts against his three daughters (all under 16) of rape, indecent assault, and causing a child to engage in sexual activity (over a 3-year period). Earl attributes the offenses against his daughters to a lack of other sexual contact and drug use. He also acknowledges that he enjoyed the power and control this gave him.

Evidence of sexual preoccupation and hypersexuality

Earl reports knowing about sex and masturbating to images of males and females several times a day from the age of 9. Aged 13 onwards, Earl frequently engaged in sexual contact and "experimenting" with male and female children in the care home. He demonstrates a very casual attitude towards sex, with only two stable partners. Aged 20, he worked as a prostitute and was repeatedly unfaithful throughout his marriage.

Earl reports that he would masturbate around 17 times a day when in the community and between two and seven times a day while in custody. He discloses having constant and intense sexual thoughts that are difficult to distract from and only ease after masturbation. He reports feeling angry and frustrated when he cannot masturbate. Earl recognizes his preoccupation and hyperarousal to be problematic and uncontrollable, interfering in his everyday activities. For example, Earl becomes aroused by vibrations from machinery at work (in custody) and finds the need to masturbate in the toilets to relieve this arousal.

Assessments

Based on the RM2000, Earl is in the medium-risk category for sexual offending and high-risk category for violent offending. No SARN is currently available for Earl.

Treatment journey

Psychological treatment programs During his current sentence, Earl has completed Enhanced Thinking Skills and engaged with CARATs (Counselling, Assessment, Referral Advice, Throughcare) to deal with his drug and alcohol misuse, which are now no longer viewed as a problem for him.

Earl has also been referred for a number of other programs: SOTP, HRP, CALM (Controlling Anger and Learning to Manage it), and HSF. He should begin SOTP by the end of 2013. Once complete the other referrals will be considered.

Anti-libidinal treatment Earl was referred for anti-libidinal medication in 2010 after disclosing, during assessment for SOTP, difficulty controlling his arousal and invasive sexual thoughts that he found problematic. It was determined that this may impede his ability to progress within group and so a referral was made.

Earl consented to taking the medication and was prescribed a daily dose of Fluoxetine (20 mg). This resulted in reduced frequency and intensity of sexual thoughts and masturbation. Earl remained on Fluoxetine for 12 months before stopping as he felt he no longer needed the medication. After 1 month, Earl requested to go back onto medication after realizing he still needed the medication to help with his sexual preoccupation and restarted on Fluoxetine (20 mg). In both Figure 19.6 and 19.7, an increase can be seen in Earl's sexual preoccupation at around the 12-month mark, possibly due to the disruption in medication.

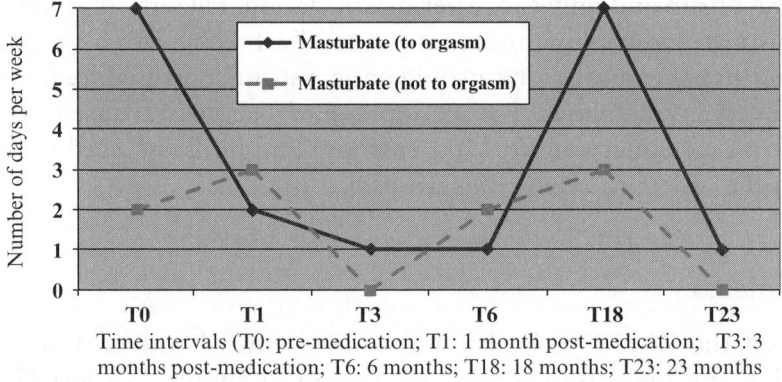

Time intervals (T0: pre-medication; T1: 1 month post-medication;   T3: 3 months post-medication; T6: 6 months; T18: 18 months; T23: 23 months

Figure 19.6   Earl's self-reported number of days in previous week masturbated.

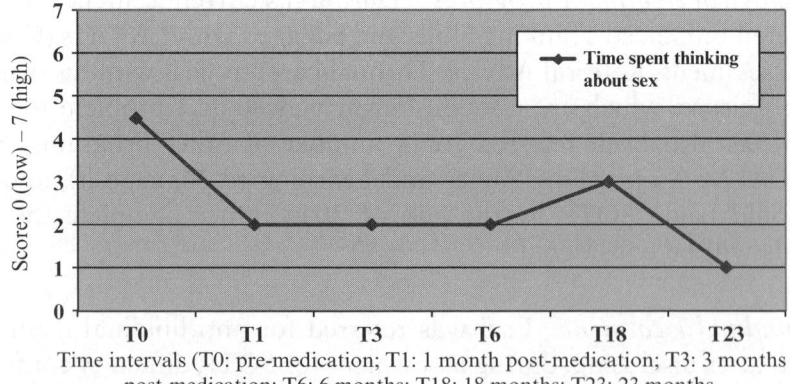

Time intervals (T0: pre-medication; T1: 1 month post-medication; T3: 3 months post-medication; T6: 6 months; T18: 18 months; T23: 23 months

Figure 19.7   Earl's self-reported amount of sexual preoccupation (time currently spent thinking about sex).

Earl reported continuing to take the medication for a further 5 months before requesting a higher dose of Fluoxetine as he claimed the medication was no longer working (again this is reflected in the figures as both masturbation and time thinking about sex increase around this time). However, Earl never collected his Fluoxetine (40 mg) dose that was prescribed and is currently not taking any medication.

Discussion

Earl is a medium-risk sexual offender with a considerable number of dynamic risk areas identified. His hypersexuality and sexual preoccupation has been a large part of his everyday life from an early age, and he acknowledges that partners have found this difficult.

Earl has had a disrupted journey on medication, coming on and off on more than one occasion. He is now no longer taking medication but reports very low sexual preoccupation and masturbation despite this. It is questionable whether this is true self-report, considering Earl's originally high need for medication.

Earl has not yet completed any treatment programs tailored to addressing his risk of sexual offending; it is hoped that participating in relevant programs will allow him to develop a deeper understanding of his risk areas and treatment needs. This may result in a more successful and less disrupted anti-libidinal treatment journey, which, due to the severity of his offending and sexual deviancy, would be beneficial.

Case 3: Stuart

Stuart is a high-risk sexual offender who was convicted of his first offense aged 15. He is currently serving an indeterminate sentence for public protection, with a history of contact and noncontact sexual offenses. Stuart was referred for anti-libidinal medication in 2010.

Demographics and personal history

Stuart is in his late 40s and of Caucasian British ethnicity. He grew up with his sister, mother, and stepfather. Stuart states that he had no friends and was bullied during his childhood due to his learning difficulties. He describes this to be an unhappy and lonely time. Stuart also reports being sexually abused by his uncle around the age of 5.

Stuart reports having seven sexual partners, with his first sexual encounter occurring when he was 17. He appears to have had stable relationships with two women. Stuart describes difficulty in these relationships, believing his partner was unfaithful and being unfaithful himself. He also had concerns that he was unable to satisfy them sexually. Stuart describes having a general lack of confidence around women throughout his life.

Offending history

Stuart has three convictions, all for sexual offenses. He committed his first offense aged 15; an indecent assault against a 6-year-old girl for which he received a 2-year probation order. His second offense, aged 36, was three counts of indecent assault on the 10-year-old daughter of his partner. Stuart was convicted for his current offenses in 2005, possessing and making indecent images of females under 16.

Stuart attributes his offending behavior and attraction to children to his own sexual abuse, loneliness, and insecurities regarding adult relationships.

Evidence of sexual preoccupation and hypersexuality

Stuart reports thinking about sex from the age of 8, and from 12 years old he was masturbating daily and often accessed pornographic magazines.

Two of Stuart's sexual partners were women he was in a relationship with, while the other five are reported to be one-night stands or casual sexual partners. Stuart reports "masturbating to everything, thoughts, visions 24/7" at numerous times throughout his life. While in custody, Stuart reports having lots of sexual thoughts about children and becoming easily aroused to children on the TV.

Assessments

According to the RM2000, Stuart is in the high-risk category for sexual offending and low-risk category for violent offending.

Strong areas of need as indicated by Stuart's SARN include: preference for sex with children; low self-esteem; difficulty dealing with life's problems; and struggling to gain control throughout his life. Stuart's offending is often associated with boredom, stress, confusion, and lack of problem solving, as well as his still apparent sexual interest in children.

Treatment journey

Psychological treatment programs After his second offense, Stuart attended a community sex offender treatment program. While he attended all sessions, he was dismissive of the program and lacked motivation, failing to increase his understanding of his offending behavior.

Since his current imprisonment, Stuart has attended all suitable treatment programs: Enhanced Thinking Skills, adapted SOTP, and Adapted Better Lives Booster. Reports demonstrate that Stuart engaged well and gained an understanding of his offending.

Anti-libidinal treatment Stuart was referred for anti-libidinal medication in 2010 by a programs facilitator due to reports that his sexual urges were very strong and sometimes difficult for him to control. Stuart consented to taking the medication and started on a daily dose of Fluoxetine (20 mg). While this initially reduced his sexual thoughts and masturbation, the effects were short-lived (see Figures 19.8 and 19.9) and after 3 months he requested to have his dose increased to 40 mg. After 1 month his dose was changed to a combination of Fluoxetine (20 mg) and CPA (50 mg) due to the 40 mg Fluoxetine not working. This resulted in a significant reduction in sexual preoccupation and masturbation, which can be seen in Figure 19.8 and 19.9. After 7 months, the Fluoxetine was stopped and CPA alone was tried. However, 4 months later Stuart reported his sexual

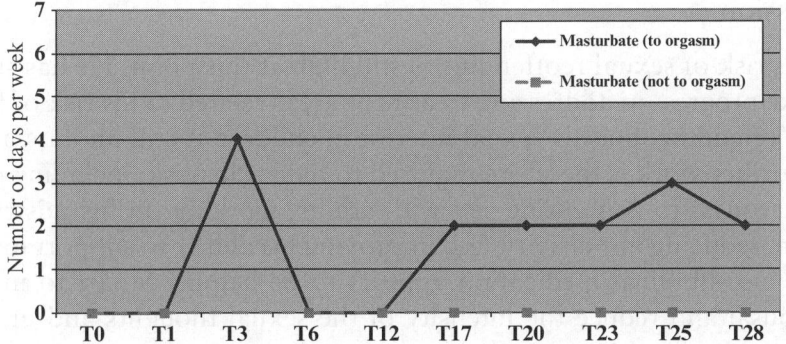

Time intervals (T0: pre-medication; T1: 1 month post-medication; T3: 3 months post-medication; T6: 6 months; T12: 12 months; T17: 17 months; T20: 20 months; T23: 23 months; T25: 25 months; T28: 28 months

Figure 19.8 Stuart's self-reported number of days in previous week masturbated.

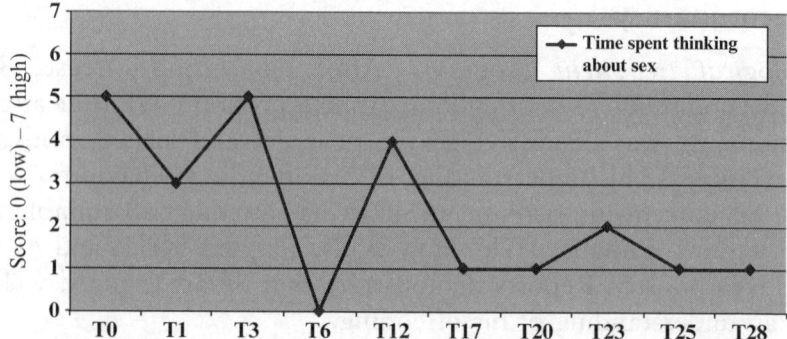

Time intervals (T0: pre-medication; T1: 1 month post-medication; T3: 3 months post-medication; T6: 6 months; T12: 12 months; T17: 17 months; T20: 20 months; T23: 23 months; T25: 25 months; T28: 28 months

Figure 19.9   Stuart's self-reported amount of sexual preoccupation (time currently spent thinking about sex).

preoccupation and masturbation had increased and so the combination of Fluoxetine (20 mg) and CPA (50 mg) was restarted. After a further 8 months on this combination, the Fluoxetine was stopped again because Stuart reported getting distressing dreams and felt this was related to the Fluoxetine. Stuart has been taking only CPA (50 mg) for the last 7 months. This continues to have a positive effect in reducing sexual thoughts, masturbation, and distressing dreams.

Discussion

Stuart's risk of sexual reoffending is still high at this point. He has started to make progress in addressing treatment areas related to his risk of future sexual offending, but his sexual interest in children is still an outstanding risk. Further work is therefore required to reduce his risk, including developing arousal to consenting sex with adults, working on his mistrust of women, reducing impulsivity, and improving his ability to support himself.

The anti-libidinal medication appears to be helping Stuart to manage his arousal and reduce the intensity of the sexual thoughts and urges he was experiencing. Despite the frequent adjustment in medication and fluctuation in sexual preoccupation and masturbation due to this, he reports being very pleased with the effects and plans to continue taking anti-libidinals after release. He does however express concerns about release, where temptations and triggers are much higher.

Case 4: Derek

Derek is a high-risk sexual offender who was convicted of his first offense aged 22. He is currently in custody following a license recall; initially serving a determinate sentence for contact and noncontact sexual offenses. Derek was referred for anti-libidinal medication in 2010.

Demographics and personal history

Derek is in his late 60 s and of Caucasian British ethnicity. He reports a "good upbringing," living with his parents whom he describes as strict, and his brother and sisters. Derek reports being abducted and sexually abused by an unknown man when he was 6, and later being sexually abused by a schoolteacher.

Derek left school aged 15 with no formal qualifications; he is unable to read or write and has a mild intellectual disability (WAIS IQ score 59). Derek has stated that he was in a relationship with a woman in his late teens, but that his partner died. Derek is not known to have had any other close relationships.

Derek has previously self-harmed both in the community and in custody (resulting in an Assessment, Care in Custody, and Teamwork document being opened) and reports previous suicide attempts. His self-harm has been reported as being the result of frustrations that he is unable to articulate.

Offending history

Derek has a total of three convictions. His first conviction, aged 22, was for theft, for which he received a probation order. His first sexual conviction occurred aged 47; this was the indecent assault and buggery of his 1-year-old male cousin. He received a 2-year sentence for this.

Derek was convicted of his current offenses aged 64; sexual assault of a 2-year-old girl and possession of sexually explicit images of children. He received a 4-year determinate sentence and was released in 2011. Derek is currently back in custody following license recall, having disclosed fantasies about the rape and murder of specific females and thoughts about approaching young children with the intention of offending against them. Within interviews and file reports, additional information relating to further sexual offenses is also detailed.

Derek reports that his own sexual abuse was formative in his deviant sexual interests, resulting in an attraction to infants and babies from the age of approximately 14 years. He reports that explicit pornographic images and videos involving young children have also fuelled his attraction and contributed to his offending.

Derek reports having a bad temper from childhood, with accounts of violence against his brother and sisters; he has three adjudications for assaulting other prisoners during his current time in custody.

Evidence of sexual preoccupation and hypersexuality

Derek reports becoming sexually aroused and masturbating from a young age (around 8). He states that he thinks about sex "all the time I'm awake" and reports strong sexual attraction to young children and infants. At the time of his index offenses, he admitted to masturbating three to four times a day, and had dolls, children's underwear, toys, and nappies in his possession.

Whilst in custody, Derek remains preoccupied with sex, reporting becoming aroused when seeing young girls on TV, and has been found with inappropriate drawings. He has also caused himself physical injury through prolonged and frequent masturbation in custody.

Assessments

According to the RM2000, Derek is in the high-risk category for sexual offending and low-risk category for violent offending.

Treatment journey

Psychological treatment programs   Derek has not currently completed any treatment programs as there was insufficient time during his initial determinate sentence. However, he is now on the waiting list for the Becoming New Me (adapted) SOTP.

Anti-libidinal treatment   Derek was referred for anti-libidinal medication in 2010 by his offender supervisor after he expressed deviant sexual fantasies and urges involving children and disclosed that he would reoffend upon release when the opportunity arose.

Derek consented to medication and began on a daily dose of Fluoxetine (20 mg). He remained on this for 5 months before being prescribed CPA (50 mg) and continued to take this in the community and while back in custody. He has been taking CPA for 21 months and has reported observable reductions in sexual preoccupation and masturbation.

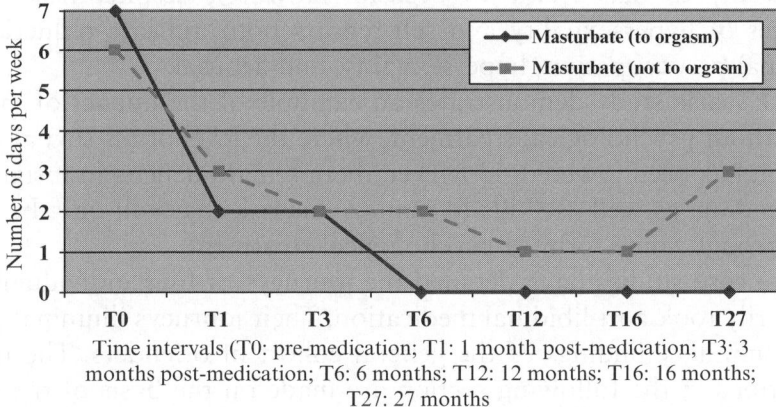

Figure 19.10 Derek's self-reported number of days in previous week masturbated.

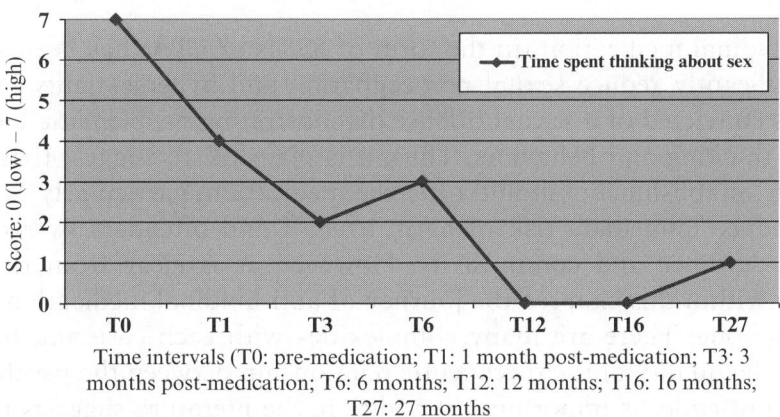

Figure 19.11 Derek's self-reported amount of sexual preoccupation (time currently spent thinking about sex).

This can be seen in Figures 19.10 and 19.11, where both masturbation frequency and time spent thinking about sex have reduced significantly from the very high scores premedication.

Discussion

Derek's deviant fantasies and uncontrollable urges are concerning dynamic risk factors. Despite agreeing to take anti-libidinal medication to help reduce this, compliance is an issue, as Derek admits missing medication occasionally to masturbate to orgasm. However, despite these lapses, measures of hypersexuality and self-reports both indicate reductions in his sexual preoccupation, hypersexuality, and arousal.

Derek's case study demonstrates an example of the impact of medication without psychological treatment, where the level of his sexual preoccupation has been lowered. However, there remain deficits in insight into his offending, as well as skills to manage his risk that will only be developed through some form of psychological treatment.

These case studies have detailed the journeys of four individuals who voluntarily took anti-libidinal medication. Their journeys illuminate some of the summary findings of the general cohort of offenders. The recommendations in the following section are made on the basis of the whole cohort to date.

Recommendations to Clinicians and Students

Anti-libidinal medication (in the form of SSRIs or CPA) has been shown to significantly reduce sexual preoccupation and hypersexuality in individuals convicted of a sexual offense demonstrating problematic levels of sexual thinking and behaviors. Thus, it is plausible to suggest that more forensic establishments should offer the medication, particularly as it can help reduce immediate risk of harm to staff and offenders by reducing sexual deviance and compulsivity. However, as is clear from the case studies within this chapter, the journey of anti-libidinal medication is not a simple one. There are many complexities with each case and for this reason the quality of the therapeutic relationship between the psychiatrist and the offender is important. In addition, the literature suggests (and is supported by this program of research) that medication must be used alongside psychological treatment and not as a replacement. Thus, considering at what time the medication will be most effective is important and this can vary case by case, for example, it may be delayed if it interferes with HRP conditioning treatment.

An additional important consideration is the throughcare of medication. The access to anti-libidinals in the community is unknown and requires further thought. More training for offender supervisors (within prison) and managers (in the community) on what anti-libidinals are may help bridge the gap between prison and community. Educating the parole board on anti-libidinals would also be helpful in this respect, promoting end-to-end offender management where all parties involved can support an offenders' reintegration into the community.

A final relevant point is the number of referrals for anti-libidinal medication at this establishment. Our research indicates that there are more offenders who have high sexual preoccupation but who are not referred for medication. Reasons for this are currently unknown, but an interesting point is the high number of intellectually disabled (ID) offenders who are referred and are taking anti-libidinals (43%). Research demonstrates that this group does not have higher levels of sexual preoccupation (Hocken, Winder, Grayson, & Andrews, 2014) and thus, the reasons for this require investigation. It may be that ID offenders are more compliant and suggestible to treatment (due to higher levels of acquiescence among ID individuals – see Gudjonsson, 1990). Alternatively, these individuals may not manage or hide their sexual preoccupation as well as higher functioning individuals. Considering the high number of ID individuals referred for the medication, the establishment has developed clear referral procedures and uses adapted information and consent forms to ensure clarity and understanding for all individuals in the consent procedure. However, the research team are considering further research into this area, not only from a clinical point of view and what this may or may not represent, but also in terms of ensuring staff are trained to explain the effects of the medication, and what it is useful for (see Lievesley, Elliott, Winder, Norman & Kaul, 2014).

In summary, anti-libidinal medication is shown to have a positive impact in reducing hypersexuality and sexual preoccupation. However, an important focal point now is to ensure that these offenders are able to access this treatment in the community. Further research is required to ascertain whether short-term benefits (reduction in sexual preoccupation) are apparent in the long term (as reductions in sexual reoffending) by these individuals.

Acknowledgements

The authors would like to acknowledge the help, support, and guidance of HMP Whatton and, in particular, Clinical Lead of SOTP Kerensa Hocken, Principal Psychologist Karen Thorne and the Governor Lynn Saunders. Thanks are given to all participants in the study who were willing to give their time and share their experiences to help with this research. The authors would also like to thank the following people for their input and support of this research: Professor Don Grubin, Rachael Lee (National Offender Management Service), Joan Scott (National Offender Management Service), and Dr. Mary Piper, (Department of Health).

References

Adi, Y., Ashcroft, D., Browne, K., Beech, A., Fry-Smith, A., & Hyde, C. (2002). Clinical effectiveness and cost-consequences of selective serotonin reuptake inhibitors in the treatment of sex offenders. *Health Technology Assessment*, 6(28), 1–67. ISSN 1366-5278.

Bancroft, J. (1989). *Human sexuality and its problems* (2nd ed.). Edinburgh: Churchill Livingstone.

Bancroft, J. (2005). The endocrinology of sexual arousal. *Journal of Endocrinology*, 186, 411–427.

Bancroft, J., & Janssen, E. (2000). The dual control model of male sexual response: A theoretical approach to centrally mediated erectile dysfunction. *Neuroscience and Biobehavioral Reviews*, 24, 571–579.

Bourget, D., & Bradford, J. M.W. (2008). Evidential basis for the assessment and treatment of sex offenders. *Brief Treatment and Crisis Intervention*, 8(1), 130–146.

Bradford, J. M. W. (1999). The paraphilias, obsessive compulsive spectrum disorder, and the treatment of sexually deviant behaviour. *Psychiatric Quarterly*, 70(3), 209–219.

Bradford, J. M. W. (2001). The neurobiology, neuropharmacology and pharmacological treatment of the paraphilias and compulsive sexual behaviour. *Canadian Journal of Psychiatry*, 46, 26–34.

Brotherton, J. (1974). Effect of oral CPA on urinary and serum FSH and LH levels in adult males being treated for hypersexuality. *Journal of Reproductive Fertility*, 36, 177–187.

Coleman, E., Gratzer, T., Nesvacil, L., & Raymond, N. C. (2000). Nefazodone and the treatment of nonparaphillic compulsive sexual behaviour: A retrospective study. *Journal of Clinical Psychiatry*, 61(4), 282–284.

Garcia, F. D., & Thibaut, F. (2011). Current concepts in the pharmacotherapy of Paraphilias. *Drugs*, 71(6), 771–790.

Guay, D. R. P. (2009). Drug treatment of paraphilic and nonparaphilic sexual disorders. *Clinical Therapeutics*, 31(1), 1–31.

Gudjonsson, G. H. (1990). The relationship of intellectual skills to suggestibility, compliance and acquiescence. *Personality and Individual Differences*, 11(3), 227–231.

Hanson, R. K., Harris, A. J. R, Scott, T.-L., & Helmus, L. (2007). *Assessing the risk of sexual offenders on community supervision: The Dynamic Supervision Project*. Corrections Research User Report No. 2007-05. Ottawa, Canada: Public Safety Canada.

Hanson, R. K., & Morton-Bourgon, K. (2004). *Predictors of sexual recidivism: An updated meta-analysis*. Corrections Research User Report No. 2004–02. Ottawa, Canada: Public Safety and Emergency Preparedness Canada.

Ho, D. K., & Ross, C. C. (2012). Cognitive behaviour therapy for sex offenders. Too good to be true? *Criminal Behaviour and Mental Health*, 22(1), 1–6.

Hocken, K., Winder, B., Grayson, A., & Andrews, M. (2014). *An investigation into the relationship between IQ and dynamic risk factors for sexual offending using the Structured Assessment for Risk and Need for Sexual Offenders.* Manuscript in preparation.

Jordan, K., Fromberger, P., Stolpmann, G., & Müller, J. L. (2011). The role of testosterone in sexuality and paraphilia – a neurobiological approach. Part I: Testosterone and sexuality. *The Journal of Sexual Medicine,* 8(11), 2993–3007.

Kafka, M. P. (1997). Hypersexual desire in males: An operational definition and clinical implications for males with paraphilias and paraphilia-related disorders. *Archives of Sexual Behavior,* 26, 506–526.

Kinsey, A. C., Pomeroy, W. M., & Martin, C. E. (1948). *Sexual behaviour in the human male.* Philadelphia: W. B. Saunders.

Krueger, R. B., & Kaplan, M. S. (2001). The paraphilic and hypersexual disorders: An overview. *Journal of Psychiatric Practice,* 27, 391–403.

Langström, N., & Hanson, R. K. (2006). High rates of sexual behaviour in the general population: Correlates and predictors. *Archives of Sexual Behaviour,* 35(1), 37–52.

Lievesley, R., Elliott, H., Winder, B., Norman, C., & Kaul, A. (2014). Understanding service user and therapists' experiences of incarcerated sex offenders receiving pharmacological treatment for sexual preoccupation and/or hypersexuality. Journal of Forensic Psychiatry and Psychology. Retrieved April 26, 2014 from http://www.tandfonline.com/doi/abs/10.1080/14789949.2014 .909867#.U5BfjPldXZ0

Lorrain, D. S., Matuszewich, L., Friedman, R. D., & Hull, E. M. (1997). Extracellular serotonin in the lateral hypothalamic area is increased during the postejaculatory interval and impairs copulation in male rats. *Journal of Neuroscience,* 17, 9361–9366.

Mann, R. E., Hanson, K. R., & Thornton, D. (2010). Assessing risk for sexual recidivism: Some proposals on the nature of psychologically meaningful risk factors. *Sexual Abuse: A Journal of Research and Treatment,* 22(2), 191–217.

Marshall, W. L., Marshall, L. E., & Serran, G. A. (2006). Strategies in the treatment of paraphilias: A critical review. *Annual Review of Sex Research,* 17(1), 162–182.

Meston, C. M., & Frohlich, P. F. (2000). The neurobiology of sexual function. *Archives of General Psychiatry,* 57(11), 1012–1030.

National Offender Management Service (2007). *Medical Treatment for Sex Offenders, Probation Circular 35/2000.* London: National Offender Management Service.

Pfaus, J. G. (2009). Pathways of sexual desire. *Journal of Sexual Medicine,* 6, 1506–1533.

Saleh, F. M., Grudzinskas, Jr., A. J., Malin, H. M., & Dwyer, R. G. (2010). The management of sex offenders: perspectives for psychiatry. *Harvard Review of Psychiatry,* 18(6), 359–368.

Ward, T., and Marshall, W. L. (2004). Good lives, aetiology and the rehabilitation of sex offenders: A bridging theory. *Journal of Sexual aggression*, *10*(2), 153–169.

Webster, S. D., Mann, R. E., Carter, A. C., Long, J., Milner, R. J., O'Brien, M. D., et al. (2006). Inter-rater reliability of dynamic risk assessment with sexual offenders. *Psychology, Crime and Law*, *12*(4), 439–452.

Winder, B., Lievesley, R., Kaul, A., Elliott, H. J., Thorne, K., & Hocken, K. (2014). Preliminary evaluation of the use of pharmacological treatment with convicted sexual offenders experiencing high levels of sexual preoccupation, hypersexuality and/or sexual compulsivity. *Journal of Forensic Psychiatry & Psychology*. Retrieved April 26, 2014 from http://www.tandfonline.com/doi/abs/10.1080/14789949.2014.903504#.U1wdM6LGCPQ.

Part V

Future Practice

20
Conclusions: Reflections and Formulations

Leigh Harkins, Tanya Garrett, and Daniel T. Wilcox

The Case Study Approach

If there was ever any doubt about the value of a case study approach, we hope that this book has been successful in changing that perception. As outlined in the introduction and exemplified in all the chapters that follow, case studies can highlight not only the heterogeneity of cases across types of sex offenders, but also the great variability within types. They can also highlight the many similarities and commonalities that are components of effective practice, not just in work with sex offenders, but in therapeutic work in general. The use of the case examples outlined here can bring to life the work involved with this challenging and vulnerable population. Although case studies cannot provide conclusive evidence for the overall effectiveness of a treatment approach, they can tell us what did or did not work when these approaches were implemented in real-life practice with individuals who have multiple needs, and this information can be used as a guide to inform future individualized work.

The authors of these chapters are recognized experts in the field of sex offender treatment, thus the insights they can offer are innumerable. The ability to see illustrations of how their expertise contributes to effective treatment for the individuals described here is tremendously valuable. But perhaps of equal or even greater value to any novice practitioners reading

Sex Offender Treatment: A Case Study Approach to Issues and Interventions,
First Edition. Edited by Daniel T. Wilcox, Tanya Garrett, and Leigh Harkins.
© 2015 John Wiley & Sons, Ltd. Published 2015 by John Wiley & Sons, Ltd.

this is the recognition that even those with years of experience and expertise still face challenges in the cases they work with. Thus, there is as much to be gained in examining challenges experienced as there is in examining successes, allowing us to see how their expertise came into play as they adapted to and overcame these challenges. Some of these are summarized below.

Challenges Experienced and Overcome

In many ways, therapeutic work with sex offenders shares common ground with any other therapeutic work. The treatment should be based on a valid and reliable assessment using multiple sources, should be able to provide a well-considered, collaboratively derived formulation and identification of treatment needs, and needs to ensure that the best-practice is adhered to in selecting the most appropriate means of addressing these treatment needs. Clients present with comorbid problems and are wildly heterogeneous, even when being treated for a common presenting problem. There is also a need to establish trust and build a therapeutic relationship. All of these factors will have a bearing on successful treatment outcomes with any population.

However, sex offenders also present a plethora of unique challenges. Some of these are commonly encountered in a forensic setting, for example, that treatment occurs in a wider legal context which the practitioner must bear in mind and that treatment can feel coercive to the offender as so much is at stake (e.g., their release from, or return to, prison) if they choose not to participate. Other challenges are specific to sex offenders. O'Donohue (2013) usefully outlines a number of characteristics that make work with this population difficult; for example, one of the primary treatment targets (i.e., sexual deviance) can be very well-ingrained and difficult to change (although successful behavioral methods for addressing this are offered by Marshall in chapter 18 and the valuable addition of anti-libidinal drugs is described in chapter 19 by Winder, Lievesley, Elliott, Norman, and Kaul). Of perhaps primary importance is how high the stakes are if treatment is not successful, as this likely means someone has been harmed. Although recent meta-analyses suggest that, on the whole, treatment is effective, especially when adhering to the principles of risk, need, and responsivity (see chapter 4 and chapter 6 for an overview of these principles; Hanson, Bourgon, Helmus, & Hodgson, 2009), the evidence is sparse in providing direction for many of the different offender types. In fact, a recent evaluation of evidence-based practice for treatment of paraphilias and sexual offending found some limited support for some sex offender types (e.g., those with child victims), but less evidence for most (e.g., those with adult victims; those with voyeuristic sexual interests; internet offenders; Harkins & Beech, 2012). Throughout this book, the authors usefully outline a variety of challenges that were encountered in their fascinating accounts of the work they engaged in with these clients. Some of those challenges that share common ground across a number of cases will be outlined here.

Several authors noted problems with offenders denying their sexual offense. For example, in chapter 5, Craig, Beech, and Ackerman, note that their client denied aspects of his arousal, Garrett (in chapter 12) and Carter and Hollin (in chapter 16) outline that their clients denied the sexual elements of their offenses, as did the client described by Rachal, Abel, and Garrett in chapter 13. However, as illustrated by the work with the client in denial described by Ware and Harkins in chapter 17, denial does not need to be a reason to preclude an offender from treatment. By taking a flexible approach to treating categorical deniers that allows offenders to consider how they came to be *convicted* of sexual offenses without admitting they committed it, many of the same treatment issues can be addressed while also developing a trusting therapeutic relationship that may facilitate disclosure down the road.

A lack of motivation for treatment was noted as a challenge in many of the case studies described here (e.g., chapters 3, 6, 7, and 17). In some of these cases, the value of motivational interviewing (Miller & Rollnick, 2013) was heralded as an important approach in assisting the clients to recognize the value they could gain from treatment. This approach helps the individual, in a nonjudgmental, empowering manner, to consider their circumstances and decide for themselves whether they need to make changes. Thus, training in this approach would seem to be of benefit to those working with most, if not all, types of sexual offenders.

There are unique challenges for the therapist as well. All work with clients who are suffering can be difficult and trying for therapists, but for those working with sexual offenders, additional considerations are needed. Therapy can involve discussion of highly emotionally charged, difficult to hear, descriptions of offenses. These can take a toll on a person. There is the added need to consider personal safety in working with some offenders. There is the temptation to feel responsible for our clients' setbacks and struggles, and any reoffenses can be especially difficult to accept. However, it is important that we recognize that all we can do is our best to help our clients develop the skills needed to make good decisions that will not bring about harm, and, in doing so, recognize that their successes (and lack thereof) come down to autonomous decisions that only they have control over and responsibility for. In ensuring that we are caring for them in helping them work towards how to go about making these right decisions, we also need to ensure we are caring for ourselves though various means. The need for self-care is extremely important, as Prescott outlined in chapter 2. Some of the methods used can include ensuring sufficient, restful sleep, and physical exercise, including yoga and meditation. For others this might mean devoted time with family and friends or allowing time to engage in hobbies, sports and other pastimes that bring enjoyment. There is also the need for therapists to recognize the potential ethical dilemmas that can arise as a result of their straddling a commitment to the client and the principles of the caring or helping profession, but also their commitment to the public and principles of the justice system. Ward, in chapter 3 outlines a valuable decision-making model that encompasses a moral acquaintance perspective that can be used as a way of guiding decisions and finds common ground amongst stakeholders.

Challenges are also noted at a wider institutional level. This includes having to work within the constraints of limited resources (such as outlined in chapter 10), which might mean that valuable group treatment is provided, but opportunities to focus on some specific needs are limited. This was also noted in terms of limited access to anti-libidinal medication (described in chapter 9 and chapter 19). Investment in ensuring wider availability would help in improving the care of the highly deviant individuals who may benefit from such medications and consequently improve public safety.

Good Practice

Each chapter represents a valuable individualized approach to addressing a client's needs, but a number of common features of good practice were also identified. An overview of some of these will be outlined below.

Although we would advocate an individualized approach to assessment and treatment, this does not mean that we believe individual treatment is superior to group-based interventions. In fact, as noted by many of the authors, group-based interventions are preferable for meeting many of the individualized needs of the offenders. As noted by Gray and Wilcox in chapter 4, clients can use the group format to develop social competence skills. In chapters, 8, 13, 16, and 17, the authors note the value of groups for providing peer support. In addition to the various psychological benefits, there are also resource-related benefits, in that group treatment is less costly than individualized treatment. However, there is the danger of resources directing services rather than vice versa so efforts must be taken to avoid this.

All of the cases described, in some way or other, illustrate the importance of the responsivity principle in guiding how therapeutic work with sex offenders is approached. This includes recognition that treatment may need to be modified or approached in different ways with some specific populations, such as adolescents (chapter 7), those with intellectual disabilities (chapter 8), female offenders (chapter 11), and those with mental health issues (chapters 6 and 12). This also includes offering treatment in a reflective manner which best suits the learning style and strengths of the client, such as in chapter 6, in which Gannon describes allowing the client the opportunities to use art and poetry to express difficult emotions, or the approach to treatment outlined by Logan and Hird (chapter 15) in addressing the psychopathic sex offenders, in which considerations like treatment-interfering factors are addressed.

The importance of ensuring a positive therapeutic relationship was noted in a number of chapters, and in several cases, as a component of that, the importance of empathy for our clients was discussed. It was noted in chapter 2 that we need to consider how few opportunities there are for our clients to exercise autonomy in their lives, thus we should do our best to afford them these opportunities when we can. In chapter 5, Craig and colleagues noted how difficult it is for our clients to do what we ask them to do (e.g., offense disclosure, report on masturbation frequency and content, and victim empathy exercises) and emphasized that we should bear this in mind. One factor in this was the need to recognize the power differential between therapists and clients. Never is the power differential more pronounced than when the professional abuses their position of trust and power to take advantage of a client. The unique difficulties in dealing with this were outlined by Rachal, Abel, and Garrett in chapter 13. However, methods of addressing this with sensitivity and professionalism, while still instilling hope, were also discussed.

Numerous cases (chapters 5, 6, 15, and 17) also noted the importance of taking a collaborative approach to assessment and treatment, such as that outlined by Marshall, Marshall, Serran, and O'Brien (2011) and Shingler and Mann (2006). Such an approach highlights the value in working respectfully with the offender to decide on, and work towards meeting, common goals. This does not mean that risk-reduction goals need become secondary or should not be addressed if the offender does not see themself as risky. Rather, work can focus on the manner in which these risk-management goals can be compatible with the offender's goals, and that these goals can be assessed and conveyed to the offender in a transparent manner that allows them to have some input. Ensuring consideration and inclusion of the offender's own goals also increases the likelihood that the offender will be more motivated in working towards them and encourages a more trusting relationship between offender and practitioner. This approach is also compatible with a good lives model (Ward & Stewart, 2003) approach to treatment, which will be considered further below.

Future Directions

Progress cannot be made without taking risks and trying out new approaches. One such approach that is recognized as a welcome change that has a positive, strengths based focus, is the good lives model (Ward & Stewart, 2003). Evidence is beginning to accumulate for the utility of this approach (e.g., Gannon, King, Miles, Lockerbie, & Willis, 2011; Harkins, Beech, Flak, & Woodhams, 2012; Simons, McCullar, & Tyler, 2006). Its use was noted in many of the cases described here (chapters 6, 8, 10, 14, and 15) and is increasingly included as a component of sex offender treatment across North America (McGrath, Cumming, Burchard, Zeoli, & Ellerby, 2010). Willis, Yates, Gannon, and Ward (2013) recently provided a detailed overview of how to implement the good lives model into practice, which practitioners will surely find a valuable resource.

The increasing role of technology in people's lives must be taken into consideration, as it comes with the potential both for tremendous risks and benefits. The risks include those described in chapter 10 by Quayle and Hayes, such as a potential avenue to initiate contact, solicit victims, and share abusive images. However, there are also potential benefits, including opportunities to utilize newer technologies such as eye-tracking and virtual reality for assessment and treatment purposes. Some researchers have found virtual reality valuable in assessing deviant sexual interest (Fromberger et al., 2012; Renaud et al., 2009). There is also the potential for such innovations to be used in a treatment context as computer-generated images and avatars of the offender's preferred victim type can be created to assist with skills practice and behavioural and cognitive modification.

Importance of Evaluation and Dissemination

As new approaches are considered, it is important that we do not accept them at face value or base their overarching utility on their relevance and success in one case, as much as there is also value in reporting on such successes as we have illustrated here. In particular, publishing case studies that showcase new approaches or unique cases can provide valuable information for all the reasons illustrated in this book. However, examining the value across a number of cases and examining them in a systematic way can increase our confidence in the generalizability and utility of the results. Guidelines for approaches to treatment evaluation have been highlighted elsewhere (Harkins & Beech, 2007), and it is worth practitioners considering how they might systematically collect outcome data that would allow them to evaluate the effectiveness of their work.

Conclusions

There is great value in looking to large-scale evaluations of treatment effectiveness, sampling hundreds of offenders over sometimes as long as decades, to direct best practice in work with sexual offenders, but, ultimately, clinicians have to decide what the best course of action is for the person sitting across the desk from them. They need to bear in mind what that person's potentially idiosyncratic needs are and what will be most effective for that individual. Of course, this should be informed by the knowledge gained from large nomothetic data sources. However, the value of the cases outlined here is to help practitioners through outlining what others have done with that person sitting across from them. We hope that the wide variety of commonalities between the cases we have outlined here and some of your own cases will be evident, but we equally hope that you will recognize the valuable learning that can come from examining the idiosyncrasies of a case as well.

We have attempted to be as inclusive as possible within the constraints of a single volume but note that inevitably some gaps remain, not least because of the incredible diversity of sex offending behaviour. For example, we were unable to include a chapter concerning treatment of a transgender sex offender (Disspain & Shuker, 2013) as well as those dealing with other subcategories of these chapters including sadistic offenders and abusers with autistic features. Relatedly, discussion among some of the authors has gravitated towards the idea of developing a continuing sex offender treatment communication and support network. It is hoped that this initiative could afford further specific guidance in the future, either through focal training to deal with particular intervention challenges or even individualized shadowing and support on especially complex cases. The editors and contributing authors will be devoting attention to this communication and support initiative and would welcome input from readers. We will also consider whether a further companion publication may be appropriate in the future to increase the comprehensiveness of assistance and guidance that can be offered to sex offender practitioners.

References

Disspain, S., & Shuker, R. (2013). Exploration of a transfemale prisoner's experience of a therapeutic community. Unpublished manuscript.

Fromberger, P., Jordan, K., Steinkrauss, H., von Herder, J., Witzel, J., Stolpmann, G., et al. (2012). Diagnostic accuracy of eye movements in assessing pedophilia. *Journal of Sexual Medicine, 12,* 1868–1882. DOI: 10.1111/j.1743-6109.2012.02754.x.

Gannon, T. A., King, T., Miles, H., Lockerbie, L., & Willis, G. M. (2011). Good lives sexual offender treatment for mentally disordered offenders. *British Journal of Forensic Practice, 13,* 153–168. DOI: 10.1108/14636641111157805.

Hanson, R. K., Bourgon, G., Helmus, L., & Hodgson, S. (2009). The principles of effective correctional treatment also apply to sexual offenders: A meta-analysis. *Criminal Justice and Behavior, 36,* 865–891. DOI: 10.1177/0093854809338545.

Harkins, L., & Beech, A. R. (2007). Measurement of the effectiveness of sex offender treatment. *Aggression and Violent Behavior, 12,* 36–44. DOI: 10.1016/j.avb.2006.03.002.

Harkins, L., & Beech, A. R. (2012). Paraphilias and sexual offending. In P. Sturmey & M. Hersen (Eds.), *Handbook of evidence-based practice in clinical psychology* (Vol. 2, adults; pp. 646–678). Hoboken, NJ: Wiley.

Harkins, L., Flak, V., Beech, A. R., & Woodhams, J. (2012). Evaluation of a community-based sex offender treatment program using a Good Lives Model approach. *Sexual Abuse: A Journal of Research and Treatment, 24,* 519–543.

Marshall, W. L., Marshall, L. E., Serran, G. A., & O'Brien, M. D. (2011). *Rehabilitating sexual offenders: A strength-based approach.* Washington, DC: American Psychological Association.

McGrath, R. J., Cumming, G. F., Burchard, B. L., Zeoli, S., & Ellerby, L. (2010). *Current practices and emerging trends in sexual abuser management.* Brandon, VT: Safer Society Press.

Miller, W. R., & Rollnick, S. (2013). *Motivational interviewing: Helping people change* (3rd ed.). New York: Guilford Press.

O'Donohue, W. T. (Ed.). (2013). *Case studies in sexual deviance: Towards evidence-based practice.* New York: Routledge.

Renaud, P., Chartier, S., Rouleau, J. L., Proulx, J., Decarie, J., Trottier, D., et al. (2009). Gaze behavior nonlinear dynamics assessed in virtual immersion as a diagnostic index of sexual deviancy: Preliminary results. *Journal of Virtual Reality and Broadcasting*, 6, urn:nbn:de:0009-6-17538.

Shingler, J., & Mann, R. E. (2006). Collaboration in clinical work with sexual offenders: Treatment and risk assessment. In W. L. Marshall, Y. M. Fernandez, L. E. Marshall, & G. A. Serran (Eds.), *Sexual offender treatment: Controversial issues* (pp. 173–185). Hoboken, NJ: Wiley.

Simons, D. A., McCullar, B., & Tyler, C. (2006, September). Evaluation of the good lives model approach to treatment planning. Paper presented at the 25th Annual Association for the Treatment of Sexual Abusers Research and Treatment Conference, Chicago, IL.

Ward, T., & Stewart, C. A. (2003). The treatment of sex offenders: Risk management and good lives. *Professional Psychology: Research and Practice*, 34, 353–360. DOI: 10.1037/0735-7028.34.4.353.

Willis, G., Yates, P., Gannon, T., & Ward, T. (2013). How to integrate the good lives model into treatment programs for sexual offending: An introduction and overview. *Sexual Abuse: A Journal of Research and Treatment*, 25, 123–142.

Index

Page numbers in *italics* refer to figures; those in **bold** refer to tables.

Sex Offender Treatment: A Case Study Approach to Issues and Interventions,
First Edition. Edited by Daniel T. Wilcox, Tanya Garrett, and Leigh Harkins.
© 2015 John Wiley & Sons, Ltd. Published 2015 by John Wiley & Sons, Ltd.